The Best American Sports Writing 2012

GUEST EDITORS OF
THE BEST AMERICAN SPORTS WRITING

The Best AMERICAN SPORTS WRITING™ 2012

Edited and with an Introduction
by Michael Wilbon

Glenn Stout, *Series Editor*

A MARINER ORIGINAL

HOUGHTON MIFFLIN HARCOURT

BOSTON • NEW YORK

www.hmhbooks.com

ISSN 1056-8034
ISBN 978-0-547-33697-8

Printed in the United States of America
DOC 10 9 8 7 6 5 4 3 2

Contents

Foreword

HERE'S HOW IT GOES:

On most days I rise early—5:30 A.M., 6:00 A.M.—just after my wife and before my daughter wakes for school. While they get ready I drink coffee, maybe tea, feed the dog, check the weather, glance over e-mails. And when they leave I go down to the basement office I built eight years ago, the one with two desks, two windows, shelves of books, and piles and boxes of paper everywhere, a place where the shades are always drawn so the room is always the same and distractions fade.

This is where I write, almost every day, something. A column for a magazine. A chapter for a title in my juvenile series "Good Sports," a note for my blog, a tweet, or something for one of my other, larger projects that sometimes occupy me for two, three, even four years at a time, require weeks in libraries, hours taping interviews, months searching online, all the time accumulating facts and details and feelings. Words by the dozen become hundreds, and thousands become millions.

I like working early, writing early, getting it out of the way before the details of life intrude. I do not understand people who work and write at the end of the day, when "what has just happened" is still at issue. By evening my eye is tired, my mind full.

Friends sometimes telephone. M. calls to talk about baseball, concrete, cycling, music, politics, and art. R. has a question, passes along a tip, parries my rants with his own. H. buries the lede, tells a story, answers a query, and in the end we talk about writing and writers, books and words, and how we do this every day.

On good days I stop by noon, or one o'clock or two. I can write for longer periods of time, but less efficiently—after five or six hours the flow ebbs and I sink, each new word written coming slow. So I take the dog outside, throw the ball, walk through the woods, and miss the one that left us last year. Sometimes we walk all the way back to the lake, to the cabin I built that floats in the swamp, just offshore, hidden in the brush. Summer nights I sleep inside and listen to the beaver gnawing on the willows 15 feet away. Then I wake before the dawn, sit in a kayak on the lake in the dark, and watch the mist and sun rising together. Winters I ski across it on the ice, aiming for the opposite shore.

We walk back home, looking for deer sign, coyote tracks, and scat. Then I climb into the truck, bounce the long quarter-mile down my gravel driveway, turn onto the road, and drive to the post office in town five minutes away.

When I open the box each day, while I never know precisely what will be there, I know what to expect—magazines and mailers, envelopes and entreaties, the raw material for this book. Sometimes the pile is small; a few thin envelopes, a magazine, a package, a plea. Other days the box is so full that I sometimes have to pry the mail out, pulling out each piece one at a time to make sure something doesn't tear or fall out the back beyond my reach.

But there is always something. I cannot remember the last time the mailbox was empty.

I put the pile on the counter and quickly sort through, separating the mail meant for this from that meant for something else; catalogs, bills, and bulk mail. Then I go home and sort the pile again, opening the envelopes and usually tossing away everything inside that is not either a story or the basic information I need to consider the story—author, publication, date, contact info. The needless rest—résumés, cover letters, CVs, pitches from agents and editors and girlfriends and husbands, and once even a 45-rpm single, the author's blues band fantasy—gets a glance and then goes unread. There is simply no time.

I'll grab a pile and then, three or four times a week, less in the summer when I can run and bike outside and perhaps more in the winter if there is not enough snow to ski, it's back down to the basement. I flick on the old TV that still pulls stations from the air, put a telephone in the cup holder of the elliptical, then climb on board, piling magazines and loose stories on the industrial-strength reading stand I built from plastic, wire, and, yes, duct tape.

You've got 45 minutes, maybe 50, as I simultaneously read and climb, Sisyphus never quite reaching the end.

Many stories I start and never finish, stumbling over the lede or something else. Others I skip to the end to see if the promising start has been sustained, some I read straight through, and some I don't quite get to yet as the pile of "still to read" grows faster by far than the "save to read again" pile that aspires to this book.

January comes, and with it, the onslaught. Like a quick winter thaw, as my deadline approaches, the words flow my direction in a flood, and I fight to keep pace with the ever-growing pile. No writing now, or not much, but bleary-eyed reading and rereading and rereading again, breaking up the occasional ice jam and wading out in the water, finding in the slush and flotsam the clear cold water running fast and true.

Then clarity. February comes, the deadline drops, and the chatter fades. Now only the strongest voices compete, whispers and screams alike sliding away into silence. I clear my ears and listen again, seeking the sounds that stop the clock, and then I know.

The survivors get copied, packaged, and sent away to the guest editor in the mail. I get back in the truck, drive home, and it all starts again.

As I attempted to describe above, each year I read every issue of hundreds of sports and general interest magazines in search of writing that might merit inclusion in *The Best American Sports Writing.* I also write or e-mail the editors of many hundreds of newspapers and magazines and request their submissions, and I send e-mail notices to hundred of readers and writers whose addresses I have accumulated over the years. I search for writing on the Internet and make regular stops at online sources like sportsdesk .org, gangrey.com, longform.org, sportsjournalists.com, ladyjour nos.tumblr.com, and other websites where notable sports writing is sometimes discussed. Yet even these efforts do not ensure that I see everything, so each year in this space I encourage everyone—readers and writers—to send me stories they believe should appear in this volume. Writers, in particular, should not shy from sending me either their own work or the work of others for consideration. However, all submissions to the upcoming edition must be made according to the following criteria. Each story

- must be column-length or longer.
- must have been published in 2012.
- must not be a reprint or book excerpt.
- must have been published in the United States or Canada.
- must be received by February 1, 2013.

All submissions must include the name of the author, the date of publication, and the publication name and address. Photocopies, tear sheets, or clean copies are fine. Readable reductions to 8½-by-11 are preferred. Submissions from online publications must be made in hard copy, and newspaper stories should be submitted in hard copy as published. Since newsprint generally suffers in transit, newspaper stories are best copied and made legible. If the story also appeared online, the appropriate URL is often helpful.

While there is no limit to the number of submissions either an individual or a publication may make, please use common sense. Owing to the volume of material I receive, no submissions can be returned or acknowledged, and it is inappropriate for me to comment on or critique any submission. Publications that want to be absolutely certain that their contributions are considered are advised to provide a complimentary subscription to the address listed below. Those that already do so should make sure to renew the subscription.

No electronic submissions will be accepted, although stories that only appeared online are eligible. Please send all submissions by U.S. mail—weather conditions in midwinter here at BASW headquarters often keep me from receiving UPS or FedEx submissions. The February 1 deadline has real meaning, so don't send things in late.

Please submit either an original or clear paper copy of each story, including publication name, author, and date the story appeared, to:

Glenn Stout
PO Box 549
Alburgh, VT 05440

Those with questions or comments may contact me at baswedi tor@yahoo.com. Copies of previous editions of *The Best American Sports Writing* can be ordered through most bookstores or online book dealers. An index of stories that have appeared in this series can be found at my website, glennstout.net, as can full instructions on how to submit a story. For updated information, readers and writers are also encouraged to join the *Best American Sports Writing* group on Facebook.

Thanks again go out to everyone at Houghton Mifflin Harcourt who supports this book, and to Siobhan and Saorla, who rarely complain about that big pile in the corner I tell everyone not to touch. Most important of all, however, is the gratitude I feel to those who write their way into these pages each year and invite me along. Many thanks.

GLENN STOUT
Alburgh, Vermont

Introduction

ONCE UPON A TIME, before Twitter and Internet and cable, the sportswriter was a pretty indispensible character. He told you, first and often exclusively, whether Ruth hit a home run the previous night, whether Citation won the third leg of the Triple Crown, whether Clay beat Liston, whether Wooden's UCLA Bruins won (again). The *Washington Post*'s Shirley Povich, perhaps the only sportswriter to write about both Babe Ruth and Michael Jordan, recalled rushing to the docks when he was a schoolboy in Maine to get the morning newspaper to learn the score of the Red Sox game, because radio wasn't yet in homes and the sports section was the only way.

A kid growing up in Washington could read Povich and Sam Lacy for decades. In Los Angeles, Jim Murray. In New York, Dick Young. Sportswriters shared dispatches from a train trip from Chicago to St. Louis with Ruth, impressions from a hotel visit with Ali the night before his bout with Foreman in Zaire, insights from a post-practice conversation with Auerbach or Wooden. And it was all real. To write for publication you had to be there, front and center, courtside, sideline, at practice, at games, in the locker room afterward, at shoot-around, in the coach's office, even if summoned. You had to *be there*—behind closed doors, backstage—to hear stuff, see stuff, to be told stuff, on the record or maybe confidentially.

Let's just say that things have changed and rather dramatically. Now anyone who can text or Tweet can be a sportswriter, in a sense, despite never having gotten any closer to ringside, to practice, the star's locker, or the GM's office than, say, a cashier at the corner grocery. There's so much to sift through now, blogs and alerts and things that loosely resemble columns, though not the stylings of Povich or Murray or the late Ralph Wiley, because who knows if subject and verb even have a chance to agree in what we call "new media."

Readers used to relish the long thoughtful profile and the 5,000-word Sunday "takeout," which have largely disappeared from the landscape. Yet as this volume shows, remarkably, in this new world of 140 characters, there is still thoughtful and insightful sports writing to be found—more of it than ever, actually, critical without resorting to ridicule.

Luckily, when you filter out all the noise, turn off the Twitter feed, and take time to immerse yourself, there are still eloquent pieces being written, pieces that command attention, and some of them in places we never used to look. There are pieces like the ones written once upon a time by Shirley Povich and Jim Murray, who had a way of making people pay attention to the biggest issues of the day as they relate to sports—to new issues such as dying hockey enforcers and football players dead by fifty with a possible new plague we know as CTE.

In these pages is sports writing as good as it's ever been: John Branch's piece about young Derek Boogard, not long ago the NHL's most fearsome fighter, who did not live to be thirty years old . . . Jeanne Marie Laskas's piece about Fred McNeil, the former NFL linebacker who went to law school while he played for the Vikings and made partner but essentially lost his memory and his mind and, so sadly, his life . . . Robert Huber's piece about the fallen star that is Allen Iverson . . . even Alex Belth's piece about a sportswriter himself, "the two-fisted, one-eyed badass" named George Kimball, whom you probably knew of only if you lived in New England.

They are not happy pieces, necessarily, but they do what all good stories should do, which is to say, they pull the covers back to show you something you ought to know but probably don't. They're complex, nuanced pieces that people confined to Twitter might find too long, too time-consuming, not instant enough. They're the kind of pieces that, back when people used phones to actually talk to one another and not to text or take photos, would have forced people to pick up a phone, call their friends, and say, "You really need to read this," the kind of pieces about which sportswriters would say, or at least think, "I wish I had written that."

And they required more from their writers than just sitting and thinking; they are pieces that required reporting, conversations, probably very difficult conversations in the cases of many. But that's always been, even more than the writing, what set apart the best sports stories. The best sports stories are based not on interviews but on conversations—conversations with people who are sometimes reluctant, sometimes in the orneriest mood, often not the most glib or polished conversationalists. But sometimes those are the people who have the most to say, the best stories to convey. And unless you were *there*, to hear them yourself, to have engaged in that conversation, you don't get to the essence of sports writing.

A handful of us who covered college basketball in the 1980s and 1990s were fortunate to encounter John Thompson, the iconic Georgetown University basketball coach, who had earned the reputation of being difficult for sportswriters. Many a scribe walked away from an attempted conversation with Thompson shaking his head, wondering what he had done to offend or enrage the coach. The answer, usually, was nothing. Thompson was neither offended nor enraged; he was probably just amused. He could ask a few of his own. More than any coach I ever got to know, as it turned out, Thompson loved to talk, loved a good story, was drawn to smart and provocative questions.

But for you to engage Thompson, he had to know you, and there were no shortcuts to reach that point. He went to some lengths back in the 1980s to find out about a writer before returning his call—what the writer believed in, whether he had the guts to take difficult stands, whether he could give a good accounting of himself in a 2 A.M. argument over politics or education or religion. J. A. Adande, one of a half-dozen writers assigned by the *Washington Post* to cover Georgetown during Thompson's run, says now, "John Thompson put me through hell covering that team. But since, I've had one of the great resources a writer could ever have. Those early days were like an initiation. It was stressful, intimidating. And then when he got to know you, if he respected your work, nobody was going to give you life perspective like John Thompson."

Nearly 20 years after covering Georgetown's Thompson for the

Post, Adande, now a columnist for ESPN.com, teaches a course on sports commentary at the University of Southern California, and he can't help but notice how few of his students want to report as he did before becoming a columnist. Most of them don't care about covering high school sports, then college sports, or working a beat for five to seven years before proving to somebody they've lived enough to merit expressing an opinion for a living. They've come of age in a world where every semiliterate with a phone is a publisher and can publish his opinion. "Everything," Adande says, "veers toward commentary now, and 99 percent of what you see on Twitter and Facebook now is opinion." Like most folks these days, students go to Adande's class not knowing the difference between a news story and a column, between blogging and spending the season with a team, between ranting from your living room and sitting with the losing quarterback after he threw a game-ending interception and trying to get him to explain through his anger what the hell happened.

Adande, who grew up in Los Angeles and worked for the *L.A. Times,* has his students read his favorite columnist, Jim Murray, even the great Grantland Rice. "They're blown away by Jim Murray," he says. "They're transfixed reading his stuff, though they weren't raised on it."

Of course, Murray, and the man I wanted to be as a writer, David Halberstam, got to know the people they wrote about in a way that Adande's students simply don't get to know 21st-century athletes. Young writers today don't get the benefit of Magic Johnson holding court 90 minutes before an NBA Finals game with no public relations person at his side. LeBron is available, yes, but like the world he grew up in, it's all so carefully managed now. So the stories, increasingly, are filed without the writer ever having seen practice, without his ever talking to one of the assistant coaches (who are increasingly off-limits), without his learning anything of substance. It's not exclusive to sports. President Obama doesn't walk to the back of Air Force One as often as President Clinton did. Why would a celebrity talk to a writer when he can profit from a reality show, control the presentation, and therefore control his own image? Every C-list celebrity can and does act as his own producer. And it's that way in sports. Why would Tiger Woods leave one sentence to interpretation if he can control the way it is perceived by issuing it on his own website?

It's made the job, certainly, more challenging. It's made sports-writers—the really good ones, anyway—search to come up with ways to separate themselves and their work from the offerings of those who have no access to real information and no real insight, those who, in other words, are limited to ranting. Gone are the days, for the most part, when we're the only ones who can tell you who won or lost, when the sports page is the primary clearing-house for what's happening that day in the world of sports. Yet it's still going to be the sportswriter who can best relate the full story of a team or a season, of the thrill of victory or the agony of defeat, of the human drama of athletic competition and how it relates to the issues of the day in the real world. The sportswriter is still the one who will bring you the conversation with the coach an hour after the worst loss of his life, or the feelings of the unlikely hero on the greatest day of his life. What used to be called stories are called "content" now, but by any other name the sportswriter is still the person who has to deliver it to the masses. If no longer indispensable, perhaps we're still, at the very least, essential.

MICHAEL WILBON

The Best American
Sports Writing
2012

DAVE SHEININ

The Phenomenal Son

FROM THE WASHINGTON POST MAGAZINE

THE FIRST THING you do is, you go over and grab one of those
iron rods—rebar, it's called—from the pile. It may weigh 50
pounds, maybe 80, maybe more. You throw it over your shoulder
and hump it over to your crew. If it's 115 degrees in Vegas that day,
it's probably 135 in the hole where you're laboring, clad in heavy
work clothes, building the foundation of another casino, feeding
the great beast of the desert. You lay the rebar down just so, tie its
ends with 16-gauge wire, and now it's ready to be encased in concrete, one more grain of rice down the beast's gullet.

They say Las Vegas is a town of phoniness and illusion. Fake pyr-
amids. Fake Manhattan skylines. Fake Eiffel towers. But Ron Harper, for 27 years a union card–holder in Reinforcing Ironworkers
Local 416—a "rodbuster," as they call themselves—can tell you
one thing: for every gaudy, phony facade in this godforsaken town,
a couple hundred men, some of them his men, bent their backs to
send it up into the sky. Watch him get one of those monthly shots
in his neck to ease his pain, and then tell him everything in Vegas
is fake.

"A lot of the new guys today are soft. They want a forklift," says
Harper, 45. "They want a crane. Hey, if you can get it—great. But
for me, nothing replaces hard work."

Once, Harper took the youngest of his three kids, Bryce, then
a precocious boy of 11, to a job site with him. It was one of those
take-your-son-or-daughter-to-work days, and it was summer, so it
was almost unbearably hot down in the hole on the famed Vegas
Strip. Bryce put on the hard hat, spent a couple of hours learning

what a rodbuster does—enough to know it wasn't going to replace baseball player atop his list of preferred careers—then declared he was ready to go home.

"I'm like, 'Bryce, we're out here six more hours,'" Ron Harper says. A stern look creeps across his face. "I wanted my kids to appreciate the hard work, the sweat."

He's out in his garage now, on a quiet cul-de-sac on the east side of town. It's full of snowboards, skateboards, and bicycles, but mostly baseball equipment bags. A half-dozen of them—stuffed with bats, gloves, catcher's gear, cleats—rise halfway to the ceiling. A baseball-size hole in the drywall above the door to the house speaks of some long-ago errant throw. A hand-painted sign above the doorway reads, WE INTERRUPT THIS FAMILY FOR BASEBALL SEASON. A tasteful array of Christmas decorations sits outside on the lawn, this being early December.

Ron digs through the equipment bags—the newest-looking of them emblazoned with a gleaming Washington Nationals logo—and through the dozens of bats, coated with the orange dirt of a thousand ball fields, until he finds what he was looking for: an old, stumpy piece of rebar, maybe two feet long, from some long-forgotten job site.

"Bryce used to swing this—still does," he says as he hands it over. It's cold and impossibly heavy. It's difficult to raise it to shoulder level, let alone think about swinging it. Exactly how heavy is this thing?

"It's about 25 pounds," Ron says, taking it back and swinging it effortlessly, with textbook baseball form.

And it is at this point, between the sheer weight of the rebar, and the determination in Ron Harper's face as he talks about his work ethic, and the amassed detritus of a childhood dominated by baseball, that you begin to see how this happened—how Ron and Sheri Harper, former junior high sweethearts now facing empty-nesthood, came to raise a prodigy.

Bryce is now 18 years old and as hard and honest-to-God real as his old man. But Bryce is also blessed with once-in-a-generation talent to hit a baseball to the ends of the earth, and he is hell-bent on greatness, and as winter gives way to spring, the Harpers are preparing to unleash him upon Washington, and upon a world less prepared for him than he is for it.

"People say Bryce is an old-school player," Ron says. "You're damn right, he is. He'd better be. And so better his brother. And his sister, my daughter, better act like that in whatever she does. Because there's nothing wrong with a little hard work. Blue-collar attitude. Strap it on, and let's go. That's the way I am, and that's the way I raised my kids to be."

What if you knew in advance that the love of your life was coming your way? What if you knew his or her identity, and the only thing still unknown was when it would happen? It is that way with Washington—or at least the segment of the metropolis that loves its sports teams and the stars who populate them—and Bryce Harper. Trust us. It is going to be silly, giddy, sloppy, head-over-heels love. We tell you this now as a public service, so you can prepare yourself for it. "My prediction," says Harolyn Cardozo, the Nationals' assistant to the general manager, who is a keen observer of the athletic psyche, "is that Washington ties its balloon to his, and they float away together."

How shall Washington, starved for a baseball champion for 87 years, love Harper? Let us count the ways. Scouts call him the best hitting prospect to come into baseball since (take your pick) Alex Rodriguez, Ken Griffey Jr., Darryl Strawberry, or Mickey Mantle. Bryce Harper has laid waste to every league he has ever seen, despite almost always being several years younger than his opponents and teammates. Tales of his prowess—500-foot home runs, the cover of *Sports Illustrated* (with the headline, "Baseball's Chosen One") at age 16—are legendary. Though he grew up playing catcher, he can handle almost any position on the diamond; the Nationals settled upon making him a right fielder.

He has pursued his dream relentlessly, leaving Las Vegas High School after his sophomore year, taking (and passing) the GED, and enrolling at the College of Southern Nevada to move up his eligibility for the Major League Baseball draft to 2010—an unprecedented and somewhat controversial move at the time—where his fate intersected with that of the Nationals, whose woeful 59–103 record the year before afforded them the privilege of drafting him with the first overall pick.

At CSN, which plays in one of the few wood-bat conferences in the country, he hit 31 homers in 2010—crushing the previous school record of 12. And he was at least two years younger than every other player on his team.

Off the field, he is polite, charming, and self-assured. When he showed up for his introductory news conference at Nationals Park last August, after signing a $9.9 million contract, he was sporting a half-grown-in mohawk. He explained that his sister, Brittany, is a beautician and likes experimenting on him—and anyway, he added with a rakish grin, "The ladies like it."

"The best way I can put it," Cardozo says, "is that he has stage presence."

This love, for now, is mostly a one-way street. Harper simply doesn't have enough experience with Washington to love it back. He is dutifully loyal to the Nationals but admits to a lifelong devotion to the Yankees. And, anyway, his love is bigger than any one team—and he speaks about it as only a moonstruck teenager can.

"I love the game of baseball," he says in the living room of the Harper house. "I'm getting chills right now about it. I absolutely love the game of baseball. If you took it away from me, I'd die tomorrow. Seriously. I'd want to kill myself. I absolutely love the game of baseball."

He is ruggedly handsome (he stands six-foot-three, 220 pounds), clean-cut (a devout Mormon, he says he has never had a drink or a cigarette, and never gambles despite having spent his entire life in Sin City), and is comfortable with the notion of fame without being consumed by it. And he is cognizant of the scrutiny he will be under as baseball's latest bonus-baby prodigy.

When he left for Viera, Florida, to join his Nationals teammates for spring training, he did not bring his brand-new Mercedes, the one indulgence he allowed himself after signing his Nationals contract, but the black Toyota truck with 130,000 miles on it.

"That's my work truck," Harper says. "I want everyone to know I'm there for work."

Harper deftly straddles the line between childhood and adulthood, just as an 18-year-old should.

He loves his dog and his mama, and says his dad is his best friend. He sleeps with his bats. He has a thing for female soccer players. At home, he's prone to invading the kitchen at 1:00 A.M. and helping himself to a bowl of Fruity Pebbles—the empty bowls frequently found in his bedroom days later. A month before he was to report to his first professional spring training, he attended a high school Sadie Hawkins dance with his girlfriend—a soccer player, of course.

This winter, three times a week, he rose at 4:00 A.M., drove half an hour across town, and reported to a 5:15 A.M. workout with San Francisco Giants outfielder Aaron Rowand, a 33-year-old former all-star. After a late-morning nap, Harper often dropped by his old high school team's practice, hoping to get in a few cuts in the batting cage. Though he looks like a man among boys in that venue, he is with his peer group: he would be a high school senior right now had he not left early.

He has a worldliness that comes from extensive traveling—frequently without his parents and occasionally overseas—for youth baseball tournaments, but a groundedness that can come only from strong parenting.

He somehow manages to pull off possessing an everyman sensibility while acknowledging his supreme gifts and sharing, with matter-of-fact bluntness, his outrageously lofty goals. This explains how his best friend and former Las Vegas High School teammate Tanner Chauncey can say, "He's real humble—a lot of people don't get that about him," then moments later reveal that Harper has often told him, "I want to be the best player ever to play the game."

"I want to be the best," Harper says with a shrug. "I want to be perfect in every aspect of the game."

Even Harper's most blatant imperfection—a competitive arrogance that borders on a mean streak—is likely to endear him to Nationals fans. Former teammates and Harper loyalists universally adore him; it's opponents who can't stand him. Why would they? And why would he want them to? He is prone to smearing copious amounts of "eye black"—ostensibly used to reduce the sun's glare—across his face, with the effect of war paint. He runs hard, slides into bases harder, and barrels into obstructing opponents harder still.

"I'm a real mean person on the field," Harper concedes. "I play the game hard, real hard. I respect everyone on the field. But if you're on the other team, even if we're buddies, I hate you. I'm trying to beat you. I'm going to knock your teeth out. I'm trying to win."

He counts as his primary baseball heroes Pete Rose, Ty Cobb, and Mickey Mantle—and it is perhaps best to forget for the moment that this hard-nosed triumvirate is also, respectively, a convicted tax-evader and gambling addict who remains banned from baseball; a notoriously ornery cuss widely considered to be the dirtiest player in baseball history; and an alcoholic and serial philanderer who died of liver disease at the age of 63.

"Bryce knows one way to play, and that's, 'I'm going to go as hard as I can all the time,'" says Sam Thomas, Harper's coach at Las Vegas High. "If someone says he's a dirty player, I say, 'No, he plays the game hard.' He's an old-school kind of guy. If his goal is second base, and you're in the way, you're gonna want to move. Trust me."

It was Thomas who, along with a couple of assistants, took a tape measure to one of Harper's gargantuan home run blasts during the latter's sophomore year in high school. By the time they traversed the outfield fence, a pair of trees, another outer boundary fence, the five lanes of traffic on South Hollywood Boulevard, and a sidewalk on the other side, the tape measure said 570 feet. Though Harper used an aluminum bat to hit it, for comparison's sake the longest home run in the majors in 2010 came in at 485 feet.

Always the best player on the field, Harper displays body language that often suggests he thinks the umpires are beneath him as well. And sometimes this has ugly consequences. Last June, in the Junior College World Series in Grand Junction, Colorado, five days before the Nationals would draft him, he protested a called third strike by drawing a line in the dirt with the end of his bat, to demonstrate how far outside he thought that particular pitch was. The umpire ejected him, and because it was Harper's second ejection of the year—the earlier one was for taunting opponents—it came with a two-game suspension.

And so it was that Harper marked the end of his amateur career alone in a hotel room while his CSN teammates lost an elimination game without him. Unable to sleep, he text-messaged his coach after midnight, saying, "I love you, coach! I'm sorry!"

When stories began appearing before the draft quoting unnamed scouts as saying Harper was a "bad, bad guy" and possessed a "disturbingly large sense of entitlement," the Nationals reacted with a mixture of amusement and indignation—suggesting privately that the unnamed scouts were from the teams that would pick directly after the Nationals and hoped Washington would pass on him.

"I like the edge he has about him," says Kris Kline, the Nationals' scouting director. "He's wired right. He's ultra-confident in himself, and he's super-aggressive."

The baseball clubhouse is a self-policed arena, with veteran players making sure rookies conform to the code. Over time, Harper's rough edges will almost certainly be smoothed—but not so much as to make him indistinguishable from the others. For this to be a singular love, Harper must remain a singular figure.

Of course, in baseball, as in all professional team sports (and, well, for that matter, life itself), you fall in love at your own risk. There is a defined window for Harper's time in Washington, running roughly from the summer of 2012—the best guess as to when he could arrive following his minor league apprenticeship—to the end of the 2018 season, when he would reach free agency.

After that, of course, love is conditional.

The question was about LeBron James, the basketball star, and it would have been understandable had Harper chosen not to answer it. The question was: how do you avoid what has happened to James—who in the span of about seven years has gone from the most heralded teenager ever to enter the NBA, to the poster child for the spoiled, detached-from-reality modern megastar?

The links between James and Harper are obvious and well chronicled. Like Harper, James appeared on the cover of *SI* as a high schooler—with the headline "The Chosen One." (Inside the magazine, the Harper piece had another headline: "Baseball's LeBron.") James turned pro at 18 and made his NBA debut two months shy of his 19th birthday.

Though few would argue that James, now 26, has been a bust, he failed to lead his Cleveland Cavaliers to an NBA title in his first seven years in the league, and this past off-season, he jilted the Cavaliers in favor of the Miami Heat—announcing his move in an ill-conceived, embarrassingly self-indulgent made-for-TV extravaganza called "The Decision."

Upon hearing the above question, essentially about how to remain grounded amid the trappings of fame, Harper launched into a defense of James—both the decision (to leave Cleveland for Miami) and "The Decision."

"Maybe he should have done it in a different fashion," Harper said. "But I don't think people know he donated all the [proceeds] from 'The Decision' to the Boys and Girls Clubs of America. That's primarily why he did it. Well—and also, he just wanted to go to the Heat. Who wouldn't? It's South Beach! Let's see—South Beach [or] Cleveland? Hmmm. I mean, he just did it to better his career."

The next day, when I spoke at length with Ron Harper, Bryce's dad, he brought up my interview with Bryce and, in particular, the question about James.

"Bryce is still learning how to speak to the media. I'm trying to teach him to be upfront and say what's in his heart," Ron Harper said. "And I want him to. I asked him how things went with you—I'm not gonna lie to you. I want to know. He's my son.

"He said you asked about LeBron and stuff. I told Bryce, 'People can twist things and turn them when they read something, so just be careful with your words and make sure you're being respectful. If you say, hey, you think LeBron did the right thing, say he did the right thing for LeBron.' He said, 'Well, that's what I meant.' And I said, 'But did you say it?'

"Bryce has already been compared to LeBron. So [fans] probably figure as he gets done [with his contractual commitment to Washington], he's going to bolt. That's not Bryce. That's not me. That's not us. I want him to be a National for the rest of his life. I would love that for my son."

Forget for a moment the opinions of a sports-crazed 18-year-old in regard to James, and go back to the original question. In this day and age, can a prodigy such as Harper achieve epic greatness and mega-fame without losing himself in the process?

Fact is, the recent history of athletic prodigies—those preternaturally talented teenagers who appear on the sports scene periodically, seemingly fated to rewrite the record books in their respective sports—is not all that great, at least in terms of image, off-the-field fulfillment, and personal journey. They may fulfill their athletic destinies, but they rarely survive with their images—if not their souls—intact.

There's James. Who else? Well, there's Tiger Woods. There's Jennifer Capriati, a former tennis prodigy who made her pro debut at 13 and won three major titles but struggled throughout her career with injuries, drugs, and other off-the-court issues.

In baseball, scouts once spoke of Josh Hamilton the same way they do of Harper. Twelve years ago, Hamilton was the number-one overall pick in the draft at the age of 18. He is now one of the best players in baseball. But in between, he battled an addiction to drugs that had him banned from the game for the better part of three years.

"To predict what a kid's going to do [when he leaves home]? You just don't know," concedes Thomas, the high school coach. "There are a hundred things that could wrong."

It isn't easy to ask a man, particularly a man such as Ron Harper, why he thinks his son won't go the Josh Hamilton route when he leaves home. But Harper isn't insulted by the question. In fact, he has thought long and hard about this issue.

"I think he'll be fine," he says. "I really do. I trust him. If he was going to do something bad, or do something against us, he would've done it by now."

Sheri Harper, who works as a paralegal and has learned over the years there is no denying the Harper men their baseball fix, has thought about this too. She's about to turn her baby loose into a mean, hard world, but other than some standard maternal angst—"I'm going to miss him like heck," she says—she has no trepidation about it.

"It starts with love in the home," she says. Give them that, "and they will respect you and be honorable. They will not purposely disgrace the name on their back."

Indeed, if something is going to save Bryce Harper—if something is going to allow him to be the one to write the blueprint for turning a prodigy's talent into both a historic athletic career and a successful personal journey through adulthood—it is the same thing that has carried him this far: Family. Upbringing. Parenting.

"I think Bryce is used to being part of a larger unit," says the Nationals' Cardozo. "That unit has been his family. It hasn't all been about Bryce. He's one of three kids, part of the unit. And if indeed that's what he's used to, and if he maintains that philosophy throughout his professional career, he's going to be fine.

"It's the athletes who come to think of themselves as the unit who get into trouble."

They were friends first, Ronnie Harper and Sheri Brooks, all the way back in junior high. They were 13 when they started dating and 21 when they got married. Neither came from any money. During high school, Sheri sometimes worked the graveyard shift at a truck shop before going straight to her first-period class. Ronnie passed up athletic scholarships—in addition to excelling at track and football, he says he was a nationally ranked BMX rider—to get his union card and go to work to help his family make ends meet. His mother had raised four kids mostly on her own.

A question about his father is met with a long pause.

"I knew him for 19 years," he finally says. "I still see him every once in a while. But he has some problems, some inner demons he has to deal with. The stuff I've been through, and my sister and my brother and my mom, it's amazing. It's amazing we've survived some—some stuff.

"But what I took from that was—you can rise from the ashes and say, 'You know what? I'm not going to be like that, and I'm not going to raise my kids like that.' I raised my kids tough, don't get me wrong. When they needed a whipping, they got it—and I'll tell anybody. But I never crossed the line."

There would be three Harper kids, and to their parents all wonderful and beautiful and challenging in their own way, but it was clear early on that Bryce, the baby, was different. At age three, he was good enough to play on his brother's five- and six-year-old T-ball team. By nine, he was being recruited to play on "travel ball" summer teams, some of them in neighboring states. More than anything else, the kid craved baseball.

Once, when Ron Harper was getting ready to leave for work around 3:00 A.M.—he usually worked a 4:00 A.M.-to-noon shift, so he could be home to pick the kids up after school—he heard rustling in Bryce's bedroom. When he went to investigate, he found Bryce, then about nine, in full uniform—down to the glove and cleats.

"Hi, Dad!" Bryce said cheerily.

"Bryce, what are you doing?" Dad said.

"Just getting ready to play."

"But, Bryce, we don't play until Friday. It's Tuesday."

Ron Harper nurtured both Bryan's and Bryce's love of baseball. For a low-impact batting practice, he'd toss small objects at them—dry red beans, sunflower seeds, bottle caps, anything that didn't fly straight—to work on their hand-eye coordination. He'd pitch real batting practice to them but write numbers on the baseball beforehand. The boys would have to call out the number as they swung—helping them focus on the ball and read its spin.

Sometimes, he admits, he'd whisper to Bryce at night, "Hey,

whaddya got tomorrow? You busy in school? You got all your work done?"

Bryce knew what that meant: "Yeah, Dad! You want to go hit? We can go hit, then get a Slurpee!" The next afternoon, when he got out of work, Ron would make up a doctor's appointment to get Bryce out of school early. He'd do the same thing occasionally for Bryan—but they always had to hide it from Bryce, or he'd be so mad he wouldn't talk to them for days.

"School is very important to me—don't get me wrong," Ron Harper says after telling that story. "But there's nothing like your family. You can't get that time back. I didn't have that time with my dad. Still don't. That kind of weighs heavy on your mind sometimes, you know? Maybe I overcompensated at times. I don't know. I didn't try to. I just wanted to be a good dad."

Bryce "played up"—with kids several years older than him—for most of his youth, which is why the family didn't think it was a big deal when the notion was raised of leaving high school two years early (he had a 3.5 grade point average), taking the GED, and playing a year of junior college ball at CSN, which would make him eligible for the draft a year ahead of his classmates. Even his high school coach embraced it.

"High school baseball wasn't even worth his time by that point," Sam Thomas says. "[Leaving] was the best thing he could've done. He was like a guy ready for his master's degree in a fifth-grade classroom."

Still, the strategy subjected Ron Harper to bruising criticism from some media members and other baseball families, who said he was pushing his son too hard, sacrificing a part of the kid's childhood for—something. His own dreams, perhaps. Or the big payday.

"I hear that all the time. But I can tell you: I've never had to push Bryce," Ron says. "He's Bryce. It's how he is. He used to drive me crazy. We'd go to a tournament, be away for a week or 10 days. We'd get back, and I'd say, 'Why don't you take some time off, enjoy the last of the summer.' The next morning, he wants to go hit. 'Dad! I need to go hit. I need to work on something. They got me [out] on that curveball. I gotta work on it.'"

It is dinnertime at the Harper house, and what's left of the family unit gathers around the small table off the kitchen, along with a couple of invited guests, for Sheri's famous tortilla soup. The first thing you do is, you break up some tortilla chips and drop them in, then spoon some shredded cheese over the top. Don't forget the fresh avocado.

It's just the three of them—Ron, Sheri and Bryce. Brittany, 24, recently moved out to Wyoming with her fiancé; they were married in late January. Bryan, 21, is a pitcher at the University of South Carolina, on a partial scholarship. (Bryce helped pay for Brittany's wedding and Bryan's tuition, and has bought both of his parents cars, out of his signing bonus.)

And, soon enough, it will be just Ronnie and Sheri again, as it was 25 years ago.

"I'm getting choked up just thinking about it," Ron says. "I love my kids more than anything. All three of them worked for everything they've got. All I want is, when they lay me down six feet under, I want to know in my heart I taught my kids the right way to live.

"Our whole lives have revolved around the kids. Sometimes, Sheri'll say, 'It's crazy—it's just me and you.' I tell her, 'Well, we'll become best friends again.'"

When the meal is over, Bryce collects the dishes from the table, and for the next 15 minutes stands at the kitchen sink, alongside Sheri, up to his elbows in dish soap.

That's right: Bryce Harper is doing my dishes. And it is at this point that my mind turns to another Nationals phenom.

It is difficult to consider Harper's wildly anticipated arrival in Washington without comparing it to another that occurred only eight months ago. Yes, if this talk of prodigies and once-in-a-generation talent sounds familiar, it's because we just went through this in 2010 with phenom pitcher Stephen Strasburg—who debuted for the Nationals on June 8 and held the city, and much of baseball, rapt until blowing out his elbow in August.

But the similarities between Harper and Strasburg end with their historic talent levels, their groundbreaking contracts—Strasburg signed for a record-setting $15.1 million out of San Diego State in 2009—and the agent they share, Newport Beach, California–based Scott Boras.

"One hundred eighty degrees," one Nationals official said about the difference in personalities. "Absolute yin and yang," another said. "They could not be more different," yet another said.

None of the team officials wanted to speak on the record about that difference, because it would serve only to paint Strasburg in a negative light—even though that wouldn't be the intention.

Strasburg, 22, is an only child, and a late bloomer who didn't realize his potential until his sophomore year in college. He's also a highly private young man whom friends have described as shy. During his rookie season, he mostly sought to avoid interaction with the media and fans—though he could be engaging and witty when he did interact—and he wasn't interested in doing promotional appearances for the team's marketing department. He had a standing rule for the media: do not attempt to call his parents.

Those things aren't necessarily negatives—he wouldn't be the first athlete to distrust the media, and he is permitted to establish his own ground rules as he sees fit—and teammates and team officials alike praised his dedication to his craft, his intense "focus" on baseball, and the manner in which he acted "the way a rookie should."

It's just that Harper possesses all those traits—okay, it remains to be seen if he has it in him to act with a rookie's humility—*and* he embraces the public component of stardom.

"I think it's fun being in the newspaper. I love talking to the media. It's a blast," Harper says. "I love people knowing where I came from and what I'm about."

Here, then, is the difference: Strasburg isn't interested in stardom, only greatness. Harper is interested in both.

And this: unlike Strasburg, perhaps, Harper is willing to let you fall in love with him. He wants you to fall in love with him. And as we already told you—you will.

So, what is to become of our prodigy, young Bryce Harper? And what is to become of the love that is as inevitable as the coming of spring? Will he make it? A generation from now, will we gaze upon his bust in the Hall of Fame? Will he realize his galactic potential, or will fate, hubris, or health stop him short? Will he fill our hearts with joy, or break them, or both? Or neither? Will we remember his name? Will we grow old together?

It's impossible to know, of course. And when it comes to young love such as this, so new and blinding and intense, it is perhaps best not to ponder those questions at all.

WRIGHT THOMPSON

Why You Should Care about Cricket

FROM ESPN.COM

DHAKA, BANGLADESH — The guy walking across the parking lot is famous. That's easy to tell from the reactions. Crowds part for him. Security guards mirror his every step. Other cricketers who made this same trip to the locker room tiptoed around the puddles. He strides over them, head up, confident. I am following an Indian cricket superstar, but I don't know who he is. That's the kind of trip this is going to be—one of constant confusion and mystery.

He's not a big man, but he's got a big aura. Fans climb the stadium wall, cheek to cheek, pressed against openings to catch a glimpse. The player looks up at the apartment buildings crowding the other side of the street, like a zoo animal in reverse, all the residents leaning over to get a peek. He waves his bat at the kids on the wall. The kids scream with joy. I grab a photographer and point.

Who is that?

He looks at me like I've got three heads.

Sachin Tendulkar.

Oh.

Chapter One: Dhaka

Sachin is both the riddle and the answer. That's what I'm told. You must understand India to understand Sachin, but you must understand Sachin to understand India. They created each other. They are the same.

This, obviously, makes no sense to me.

How could it? Just a few hours ago, on a mid-February morning, I landed in Dhaka. I came with a copy of *Cricket for Dummies*. The 2011 Cricket World Cup starts tomorrow, India at Bangladesh, and I know nothing about the sport, not even about the tremendous pressure on the Indian National Cricket team to win its second World Cup after a three-decade drought. How tremendous? The *Hindustan Times*'s logo for their cup coverage says, every day, in enormous letters: "A Billion Dreams . . . 28 years of yearning."

I don't understand that the sport itself is at a crossroads, in crisis even.

I don't realize that Sachin Tendulkar is likely playing in his final World Cup, still searching for his first title. Tendulkar is probably the most famous man in India. He's so famous that people who worked for him are famous: a Bollywood movie character is based on his first agent, Mark Mascarenhas, who died in a car wreck. Billboards with Sachin's photo blanket India's cities; every other commercial on television features his face. He's wildly rich. He is the greatest cricketer in the world. One of the greatest ever.

I know none of that.

At the moment, I'm too busy trying to figure out the definition of a wicket.

Is it the manicured area in the center of the field?

Is it the stumps on either end of that manicured area?

Is it when a player gets out?

(Turns out, according to my book, it's all three.)

Cricket, like India, had long intrigued me from afar. It seemed so mysterious: a game with strange rules, and stranger vocabulary, one that can last for days, captivating billions but meriting only an inch or two in the papers at home. Only madness made it to my radar. *Fan hangs himself after India loss. . . . Pakistan's coach allegedly murdered after upset defeat.* There seemed something pure and savage that was missing from the glossy sports I follow at home.

My first day in Bangladesh, I'm sitting in the press box considering the journey ahead. Sambit Bal, the editor of ESPNcricinfo, sits next to me. If you are looking for someone with the opposite of my cricket knowledge, he's it. Back home, an Alabama fan had killed the trees at Toomer's Corner, and I was trying to explain the significance to him. This was big news to me. I'm a Southern boy, and I tend to believe that SEC football is the most important thing in the world. Only, Sambit has never heard of Auburn, or Alabama, doesn't know that they play college football, or that they are rivals. I fumble around. This is perhaps America's most intense rivalry. A fan just poisoned two 130-year-old oak trees. It's serious. I need an analogy.

My first thought: it's like India-Pakistan in cricket.

Except, you know, for the four wars since 1947 and the constant threat of nuclear holocaust. Other than that, Auburn-Alabama is just like India-Pakistan.

This is my first day in the world of cricket.

I have a lot to learn.

NO MAGIC MOMENT TODAY

Game day outside the stadium is wild. People fill the streets for blocks. A drum beats somewhere in the distance. Vuvuzelas are the horn section. The roar of the mob gets louder and louder until it's just white noise. Chaos is the new normal. Loud is the new quiet. Dhaka has ceased to function.

The stadium fills up. India is the favorite to win the tournament. The team's lineup is stocked with sluggers. The first two swagger to the center of the field: Virender Sehwag and Sachin Tendulkar. They are really here, waddling in pads, giving fist bumps. The crowd is bubbling now after months of anticipation, after years of hunger for their country to be seen as more than its disasters.

The first ball brings a crescendo.

I'm trying to follow the game. I know Tendulkar is a star, so I focus on him. I cannot tell what makes him special. Then, before I know it, he's out, finished for the day. I don't really understand why. The fans rise to their feet as he walks off. He's scored 28 runs. It all happened so fast. I feel cheated.

Sehwag stays in. He crushes ball after ball. It's like watching Mark McGwire take batting practice. The dude has Popeye arms, and he's pounding the thing all over the yard. Sehwag is called "the Butcher of Najafgarh." He puts on a show. The cricket-mad Bangladeshi crowd oohs and aahs, just happy to be seeing the game in person.

Sehwag finally gets out with 175, an incredible total. After that, the game slows. India wins, and it's a little boring, frankly. Maybe it's because I don't know the rules, or because the scene in the street was exponentially more dramatic than the one in the stands, but the game itself seems anticlimactic. I've flown halfway around the planet, and I'm after more than an intellectual understanding of why cricket matters. There's a mystic place beyond the assignment. When the books are closed and the conversations about culture and history are over, I want to sit in a stadium and have the game explain itself to me.

That didn't happen tonight.

INNOCENCE LOST?

One thing did happen—a press-box conversation during the game that will eat at me for the next week. I'm sitting with Sambit, and a guy comes up to chat. He's a former Indian cricket player turned broadcaster, Sanjay Manjrekar, and he's been captivated by Bangladesh's reaction to this World Cup opening in its capital. This pure love for cricket transports him to his past.

"There is a certain amount of innocence here," he tells us, "which I think India has lost."

The entire exchange lasts a minute or two. His lament, and the place from which it comes, are beyond me.

I don't yet know enough to recognize a eulogy when I hear one.

Chapter Two: Ahmedabad, India

I'm taking a retired physics professor named Kumar Bhatt and his brother Bankim to the next game. Kumar taught at Ole Miss, Kentucky, and Texas. Most of that time was spent in Oxford, Mississippi, where I live. Before he moved back to India, his house was a few blocks from mine. If anybody would understand where I am coming from, it's a former neighbor.

We find our seats, and the game begins: a slow affair, plodding, with the powerful Australians still finding their legs and the overmatched Zimbabweans playing defensively, taking no chances.

The stadium is mostly empty. It will remain that way. I think of Manjrekar's press-box lament.

Kumar tells me about the history of the game. When he was growing up, championship cricket meant a Test match. White uniforms. Breaks for high tea. Unlimited overs. (An over is a set of six balls, sort of like an at-bat.) Games lasted for days. Sometimes nobody won. Cricket was designed to be played, not watched. "After five days," Kumar says, "it was frustrating for the spectators."

Modern attention spans began shrinking cricket. First came the World Cup format, which could be completed in a day and is now 50 overs. More recently, the 20-over game has become popular with paying customers, an event stripped of nuance, played in the same amount of time as a baseball game.

We sit in the lower bleachers, the entire circle of green in front of us. An Australian player muscles a ball toward the boundary. A ball that hits or bounces over the boundary at the edge of the field is four runs; a ball that crosses it on the fly is six. Some Aussie hits are seen as gauche. Kumar clucks disapprovingly. I ask why. Old-school cricket fans don't like it when players cross the bat, which for baseball fans would be like if a right-handed hitter got an outside fastball and, instead of going the opposite way, turned and pulled it. It's vulgar. The ball should be hit in the direction from which it's pitched.

"You are to play gracefully," Kumar says, "and give respect to the ball."

Have you ever heard that something "isn't cricket"? That's where the phrase comes from. To cross the bat isn't cricket. Sehwag crosses the bat. Constantly. He wants bombs. Fours and sixes. Sehwag revels in his vulgarity. Tendulkar, although a big hitter, plays with an old-school respect. Kumar loves Sachin.

"Grace has a place," Kumar says.

"The players have gotten soft," Bankim grumbles.

"Australia relies mostly on fast bowlers to win," Kumar says. "We don't consider it fair."

The sparse crowd gets behind Zimbabwe, which steals a couple of wickets. Fans whistle at the departing Australians, waving goodbye. Australia completes 50 overs with 262 runs.

"Not a good score," Bankim says.

Zimbabwe comes to bat. It's already been a long day. Kumar is 78 years old. "Would you like to leave?" he asks.

Bankim ignores him for a bit but gets the message. We pack our stuff. I check the scoreboard and work out some numbers. Zimbabwe is scoring 5.25 runs an over. It needs 5.26. It has a chance at the upset. I head up to the press box. I need to keep watching cricket, in person and on television, if I want a revelation. There will be a moment when it all becomes clear.

Maybe that will happen tonight.

That is one of many miscalculations I will be guilty of today. The Zimbabwe team slows down, needing 26 overs to reach 100 runs, but in the well-lit press box I hold out hope, doing the math on my phone, figuring out the run rate. At least I'm taking steps, learning the nuances of the game. I divide the runs by the overs. Repeat. Then the wire-service reporters stop watching the game and begin typing. Hope is gone. There are many ways to know when a game is over, but the most reliable is to find the correspondent from the Associated Press. The AP guy is sitting next to me. He taps furiously.

There will be no magic.

Chapter Three: New Delhi

My New Delhi cab driver's name is Deepchand Yadav. He loves cricket. Once, the captain of India's 1983 World Cup champion team, Kapil Dev, rode in his car. *Can you imagine?! Kapil Dev, in my cab!* He hopes India will win this year's tournament. Everyone is very nervous. A billion dreams. Twenty-eight years of yearning. The team must win, for the billion, for its star.

"I'm fans with Sachin," he says. "Sachin is mentally cool."

Deepchand moved to Delhi from his village 18 years ago. Yadav is a caste name. His caste members are traditionally cow herders, and as India has changed, they've spread through the nation, taking any job they can get, sending money back to the villages. He is part of post-caste India. Anything is possible through hard work. He grinds, trying to hang on to the first rung of a lower-middle-class life. He's a smart guy, with a big smile and a luxurious mustache.

Six years ago, worried about the lives of his wife and three children, he brought them to Delhi with him. "My family actually likes village," he says, "but I like Delhi because business purposes is good." Six years ago, he played cricket—captain of his village team. But since his family came to the city, there's no time. He's never played cricket with his son.

His son is 10 years old. The boy plays cricket with friends in the street, wherever they can find a little space, five or six sharing a bat. The wheels turn. I ask Deepchand if I could play with them tomorrow. I've watched cricket, but I've never held a bat or struck a ball. Books take you only so far. The best way to know a sport is to play it with children.

"What's your son's name?" I ask.

"Sachin," he says.

"IF CRICKET IS A RELIGION, SACHIN IS GOD"

Deepchand chose this name carefully. A name is very important in Hindu culture. The right one, it is believed, can lead a child to immortality. A name is a compass. It points a person in a specific direction.

Of his three children, Deepchand got to name two of them. The girl he called Sonia, after Sonia Gandhi, a politician, "an honest and powerful woman." He wants his girl to be like her. He wants his son to be like Sachin: strong, sincere, poised. Sachin represents so many things for Indians who aspire to a better future while not losing their past in the exchange. The name literally means "pure."

"He never behaves badly," says Rahul Bhattacharya, once a popular young writer on cricket, now a novelist, "which Indians find very appealing. He's not had scandals with women or drugs. He's the idol for our children."

Before Sachin, typical Indian cricketers took few risks. For the first hour, shots were deflected, frustrating the bowler, tiring him out, forcing him into mistakes, a perfect sporting ethos in a country known for vein-popping passive-aggressiveness. Sachin changed that. His style was new. He swung a thick bat, heavier than Indians had used before.

He wasn't passive-aggressive.

He was simply aggressive.

He played with respect, but he also played with power. A recent book, *If Cricket Is a Religion, Sachin Is God,* finds an important corollary to India's history in this. Before, because of a stagnant economy, nutrition was a problem. India couldn't outslug rivals. It needed spin bowlers and crafty batsmen. An inferiority complex developed. Despite his greatness, somewhere deep inside, Indian legend Sunil Gavaskar, who retired two years before Sachin debuted, seemed terribly insecure. After he became famous, he turned down a membership to London's exclusive Marylebone Cricket Club—the Royal and Ancient Golf Club of cricket—because, once, a guard there didn't recognize him. The slights burned until they became a part of him, his pilot light, defining both him and the nation he represented.

Sachin isn't from that India.

His international debut came a year before India opened up its economy. His rise mirrored India's early-'90s rise, when foreign corporations arrived in India for the first time, accounts swelling with advertising dollars, looking around for a face. They found Sachin.

He was India's first modern sports star, a combination of Babe Ruth, Muhammad Ali, and Michael Jordan, because his rise mirrored a nation's economic rise, and he forever changed sports celebrity and marketing in India. Once, when an American company executive contacted his agent and wanted to understand what place Sachin held in Indian culture, the agent didn't quote the number of Test wins, or international centuries. He said, simply, that Sachin endorsed Audemars Piguet watches, and that the company made a model just for him. The executive was sold.

Sachin has been a star since he was a boy. Cops had to stand guard outside his 12th-grade exams. Despite the attention, he's remained dignified. There are no porn stars. He grants few audiences. He is the man Indians count on when things are at their worst.

Two weeks after the Mumbai terrorist attacks, India's 9/11, with the country reeling, India played a Test match against England. Sachin anchored the match, his performance rising to meet the stakes of the day, scoring more than 100 runs without getting out, which would be like dropping 50 in the NBA Finals. A century, it's called. His success, which he dedicated to those suffering in his hometown, added to his legend. Over coffee one evening, his current agent asked me, essentially, if Derek Jeter had a Secret Service detail. He was completely serious. I laughed out loud. No, I told him. He seemed surprised. Everywhere Sachin goes, the government of India protects him.

He's a national treasure.

Now his career is nearing its end, and fans are left with beautiful memories, to be sure, but also questions.

What does Sachin's retirement mean for cricket?

What does it mean for India?

ELEPHANT IN THE SLOW LANE

The highway runs past ancient ruins, and the lights of the cricket ground. Tomorrow, I'll see South Africa–West Indies. Today, I'm going to play cricket with little Sachin and his friends. I've brought a surprise for him. It's a Sachin Tendulkar signature series cricket bat made from pure English willow. It'll be his first proper bat, and when Deepchand told him about it last night, Sachin had trouble going to sleep. We ride out toward the suburban slums. I'm twisting around to see the wrecked castle when Deepchand shouts, "You see elephant?"

What? I turn around. There's an elephant in the slow lane. Cars whip past and the elephant just lumbers, oblivious, carrying people patiently to their destination. *There's a freaking elephant in the slow lane.*

"What happens if a car hits the elephant?" I ask.

"The car is damaged," Deepchand says. "The elephant is okay."

LIKE AMERICA IN THE '50S

There are elephants on the highway. There are elephant-sized metaphors shuffling alongside. This is a nation with a foot in both the past and present. India is at an end and a beginning. Over drinks in Delhi with my friends Candace and Lydia, we talk about this. Lydia is a correspondent for the *New York Times* and one of the world's experts on developing nations. Talking journalism with her is like talking cricket with Sachin. She cautions me to avoid trying to figure out what India is, or what it isn't, or to draw conclusions. "It leads you down all of these blind alleys," she tells me. "It defies all efforts to simplify."

She's right. I'm not sure what any of this means, or how cricket or Sachin fits into it, or even if he'll actually retire, but this is a critical time for the nation, just as it's a critical time for cricket.

Their ambitions and threats are the same. Anyone who's here for even a few days can tell that. India today seems a lot like America in the mid-'50s.

This is largely a pre-ironic society. Yes, there is a rich history of satire, and modern exceptions—the '50s also produced Jack Kerouac—but the earnestness with which people love Sachin is reflected in many aspects of the culture. There's no place, yet, for an Indian *Daily Show*. Elephants aren't for statues representing a bygone era, like the blue mustang outside Denver's airport. They are for the slow lane.

Movies are expected to end a certain way. Heroes in those movies are expected to behave a certain way. In his definitive book on Mumbai, *Maximum City,* author Suketu Mehta describes an Indian audience's reaction when the hero of a film turned out to be a terrorist. They ransacked the theater. It does not seem strange to an Indian filmgoer that the songs in the movies have nothing to do with the plot. Mehta writes:

> The suspension of disbelief in India is prompt and generous, beginning before the audience enters the theater itself. Disbelief is easy to suspend in a land where belief is so rampant and vigorous. And not just in India; audiences in the Middle East, Russia, and Central Asia are also pre-cynical. They still believe in motherhood, patriotism, and true love; Hollywood and the West have moved on.

Commercialism is a new mistress in sports. The Indian Premier League, which plays 20-over cricket, started three years ago. The creation of the IPL is India's Dodgers-leave-Brooklyn moment. Money is changing the sport. The change is seen by most as good. Any achievement by an Indian is good, something to be admired in the light. For many Indians, especially those who speak English and are trying to navigate the brave new world of economic revolution, the issue of identity is an important one. Excellence is tied up in that search. Indian writers are judged by the size of the advance, not the magic of their words. Indian artists are judged by the price fetched at auction, not the feelings they create in someone who stands before their canvas. Open the paper any random day to find an example. When famous Bollywood actress Aishwarya Rai met Dustin Hoffman at a Lakers game, the tabloids report, she talked to him about "new market-tapping agendas and global trends." Not acting. Not his construction of Benjamin Braddock or Ted Kramer. They didn't talk craft. They talked money.

Over drinks, Lydia tells me one I hadn't seen. Indians are obsessed with the *Guinness Book of World Records*. Obsessed.

India still believes in the simple beauty of success.

Irony and cynicism come next.

"Irony requires a certain amount of self-confidence," Lydia says. "You have to have built enough of an identity to turn around and reject it, or to laugh at it. I think that's something that takes time."

THE KIDS ARE ALL RIGHT

The kids see Deepchand and me walking down the street and furiously make preparations. One of them yells, "Wickets!" and they spring to action, setting up a stack of bricks. Our field is the only greenish space in the neighborhood, dirt, really, strewn with bits of trash. The kids introduce themselves. There's Sachin. He's quiet, with a wide smile and a laugh that comes out a chortle, rushed, almost as if it's surprised him. Another one, the most confident, tells me his name is Sunny. That's Sunil Gavaskar's nickname. He's 13. The brashest kid, the cockiest, is named Deepak.

I pull out the bat.

A neighborhood kid winds up and bowls to me. The first few, I deflect. Then I get into one, a full baseball-style turn, and wallop it over the crumbling brick fence at the end of the field. Six!

"Good knock!" one of the kids tells me.

When I pop out, Sachin bats next. He crushes a high-arcing drive that lands in the trash-strewn woods. The kids hunt in the mud for the ball. The day fills with laughter. The old women sitting in the shade of a tree watch the game. Deepchand and Sachin are playing cricket for the first time together in Delhi. They are happy, tossing the ball, dad bowling and son batting. The cab driver seems suddenly lighter.

"You're a kid again!" I yell at him across the field.

He throws back his head and laughs.

The boys fight over who'll bat next. They race back to the wicket. Sachin wins. They want me to bowl. The first time, instead of windmilling with my arm locked, I throw it like a baseball. That's a no-no. It's called chucking. I'm a chucker. Sunny explains.

"Full-arm action," he says. "Can I show you?"

He places my fingers along the seams. I wind up and clean bowl Deepchand. I've gotten him out. The kids give me high-fives. "Pretty good," Sunny says.

The game is no longer tedious. It's alive, inside me, in these children, even in the women grinning at us from beneath the tree. I look down at the end of the field and catch Sachin staring at his new Sachin signature bat, showing it off to his friends.

The kids decide we should play a game—five overs, two teams of four. Sachin and I go first. One player stands at each edge of the makeshift wicket. To score a run, each runner has to make it safely to the other end. The farther the hit, the more times we can complete the circuit.

I put my notebook down. The sky is blue. The sun pans across my face, warming the afternoon. The boys are happy. Deepchand is happy. I am happy too, playing with the neighborhood kids, although when I am bowled, when I'm out, I feel like I've let a 10-year-old down. Cricket, like most team sports, is a personal game but also one of intense connection. It is both individual and communal. I'm left to watch. Sachin crushes it, six after six. Sunny kills it too, spraying the ball around the makeshift field, over the fence. We finish with 49 runs. That's the target.

The next team scores fast too. Deepak is a beast. He's barrel-chested. He hits a booming six, and when the ball is finally found, he hits another. He hits a third one, high into the air, which will come down in the trees and in the trash, a ball that will never be found, ending our match in a draw. He watches it sail into the Delhi sky, and he poses.

"I am Sehwag!" he says.

WHERE PURE AGGRESSION COMES FROM

I am Sehwag.

As Sachin grew up watching Sunil, Sehwag grew up watching Sachin. He saw Sachin's aggressive stance. He took what he saw, internalized it, and spat out something new, something dangerous even. There's a reason some old-school fans find him vulgar, and Deepak screams his name.

Where does something like that come from?

We leave Deepchand's house and drive toward the airport, past the endless storefronts featuring posters of bodybuilders. Strength is in. Out on the edges of Delhi, huge apartment buildings stretch to the horizon. Ugly concrete boxes, row after row of them. If Bruce Springsteen were from India, he'd sing about these streets. There are things being built here. There are things being torn down. A shepherd drives a flock of sheep down the road, turning them into a weedy lot, the proposed site of a cultural center. He wears a red turban, carries a staff.

Sehwag grew up in these badlands. He saw Sachin through the prism of the gritty world around him, looking past the grace to the power. Before Sehwag, Indian opening batsmen were supposed to take the shine off the ball. That's the cricket phrase. Take the shine off. Break it in. Wear down the bowler. Sehwag would take the shine off by going for fours and sixes. He got a reputation for dogging it on singles. And if Sachin gave birth to Sehwag, then a whole group of younger sluggers have taken it a step further. At least Sehwag still plays Test cricket. Some newer stars don't.

The Indian team is a blunt object, 15 men created not in the image of Tendulkar, exactly, but in the image of the new India that he both inspired and represented. Sachin carried the team alone in the '90s, but in the past decade a generation of hyper-aggressive Indian stars came of age. Former captain Sourav Ganguly ripped off his shirt and twirled it above his head on the balcony of the uptight Lord's Cricket Ground in London.

They are celebrities now. They frighten opposing bowlers. They themselves are not afraid. Two years ago, the team changed its jerseys from powder blue to a deeper color. It seemed less meek.

I am Sehwag.

"The aggression, the brashness," says Bhattacharya, the cricket writer turned novelist. "It's now something which Indians see that this is what we have to do to assert our place in the world. We've been f——ed over for thousands of years. Everyone has conquered us. Now we're finding our voice. We're the fastest-growing economy in the world. We are going to buy your companies. Our cricket team is like going to f——ing abuse you back, and we're going to win and we're going to shout in your face after we win. People love that."

We turn on Najafgarh Road. Shop workers give us directions. Everyone knows The Butcher. In the midst of this urban blight, there is a single planted field. This all used to be farmland. Now there are big piles of sand, the dust of something old waiting to become something new. White smoke rises from burning trash. Mechanics fixing motorcycles on the sidewalk tell us to take a right at the feeble old tree past the shrine to the monkey god.

This is Sehwag's street.

When his father died, the neighbors tell us, he moved his mother to a nice place in central Delhi. Other family members live in the house now. There, they point. That's his aunt. The home is down an alley, where Sehwag used to pound cricket balls. "He was always a long hitter," a man says.

The house has a big black gate and a bamboo fence to offer privacy for the patio. There's an orange lantern and a rooftop terrace. It's the middle-class home that Deepchand dreams of for his family. This is the home of a grain merchant who moved to the city from a village, wanting to build a new life.

Sachin is the son of a poet.

Sehwag is the son of man who sold wheat and rice.

THE LAST OF A DYING BREED?

"In the golden age of cricket," Bhattacharya says, "you'd never be without *rotis*."

Halfway around the world, I feel at home here, a group of sportswriters at dinner. We're crowded around an upstairs table somewhere deep inside the alleyed maze of Old Delhi. It could be Augusta, Georgia. They've brought our food but not our bread. No *rotis*? Bhattacharya hits the running joke. Gallows humor. In the golden age of cricket, the *dal* wouldn't be bland. In the golden age of cricket, there wouldn't be so much grease in the mutton. It's never far away. Any conversation about cricket quickly arrives here: are the changes designed to help cricket exist in a modern world actually killing the game?

They tell a story of Sunil Gavaskar crushing a six in a long-ago Test match and stepping back to curse himself. He knew he needed to calm down, to play for the long haul, not just one six-and-out. Adrenaline and aggression are enemies of Test success. Now some of the artistry has been bred out. The new formats have given birth to dramatic changes in strategy and in the skill set required. For football fans, imagine if a television network asked the NFL to shorten a few games a year to 15 minutes. Then imagine if, because of the success, it seemed inevitable that soon all football games would last 15 minutes. Now imagine if everyone who played football lost the ability to play the longer game.

"That's one of those existential cricket dilemmas," Bhattacharya says. "We don't know. We all live in fear of Test cricket perishing at the hands of Twenty20. It's something we all worry about. We don't actually know."

So, when Tendulkar retires, will he take an era of cricket with him?

"Sachin's symbolic value is very strong," Bhattacharya says. "He might be the last one."

Sachin is a bridge in a sport that my friends fear is burning its bridges.

A DELICATE SORT OF QUESTION

The next afternoon we are all at the game. Bhattacharya sits next to me. His first book, a cricket travelogue called *Pundits from Pakistan,* has been my faithful companion on this journey. He has a big day tomorrow. *People* magazine just called. It needs to take his picture at 8:00 A.M. His novel *The Sly Company of People Who Care* is hot here in India. He has a face made for a photographer, in that writerly way, delicate, almost pretty, except for the crooked nose that hints at a stormy past. He's arrogant as hell, but in the same way I am, so we get along great.

I'm learning the rules. I feel more at home every day. The stadium is like any American stadium: (too-)loud music and ham-fisted promotion. The fans sit quietly until a JumboTron camera finds them, then they go nuts. Look! Everyone's a celebrity!

But there's something missing.

The stands are half-empty. These are two great teams, elite sides, evenly matched, on a beautiful Delhi day, in a city of 14 million people, and most seats are empty. They'll stay that way. It's not just Delhi. When India's not playing, the stadiums are pretty dead. That game has explained itself, all right: Indians aren't as cricket-mad as I thought. There is a surprising lack of street-level buzz. Sure, the televisions are going mad, and the newspapers and radio programs and billboards. The hype machine is kicking at max RPMs. But it seems just that. Hype. A mile wide and an inch deep. The former Indian player's press-box eulogy makes sense.

India has gained an impossible amount in the past 20 years. Has it lost something too?

I turn to Rahul. "Do Indians still love the actual game of cricket?"

There's a pause.

"It's a delicate sort of question," he says.

Another pause.

"The thing about Indians' love for cricket is, a lot of it is having something to support India at," he says. "A lot of it is celebrity. People in love with [team captain M. S.] Dhoni instead of the actual sport. It happens all the time. In the past five years, you find that matches not featuring India don't draw crowds. It does seem on some level the love is not for the sport itself but for some of the things it stands for."

Cricket is everywhere. It's on 24/7. It's on red carpets with Bollywood bombshells and in corporate boardrooms. But the more it is, the less it is.

"We've been so neutered by cricket now," Rahul says. "There's so much of it. It's reached a point where you can be oblivious to it. Indian fans now just watch India."

The afternoon unspools. Friends come and go. Many jokes, and a few serious conversations. Rahul is quiet. An hour or two passes. He turns to me. "The question you asked me. . . ."

He's been thinking. India leads you down blind alleys. It is a place with many different regions and religions and cultures. The Indian national cricket squad binds them. You must understand that to understand the mania surrounding the team.

The team's rabid popularity, he says, is a reflection of rising national ambition, of pride in national achievement. *The Guinness Book of World Records,* squared. In a republic with a short history and a thin national narrative, cricket and Bollywood are India's baseball and apple pie. Rahul makes air quotes and says, "Indian culture."

"People think if I'm Indian," he says, "I have to access this part of our culture. It's in our blood."

More time passes. The game continues to drag. I think about tomorrow's flight and my trip to Bangalore. In a few days, I'll finally see India play in India. That's ground zero. I'm ready to see the obsession up close, see if I'll find passion or more hype. Next to me, Rahul is in thought too. Something's bothering him.

"I wonder," he says, "if I've been too cynical about India and its passion for cricket."

Chapter Four: Bangalore Hype

Morning dawns ghost-white. We drive into a wall of smog. Pollution is the price of progress. One of the prices anyway. Some drivers pull over. Jets scream overhead. We cannot see them. The New Delhi airport is nearby. We cannot see it either. Soon we can't even see the car directly in front of us. Two disembodied red lights float in the chemical haze. The driver slows. He finds the turn at the last minute and screeches to the terminal. I'm dreading the usual chaos of an Indian airport.

But once inside, I am transported. Is this the future? The place is new and serene. The floors are shiny. A fancy coffee kiosk teems with undercaffeinated commuters. The food court has a Subway, a Baskin-Robbins, a McDonald's, a Yo!China. There's a bookstore. A bronze elephant towers in the lobby.

That's when I see it.

There's a restaurant named Dilli Streat. It's a take on Delhi's famous street-food scene. It has slightly dressed-up versions of blue-collar classics. The concept is an ironic mixture of old and new, with a winking nod to a past seen as quaint yet valuable. Cynicism and irony, on back-to-back days.

India is changing at lightning speed.

THE NEW CAMERA-SMASHING INDIAN HEROES

Players walk through the lobby of the Royal Gardenia Hotel. Wide-eyed young fans and gossip-hunting reporters slowly circle, the light and dark of fame. I'm sitting on a couch. A woman approaches. She's from a local tabloid. She wants me to take a paparazzi picture of an English cricket player, a wealthy Indian liquor tycoon, and the tycoon's son. They're together in the bar. She wants me to be her Trojan horse.

"We have a lot of pressure from our editor in chief to get the story," she says. "You know that pressure? Okay. So I need a picture. I'm local. They've seen me. They know my face. And, um, so we would like to take their pictures to publish. To print. So . . . we wondered if you could help us."

"I can't do it."

"I just want you to take a picture. That's it."

"No."

"No? It's just a picture."

"Then you go take it."

I tell her that I'm a reporter too, a professional, not a tourist, and I cannot be talked into anything, much less this.

"I could go take the picture myself," she says. "I just don't want my camera smashed. That's the issue."

"They won't smash your camera," I say.

"Of course they will," she says. "He's done it before. The kid."

Her editors don't want cricket info. They want to know about the players' lives. This is a fairly recent development. Everything is changing. Lines must be crossed, ethics blurred. The newspaper industry is still rising here. Competitive celebrity gossip is corrosive, and it leads, almost inevitably, to the taking down of heroes—the end of heroes, even, for deep earnestness cannot survive a daily diet of snark. I think of Jane Leavy's magnificent book about Mickey Mantle, and her documenting the moment when Americans began viewing our idols differently. India, it seems, is approaching that day. Another question about Tendulkar arises: is he the final star athlete created by that deeply earnest society, the one with its suspension of disbelief fully intact?

Is he the last hero?

Cricket is Bollywood by a different name. The match-fixing scandal of the late-'90s was the end of an innocence about the game, and Sachin's role in steadying the ship afterward is part of people's great love for him. But the lid is off. The readers demand information. The pressure is great. Where do they eat dinner? Whom are they dating? What movies do they like? What's their favorite food? What's to come? Are they on drugs? Are they taking steroids? What are their failures and weaknesses and scandals?

"Are they the same as us?" the tabloid reporter asks.

They will be soon.

KIDS IN THE LOBBY

The thirst of a tabloid reporter and the love of a starstruck child are fruit from the same tree. Maybe the difference is intent, and maybe it's innocence, which sounds like the pitter-patter of tiny feet on marble floors. Kids chase their favorite cricketers around the hotel. Their joy restores faith, washes away cynicism. Maybe the soul of cricket can survive this landslide of change. Maybe there's more than hype.

To the cute little stalkers, there are many heroes besides Sachin. Parents hover nearby, briefly children again. Virat Kohli is eating in the coffee shop against the back wall covered with ivy. He's got a woman with him. Kids hang by the door. Ten minutes is an eternity to a child who's a few feet from his hero.

Vineet Sethi sits with his daughters, 15-year-old Radhika and nine-year-old Nandini. The girls started plotting the moment this game was announced for Bangalore. High-level strategy. When Vineet got home from work, the girls were ready to go. It's D-Day. Who will they meet?

Finally, mercifully, Kohli stands to leave. The girls rise to meet him at the door. Kohli has a faux-hawk and a tight black T-shirt. He signs. His date carries a designer handbag. Radhika is checking out the signature when Nandini's eyes widen. *OMG!*

It's Sehwag.

Up close, he's stocky and balding. He stops to sign. Then Gautam Gambhir comes down the hall. The girls are losing their minds now. Dad asks if he'll pose for a photo. Gautam smiles for the camera.

"I'm gonna faint," Radhika says.

The girls can't stop looking at the autograph book, then leaning into each other, then giggling, then looking, then giggling. "I cannot believe you told Virat Kohli that I'm in love with him!" Radhika says.

Vineet laughs.

"I only like Gautam," Radhika says. "I don't like Virat Kohli anymore. I used to like him a lot, but he was with a girl. A nice one."

Dad is still laughing but has that worried-dad look on his face.

"Why not Sehwag?" I ask.

"He's married," Radhika says. "And has two kids."

Vineet looks a bit pale. "I'm not listening," he says.

The girls cover their faces with their hands, tapping their feet, tingling with nervous energy. I feel it. The passion I looked for at the other cricket matches doesn't exist around the sport, but it does in the Royal Gardenia lobby. Indians might not be obsessed with the sport of cricket per se, but they are with the Indian cricket team. They are unhealthy, myopic, and without measure or self-control, and that's just when they see their idols in the flesh.

I cannot imagine what it's like when they're actually watching them play.

Chapter Five: Game Day

The morning of the India-England match, I wake up anxious. No newspaper, no television. No more hype. The more someone tells me something matters, the more suspicious I become. The game stands on its own today. It could bring my moment of rapture — or deep disappointment. What if the thing I'm hungry for is too rare to just happen upon? What if it no longer exists?

The driver picks me up outside the hotel. The traffic is terrible as we make our way toward the stadium. I can see the light stanchions in the distance. I wonder what they'll shine on today. Somehow, on a lark to be introduced to a new sport, I've stumbled into a rapidly changing world. Things are being gained, and things are being lost. What if I've come to cricket too late? Other cricket reporters sense this fear; one asks me if I'll be writing a positive or negative story. I'm not sure. It seems that the sporting future in India is the present in America. I can see their tomorrow.

The driver drops me at the main gate. I walk around for several hours. The air smells like fried food. Vendors sell Indian snacks and sugarcane juice. Cops, wary of another cricket riot, whack sticks against trees whenever someone stops. There is no still today.

"Sachin!" a man yells. "Sachin's last World Cup!"

"He will not retire after the World Cup," another insists. .

A group of fans are being interviewed by a television reporter. They're young and funny. They're intentionally extreme, with knowing smirks.

"After 300 years of them ruling us," one says, "it's time we gave it back."

"We're gonna trash the English," another says.

"They play like little boys," says the third.

They seem so confident, not people who need any outside validation. Maybe Sachin isn't needed any longer. Maybe Sehwag is more representative. That hasn't occurred to me until now. Later I'll talk to an Indian journalist, Vaibhav Vats, who is writing about cricket as a window into national self-esteem. He thinks Sachin isn't as important as he used to be.

"It's about wealth," Vats says. "So you don't look for external things to shore up your own sense of identity. There isn't the identity crisis there was then."

Fans wave Indian flags. For 10 rupees, about 22 cents, dozens of entrepreneurs paint Indian flags on people's faces. Other kids take blue paint and, emulating a famous billboard around the country, tag themselves "Bleed Blue." Sports marketing creating fan behavior creating more sports marketing: a snake eating its tail.

A man chases me down. He's wearing a long robe with the Indian flag painted on it, along with the cricket alpha and omega: *Sachin* and *Sehwag*. There's a young boy with him. The boy opens up a binder. It's full of stories about the man wearing the robe. They point to one. He's offered to trade his kidney for a ticket to this game. He says he wants to watch cricket. I think he wants to be a star.

Finally, I slip through a gate.

It's almost time.

FINALLY, THE GAME IS AT HAND

We hear the cheers as the Indian bus gets closer. The soldier on the tower with the rifle stands up from his red chair. Radios squawk. The bus pulls to a stop. Submachine-gun-toting troops in tight T-shirts and khaki fatigues form a wall of flesh and metal.

Sachin Tendulkar is third off the bus. I recognize him now. He's wearing headphones, yesterday's smile replaced by determination. We enter the stadium behind the team. The place simmers with anticipation. I trade my press-box seat for one in the bleachers. Today, I'm a fan. Andy Zaltzman, a cricket-mad British stand-up comedian, sits next to me. The speakers play music so loud we cannot talk when it's on. "Don't need it," Andy says every time there's some marketing flourish. The broadcast people interview some fans. "Dhoni's hot," a young woman says.

The broadcast people interview Dhoni. "How are you coping with the hype and the pressure?" the man asks.

"We're looking forward to the national anthem," Dhoni says.

The music begins, and the crowd comes to its feet. Here we go. Andy saw a game in this stadium on television once, India versus Pakistan, and the cacophony when an Indian player bowled his opponent seemed to come out of his television and transport his London home across two oceans and several lesser seas. That noise is something he cannot forget. He's chasing that ghost, left a wife and two kids at home for six weeks to chase it halfway around the world. I'm chasing something too. The appointed hour has arrived. I've heard it all week, from fans and writers, and now I hear it once more.

"Wait till Sachin comes to bat," Andy says.

IN CASE YOU WERE WONDERING: HERE, NOW, THE RULES

This time, I'm ready for whatever is about to happen.

After 10 days I know the basic calculus of cricket. Each team has 50 overs and 10 wickets. For baseball fans, think of it as 50 at-bats and 10 outs. All overs last six balls, whether any of them are hit or not. A player is out if just one of his hits is caught, or if he misses the ball and it strikes the wicket behind him, or if a fielder throws the ball into the wicket before he completes a run.

When either the overs or wickets are gone, the innings is over; an innings is a set of 50 overs, and each team, in one-day cricket, has one. Wickets and overs are the two resources a team has when setting a target, or, if it bats second, chasing it. Figuring out when and how to risk them is the chess match. A wicket can be gone with one moment of carelessness.

Sachin's agent once brought a business partner to a game only to have Sachin get out on the first ball. The ball doesn't care that there are executives in a luxury suite. There are 11 opponents constantly shifting around the green field, looking to trick, to trap, to slide into a spot where a ball is coming.

The cricket pitch is a dangerous ocean. The batsman is a tiny boat.

CONSTRUCTING MAGIC

Sachin's name is lost in the cheers. The crowd roars even in anticipation of it. Once again Sachin walks onto the field. Sehwag is with him. They are leading off, alternating at-bats, an entire modern history of a country between them. Sunil begat Sachin begat Sehwag. From insecurity to confidence to aggression. Which will be best today?

Sachin looks up at the crowd. He rubs his hands together. Spits on them. Sehwag takes one practice cut. It's time. Sehwag hits an immediate four, one that's almost caught. The Indian fans jump, then laugh. Sehwag pops up, and it is again almost caught. He's swinging for the fences.

Sachin plays slower, taking his runs where he can get them, defending the other pitches away. Shades of Gavaskar? "Sachin has this aura of calmness around him," Andy says. "Federer has it. Brady seems to have it."

Then, a victim of his own aggression, Sehwag is out. He slams the bat down. Gambhir, the hotel girl's idol, comes in. As he gets comfortable batting, Sachin slows down more, protecting himself. When he sees a pitch to drive, he steps into it. His first four of the day. The speakers play Bon Jovi's "It's My Life." Sachin hits another one, then gets conservative, taking no risks. He's trying to bat 35 or 40 overs, to anchor his team, to give openings to the other batsmen by consuming the attention of the bowlers. The crowd senses something special and chants, "Sachin! Sachin! Sachin!"

A feeling arises, a rare one, that you are part of a group watching something special. The power of sport is that, on occasion, it redeems the messes we create around it. Cricket can be stronger than the forces changing it. Victories are fleeting, but the poems are what matters. I don't know if cricket is about to be ruined, or if Sachin is no longer needed, if he's retiring, or if he'll defy expectations and play 10 more years. These are things we can guess about but never know.

I do know this: I am a fan. I am sunburned but do not care. I lose track of time. That's not a narrative flourish. Hours seem like moments.

Rapture comes to the people here. I see Sachin constructing a score, and I understand the planning, and the years of experience, that lead a man to this field on this day, and to the artistry he now holds as part of himself, like a chamber of his heart. We are congregants in a church. We are watching the son of a poet. The stand-up comedian is serious. This is a perfect at-bat, Andy tells me. This is art, and I am lucky to see it. Soon, Sachin will be gone.

This feeling will be gone. Right now, it is alive. It has the power of a name, immortal and pure.

"You don't have to know anything about it," my friend Gokul says.

"It's almost a religious experience," Andy says, "seeing Tendulkar play so well in front of his home crowd. It's a communal worship."

England sends in Graeme Swann, the best spin bowler in the world. They are targeting Sachin. One mistake and he's gone. The crowd grows tense. Swann winds up. The roar of the crowd rises, like the start of a football game. The ball arrives. The crack echoes through the stadium.

Sachin has hit it off the scoreboard.

It's an uppercut. A knockout blow. A roaring *Up yours!* A six. Flags wave and shake. Three fans wearing clown wigs blow their whistles over and over.

Swann winds up again.

Sachin crushes it, another uppercut, over the fence. Two pitches, two sixes. The air is sucked out of the stadium, and Bon Jovi is played again. But now, incredibly, the crowd noise is louder than the sound system. The real finally trumps the fake. Swann looks broken.

Sachin is building toward a century. The crowd wants it for him, for themselves. The noise doesn't ebb between bowls. He's got 72, then a four gives him 76. The clown wigs go batty. Sachin goes up high to get 78. The crowd needs this. A wave passes five full revolutions around the grandstand. Eighty-two. Eighty-six. The people behind me are barking now. The noise is constant. I am inside the soul of cricket. I get it. I will be back again, like Andy, chasing this ghost. Across town, Sachin's agent's BlackBerry buzzes. "Wonderful moment," one reads. An English friend writes, "Sachin is killing us. Awesome." One executive wants to put his company logo on Sachin's bat. The sister of Sachin's first agent, the man who died in the car wreck, writes, "Hope this one was for Mark."

Sachin gets to 98.

The sound system plays, "We Will Rock You!" The crowd pronounces the last two words as one. *Rockyou! Rockyou! Rockyou!* Everyone in the stadium is standing, again, and typing this 25 hours later, I get chill bumps. Again.

Sachin hits a four.

He's done it. A century. I've never been in a stadium that feels like this one. Hindus and Muslims, Sikhs and Christians, people from different castes and classes, speakers of a dozen languages, all citizens in the Republic of Sachin. The stern cops give wide smiles and thumbs-ups. The chant goes from "Sachin! Sachin!" to "Hoo . . . ha . . . IN-DI-A!" They are interchangeable.

Finally, at 120, Sachin pops out. He walks off, and the crowd rises once again. The people lean over the railings, trying for one more moment with their hero.

He waves his bat and disappears.

Sachin's gone.

FALLING APART

The Indian players collapse without him.

They leave too many runs on the table, lost without their anchor. Their score is 338. They cannot play defense or bowl, and England steadily mounts a comeback, putting up run after run. The worrying begins. The fans sense something, a fatal flaw built into this team of sluggers. They can all hit the ball a mile, but they can't get anybody out. Power has its limits. They are wasting Sachin's brilliance. The noise dies down. The stadium is still. People look into themselves. The team is a proxy for the nation, so what does an Indian collapse tell them about India? About India without Sachin?

England scores, off big hits, off bad pitches, off lazy defense. The India outfielders don't run down balls that go for fours. Next to me, Andy finds hope. With 15 overs left, England needs 102 runs off 90 balls. "It's bizarrely easy," Andy says.

An Indian writer shakes his head. "We've lost this game," he says.

The fans agree. People file, en masse, to the exits. The wire-service reporters type their stories. I'm spinning from the reversal in fortunes. A fourth of the seats are empty. Now a third. England needs 61 runs from 54 balls. Now 59 from 48.

Then India gets a wicket.

Then a second in a row.

The crowd comes alive. What does this revival tell them about their nation? About themselves? Andy shifts uncomfortably. The place shakes. The whistles are back out from the clown wigs. The barking returns. People howl. England needs 57 runs from 39 balls. An Indian player makes a huge diving catch. Hustle has returned. India has returned.

"I didn't see this coming," Andy says.

There is dancing in the aisles. The Indian team is getting more wickets, which eliminates the strongest English batsmen and puts pressure on the bottom of the lineup. England needs 50 from 28. Now 29 from 11. It seems finished. The local in front of me tweets: "It's amazing to watch India in India."

Suddenly, England counters. Two big-bang sixes, and it's 14 runs from six balls. One more over. I can barely breathe. Nobody can. The noise is deafening now, rising in crescendo before each bowl. Imagine a football kickoff every 30 seconds.

The Indians are going to win. England needs 12 from five, then 11 from four. The "India" chant returns.

Then England hits a six, crushed, into the stands.

"Unbelievable," the Indian writer says.

The target is now five runs from three balls. England singles. It's four runs from two. The English get a double. We are down to the last ball. Two runs from one. That's it now. All the hype, and the planning, and all these hours, down to a moment. The infield comes in. The crowd rises.

The stadium quiets.

A man folds his hands in prayer. The clown wigs are silent. One sits down. The local reporter puts up his notebook. The Indian bowler winds up, the English batsman swings, makes contact, crack, it's happening so fast, the fielder rushes over, gets the ball in. England scores only one. India did it!

In the moments after the end, there's confusion. I'm confused. The crowd noise is strange. I look around. The scoreboard is hard to read. We've spent eight hours and two minutes in these seats. Has India won? Has England? What happened? I'm looking to Andy, trying to understand. That's when I realize: I did the math wrong. Two to win, which means, after all that drama, my God . . .

It's a tie.

CARRYING THE HOPES OF A BILLION COUNTRYMEN

One last stop remains before the airport. "We've got 30 seconds," his agent says.

A special key card grants access to the 18th floor. Three plain-clothes bodyguards look us over. A sign hangs on the door. SHHH, it reads, I'M SLEEPING LIKE A BABY. The agent knocks.

Sachin Tendulkar opens the door. "Come, come," he says.

A tangle of wires covers the bedside table closest to his pillow. There's a Diet Coke and a bottle of water. A Hindu shrine is on the other side. There's a book across the room, *The Last Nizam,* about the end of one era and the beginning of another, about a king who lost his throne in a time of great change.

His agent explains my journey to Sachin. "He didn't know anything about cricket before he came," he says.

Sachin looks at me. He seems confused. "Hmmmmm," he says.

His phone rings. The ringtone is U2. We chat, and he loosens. He doesn't overtalk. It's strange. There actually is an aura of calm around him. It must be how he's survived. At the center of this mania is a reservoir of peace, focus, and determination. I ask if he spends a lot of time in America.

"Not really," he says. "I have a lot of friends there, but it's too far for me to travel."

"I'm about to get on a 15-hour flight," I say.

He laughs and grimaces with me. A trip to the States, he says, needs several weeks to be worth the flight. "I don't have 15 to 20 days," he says.

He's carried the burden of a billion people for more than 20 years. Just outside the hotel is a billboard with his stern face looking down on the city. Its tagline is direct: WE'VE WAITED 28 YEARS TO HOLD THE CUP. HOPE THAT WAIT ENDS NOW. Heroes don't punch clocks.

Sachin Tendulkar says good-bye and closes his door, while, in every direction, a vast nation sees its hopes and dreams in him, for at least a little while longer. I step into the elevator, then a car, then three flights, then my car, then my house. I return from blind alleys and brightly lit fields, having found my moment of rapture and, at the end, the man who created it. I've found both the riddle and the answer, and I wonder what it must cost someone to be both of those things. One part of my conversation with Tendulkar will return to me every time India plays in this World Cup.

His agent told me he's aware of what he means to people, of the symbolic importance of being both the beginning and end of something. He is a bridge, and it is vital to the psyche of a nation that he remains intact. He gets it. That's why he never loses focus. Nothing, it turns out, is effortless. In his room, he seems tired, worn out mentally and physically. He needs a break. I ask when was the last time he had 20 days off in a row with nothing to do. No balls to hit or billions to represent.

"I'm waiting for that time to come," he says.

ROBERT HUBER

Allen Iverson: Fallen Star

FROM PHILADELPHIA

I AM IN ISTANBUL. All I know is that Allen Iverson is here—in this city of 13 million, with one foot in Asia and one in Europe—to play basketball. His manager keeps saying no, that Allen won't talk to me. So I ask the concierge in my hotel: if you're Allen Iverson—the greatest thing to ever hit Turkish basketball—where do you go to meet women?

"Reina," he tells me. "Yes, Club Reina—on the Bosphorus."

Reina is a place with a metal detector at the entrance, and chandeliers and fireplaces and lighted floors and a DJ and lovely people on the inside. You can walk out onto a pier to check out the lapping Bosphorus River, which connects the Black and Mediterranean Seas, and gaze up at the Asian moon, and sip drinks for 20 lira.

I go up to a young woman in a tank top and impossibly tight jeans and three-inch shiny black heels, who's having a drink with another woman and a man. She is dark and beautiful. I ask her if she speaks English. *Yes.* I tell her I'm in Istanbul to write about Allen Iverson. She smiles a bit of a devilish smile.

"I met him last night."

The hottest girl in the hottest club, 24 years old. Allen Iverson has already met her. She's a dead ringer for the character Sloan in *Entourage*—the same prettiness and almost over-the-top sexiness coupled with sweetness and, I quickly find out, smarts.

Along with her friend, the silent Turk to my right, she went to Iverson's first game in Istanbul the night before, in a home arena so tiny—it seats 3,200—she could easily find Iverson's manager,

Gary Moore, and tell him how she studied at Georgetown. Iverson's school! So Moore naturally invited her to join Iverson and his crew at their postgame haunt, the place where he's been hanging out with his slightly downsized America-to-Istanbul posse, in this lovely ancient city:

T.G.I. Friday's.

That's where Iverson lands every night, for all of his first week in Istanbul. *Friday's.*

Of course she went, and spent a couple of hours. She found Iverson kind of cold. He said hello, but that was about it. He played cards. He drank Corona. She ended up talking to Moore. Clearly she wanted a little more than that.

I tell her about Iverson's nightlife in America—how he used to go to a Friday's on City Avenue all the time, and when things got a little chaotic there, when it was no longer so cool for Iverson to drink 40s out of a bag, leaning against his Bentley parked in a handicapped spot, he slipped across the street to Houlihan's. He would show up with two or three or five guys, sometimes popping in around midnight after a game, drink Coronas, play poker with his boys at the bar. And the women would show up. They would line a low wall behind him. A half-dozen. Ten. Twelve. Fifteen. They would preen and wait. Finally, Iverson would nod to one of his posse, and his guy would go over to the one in the line he wanted and tell her to join them. She'd have a drink with Iverson. In a little while, he would leave. And then she would, a moment later.

I tell the woman at Club Reina all this because I'm wondering if Iverson might have women at his beck and call here. Would they be so aggressive?

She smiles. "We would be . . . what is the word? . . . more discreet."

"Turkish women wouldn't line up like that?"

"No."

"But sex is . . ."

She smiles again—a different smile—the prettiest girl in the hottest club. Istanbul is a big, busy, cosmopolitan city, and Allen Iverson won't be merely playing cards and drinking Coronas at the Istanbul Friday's while trying to resurrect his basketball career. Unless he's a changed man.

*

Iverson is at a crossroads in his life. There is no going off into the sunset for him, no taking his vast millions and his fame and finishing off the job of raising his five kids in splendor and ease. Nothing works that way for him.

In fact, last spring—just after Iverson abandoned the Sixers following a short second stint with the team—Gary Moore said publicly that things were very bad for Iverson. His young daughter Messiah was quite sick with an undisclosed illness. His wife had filed for divorce. There were stories that he was gambling and drinking himself into oblivion. At one point, Moore beseeched a reporter with a chilling request:

"Please pray for us. We need all the prayers we can get."

Iverson had hit rock bottom. At 34—having nearly exhausted his athletic gifts—he'd washed out of the NBA, largely seen as too troubled and demanding to finish his career with some team needing to get a few more fannies in the seats. That failed last year in Philly, after Iverson had already been pushed out of Detroit and bolted from Memphis. His career seemed done, and maybe he was too.

So he has come to Turkey to resurrect not only his basketball career, but his life. In . . . *Istanbul?* How is he going to survive camped out in a Friday's in Istanbul?

As one NBA official put it, the guy spent the past five years pretty much living in either bars or casinos. But word has it that his family is coming, that he and Tawanna have reconciled and she's about to arrive with all five kids, ranging in age from two to 16. The team has checked out schools and is finding the family a villa to live in. It's a new beginning.

On this night, after my conversation at Reina, I head to Friday's, which even in Istanbul looks like Friday's everywhere, with stained-glass lamps, and TVs viewable from every angle (soccer!), and signs on the wall for the Farmers' Almanac 1879 and Frank's Cattle Manure.

Iverson was in earlier, a waiter tells me, he and his boys, drinking Corona and playing cards. "He's a nice guy, Allen Iverson!"

But now, 11 at night in Istanbul, he has slipped away.

He is extreme. He always has been. His beginnings might be familiar to us, but require understanding to fathom him now. Iverson comes from nothing—he's said that himself—or, more precisely, from Hampton, Virginia, born of a single mother, Ann, who had him at 15 and supported herself however she could. Cousins and uncles piled into one tiny house. Sometimes there was raw sewage on the floors. He was called Bubbachuck, and Ann believed he had something special—something extreme—from day one. She marveled at his long arms and his long fingers even while he was an infant. He was going to be a ball player. A great ball player.

And he was—in football, baseball, and basketball. He was lightning-quick and fast and fearless. Men around him—uncles, coaches—saw what he had. Their Hampton neighborhood was violent, riddled with drugs. He was too good to let slide away. They protected Bubbachuck, a star from the time he was a child. School—well, school didn't matter. Often, he didn't go. Often, he had to stay home to take care of his younger sister when Ann wasn't up to it.

Then he became even more famous, at 18, way beyond Hampton.

There was a fight in a bowling alley. Accounts still differ. Bubbachuck and some black friends from the basketball team got into a melee with white kids. Punches were thrown, a chair was cracked over someone's head. And Iverson, at 18, was sentenced to five years in prison. There were racially charged "Justice for Bubbachuck" rallies. The story hit the national press.

Prison at a Newport News, Virginia, work farm pushed him deeper into his own world. His friends would appear outside the prison yard, as a show of support. Bubbachuck never made eye contact with them, but he knew they were there. His girlfriend, Tawanna, would come too, to show him she still believed. But as far as he knew, there was nothing to believe. His God-given dream of the NBA, his ticket out, his family's ticket out, had been snatched away.

And then it was given back in late 1993, when Governor Doug Wilder, just before leaving office, granted Iverson clemency after he had served less than six months.

"I learned a lot about people from that experience," Iverson would say later. "I really didn't know how people were, or how they could be. I feel no pressure anymore. About anything. I know what time it is."

Those half-dozen friends who came to see him at prison—his

posse—Iverson would keep tight. He and Tawanna started having babies. He played two years at Georgetown, lighting up the Big East with his free-flow game, then joined the Sixers.

He was an electric player, one of the smallest and fastest, fearless in charging to the basket, smacked to the floor again and again by players who weighed almost twice as much as his buck-65. He never got angry at opponents. He simply kept attacking. He hogged the ball, often ignoring his teammates, but the speed and relentlessness made him impossible to stop, by either an opponent or his own coaches. He was going to do it his way, and we had never seen anything quite like it.

The NBA would not publish the photo of Allen Iverson being named Rookie of the Year: he showed up at the award ceremony in a white skullcap. Then it was cornrows. And heavy jewelry. And tattoos that crept all over his body.

In Philly, we ate it up. It was his defiance, and skill, and something even better: he was incapable of hiding, of not being himself. No other athlete is like that. He became infamous for a press conference where he defended himself for skipping and showing up late for practice (and, occasionally, hungover). It was a press conference in which he uttered the word "practice" 26 times dismissively, as in "We're talking about *practice*," and at the same time, with each of those 26 "practice"-es, his wide child's eyes showed just how bewildered he was to be judged in a way he couldn't quite fathom. In his world, practice didn't count. But even in defiance he looked wounded. That too was riveting.

Other stories hit the press. He was stopped by cops in Virginia while riding in a car's passenger seat with a registered gun on the floor and in possession of marijuana. He was sued by a guy who wouldn't leave a VIP area in a lounge and was beaten up by Iverson's bodyguard as Iverson impassively watched. (The guy won $260,000.) He got into a scrape with Tawanna in which he supposedly threw her, naked, out of their house in Gladwyne—then showed up at a cousin's place in West Philly looking for her, allegedly with a gun in his pants. (The allegation fell apart in court.) All of this was momentarily shocking, but not surprising; the only issue was whether he'd tumble into a scrape he couldn't roll out of. Whether he was a heart-on-his-sleeve man-child or a thug, either way, we couldn't get enough of him.

He thrived on movement and chaos, on testing the limits. Close observers noticed that he seemed to play *better* the night after staying out until all hours or gambling huge amounts down at the Taj. A very mediocre Sixers team would ride him all the way to the finals in 2001, the tiniest guy with the biggest will.

His way: When the team was on the road, Iverson and his posse would move the mattresses off their beds to the floor in their hotel rooms. Because it helped them feel comfortable. Because that's how they'd grown up.

Istanbul doesn't feel like an ancient city, just that it's 1974 in some ways: laundry dries from apartment balconies; nobody wears seat belts; the men smoke; older women, especially, wear head scarves. It is pretty and hilly and crowded and very friendly. The men have a hard look, as if they just might pull out a sword and give you a hack, but a mere hello on the street stops all the locals—they smile, they'll break out their English for a little chat. It is a city, and country, moving westward.

But Allen Iverson—at least, the one who once got so drunk at Bally's that he pissed in a potted plant for all the gambling world to see, and who was lovingly written up in a Power 99 DJ's memoir for having sex in the front seat of his Bentley while he drove—seems *way* too West.

Gambling is illegal in Turkey; Iverson would have to hop a plane for an hour to Bulgaria or Cyprus to throw dice. Worse, his team, Besiktas, often practices twice a day, there's no break for Christmas, and the off-season escape back to America lasts all of two months. Training camp features early-morning team-spirit-building runs through the woods.

All this seems antithetical to the Iverson mode of living, yet as I finally get within shouting distance of him during his Besiktas practices, he's the most spirited teammate. During a scrimmage he claps and laughs and encourages across the language barrier and breaks into a Marvin Gaye falsetto for a moment; after one missed fast-break pass, he leaps onto the back of a teammate in a rousing we're-all-in-this-together show.

His first game in Turkey, played in the Besiktas home arena that is smaller than Iverson's high school gym, features the loudest crowd I've ever sat among, with stomping and clapping and hooting. It's an indoor soccer match.

Iverson's scaled-down posse is easy to spot in the stands: two large black guys, one with a big diamond earring, one with a deeply lined face and a baseball cap pulled low, with a gorgeous, eye-blinking biracial woman in tow, and a mixed-race buddy with a red ponytail, diamond-shaped earrings, and heavy silver chains. I point out these particulars because it is impossible *not* to stare at them, which seems like a dangerous thing to do even in Turkey. Their standout presence is so at odds with both Iverson's careful, controlled first game and the crowd's careful, nervous solicitation of him. He is clearly rusty; when he drops a little stop-and-go move into the basket, scoring his first points, the crowd goes berserk and then *shh-shh-shh*'s itself to give Iverson complete quietude while he contemplates the ensuing free throw. When he makes it, everyone goes berserk again.

Basketball, though, is still a niche sport in Turkey, and the skill level of Iverson's team, I'm judging, is on the level of a middling Division I college program here; Besiktas plays in the Turkish league, not in the superior Euroleague. I ask people on the street, in hotels, in cabs, what Iverson's coming means to Turkey; a lot have no idea who he is. One cabbie says, "Iverson! Yes!" and then turns up the radio he turned down when he picked me up—a game blared. "This is the sport here," he says. "Football!" Soccer, in other words. Allen Iverson, basketball star, is in a foreign place.

The third day I go to practice, Iverson is sitting alone on the bench, and it's time to desist with managers and handlers. I go up to him and ask if we can talk.

"About what?" he says, his voice deep and terse, his arms on the back of the bench. He tells me to talk to his manager about it.

But the next day, Iverson agrees to talk, and he surprises me. After practice, I follow him up into the empty stands. Later, people who know him well tell me that once he believes somebody is okay and not out to hurt him, the wall comes down, and that's what I discover: a friendly guy.

He's touched, he says, by how nice everyone has been in Turkey. "That was one of the biggest things coming to Istanbul," he says. "Somebody wanted you." When nobody in the NBA did. When it was the only overseas offer made in writing, $2 million a year for two years.

I kid him about going to Friday's in Istanbul, though he doesn't seem to see it as teasing:

"Man, listen," he says. "I didn't know that the Philly cheesesteak wrap was that good when I was in Philly. I tried them when I got out here and every day since then. Every day since then!"

Iverson is startling, both handsome and almost cherubic. His eyes, the irises and pupils very nearly the same color, are vast. He laughs easily. What was for a decade a hopeful wisp of a mustache on a boy is now several days' growth in full Fu Manchu mode. I'm talking to somebody I don't recognize: a 35-year-old man, calm and measured. And he really is willing to talk.

"Everybody is making a big deal out of the money and making $2 million—what do people want me to do? Sit at home and just watch basketball, or play at the YMCA? I had to do what I had to do to continue playing basketball."

Ah, yes, two big issues there. First, whether he is broke—a guy who has pocketed some *$200 million* in salary and endorsements over the past 15 years. It would emerge a week or so later that Iverson is selling some of his collected memorabilia on eBay, and a lot of people are saying he's gambled and partied and supported hangers-on to the point of going through all that cash. But Iverson laughs softly, high up in the Besiktas stands:

"I would be a damn fool to blow that much money and have five kids to take care of. One thing I do have, and I can say, is that I do have money. A lot."

But on the matter of what he had to do to keep playing basketball, that's a little more complicated. It really begins with Iverson washing out of Philly in late 2006. The previous spring, the team tried to trade him, but a deal fell through. Yet the specter of a trade could never be, for Iverson, merely about changing his city of employment. It would be about control, and loyalty, and love.

Which is why, in very short order, he verbally lashed coach Mo Cheeks at a practice and walked out, blew off a mandatory team function, and pulled himself from a game in Chicago complaining of back spasms.

The team told him to stay home. A week later, he was playing for Denver.

But something funny happened in Denver, in the soft mountain air. Iverson was ready to start over. He listened to coach George Karl (and still hoisted a lot of shots). He went to practice. He was out and about, but kept his late-night high jinks under wraps. He liked the schools in Denver for his kids. And he liked the possibility that he and fellow star Carmelo Anthony could make a run at a championship.

It was all good except for the last part. The Nuggets washed out of the playoffs in the first round two years running, and at the beginning of the third year, Iverson was traded to Detroit, because the Nuggets believed that at 33, he was slowing down.

With that, it all came crashing down, very fast. Detroit wanted Iverson to be a substitute, to not even freakin' *start*.

The problem, Iverson says, was that he was lied to by rookie coach Michael Curry, who told him he'd never ask him to *come off the bench*. Then, not even a week later, he was no longer a starter. He was a role player. He was *ordinary*. And from the time he was an infant, from the time his mother Ann saw his arms and hands and *knew* what he was going to be, Iverson had never been ordinary.

It was the moment almost all pro athletes, especially big-time pro athletes, can't come to grips with when it hits: their bodies are winding down. To Iverson, a tiny man in a big man's world, his game built not just on speed but on a survivor's arrogance that he must be the very best—this was not something he'd stomach.

I can feel it now, talking to him, his pain and arrogance both: still in his practice uniform, he pulls his sweatband over his eyes, cradles his head in his hands. This moment for him came on so fast.

What was Iverson without his athletic superiority? He sulked and fought with Curry. The *Detroit Free Press* blogged that he was banned from two Detroit casinos for throwing chips at dealers and spitting at them and even trying to cheat. (The casinos, ever concerned about PR, deny that he was banned, and the *Free Press* took down the blog post, but the reporter who broke the story says now that he was privy to at least 15 people regaling him with stories of Iverson drunk and unbearable in casinos.) Iverson believes no NBA team wants him for a simple reason: Detroit general manager Joe Dumars put the word out that he was too much trouble. "I think that situation basically destroyed my NBA career," he says. "I honestly believe that."

I ask Iverson if he has a gambling problem. From his days with the Sixers, there are myriad stories of him dropping big money in A.C. at the Taj and Bally's, getting drunk and being rude to dealers. The stories smack of him throwing his money around recklessly, even dangerously.

"You find out when dealing with people that doesn't have nowhere near as much money as you," Iverson says, "that a lot of people who don't have that money and can't fathom it, would never understand. If I had that much to lose and I know it, then it's not a problem for *me*."

How about drinking? "Everybody I know, damn near, drinks. How is it a problem for me? I don't remember getting any DUIs or going to jail for getting drunk in public." Iverson laughs, because, really, are we talking about *drinking*? "I've never been reprimanded or anything, with any team or anything like that, because of any drinking."

In late 2009, he tried to resume his NBA career in Memphis. Just as the season was starting, the team was practicing in L.A., and coach Lionel Hollins cleared the gym of onlookers so he could address his players. And then he lit into Iverson for caring only about himself—the player famous for playing his heart out, admonished for not giving enough. Iverson was out of there after the next game. He signed back here, and played 25 games with the Sixers. But he'd not only lost a step; worse, his mind was no longer in the game, and that had always been one of his gifts: using the gym to escape from his life.

Iverson's daughter Messiah was sick. There was another, even graver problem: Tawanna had filed for divorce.

They have been together, Iverson says, for more than half his life. An old family friend from Hampton, who has known him since he was eight years old, understands what Tawanna saw in him before he had two nickels to rub together: "She was a sweet girl—she didn't know anything of the streets. Bubbachuck was an athlete, a humble sweet little kid, and she saw an innocent boy who was gifted and had nothing but wanted something. She saw that, and fell in love with that dream. It's a hell of a love story. And she didn't leave the dream—she kept dreamin', like Hollywood. Some dreams happen, some don't. She kept dreamin' one day, somehow, Allen would be the innocent boy she met when she was very young."

When the Sixers let Iverson go home last February, it was to sit down with Tawanna, to see if they could, somehow, get back on track. For Iverson, his marriage—maybe more than anything else—is paramount to his survival.

"I'd die for her," he once said about Tawanna. "I'd die without her."

Sitting up in the stands in Istanbul, Iverson tells me, "It's 360 degrees better now," and this is the effect he has, despite all his excesses, or maybe because of them: I really hope, for his sake, that it is better.

I ask him how Tawanna feels about making the move from Atlanta with five kids. (Messiah is well now.)

Iverson smiles ruefully. They are a work in progress.

On the day I talked to Iverson, I'd gone for a long, winding walk. Far above a four-lane highway, a hard-sounding Turkish voice blared. I walked up the hill to the voice and found a mosque, the imam's incantations broadcast from speakers.

I peered in an open door. Shoes were lined in a vestibule. I took mine off, and slipped to the entrance of the main room, where 15 men in robes knelt in a row and touched their foreheads to the floor, as the imam chanted and imprecated.

Suddenly, a cell phone rang. I panicked, reached down—but it wasn't mine. A man in the middle of the row of worshipers got up, turned, came toward me, reached into his white robe, and answered his phone.

I went back out into the sun, laughing, and watched women go in their own separate entrance. One second I was taking a peek into the Ottoman Empire, the next—well, it's a rapidly shifting world.

Does Allen Iverson have a prayer of making it here? People who know him in America, or think they do, seem to find the idea laughable. How do you go from practically living in casinos and drinking heavily to Istanbul?

"I'm not like I was when I was in Philly," Iverson says, "when I was 21. I didn't have five kids. I didn't have the responsibilities I have now."

His old teammate Eric Snow tells me he *knows* Iverson wants to get back to the NBA. But Iverson says no. He's done that, had his career there. He's in a new place now, a city and country that have embraced him. There are millions more fans out there, all over Europe, that he can play for. And that's what he intends to do, because the truth is, Allen Iverson has nowhere else to go.

Bad Nights in the NFL

FROM SPORTS ILLUSTRATED

THERE WAS A YOUNG millionaire in Denver whose white limousine came under gunfire on a snow-lined boulevard in the dark of a winter morning. When the shooting began he had about one minute to live, and he spent that minute surrounded by the tangible signs of his newfound wealth. The black leather seats held nine women in short dresses and fur-trimmed jackets, as well as four rappers from Texas whose T-shirts advertised their collective name: *Billion Dolla Scholars*. But the most dazzling sight in the Hummer limousine was the young millionaire's gold chain. Dangling from it was a medallion about the size of a compact disk with a white crust of diamonds that spelled the name of his record label, *Ryno Entertainment*, and his nickname, *D Will*, short for Darrent Williams, starting right cornerback for the Broncos. The chain was worth about $50,000, and those who had worn it said it felt heavy around the neck. In the last 10 minutes the chain had been lost, then found, and the reasons for that brief disappearance would make the difference between life and death.

Many theories have surfaced in the four years since the shooting, many prisms through which to view the events of New Year's Eve 2006. Most have some basis in fact. You would not be wrong to blame new money, unaccustomed celebrity, old-fashioned jealousy, Napoleonic insecurity, or an airborne mist of champagne. You could even surmise, as a judge did, that the bullets were probably meant for a different Bronco in a different limousine. But Darrent Williams was no mere bystander in the sequence of events that led to his death. He chose to help a friend in distress—chose to take off the heavy gold chain to do so—and that choice cost him his life. You would not be wrong to say he died from the .40-caliber bullet that tore two jugular veins and opened his right carotid artery. Nor would you be wrong to say Darrent Williams died of loyalty.

You could even call it predestination. Williams came from Carter Park, a battleground in Fort Worth, Texas, where loyalty is a means of survival. He wasn't close to his father, and his mother's fiancé was shot to death in a Burger King parking lot when Darrent was 10, but it would be too simple to call Rosalind Williams a single mother. She was one of seven children, and they all raised their own children together, side by side. Thus, when Darrent's name appeared in police reports, it usually had something to do with familial defense. At age 15 he confronted Hispanic gang members about speeding in front of the house of his grandmother, Easter Williams; they later came back and shot up the house with a high-powered rifle. When a man came to Granny's door asking for money, Darrent chased him away with a dog that bit a hole in the man's forearm. When Darrent signed with the Broncos, he bought his mother a new house and Granny a new Lincoln Town Car. When he shopped for himself he took friends along, and when he bought Air Jordans, he bought them for everyone. Williams was not the only man in the white limousine wearing a diamond chain. He'd bought smaller ones for each of the Billion Dolla Scholars.

The only man in the limousine with more money and fame than Williams was Javon Walker, a teammate on the Broncos, and one of the last things Williams heard before the gunfire was a lecture from Walker on how a rich man should guard his possessions.

"Don't hang your chain with somebody who can't cover it," he said, referring to the diamond chain that Williams had recently lost and found. Those within earshot understood what Walker meant: don't let anyone hold the chain unless he has the cash to pay for it. Walker had played five years in the NFL, three more than Williams, and he led the Broncos in receiving yards in 2006. Walker looked across the limousine at the Billion Dolla Scholars, old friends of Williams's from Fort Worth, who were much less wealthy than their name implied. "Not to be disrespectful to y'all," he said, "but I can cover it."

A minute or two later, as the limousine rolled northwest on Speer Boulevard, a white Chevy Tahoe pulled up in the lane to its left. Bullets sprayed from the Tahoe's open window. At least 15 struck the limousine. Miraculously, only three of the 17 passengers were hit, and each was hit just once. One Scholar took a round to the buttocks, and a young woman suffered a shallow head wound that might have been fatal had she not leaned forward an instant earlier to answer her ringing cell phone. Darrent Williams got no such phone call, although for weeks thereafter his high school sweetheart regularly dialed his number just to hear the recorded sound of his voice. At the funeral their seven-year-old son asked if Daddy had his cell phone in the coffin.

The limousine veered off the road into a snow-covered patch of grass. As women screamed and men dove for cover, Javon Walker found his teammate. Walker stood six-foot-three and weighed 215 pounds; he was six inches taller and at least 30 pounds heavier than Williams. He picked Williams up and held him like a baby, covering the wound with his hand, begging him not to die.

In the video of Javon Walker's first interview with Denver police, just under two hours later, it's all Walker can do to stop crying, raise his head from the desk, and look at the officer.

> SGT. MATT MURRAY: Javon, is there anything else you can think of that might help us to sort this out?
>
> WALKER: I couldn't tell you, because I'm the most non-controversy-conflict person whatsoever, and I don't deal with everything. Like . . . I walk away from conflict. And if I'm dealing with someone who's my friend, and—when I was dealing with Darrent Williams, he gave me all his jewelry. Which is right here. . . .
>
> *Walker reaches into the left front pocket of his bloodstained jeans and pulls out the $50,000 diamond chain. The gold rattles softly in his fingers.*
>
> MURRAY: Why would he do that?
>
> WALKER: Because I'm a trustworthy person. So you can't trust too many people. So I say, "Gimme your jewelry." I put it in my pocket, just like this. . . .
>
> MURRAY: I don't understand.
>
> WALKER: Well, you know what? He lost his jewelry, because he didn't know where it was. And whenever they found it, when they found it, his mutual friends found it, we found it, and I

said, "Okay, I'm taking it. . . ." [*The sergeant never asks why the chain was lost.*] You never understand it, if you're an athlete. Because a lot of people get jealous. And we can't stop doing what we're doing because somebody else is upset about it. And that's what's hard about it. . . .

MURRAY: I know.

WALKER: It's like you're damned if you do, damned if you don't. But you're doing something you love. But all of a sudden you get cursed by doing what you love.

This curse goes back to the first page of history. It comes of getting what you want, having more than your neighbor and feeling the compulsion to show it off. The curse is an epidemic in modern American sports, which turn poor young men into millionaires overnight and leave them overwhelmed with the complications. There may be quiet satisfaction in watching your personal accounts fill with cash. But for some of the overnight millionaires, the simple condition of being rich is not enough. They have to show everyone. Then comes the curse. You heard Javon Walker: people get jealous.

At least six Broncos and two Nuggets celebrated New Year's Eve 2006 at the Safari nightclub in downtown Denver, and Williams did not win the contest for most expensive piece of jewelry. A rookie wide receiver named Brandon Marshall later told police he was wearing a chain worth $57,000 that night. And although his chain didn't play an important role in the events that led to the shooting, Marshall did. He told a detective he didn't feel safe after the shooting, said he couldn't go to nightclubs anymore, asked about the legal procedures for carrying his gun. "We were outside that limo, so that's probably why they shot at that limo," he said. "If I didn't act rowdy outside the club? It probably wouldn't have happened."

Marshall declined interview requests for this story, but he was obviously shaken by the incident. Ten months later Denver police stopped him for allegedly driving drunk and going the wrong way on a one-way street. On the way to the drunk tank, according to an officer's report, Marshall said, "Why ain't you guys out looking for Williams's killer? I hate Denver. I hope I get traded. I hate this f—— city." Last year Marshall finally got his wish, escaping Denver to play for the Dolphins nearly 2,000 miles away.

Almost two years passed without an indictment in the Williams murder case. Not long before that, Javon Walker made the news again. He'd been found lying on the ground near the Las Vegas Strip, beaten and unconscious.

On June 15, 2008, Walker went out drinking in Vegas. He wore jeans, black sneakers, a stylish black T-shirt, a black ball cap, and enough precious stones and metals to buy a small house. He had a platinum earring with a two-carat diamond in each ear, a Jacob & Co. watch with a wall of diamonds on the face and a platinum chain that was also studded with diamonds. His pockets were full of cash.

Flanked by an old buddy from his hometown in Louisiana and two women he described as friends, Walker left the Bellagio and headed for a nightclub called Body English at the Hard Rock Hotel and Casino. Walker paid for everyone. He'd made many sacrifices to become a professional athlete and took pleasure in sharing the rewards. When he wanted a haircut, he flew in his old barber from out of state. When the Boys and Girls Clubs of Metro Denver needed funds to complete the Darrent Williams Memorial Teen Center, Walker cut a check for $30,000. He was known around Las Vegas as an exceptional tipper.

Walker strolled into Body English just after midnight ahead of a long line of ordinary people and met a large man named Joel Abbott, who would serve as his bodyguard at the club. Management had reserved him a table by the dance floor, next to Floyd Mayweather Jr.'s table. Walker ordered a bottle of Patrón tequila, at least two magnums of Grey Goose vodka, and at least two bottles of rose-colored Dom Pérignon champagne. He did not like champagne.

In Las Vegas and everywhere else, the rich play by other rules. Not just anyone can skirt the line outside a club, get a VIP table by the dance floor, or stand on said table raining foamy beverages upon other patrons with the tacit approval of management. Walker spent nearly $18,000 on drinks that night, and this bought him many rights. The club activated its special champagne-spraying protocol.

"A lot of times," Abbott, the bodyguard, testified in a later court proceeding, "the management can get their arm turned to say, 'Okay, let's let this guy order five bottles of this very expensive champagne, and if he wants to spray them or shake them up, that's fine, as long as we have advance notice.' Now, if a regular person might just grab and start spraying without any notification, there might be an issue. But never with him. . . . And as we kinda back up the crowd, saying, 'Hey, there's gonna be some champagne sprayed,' some, usually females, that's just how it is, will say, 'Oh, I'm fine with that,' and wanna actually get closer."

After sharing his wealth with the women of Body English, Walker stopped at the blackjack tables and then went to the penthouse for some drunken bowling. He paid the deejay something like $500 to play a particular song. He fell down when he tried to throw the ball. His friend and the bodyguard tried to escort him outside, but it took forever because Walker kept stopping to talk to strangers. He wanted to thank the waitresses and the busboys, to give autographs and pose for pictures. People tell stories all the time about meeting their sports heroes and being terribly disappointed. If you had met Javon Walker that night, you probably would have loved him.

But Walker left his friends that night, and that's where it all went wrong. He took offense at something his buddy said on the way back to the hotel, and he jumped into the street before the Cadillac Escalade came to a stop. A few minutes later, after he'd returned to the Bellagio, he was standing outside the hotel when a stranger called his name: "Javon!" Walker saw two men in a black Range Rover. They promised to give him a ride to meet up with his friends again at an after-hours club. He got in. Walker is a big man, sharp with muscle, but his blood alcohol level—estimated at 0.39—could have killed him all by itself. The hustlers took his money and jewelry. One of them hit him so hard in the right cheekbone that his eye socket fractured.

Walker was recently asked when he began wearing diamonds, and his answer was simple: when he could afford them. His mother, Bernita Goldsmith, was a sharecropper's daughter who grew up picking cotton in the humid fields of Louisiana, and after Javon was born, she worked two jobs to keep him fed. At night she served champagne to the oil barons at The Petroleum Club in Lafayette, and then she picked up Javon from his grandmother's and they went home to their one-room efficiency apartment and fell asleep in the same bed.

So Javon Walker wanted diamonds. And he never stopped pay-

ing for them. He paid at Florida State, when he gave up the life
of a normal fun-loving student for an existence that involved little
more than sleep, classes, workouts, and football practice. He paid
during the NFL season, when he abstained from alcohol, went to
bed at 9:00 P.M., added or dropped eight pounds in a given week
to maximize his competitive advantage against the cornerback he
would face that Sunday. He paid in relationships, in the loss of
common ground with some of the people he'd known the longest.
He paid at restaurants, because others assumed he would, and if
he could help out with the mortgage and electric bill too, that
would be much appreciated. He paid at home, when contractors
charged him double the normal rate, and at work, where fans and
sportswriters tore into him for every mistake. And of course he
paid in Las Vegas, where he asked the hustlers not to tear his ear-
lobes when they took the diamonds from his ears. Then he paid
again, in public shame.

Today some people see Walker's misadventure in Las Vegas as
a direct consequence of the terrible night in Denver—as a symbol
of everything that went wrong for him after Darrent Williams bled
to death in his arms. True, his promising football career disinte-
grated soon after the shooting: he caught 30 touchdown passes
before that night and only one thereafter. But he says this is a coincidence. His right knee failed early in the 2007 season, as knees
often do in the NFL, and his window of opportunity closed.

Walker's mother believes he went drinking that night to drown
his sorrow. But Walker insists he just went out to have a good time.
Even now he sees no mistake in walking around in public with a
heavy load of diamonds. If this proves anything, it's the insidious
nature of the curse. It seems no loss will be great enough to keep
Walker from the lifestyle he has earned with his sweat and blood.

Walker made a full recovery in time to testify against one of the
hustlers. During the trial he faced cross-examination by defense
attorney Betsy Allen. "There was an incident in Denver," she said,
"where you had sprayed champagne at a nightclub."

"No," Walker said. "No. No incident in Denver. That was nothing to do with me."

The prosecutor objected, and the judge intervened. "The incident in Denver is irrelevant," he told Allen, "and you'll move on,
please."

*

The incident in Denver remained mysterious to the public for more than three years. In October 2008 a grand jury indicted a local gangster named "Little" Willie Clark for the murder of Darrent Williams. The indictment said Clark fired the bullet that killed Williams, but it didn't fully explain why. And the full explanation didn't come until February and March 2010, over the 14 days of Little Willie's trial.

By then it was possible to see New Year's Eve 2006 as a turning point in many lives. In almost every case, the change was for the worse. Nicole Reindl, the young woman saved by her ringing cell phone, still had part of a bullet lodged next to her skull. Brandon Flowers of the Billion Dolla Scholars still had his bullet too; he could feel it in his leg whenever he climbed the stairs. Rosalind Williams could no longer enjoy New Year's Eve, or Mother's Day, because without Darrent she had no children. When the trial began, Darrent's eight-year-old daughter, a competitive runner named Jaelyn, had only recently recovered from her fear of the starter's pistol. Her 10-year-old brother, Darius, wouldn't stop playing an old copy of a football video game that let him use the avatar of his father.

And then there was Brandon Marshall, the Broncos' receiver, whose fortune turned the other way. On the night of the shooting he was a fourth-round draft pick who had just finished an uneventful rookie season. Over the next three years he made 307 catches. Defenders called him "the Beast" because his chiseled six-foot-four, 230-pound frame was so hard to bring down. Now, taking the stand as a crucial prosecution witness in Little Willie's trial, he'd become one of the best players in the NFL. He raised his large right hand and swore to tell the truth.

PROSECUTOR TIMOTHY TWINING: New Year's Eve, December 31, 2006, in the early morning hours of January 1, '07. Do you remember that night?
MARSHALL: I think about it every night.

Marshall went on to describe the Third Annual Safari New Year's Eve party, which offered regular people a chance to meet professional athletes for a $20 cover charge. The advertised hosts included Kenyon Martin and J. R. Smith of the Nuggets as well as Darrent Williams and Brandon Marshall of the Broncos. It was 18 degrees outside around 11:30 P.M. when Marshall and his crew arrived in a Town Car limousine to find a crowd waiting in the cold.

Remember how Javon Walker the exceptional tipper was treated at the club in Vegas: security quietly escorted him past the line to meet with his personal bodyguard, and hardly anyone noticed. Brandon Marshall the rookie fourth-rounder got no such treatment in Denver. In fact, when he waved to the bouncer, the bouncer put up a hand as if to hold him back. And Marshall lost his patience.

"Damn," he said. "I put my name on the flyer and make them money off my name, and y'all going to, you know, leave me out here?" By the time the bouncer recognized him and escorted him to the entrance, Marshall and his friends had drawn the attention of at least two people waiting to get in the club. One was Little Willie.

Entire books could be written about Little Willie and the Tre Tre Crips, the cocaine-dealing gang from eastern Denver; the 11 unsolved murders that authorities suspected them of committing; the killing of a witness less than a month earlier; and the gang's eventual crippling in an April 2007 raid that was called the largest combined law enforcement operation in Colorado history. Suffice it to say that Little Willie was raised by his grandmother; when he was 12 street thugs beat him with a gun and stuffed him in the trunk of a car; and now, standing five-foot-seven at age 23, he took immense pride in a set of possessions that included a $1,000 pair of jeans and about 25 pairs of expensive sneakers. He called himself Boss Money.

So Little Willie saw Brandon Marshall cutting through the crowd. And, according to trial transcripts, Little Willie said something like this: "We street n——, we got money too." And Marshall, trying to defuse the situation, jokingly threw it back: "Well, if I ain't the only one with money, then drinks on y'all tonight."

Little Willie didn't laugh, although his friend did, and Marshall told them to meet him at the bar. "Make sure those two guys get in," Marshall told the bouncer. Then he and his buddies went inside.

Upstairs in the VIP section they saw Darrent Williams, wearing that big diamond chain, and his five friends from Texas, wearing smaller ones.

*

Say what you will about the modern pro athlete and his entourage. But it serves an actual purpose. If Williams had gone wild in Vegas, there is virtually no chance he would have been kidnapped or robbed. His friends wouldn't have let it happen. Williams survived his childhood in Carter Park because friends and relatives shielded him from its ever-present dangers. And if he found some trouble now and then—like the time he allegedly shoved his high school sweetheart while they were fighting about their one-year-old son—most people were more surprised by the amount of trouble he avoided.

Given neighborhood conditions and his business acumen, Williams probably could have made a lot of money selling drugs. In other words, he could have become Little Willie Clark. Instead he got a job in the kitchen of a Southern restaurant called Grandy's, where he scrubbed chicken-fried steak crust off dinner plates for $4.75 an hour. He knew he'd make his money later, the right way, because he could return punts and interceptions as if fired from a gun. And after the Broncos drafted him in the second round out of Oklahoma State in 2005, he rode around Carter Park in an old Mitsubishi Montero, standing up, head poking through the sunroof, like a king surveying his kingdom. Carter Park rejoiced. His mother doused him with champagne.

That summer he signed a four-year contract worth about $2.2 million, including a signing bonus of about $1.3 million, and he did all he could to spread the wealth. That was the unwritten law of Carter Park. You always took care of your friends. Once, when a guy broke into a friend's car, Williams tracked him down and beat him up.

It worked the other way too. One day in February 2006, after his first season in the NFL, Fort Worth police pulled Williams over in the Chevy Impala he was driving and found a glass jar of marijuana in the center armrest. Another young man was riding in the front seat, but the police let him go. The young man asked an officer if he thought Williams would be arrested. "Yes," the officer replied. The young man walked away and returned a moment later. "The weed's mine," he said, surrendering to the officers, and Williams was not arrested.

For Christmas 2006 Williams's high school sweetheart, Tierria Leonard, brought their two children to visit him in Denver. Darrent loved the children, but he and Tierria had been off and on for nearly a decade. Now, near the end of his second season with the Broncos, he'd become one of the best young cornerbacks in the league. He and Tierria sat together on the couch in his condo with snow lying in fresh drifts outside and Darius lying across their laps, pretending to sleep. Darrent gave Tierria diamond earrings, a three-carat diamond tennis bracelet, and a gold ring with a swirl of diamonds. "That's your engagement ring," he said, and when she and the kids flew back to Texas, she had to borrow his suitcase to hold all the gifts.

On December 29 the four Billion Dolla Scholars and their manager arrived from Fort Worth, bringing the matching diamond chains that Williams had bought them. As chief executive of their record label, he wanted to introduce their music to Denver. On the evening of December 31 they put on their jewelry and their custom-painted graffiti T-shirts. At 10:00 P.M. they got into a rented white Hummer limousine and rode downtown.

In the story Brandon Marshall told under oath at the trial, he tried to make peace in the VIP room. He was minding his own business when two guys started trouble. They were the same two guys who had hassled him outside, only now they were antagonizing Darrent Williams and the crew from Fort Worth. They were throwing gang signs and spoiling for a fight. So Marshall and another teammate, Elvis Dumervil, ran over to break it up.

"Man," Marshall told the troublemakers, "we got all these bottles of champagne up here, all these women, it's New Year's, man, everybody chill out. It's not that serious, and just party with us." And the guys chilled out, and the party went on.

When Marshall finished telling this story at the trial, the prosecutor asked him to clarify the following point.

TWINING: Brandon Marshall, did you see any champagne being sprayed?
MARSHALL: No.

But in a previous videotaped interview, a detective had asked him virtually the same question, and Marshall had given a different answer: "I remember D-Will was spraying champagne. I made a comment like, 'Man, pop the bottles, New Year's or whatever, lemme show you how to do it,' and when he sprayed it, we in our own section, there was nobody else around. Just us and our section, that's it."

The reason Marshall changed his story about the champagne might be the same reason he changed his story about who rode with him to the club that night: he was protecting someone. In his first interview with the police Marshall said three other people rode in his limousine. It was actually five. And one of the people he left out was his cousin Blair Clark, a man who played a pivotal role in the events that led to the shooting.

On the witness stand Marshall admitted that his cousin was at the club that night. But he maintained that Blair Clark was elsewhere in the club during the controversy with the locals. And even this story didn't quite match the story his cousin told the police. Asked where he was when the clock struck midnight, Blair Clark said, "I was upstairs. But no champagne got sprayed when I was up there."

The more you think about this claim, the less sense it makes. Even Marshall—in one of his stories—admitted that champagne was sprayed. And if champagne was sprayed at any time on New Year's Eve, it would have been at midnight. Which is exactly what the men from Fort Worth said. Champagne went everywhere at midnight. It splashed around. It spilled all over the floor.

All five friends from Texas named Blair Clark as the sprayer-in-chief. Another Bronco blamed one of the men from Texas. In one of his stories Marshall said it was Williams, and he even hinted that he'd done some spraying himself: *Man, pop the bottles. . . . Lemme show you how to do it.*

One thing is certain, though. Javon Walker had nothing to do with it. He was in his own limousine full of women at midnight, still on his way to the club. In fact, it might have been better if Walker *had* been there. He had more money and experience than everyone else there, and he knew the right way to spray champagne: You notify management ahead of time. You get security to create a perimeter. You make sure all men are out of the blast radius. Only then do you pop the cork.

It's not clear how the two Denver Crips got into the VIP section—perhaps Marshall's endorsement helped—but Little Willie and his friend did get in. By several accounts, they were sprayed with champagne. And they were furious. Willie fancied himself as a big-spending rapper: lyrics found in his jail cell included the phrase, *we pop bottlez n clubz cuz ya kno who it iz*. And now these strangers had rolled in on one of the biggest party nights of the year and stolen the spotlight. Football players are less recognizable in public than other pro athletes because they usually wear helmets on television, so Little Willie may not have recognized Williams. All he knew was that Williams and his friends weren't from Denver, the city he loved so intensely that he had its area code, 303, tattooed on his chest. Willie loved the Broncos too, but Williams didn't wear Broncos clothing. He'd come out that night to represent Texas, with a white Texas Rangers hat and a tattoo that read *Carter Park*.

No wonder the Crips felt the need to announce themselves. Little Willie's friend started yelling things like "Eastside!" and "Denver!" and "Tre Tre!" referring to their point of origin, 33rd Avenue.

In the version of the story told at trial by one member of the Texas crew, Little Willie approaches Darrent Williams to ask him who sprayed the champagne. In this telling, of course, the sprayer is Marshall's cousin. "He's good," Williams says. "He's with us."

"Who are you?" Little Willie says.

"I'm Darrent Williams," he says, "27 for the Broncos." And Little Willie shakes his hand.

But the other Crip won't let it go. He keeps yelling about Eastside Denver. The commotion continues. Bouncers arrive. They take the side of the champagne-spraying strangers. And through little fault of his own, Little Willie gets thrown out of the VIP section of the club, on New Year's Eve, in his own city, and that guy in the Texas Rangers hat keeps dancing, and he's holding that big diamond chain.

Sometime later, in another part of the club, Little Willie punches a woman in the face. He has mistaken her for a man. The incident begins when someone drops a cell phone in a crowded hallway and, while helping to find it in the dark, a woman holds up the line. Little Willie says something offensive about it, and the woman's female companion gets in his face, and Willie slugs her in the jaw. He later comes back and apologizes. He says he never would have done it if he'd known she was a woman.

The lights come on and the club shuts down. The two women

are walking out when a tall man in a Pepsi jacket comes up behind one of them and grabs her rear end. The tall man will later be identified as Blair Clark, Brandon Marshall's drunken cousin. The angry women pursue Blair Clark down the sidewalk. He loudly encourages them to offer him a certain personal service. And then an unlikely defender appears: Little Willie, who is not about to let some drunken out-of-towner speak to Denver women that way. He puts a hand inside his shirt, as if he were reaching for a gun.

"That's the wrong move," he tells Blair Clark, who is nine inches taller than he is. "You might not want to do that."

Throughout the evening, the actions of Marshall and his cousin have blurred together. They are both six-foot-four African Americans, born less than a year apart, with moderately dark complexions. They've often been in the same place, doing similar things. In the VIP section a witness thought he saw Marshall spraying champagne; he later changed his mind and said it was Blair Clark. The woman leaving the club initially identifies Marshall as the man who molested her, but Blair Clark later admits *he* did it. Outside the club the cousins confront Little Willie, the Denver Crip with the newfound sense of chivalry, and although one of the women says Willie points an imaginary gun at Blair—she knows this because he's the same guy who did the grabbing—both Blair and Marshall say Little Willie pointed the imaginary gun at Marshall. This distinction matters, because prosecutors have suggested that either Blair Clark or Marshall delivered the final insult to Little Willie—the assault on his fragile pride that turned him from angry to murderous.

In Marshall's account of his last encounter with Little Willie, he escalates the hostilities. "Man," he angrily tells Willie, "I done offered you guys drinks twice tonight." And when Willie points the imaginary gun, Marshall says, "Man, you ain't got no f——' gun." Marshall tries to climb a snowbank to go after Willie and his friends, but he slips before he can reach anyone, and the other Denver Crip punches him in the face. But neither Marshall nor his cousin lays a hand on Little Willie.

Here's another version of the story. It comes from the woman who saw Little Willie point the imaginary gun at Blair Clark: "The dude that grabbed my girlfriend's butt, some dude ran up on him, and he, like, palmed him, and dropped him in the snow, he, like, pushed him in the snow, and was just holding him there." The palmer, of course, would be Blair Clark. And while the witness doesn't say who got palmed, prosecutors believe it was Little Willie.

Surveillance video time-stamped 2:10 A.M. shows Little Willie forcing his way through the crowd outside the club, apparently in a hurry. Marshall has seen situations like these before. When a guy runs away in the middle of a fight, it's called *going to the trunk*. He's pretty sure Willie's going to get a gun. Marshall and his cousin hustle to their Town Car.

You would not be wrong to call the murder of Darrent Williams a simple case of mistaken identity. The evidence suggests that Little Willie meant to open fire on Marshall's limousine—that he thought the white Hummer was Marshall's limousine. The trial judge found this a likely explanation, and so did Marshall when he talked to the police. While educated guesses can be made about how this knowledge affected Marshall (an ESPN report showed he had some 12 encounters with police in the 27 months after the shooting, most of them domestic disturbances), it didn't stop him from becoming a superstar. Darrent Williams's friends believed Williams was destined for the Pro Bowl. Brandon Marshall went instead, and last year he signed a five-year deal with the Dolphins worth more than $47 million.

But Marshall and Williams didn't trade places by chance. It happened because of a decision Williams made, in keeping with the unwritten law of Carter Park. When Javon Walker said, *All of a sudden you get cursed by doing what you love,* he could have been describing Williams and the fierce loyalty that may have saved Marshall's life.

This is how the chain disappears.

Six men from Fort Worth leave the club at 1:56 A.M. The surveillance camera catches them on the sidewalk, heading for the white Hummer limousine. Williams stops to sign autographs. They cross the snowbank and congregate by the limousine.

At 2:07 the second Denver Crip crosses the snowbank and heads for the street. He's going to pick a fight with the men from Fort Worth. The Crip yells epithets and goes on about Denver. The men from Fort Worth yell back. Williams waves the diamond medallion and says something about Texas. But the provocation fails. Nobody fights.

At 2:08 Marshall enters the frame, moving quickly along the snowbank toward the disturbance involving his cousin and Little Willie.

At 2:09 the second Crip pushes through the crowd. He appears to have given up on the men from Fort Worth. He is heading toward Marshall.

At 2:10 the street is nearly empty by the Hummer's right rear side. It seems the men from Fort Worth have gone inside their vehicle.

If you go northeast from downtown Denver today, to the Boys and Girls Club on Crown Boulevard, you'll find an eight-foot bronze statue of Darrent Williams facing the Rocky Mountains. The inscriptions never mention a curse. But a kid who dreams of being rich like Williams could wind up like Little Willie, serving life plus 1,152 years with the Colorado Department of Corrections. And even if the kid catches a few touchdowns and a few breaks, he could become Javon Walker, broken on the asphalt in Vegas with the diamonds taken from his ears; or Brandon Marshall, haunted at night by misdirected bullets; or even Darrent Williams, gone at age 24. Williams was just a man, not a hero, and he turned to bronze through the alchemy of football and untimely death.

But let this be said about the king of Carter Park. The diamonds never changed his heart. He was always a true friend. This is why he lost the diamond chain, and why he lost his life.

At 2:10, with the white limousine full of people and almost ready to go, Williams looks through the rear window and sees his friend and teammate Marshall caught up in a fight on the snowbank. Little Willie is out there too, preoccupied, nowhere near his own vehicle, which means the white limousine is poised for a clean getaway.

Williams takes off his chain.

About five minutes from now, Walker will tell Williams how a rich man should guard his possessions. He'll say you should never hang your chain with anyone who can't cover it. He'll lay out the difference between himself—a trustworthy man with deep cash reserves—and the old friends Williams has brought along for the ride.

But Williams doesn't need friends who can cover the chain. He needs friends who will cover him, just as he covers them, just as he prepares to leave the white limousine and go cover Marshall.

And so, when he takes off the diamond chain, he hands it to his old friend John Sheppard for safekeeping. And when Sheppard takes the diamond chain and sees his friend get out of the white limousine, he throws the chain under the seat and follows him. The other friends go too. There are many accounts of what takes place on the snowbank, but this fact is certain: Walker is not there. When he tells the police he avoids conflict, he is telling the absolute truth.

Williams approaches the fighters. He tells them to break it up and go home. His friend hears him raise his voice and tell Marshall, "Come on, get in the limo," thus deepening the connection between Marshall and the white Hummer. But the fighters won't listen. Marshall's cousin slaps Williams's hands down and says, "Nobody touch me."

Finally Williams gives up. He tells his friends to get back in the limousine. They get back in. Little Willie heads down the sidewalk with good reason to believe that Marshall is riding in the white Hummer. As Little Willie goes to the trunk, Marshall goes to the Town Car and flees for the suburbs.

At 2:13 the white Hummer limousine begins to pull away from the curb.

A few seconds later it stops. The diamond chain is missing. They can't leave until it's found.

Around this time, a man fitting Little Willie's description is seen in a Chevy Tahoe idling on Broadway, in position to follow the white limousine.

The chain is found under the seat. Javon Walker puts it in his pocket and promises to keep it safe. The white limousine takes off. On the boulevard, a woman hears a sound like fireworks.

JOHN BRANCH

Punched Out: The Life and Death of a Hockey Enforcer

FROM THE NEW YORK TIMES

Part I: A Boy Learns to Brawl

DEREK BOOGAARD WAS SCARED. He did not know whom he would fight, just that he must. Opportunity and obligation had collided, the way they can in hockey.

His father bought a program the night before. Boogaard scanned the roster, checking heights and weights. He later recalled that he barely slept.

A trainer in the dressing room offered scouting reports. As Boogaard taped his stick in the hallway of the rink in Regina, Saskatchewan, he was approached by one of the few players bigger than he was. Boogaard had never seen him before. He did not know his name.

"I'm going to kill you," the player said.

The scrimmage began. A coach tapped Boogaard on the shoulder. Boogaard knew what it meant. He clambered over the waist-high wall and onto the ice.

He felt a tug on the back of his jersey. It was time.

The players flicked the padded gloves from their hands. They removed the helmets from their heads. They raised their fists and circled each other. They knew the choreography that precedes the violence.

Boogaard took a swing with his long right arm. His fist smacked the opponent's face and broke his nose. Coaches and scouts laughed as they congratulated Boogaard.

He was 16.

Boogaard was exhilarated, exhausted, relieved. Maybe the fear was extinguished, but it always came back, like the flame of a trick candle. One fight ended, another awaited. It was a cycle that commanded the rest of his life.

There is no athlete quite like the hockey enforcer, a man and a role viewed alternately as noble and barbaric, necessary and regrettable. Like so many Canadian boys, Boogaard wanted to reach the National Hockey League on the glory of goals. That dream ended early, as it usually does, and no one had to tell him.

But big-time hockey has a unique side entrance. Boogaard could fight his way there with his bare knuckles, his stick dropped, the game paused, and the crowd on its feet. And he did, all the way until he became the Boogeyman, the NHL's most fearsome fighter, a caricature of a hockey goon rising nearly seven feet in his skates.

Over six seasons in the NHL, Boogaard accrued three goals and 589 minutes in penalties and a contract paying him $1.6 million a year.

On May 13, his brothers found him dead of an accidental overdose in his Minneapolis apartment. Boogaard was 28. His ashes, taking up two boxes instead of the usual one, rest in a cabinet at his mother's house in Regina. His brain, however, was removed before the cremation so that it could be examined by scientists.

Boogaard rarely complained about the toll—the crumpled and broken hands, the aching back, and the concussions that nobody cared to count. But those who believe Boogaard loved to fight have it wrong. He loved what it brought: a continuation of an unlikely hockey career. And he loved what it meant: vengeance against a lifetime of perceived doubters and the gratitude of teammates glad that he would do a job they could not imagine.

He did not acknowledge the damage to his brain, the changes in his personality, even the addictions that ultimately killed him in the prime of his career. If he did recognize the toll, he dismissed it as the mere cost of getting everything he ever wanted.

THE BIGGEST KID, BUT NO BULLY

There were times, as a boy, that Derek Boogaard's skates broke, the rivets attaching the blades giving way under his heft. His awkward size and movement led to teases from teammates and taunts from fans. He heard the whispers of parents saying that this over-size boy—too big, too clumsy—had no rightful place on the team.

Boogaard never fully escaped such indignities. But there was one place where he could reliably get away.

Youth hockey in western Canada is a perpetual series of long drives across dark and icy landscapes. For Boogaard, that often meant riding shotgun in his father's police car.

It meant stopping after school for gas and a Slurpee as the winter dusk settled early on the prairie. It meant a postgame meal of rink burgers, the snack-stand staple that warmed the belly against the bitter cold. It meant a radio usually tuned to hockey—maybe the Toronto Maple Leafs, Derek's favorite team, or the hometown junior league team, the Melfort Mustangs. And it meant falling asleep in the dark of a winter's night, awakened by the warm light of the family garage.

"I think the best part of playing hockey for ages 3 until 16 was the little road trips with dad," Boogaard handwrote a few years ago, part of 16 pages of notes found in his New York apartment after his death.

He remembered the blue and white jerseys of his first team. He remembered his grandfather tapping the glass to say hello. He remembered scoring his first goal—against his own goalie.

"I remember when I would sit in the bench I would always look for my mom or my dad in the stands," Boogaard wrote.

During the first shift of his first game, Boogaard skated all the way to one end, alone, away from the puck and the other children, looking for his family.

"And he finally saw us," his father, Len Boogaard, said. "He had a big smile on his face and he was waving at us."

Derek Boogaard was born on June 23, 1982. He was the first of four children of Len and Joanne Boogaard, three boys then a girl, spaced evenly two years apart.

Len Boogaard, a member of the Royal Canadian Mounted Police, mostly worked his beats in small towns on the Saskatchewan prairie. RCMP policy dictated a move every few years so that familiarity in one town did not breed comfort or corruption. It cast his family, like those of other officers who are part of the sprawling Canadian carousel of small-town law enforcement, into roles as perpetual outsiders.

The Boogaards lived in Hanley, Saskatchewan, population 500, when Derek was born. After a couple of years near Toronto, the family moved to Herbert, Saskatchewan, a town of fewer than 1,000 people, predominantly Mennonite. Whether Len Boogaard was issuing traffic tickets or investigating domestic disturbances, the grievances "would ultimately come back to the kids at some point," he said.

No one was more affected than Derek, who spent a childhood trying to fit in. The biggest kid in class, shy and without many friends, Boogaard was often tagged as a troublemaker and dismissed as a distraction. A grade school teacher, the family said, routinely relegated Boogaard to a closet.

Boogaard had a restless, inquisitive mind, but struggled to follow directions. He labored through reading assignments. On an application for a hockey team in ninth grade, the Boogaards said that Derek had an average grade of 65 percent. They also noted that he was six feet four inches and 210 pounds.

He was hardly a bully. Paradoxically, he was picked on largely because he was so big. At age 11, after another family move, he was quickly challenged to a schoolyard fight by a boy named Evan Folden, who considered himself king of the school jocks.

Boogaard won his first fight. He bloodied Folden's nose.

He was continually targeted by older kids and challenged by classmates wanting to build a reputation. Even his younger brother Ryan and Ryan's posse of friends ganged up on him, like Lilliputians on Gulliver.

The family feared for Boogaard's safety because he often acted without considering the outcome. He once moved a friend's new trampoline close to the garage, climbed to the roof and belly-flopped onto the canvas. The springs broke, the frame collapsed, and Boogaard hit the ground with a thud, bruising his ribs.

"There were some cognitive issues and behavioral issues that made it difficult, as well, trying to understand what he was doing sometimes," Len Boogaard said. "He would do stuff and he wouldn't appear to know the consequences of what he was doing—or why he was doing it, what sort of impact it would have on him or other people around him."

The family was determined to provide positive reinforcement. Hockey was one way.

"It's something that he really enjoyed to do," Joanne Boogaard said. "And because he struggled so much in school, we bent over backwards to give him every opportunity that you could for him to do what he liked to do."

That is why, after a separation from Len Boogaard when Derek was 16, she took out a second mortgage on the house, to finance the sports her children played. It is why Len Boogaard repeatedly drove Derek 90 minutes each way to Saskatoon for skating lessons, then boxing lessons to teach him to be a better fighter on the ice.

Len Boogaard, a quiet man smoldering with a cop's intensity, sometimes saw that his son needed a boost. So he would pull into an icy parking lot and spin the police car in a dizzying series of doughnuts. Or he would park at the edge of a pasture and moo at the cows through the loudspeaker. Or, with the backseat filled with boys, he would shout for them to look up before hitting the brakes, smashing the smiling faces into the clear partition and sending the boys into shrieks of laughter.

Derek Boogaard loved that part of hockey.

A MEMORABLE NIGHT IN MELFORT

Melfort, Saskatchewan, has about 5,000 residents. It is surrounded by horizons of flat, windswept fields, covered in grain in the summer and snow in the winter, crosshatched every few miles by two-lane roads. It rests under the dome of an impossibly wide sky, pierced by the occasional water tower or silo.

The Boogaards and their four children arrived in 1993, when Derek turned 11, moving into a split-level house at 316 Churchill Drive. There were hockey games in the street, wrestling matches on the front lawn, video games in the basement, and family dinners around a cramped kitchen table.

"It seemed so small because they were all so big," said Folden, who became a teammate and friend of Boogaard's after their schoolyard fight.

They were rough-and-tumble days, and even Krysten—the youngest, on her way to six-feet-five—was pulled into the scrums. "Cage raging" began in elementary school and continued in hockey dressing rooms as teenagers.

"It's where you put your gloves and helmet on and just go at it like a hockey fight and the loser is the one on the ground," Boogaard wrote. "This is where you kinda learn how to punch."

In eighth grade, Boogaard had an assignment: describe what

you want to do for a living. He wrote that he wanted to play in the NHL, envisioning himself among the class of gritty players with scoring punch, like his hero, Wendel Clark, who grew up in Saskatchewan and became captain of the Toronto Maple Leafs.

The teacher asked Boogaard for an alternate plan. Boogaard said he did not have one. Their ensuing debate landed Boogaard in detention.

"He didn't have a Plan B," Len Boogaard said. "Plan A was to play hockey. There was no backup plan."

And what if hockey did not work out?

"I have no idea," his father said. And neither did anyone else.

Boogaard's size, if not his skill, provided roster spots on top-level youth teams. At 13, a team photograph showed Boogaard among the tall boys in the back row, with a round, cherub face. Two years later, it was as if Boogaard had been stretched by a rolling pin. He towered over his teammates. His knees ached from the growth spurt.

Floyd Halcro, a coach who helped talk Boogaard into playing after he had quit hockey at age 14, heard all the concerns, from parents of teammates and opponents alike.

"He would get penalties that were not, in any way, shape, or form, his fault," Halcro said. "I'm five-foot-nine, and a little guy my size would take a run at Derek and run into his elbow, and the refs would give him a penalty. He got so many penalties because he was six-foot-three, six-foot-four at that age. And he was actually picked on by other teams, by other referees, other communities, simply because of his size. Derek would certainly stick up for the team, he would stick up for his teammates, but wasn't mean at all."

That is what made one particular episode so memorable. The old rink at the corner of Stovel Avenue and Manitoba Street, covered in pea-green aluminum siding, squats low next to Melfort's curling club. Built in 1931, Main Arena has low-hanging fluorescent lights above the ice and orange-glow heaters above three rows of bleachers.

Exactly what happened that winter's night has been left to the rusty memories of the few dozen in attendance. This much is clear: Melfort was losing badly, and 15-year-old Derek Boogaard was suddenly inside the other team's bench, swinging away at opposing players.

"It felt like I had a force feild on me," Boogaard wrote. (His notes had occasional misspellings.)

Players scattered like spooked cats, fleeing over the wall or through the open gates.

"He had gone ballistic," Len Boogaard said. "It was something I hadn't seen before."

Eventually subdued and sent to the dressing room, Boogaard re-emerged in his street clothes. He sidled up to his seething father, who was dressed in his police uniform.

"Dad just kinda asked me what the [expletive] are you doing?" Boogaard wrote. "So I stood by him for the rest of the game."

Len Boogaard nodded toward the few unfamiliar faces in the bleachers. There were about 10 scouts from teams in the Western Hockey League, a junior league that is a primary gateway to the NHL. Among them were two men representing the Regina Pats—the chief scout, Todd Ripplinger, and the general manager, Brent Parker.

"All the Western League scouts' jaws are down like this," Parker said. His mouth fell open at the memory.

Ripplinger and Parker scribbled a note saying that the Regina Pats wanted to add Derek Boogaard to their roster. They stopped at the Hi-Lo Motor Inn on the edge of Melfort and used the fax machine to send the note to the WHL office in Calgary. Then they drove three hours back to Regina.

"Me and Brent talked all the way home about how we'd never seen anything like that before in our lives," Ripplinger said.

Ripplinger arranged to visit the Boogaard family a few days later. Boogaard sheepishly made just one request: could the Pats provide some extra-large hockey shorts?

Derek Boogaard had outgrown his.

LEARNING HIS FUTURE: HIS FISTS

The Western Hockey League has 22 teams flung across western Canada and the northwestern United States. The players, ages 16 to 20, have their expenses paid, receive a small stipend for spending money, and can earn scholarships to Canadian colleges.

Most harbor hopes of playing professionally. On a typical roster of two dozen, a few will advance to the National Hockey League.

And in today's NHL, about one of every five players once played in the Western Hockey League.

It is one of the three top junior leagues in Canada, the others based in Ontario and Quebec. In many regards, the WHL is the toughest. Not only are franchises stretched 1,500 miles apart in some instances, making travel part of the teenage tribulation, but they also have produced some of hockey's most notorious enforcers—from Tony Twist and Stu Grimson to Colton Orr and Steve MacIntyre. Veteran executives recall games where the only way to stop the brawls was to shut off the arena lights.

The teams are not affiliated with NHL teams, so player development is less a goal than profit. Fighting, an accepted and popular part of the game, is seen as a way to attract fans.

Efforts to ban fighting in the NHL have long been stymied, in part by the popularity and tradition of it in the junior and minor leagues. Websites are devoted to the spectacle, often providing blow-by-blow descriptions, declaring winners and ranking the teenage fighters.

Boogaard stepped into this culture when he was 16. The unwritten rules were well established.

Both players must agree to the challenge. Gloves are off. Until a few years ago, helmets were removed as both a sign of toughness and consideration to the unprotected knuckles of the combatants. When the leagues made helmet removal illegal, players learned to delicately remove each other's helmets before the fight began—a concoction of courtesy and showmanship. Players knowingly drifted to the center of the rink. Some, like professional wrestlers, paused to pose or fix their hair.

The reaction of the scouts that winter's night in Melfort made it clear what to expect when Boogaard went to his first WHL training camp in Regina in the fall. If Boogaard wanted to advance in hockey, he would need his fists.

"He knew," Ripplinger said. "He was a smart guy. He knew he wasn't going to be good enough to make it on skills alone, and he used his size to his advantage. I remember him at 16 years old, pushing weights and boxing and stuff like that. He knew his job."

Boogaard's first fight was the one-punch nose-breaking knockdown of the reigning tough kid during Regina's first team scrimmage. But Boogaard, seen as a fighter, not a player, played little during the preseason. Finally, he was told he would play one night in Moose Jaw, against the Pats' primary rival.

The family drove four hours from Melfort. Ryan Boogaard, two years younger, researched WHL fighters, a brotherly scouting service that continued through Boogaard's career. He warned Boogaard of a player named Kevin Lapp, rated as the league's number-two fighter. Lapp was nearly 20. Boogaard was 16.

Moments into Boogaard's first shift, Lapp asked if he was ready. Boogaard said he was. He was not.

He heard the older players in the back of the bus making fun of him on the way home. The next day, Boogaard was reassigned to a lower-division team in Regina.

Len Boogaard told his son he was proud of how far he had made it.

"When all the people in Melfort said that I wasn't any good," Derek Boogaard later wrote, "he said I shoved it up their [expletive] already."

The next team also had little use for Boogaard. During a game at a tournament in Calgary, Boogaard watched teammates take turns on the ice while he sat, unused, on the bench. Frustrated at being forgotten—or viewed as something less than a hockey player—he finally turned to the coach.

"I'm good, I can play," Boogaard cried. "I'm right here in front of you."

He later lashed out at the coach in the hallway and quit. Joanne Boogaard came from Saskatchewan to retrieve him. She drove him eight hours home.

"For your son to cry halfway from Calgary to Regina, just to be beside himself with, 'Why does this have to happen?'" Joanne Boogaard said. "All he wants to do is play. All he wanted was to have his fair share, to show people."

Boogaard thought his hockey career was over. His parents were divorcing. Len Boogaard was reassigned to Regina, the provincial capital. Joanne Boogaard, a Regina native, moved from Melfort too. Derek Boogaard was failing classes at his new high school. The family worried about the people he hung around.

Just 16, he and two friends got into a fight outside a bar. Boogaard later wrote that they beat up seven 30-year-olds. He came home at 2:30 A.M. with no shirt and his body splattered in blood. One eye was black by morning.

By the fall of 1999, the 17-year-old Boogaard had grown a few more inches, to six-seven. The Regina Pats wanted him back in training camp. Desperate to prove himself, he fought teammates 12 times in four scrimmages.

Called into the coach's office one day, he thought he would be cut from the team. Instead, he was told he would play that night against the Kelowna Rockets.

Kelowna featured a six-foot-seven enforcer named Mitch Fritz. Ryan Boogaard provided the scouting report. Fritz had an overhand punch that reminded the Boogaards of the villainous ape in the Donkey Kong video game.

Fritz won. Boogaard was traded. There is not much use for an enforcer who loses fights.

STRUGGLING WITH EVERYTHING

Prince George, British Columbia, where Boogaard had been dealt, was curious to meet its new teenage enforcer, but not quite prepared. Boogaard's jersey had to have extra bands of cloth sewn to the bottom and at the end of the sleeves.

After his first practice with the Prince George Cougars, Boogaard met with general manager Daryl Lubiniecki.

"If you win a few fights in this town you could run for mayor," Lubiniecki said.

The local paper, the *Prince George Citizen,* ran a full-page photograph of Boogaard with a Boogeyman theme. The family name had always been pronounced "BOH-guard." With Derek, some were starting to say it as "BOO-guard." Boogaard was expected to step into the character, leading with his fists.

"It bothered me," Joanne Boogaard said. "I didn't want him to fight. He knew that. He would always be: 'Oh, Mom, it's okay. It's my job now. It's what I'm doing.'"

Prince George is a city of 80,000 about 500 miles north of Vancouver. It spills out of a valley amid a wrinkled landscape of mountains carpeted with evergreen forests. Bears and moose are common backyard visitors. For the Cougars, the nearest opponent is a six-hour drive. It is not uncommon for the team bus to roll into town at midday after a road trip.

"Prince George, it's not a dirty town, a rough town, but it's an honest town," said Jim Swanson, the local paper's former sports editor. "And people didn't mind seeing two guys who were willing to drop the gloves and go at it."

For Boogaard, instantly homesick, the season started poorly and got worse. He lost his first fight to Eric Godard, a future NHL enforcer. Quickly tagged with a reputation for poor balance and wild swings, Boogaard lost most of the rest of his fights too. Online voters gave him a 6-9-1 record.

His private struggles were just as profound. Junior hockey is considered a rite of passage for Canada's most promising young players. It is a wild, frightening, competitive, and lonely voyage into the world of frenzied fan bases, full-time coaching staffs, cross-province bus travel, and host families, known as billets.

Boogaard got tangled in all of it. He was awed by the ferocity of fans. ("That's the worst I have ever heard people yelling and screaming," he wrote of a game in Swift Current.) His spirits flagged under the callousness of coaches pressured to win. His inexperience meant that he spent overnight bus trips sitting near the front, not sleeping in the bunks in back reserved for veterans. And Boogaard bounced from one host family to another, unable to create a facsimile of his once-stable home life.

"It was a very long year for me," Boogaard wrote. "I struggled with everything it seemed."

Boogaard was hardly a model citizen. He quietly rejected authority figures—teachers, coaches, host families—who treated him with what he sensed was distrust. He disobeyed rules, particularly curfews, and rotated through several families. He never completed 10th grade.

"He was a boy in a man's body," said Dallas Thompson, then an assistant coach for Prince George. "Everything was in a hurry. He knew what he wanted to do: he wanted to play in the NHL. A lot of things, like school and growing up, got accelerated a bit, and I think it overwhelmed him at times."

In March 2000, during a home game against Tri-City, Boogaard was hit in the face by an enforcer named Mike Lee. The two were ushered to the penalty box.

"I sat in the box for the five mins and I couldn't close my mouth," Boogaard later wrote. "My teeth wouldn't line up."

Boogaard went to the hospital, where his jaw was wired shut.

The Cougars put him on a liquid diet and sent him home to Regina.

"He was missing a tooth," Len Boogaard said. "He could fit a straw through there. Then he realized, too, in that space, he could shove food down as well. So he would cut up little pieces of steak and slide it through that hole. Instead of losing weight, he gained about 25, 30 pounds that summer, while his jaw was wired shut. It was incredible."

The father laughed at the memory.

"He'd go to McDonald's and shove fries through that little hole there."

THE PHONE RINGS. IT'S THE NHL.

Boogaard ultimately found refuge at the home of Mike and Caren Tobin, owners of a Prince George jewelry store and longtime hosts for the Cougars. Boogaard trailed a teammate to their house and never wanted to leave.

"Derek was shy—oh my God was he shy," Mike Tobin said.

The house became Boogaard's sanctuary. He played video games in the basement and made himself comfortable in the kitchen. He brought other teenagers—not teammates, usually, but assorted misfits he befriended at school. He went to action movies with Mike and tagged along on family outings. He helped run the birthday party when the Tobins' twin daughters turned five and had a giant bounce house in the front yard.

Boogaard felt an instant kinship with Mike Tobin—an affable man who treated Boogaard less like a son than a little brother, who did not finish school but built a successful business, who drove nice cars and had a stately home on the edge of town.

"He hated, hated, hated school," Tobin said of Boogaard. Imitating Boogaard's deep voice and sideways smirk, he added: "'Look at Mike. He didn't finish school and he has a Porsche.'"

Boogaard, with a backlog of frustrations, wanted to quit during training camp in 2000. He was 18. He called his father to tell him. He told his teammates he had a plane ticket home. Tobin ultimately persuaded him to stay.

And, suddenly, Boogaard started to win fights.

"His first year in the WHL, I think, it was mostly adjusting to his frame, not knowing how to use his reach," Ryan Boogaard said. "I think he felt more comfortable with that frame in his second year in the WHL, and he did a lot better."

He quickly avenged his broken-jaw loss to Mike Lee. He beat Mat Sommerfeld, a rival who had torn Boogaard's name from the back of his uniform and held it over his head after an earlier conquest. One website put Boogaard's record at 18-4-4 in fights that season. One poll named him the toughest player in the WHL's Western Conference.

When Boogaard took the ice, a buzz rippled through Prince George's arena, which routinely had capacity crowds of 5,995. One side of the arena would shout "Boo!" and the other would shout "Gaard!"

He scored only once in 61 games for Prince George in 2000–2001. He recorded 245 penalty minutes, ranking eighth in the WHL. He was, finally, an enforcer, appreciated by one team, feared by all others.

"Whenever he would score or get a point, they would cheer like it was the greatest thing," Swanson, the former sports editor, said. "It just wasn't something they expected. Whenever you heard the name 'Derek Boogaard' announced, you expected it to be followed by, 'Five-minute major for fighting.'"

Yet, improbably, Boogaard found himself on the ice during overtime of a playoff game.

"I was standing in front of the net and I turned around and the puck was just sitting there while the goalie thought he had the puck," Boogaard wrote. "I backhanded it into the net and the game was over. It was an unbelievable feeling. The guys came out of the bench and the place was going nuts. It was the best feeling I had the last 2 years."

The television announcer called it "a miracle on ice." It remains a highlight in Prince George hockey history.

"I don't think I ever saw our rink, or Derek, that happy as the time he scored that goal," said Thompson, the former assistant coach.

The 2001 NHL draft began on June 23, Boogaard's 19th birthday. Now of legal drinking age, he spent the night mostly at the Iron Horse Bar in Prince George with a couple of friends.

The next day, the phone rang at Joanne Boogaard's house in Regina. It was Tommy Thompson, then the chief scout of the Minnesota Wild.

"I told her I was calling from the Minnesota Wild and that we had drafted Derek," Thompson said. "She clearly was not expecting this call. She said he was already on a team, in Prince George. I said, 'No, the NHL draft.' She said: 'NHL? You've got to be kidding.'"

Caren Tobin answered the ringing telephone in Prince George moments later. She ran upstairs to the bedroom where Boogaard was sleeping. She pounded on the door. Boogaard answered in grunts and asked her to take a message. She coaxed him out of bed and downstairs to the phone.

"In typical Derek style, he goes, 'Uhhuh, uh-huh, okay, yeah, okay, thanks,'" Tobin recalled. With little emotion, he hung up and said he was drafted by the Wild in the seventh round, number 202 over all. The Tobins screamed in excitement.

Boogaard said he was going back to bed. He had a headache.

A month later, he was in St. Paul, home of the Wild. An arena worker let him into the team dressing room. For the first time, he put on an NHL uniform.

And it fit.

Part II: Blood on the Ice

> I didn't see it coming at all. I was in a bad position and he hit me hard, hardest I've ever been hit. Instantly knew it was broken. I didn't lose consciousness, but I went straight on the ice. And I felt where it was, and my hand didn't rub my face normally. It was a little chunky and sharp in spots and there was a hole there about the size of a fist.
> —Todd Fedoruk, former NHL enforcer

The fist belonged to Derek Boogaard. Whenever he opened his right hand, the fingers were bent and the knuckles were fat and bloody with scar tissue, as if rescued a moment too late from a meat grinder. That hand was, until the end, what the family worried about most with Boogaard. How would he write when he got old?

When Boogaard closed his right hand, though, it was a weapon, the most feared in the NHL. The thought of Boogaard's right fist kept rival enforcers awake at night. It made them alter their strategy and doubt their fighting acumen. And, in the case of Todd

Fedoruk, that fist shattered his face and dropped him to the ice, all while officials and teammates watched, an arena full of hockey fans cheered, and Boogaard's Minnesota Wild teammates banged their sticks against the boards in appreciation.

No single punch announced the arrival of a heavyweight enforcer the way it did on October 27, 2006. Fedoruk, six feet two and 235 pounds, had built a career as a nuisance and willing combatant. Trying to avenge a hit that the six-eight Boogaard had laid on an Anaheim Ducks teammate, Fedoruk chased Boogaard down the ice. He baited him with tugs on his jersey.

Seven seconds after their gloves dropped, the damage was done. Surgeons inserted metal plates and a swath of mesh to rebuild the right side of Fedoruk's face. His career was never the same.

Message sent. Players around the league took notice of the Boogeyman.

"I knew sooner or later he would get the better of me," said Georges Laraque, long considered the toughest man in hockey. "And I just—I like my face, and I just didn't want to have it broken."

Boogaard was 24, in his second NHL season. He was already established as a fan favorite in Minnesota and a man to avoid everywhere else in the dangerous, colorful, and sometimes unhinged world of hockey enforcers.

> I never fought mad. Because it's a job, right? I never took it personally. Lot of times when guys fight, you just ask the other guy politely. Because the job is hard enough. Why make it harder by having to insult anyone? We know what the job is.
> —Georges Laraque, former NHL enforcer

There has been fighting in hockey for about as long as there have been pucks. Early games, on frozen ponds and outdoor rinks, were often scrumlike affairs with little passing. Without strong rules, scores were settled with swinging sticks and flying fists.

The NHL, formed in 1917, considered a ban on fighting. It ultimately mandated that fighters be assessed a five-minute penalty. That interpretation of justice, now Rule 46.14, still stands. It has never been much of a deterrent.

The best way to protect top players from violent onslaughts, teams have long believed, is the threat of more violence, like having a missile in a silo. Teams employ on-ice bruisers, the equivalent of playground bodyguards. Hurt one of us, and we will send out someone bigger, tougher, to exact revenge.

"Having another player in the bench that is willing to come over and willing to punch you is a good deterrent for other violence on the ice—as crazy as that sounds," said Matt Shaw, an assistant coach for the NHL's San Jose Sharks.

Teams did not hesitate to promote the prospect of a ruckus. Fighting was not just necessary, they believed, but also part of hockey's allure. Nearly half of NHL games, 600 or more in a typical season, pause for a two-man brawl.

"I went to a fight the other night and a hockey game broke out," the comedian Rodney Dangerfield used to say. Everyone still gets the joke.

Imagine in football, if a linebacker hit a quarterback with what the quarterback's team believed was too much force. The equivalent to hockey's peculiar brand of justice would be if those teams each sent a player from the sideline—someone hardly valued for his skill as a player, perhaps rarely used—and had them interrupt the game to fight while teammates and officials stood back and watched.

In football, as in most sports, such conduct would end in ejections, fines, and suspensions.

In hockey, it usually means five minutes in the penalty box and a spot in the postgame highlights.

Fighting is not tolerated in most hockey leagues around the world. It is not part of college hockey in the United States and Canada, nor international tournaments like the Olympics.

But it is a mainstay of North American professional leagues, stretching from the NHL to small-town minor and junior leagues. Proponents believe the sport is so fast and so prone to contact that it needs players to police the shadowy areas between legal hits and dirty play.

With a mix of menace and muscle, enforcers settle grievances and slights between teams, be they real, imagined, or concocted as an excuse for disorder. Sometimes fights are spontaneous combustions, a punch thrown to avenge a perceived cheap shot. Others are premeditated affairs, to settle simmering disputes—whether from last period or last season. Some are intended to reverse the momentum of a lopsided game. Some are a restless player's way of proving himself to his team.

But there is generally order to the chaos, unwritten rules of engagement, commonly called "the code."

It covers everything from how a fight originates (both players must agree, and they usually do because of a fraternal bond of responsibility) to how it ends (with a modest glide to the penalty box).

No sticks. Hands must be bare. Face-protecting visors are not worn by most enforcers to indicate that their face is open for business.

The fight ends when a player falls or the action slows to a stall, like popcorn after all but the last kernels are popped. Officials slide between the men and steer them away. Teammates cheer their own, regardless of the outcome.

"There's no better feeling when the boys get a rise from you showing up, putting yourself out there," Fedoruk said. "I'm getting chills right now just from talking about it."

When his cheek was crushed by Boogaard in 2006, Fedoruk's first thought was to "save face" and skate off the ice. He did.

"Their bench was cheering like you do when your teammate gets a guy," Fedoruk said. "I remember skating by their bench.

"Their faces kind of lost expression because I think they seen—you could see it. You could see the damage that was done because the cheekbone, it wasn't there anymore."

> Derek would take two or three punches to land one good one. He wasn't a defensive fighter. I remember he said: "I hate guys that hide. When I fight, I'm going to throw, and I'm going to throw hard. I don't have an off switch." Anytime a fight didn't go his way—a draw or maybe he thought he lost—that would eat at him.
> —John Scott, NHL enforcer

D. J. King has watched the video dozens of times. He still pauses the fight on the part where the Minnesota Wild's Derek Boogaard, a second after getting his nose broken, slugged King on the head and sent his helmet flying.

King has tried to count the number of revolutions his helmet made before it hit the ice behind him. He thinks it was 12.

"The punch flung it about five feet in the air, I think," King said, with a tinge of awe.

It was March 14, 2010. The game between the Wild and the St. Louis Blues was minutes old. King and Boogaard, both from rural

Saskatchewan, knew each other from the Western Hockey League,
when they were teenagers and their ambitions were similarly reli-
ant on their fists.

They barked in the casual language of enforcers: *You wanna
go? Let's go.* Each man dropped his stick from his right hand. They
shook their gloves, worn loose for such occasions, to the ice. They
pushed up their sleeves. It was just another fight—yet memorable
and telling.

King drifted to center ice, caught up by the spectacle. Boogaard
stopped halfway there, leaving the men comically far apart.
Boogaard stood firm, a matador awaiting the bull. King, six-three
and 230 pounds, drifted toward him, as if pulled by Boogaard's
gravity.

"The referee just looked at them and said, 'Okay, boys, let's get
it going here,'" one television announcer said.

"This is a super-heavyweight bout," his broadcast partner said,
his voice rising with excitement.

Boogaard liked to grab opponents by the collar with his left
hand and lock his arm. From that distance, opponents could not
reach Boogaard's face with a swing. But he could shake them off
balance or torture them with jabs of a left fist full of jersey until he
found a chance to uncoil his cocked right arm.

"I want to get in tight," King said, analyzing video of the fight. "I
want to come and switch up, throw some lefts right away and then
go back and throw rights. All I want to do is be tight and throw as
much as possible."

Boogaard stood in place, turning slowly. King orbited. He batted at air, gauging distance and reach. Finally, King stabbed with
his left hand and, head down, swung at the bigger man with his
right.

Boogaard blocked it. He grabbed King with a left arm bent at
the elbow. King delivered two left-hand punches to Boogaard's
face, "just to get him thinking," King said.

The announcer's voice rose to a shout.

"Boogaard fighting back!" he said as Boogaard, half a foot
taller, thundered a couple of right hands on top of King's head.
The helmet absorbed most of the beating. King felt it only after
the adrenaline faded.

"It's the hardest bone in the body and it's not going to daze you as much as getting hit, especially, like, in the temple area or the chin area," King said.

King blindly threw three right hands that punched the air. A fourth bashed Boogaard in the nose and broke it.

More than anything, Boogaard hated getting hit on the nose. It had been surgically repaired less than a year before.

"Oh! And King stuns Boogaard," the announcer shouted. And just as he said it, Boogaard threw a right hand that struck King on the forehead. King's white helmet flew from his head.

The crowd roared.

The players had been swinging at each other for only eight seconds. Boogaard hit King on top of his bare head. King tagged Boogaard in the face again. A "Tale of the Tape" graphic, showing heights and weights of the fighters, popped onto the screen of the television broadcast.

King steered Boogaard toward the boards. Boogaard took a few more swings, but King was content to cling tight. Finally, as they came to rest behind the goal, officials slipped between them. Boogaard's nose was bleeding, and blood was smeared across his forehead.

The fight lasted about a minute.

"That was a dandy!" the announcer said, and his partner laughed.

Replays were shown. Rink workers repaired the gouges in the ice and used shavings to cover the blood.

King went to the penalty box and wrapped an icy towel around his bloodied hands.

"The scar tissue in the hands builds up so much that when you get hit it just comes off in chunks now," King said.

Boogaard headed to the locker room. He missed the next five games.

> When a team scores, the fans of the team that scored will get on their feet. But when there's a fight, everyone gets on their feet.
> —Georges Laraque

Among the hundreds of Boogaard hockey clips cataloged across the Internet, almost all of them fights, one is a favorite of family and friends. It is from the final minutes of a Wild playoff game against the visiting Anaheim Ducks on April 17, 2007.

The teams stirred a dislike for each other during a series of hits and taunts. Bickering continued through a time-out. The Wild led, and Boogaard stood and jeered—or chirped, in hockey parlance—from the bench. The Ducks chirped back.

Tension built. The crowd chanted Boogaard's name. Finally, coach Jacques Lemaire gave the signal. Boogaard slid onto the ice and skated casual arcs near the benches. He looked at the Ducks, smirked, and shrugged.

"If the roof wasn't screwed down, it would have flew off," said Joanne Boogaard, Derek's mother.

Never had Boogaard felt such love. And it was not because he had smashed someone's face. It was because he could have.

"He didn't have to fight, he didn't have to get hurt, he didn't have to hurt anybody," Joanne Boogaard said. "That was the best. He could just go out there and skate around."

Boogaard had size and determination, but not much else, when the Wild chose him in the seventh round of the 2001 NHL draft. He trained with a Russian figure skater. He continued lessons to bolster his boxing. He was sent for seasoning in the minor leagues, where Wild officials told the coaches to mold Boogaard into an NHL enforcer.

His minor league coaches did not have such vivid imaginations.

"We didn't give him a chance, and we were the guys trying to help him," said Matt Shaw, who coached Boogaard in the minor leagues and the NHL. "Give him credit. This guy willed his way to the NHL."

At his first camp after being drafted, Boogaard aimed his body at an opponent, who ducked at the last moment. Boogaard hit the glass and shattered it. His body tumbled out of the rink.

At 20, Boogaard was assigned to the Louisiana IceGators of the East Coast Hockey League. Within a year, he battered his way to the Houston Aeros of the American Hockey League, one rung below the NHL.

Hard work endeared him to coaches. In the summer heat of Houston, Boogaard tirelessly ran up hills near the practice rink. He stayed late after practice, awaiting further instruction. Alone, he skated, shot, and practiced the basics, hoping coaches would trust him enough to put him in the game.

Most important, Boogaard won fights. The Aeros replayed bouts on the video board and called it "Boogeyman Cam." They had a Boogaard bobblehead promotion, and the fists bobbled too.

Boogaard skated well for a big man, but he turned like a loco-motive. When he aimed his body at players and missed, the rat-tling boards echoed an intimidating message. One coach told the Aeros staff that Boogaard was their most valuable player, because his team was frightened by his mere presence.

"That's when it hit me," Shaw said. "I went: 'Good God. This guy's going to play.'"

Still raw, Boogaard went to the Wild's training camp in 2005. He beat up an enforcer from Buffalo, then one from Chicago in pre-season games. Lemaire, the Wild coach, saw the impact Boogaard had on other teams. He never played in the minors again.

In his first regular-season fight, on October 16, 2005, against Anaheim, he pounded Kip Brennan before dropping him with a big right hand. Boogaard won again, then again. With each fallen opponent, the rookie's popularity grew.

Such adoration is not unusual. The enforcer, sometimes mocked as a goon or euphemized as a tough guy, may be hockey's favorite archetype. Enforcers are seen as working-class superhe-roes—understated types with an alter ego willing to do the sport's most dangerous work to protect others. And they are underdogs, men who otherwise might have no business in the game.

Boogaard went nearly five years between NHL goals and scored three times in 277 games. He spent 1,411 minutes on the ice and 589 minutes in the penalty box.

But he was quick to do an interview or sign on for charity work. He was huge and imposing, yet laughed easily and always kneeled to talk to children. His personality was an understated counter-weight to his outsize reputation as a fighter. His number 24 be-came a top-selling replica jersey.

"It was the fierceness of his brand and the gentleness of his character," explained Tom Lynn, a former Wild executive.

Lynn was among those who noticed lifestyle changes as years passed. Boogaard signed his first contract with the Wild in 2003 and spent most of the $50,000 bonus on a GMC Denali. He liked the status it signaled in the players' parking lot.

"Before he got to the NHL, Derek would walk around with his two teeth out, because he was missing those two front teeth," said Janella D'Amore, Boogaard's girlfriend through several years in the minor leagues and his first season with the Wild. "His hair would be a mess, he would wear the same T-shirt. He didn't care. He was just happy. Then he got to the NHL, and it was about having to wear the designer clothes and having the perfect haircut and the perfect designer glasses. I think he felt he had to fit the part."

Len Boogaard accompanied his son on a three-game trip to the West Coast in November 2006. Hungry after a movie in San Jose, California, Len recommended a fast-food place across the street. Derek wanted room service.

"So I got a pita for six bucks, and a Coke, and went back to the hotel room," Len Boogaard said. "Room service finally showed up, and he had a steak, very small, some veggies on the side, and a Coke. And it was 95 bucks. I said, 'What?' And that's when he put up his hand and said: 'Don't worry about it, Dad. It's the lifestyle.'"

In juniors, Boogaard usually received about $50 a week for spending money. In his final year in the minors, he made $45,000.

Now his salary was $525,000. It was a long way from the dark drives across the icy prairie of western Canada, fueled by rink burgers and the sound of the radio.

"Anytime I would question what he was doing, the hand would come up, waving," Len Boogaard said. "'Don't worry about it, Dad. It's the lifestyle.'"

> My back wakes me up. I get on the floor every morning. My left hand has been smashed and broken so many times I'm missing a knuckle. From the concussions, my memory—I have a lapse with my memory at times. It's just little things, and important things. If you look at the fights I've had since I was 16, I've had about 300. These aren't boxing gloves. These are fists. There has to be an impact.
> —Brantt Myhres, former NHL enforcer

The worry was always about the hands. Like those of most enforcers, Derek Boogaard's giant hands were mangled—especially the right one. But that was the most obvious cost of his work. The rest of the damage, physical and mental, he liked to hide.

His sore right shoulder had ached since he broke his collarbone at 13. His nose, crushed too many times to count, was bent, like that of a cartoon character who smells something delicious in that direction. In the minor leagues, his back was so perpetually sore that he once could not stand up after lacing his skates.

"Being the guy he was, he couldn't show that pain and stuff like that, so he was kind of sucking it up a lot," said Todd Fedoruk, who was signed by the Wild about a year after absorbing the face-crushing blow from Boogaard in 2006.

The men became friends, not divided by their bout but tied together by their roles. They roomed together on road trips in 2007–2008. It was only there that Boogaard asked for help: Todd, can you put a couple of pillows under my feet?

"I was kind of a nurse for him in the room, because around the rink he wanted to play," Fedoruk said.

A couple of years ago, a friend in the Wild locker room watched as a trainer sat on Boogaard's chest, tugging and twisting Boogaard's nose after a fight.

In the fall of 2009, a doctor asked Boogaard to name every word he could think of that began with the letter R. He could not come up with any.

Last winter, a friend said, a neurologist asked Boogaard to estimate how many times his mind went dark and he needed a moment to regain his bearings after being hit on the head, probable signs of a concussion. Four? Five? Boogaard laughed. Try hundreds, he said.

Any boy's dream of the NHL intersects with the reality of skill, usually in the teens. For a few, fading hope depends on a willingness and ability to give and absorb beatings.

"If you're playing pond hockey, six or seven years old, and somebody said, 'Hey, Brantt, the only way you're going to make it to the NHL is fighting your way there,' you think I would have done it?" the former NHL enforcer Brantt Myhres said. "No way. I would have done something else."

There is pain, of course. But fear too.

"Imagine you go pick a guy that's six-four, 220 pounds, and say, 'Why don't we meet here on the street in two days, and we'll slug it out and see how it goes?'" Myhres said. "I guarantee you'll be a mess."

Add the pressure of thousands of fans in the arena and countless more watching on television and judging on the Internet, of teammates and coaches, roster spots and contracts, and of knowing that any fight could be the end of a career.

More than most players, enforcers gaze ahead on the schedule.

They know that the game in Calgary will entail a rematch of a fight lost last time. That game against Edmonton will need an answer for the cheap shot laid on a star player.

"I've had times where, going into a game, I know I'm going to get into a fight," the Chicago Blackhawks enforcer John Scott said. "Just the thought of getting into a fight, I just lay there, awake. 'Okay, what am I going to do?' I'm nervous. I've got butterflies in my stomach. I'll probably get one hour of sleep. It's exciting, nerve-racking, and terrifying all at the same time."

There is no incentive to display weakness. Most enforcers do not acknowledge concussions, at least until they retire. Teams, worried that opponents will focus on sore body parts, usually disguise concussions on injury reports as something else. In Boogaard's case, it was often "shoulder" or "back," two chronic ailments, even when his helmet did not fit because of the knots on his head.

"I hid my concussions," said Ryan VandenBussche, 38, a former enforcer who estimates he had at least a dozen concussions, none of them diagnosed. "I masked them with other injuries. I'm not a huge guy, by no means, but I fought all the big guys. And I certainly didn't want to be known as being concussion-prone, especially early in my career, because general managers are pretty smart and your life span in the NHL wouldn't be very long."

Myhres said he had concussions diagnosed twice but estimated he had more than 10 in his career. Now 37, he feels his memory slipping.

Mat Sommerfeld toppled Boogaard the first time they fought in the Western Hockey League. He was only six-two and 200 pounds, but was drafted by the Florida Panthers to be an enforcer.

Concussions ended his career. In his first rookie camp, his face was so swollen after a fight that he had to sleep sitting up for a few days. There were times he took the ice still woozy from a blow, only to be leveled again.

Now married with young children, working the family farm in Saskatchewan, Sommerfeld has had bouts of depression serious enough to warrant professional help.

"I don't know if it's worth it," he said. "It wasn't for me."

On January 9, 2007, in Calgary, Boogaard fought Eric Godard, a longtime rival called up from the minor leagues specifically as a counterweight to Boogaard. Godard landed a series of punches to the left side of Boogaard's head. Boogaard twice fell to one knee. Dazed, he skated to the wrong penalty box.

He was placed on injured reserve with a head injury. He returned in time to fight Godard again 17 days later. The men knocked each other's helmet off and traded punches to the face.

Boogaard likely had dozens of concussions before his death in May. No one knows.

But the hands? All it took was one look. Even the medical examiner who performed Boogaard's autopsy noted the scars.

"He would fight and his knuckles would be pushed back into the wrist," Len Boogaard said. "And then he'd have to have it manipulated and have his knuckles put back in place. His hands were a mess. My concern was always, okay, he's going to suffer with this later on in life, in terms of arthritis. It was his hands that I was more worried about."

> Obviously, I've used painkillers, with injuries and stuff. Get your shoulder rebuilt, get your knee scoped. It's hard to go out that next night and fight that world-class guy with broken knuckles. I've gotten into the drugs. Not going to lie. I'm sure people think, "Oh, he's making $1.5 million, how bad can it be?" But they've never been in his shoes.
> —Mitch Fritz, former NHL enforcer

It was the middle of the 2007–2008 season, and Boogaard knew that Fedoruk was in the midst of a decade-long battle with alcohol and drugs. Boogaard was taking prescribed pain medicine for his aching back.

"He's like, 'Man, these things work really good,'" Fedoruk recalled.

Boogaard and Fedoruk met as boys at camp for the Regina Pats in 1998. Almost a decade later, Fedoruk, three years older, was a teammate, mentor, and confidant. And Boogaard wanted to know about painkillers.

"Him knowing my history, I think he knew he could trust me," Fedoruk said. "He could open up to me and maybe try and find out some things about that. He was asking questions like, 'You're taking because you like it?' Stuff like that."

Fedoruk said his advice was simple: be careful.

Two years later, Boogaard was in substance abuse rehabilitation. Fedoruk would follow, for the second time in his career.

That kind of arc gnaws at Tom Lynn. He spent eight seasons as a Wild executive and is now a player agent.

"I started to notice, as I got to know the players in these roles, that some of them came in in a much more gentle way—some of them came in as different people than they were later on," Lynn said. "After fighting for a while, they seemed to have susceptibility to personality issues such as depression or anxiety and addictions."

As a teenager, Boogaard was a bingeing beer drinker, but it never seemed unusual in the culture of Canadian junior hockey.

In the minor leagues, he began taking Ambien, a prescription sleeping pill. It has long been doled out in training rooms to players struggling to cope with chronic aches and the demands of the schedule.

"I've been on teams where it's pretty out in the open, and guys will say: 'I have Ambien. Need an Ambien?'" said Mitch Fritz, a teenage rival of Boogaard's who has played mostly in the minor leagues.

On April 14, 2009, Boogaard had nose surgery. Seven days later, he had surgery on his right shoulder. He was prescribed Percocet, a combination of acetaminophen and oxycodone.

"He's such a big guy," Boogaard's brother Aaron said. "The doctor told him it took about twice as much medicine to knock him out as for most people. He'd go through 30 pills in a couple of days. He'd need eight to 10 at a time to feel okay."

John Scott, a six-foot-eight teammate of Boogaard's now playing for Chicago, was prescribed oxycodone after nose and knee operations.

"It just dulls you right out," he said. "Totally numbs everything. You don't feel anything. You're in no pain, but you're not yourself. There's no senses. Nothing. My wife was like: 'This is creeping me out, man. You've got to stop taking those.' And so I stopped."

Boogaard did not. One September afternoon during the Wild's preseason, disoriented while driving around Minneapolis, Boogaard was rescued by a police officer he knew. Boogaard slept on the officer's couch.

Late one night soon after, at home with his fiancée, Erin Russell, Boogaard said he took four Ambien. She knew it was something more.

"I was scared," Russell said. "I had never seen him that drugged up—falling all over the place and running into walls."

A few phone calls and a day later, Boogaard was on a plane to California, headed to a substance abuse program in Malibu.

"He just left," Scott said. "He never told anybody he was leaving. I remember talking to him and everything was fine and then all of a sudden he was just gone. They told us he was getting surgery, or it was a concussion or something. They made up some excuse and they never told us what happened. But we all kind of figured it out. It's not that hard to see."

Part III: A Brain "Going Bad"

Through the night and into the next day, as the scrolls across the bottom of television screens spread the news of Derek Boogaard's death last May, the calls of condolences came, one after another.

Among them was a call from a stranger, first to Joanne Boogaard in Regina, Saskatchewan, then to Len Boogaard in Ottawa. It was a researcher asking for the brain of their son.

An examination of the brain could unlock answers to Boogaard's life and death. It could save other lives. But there was not much time to make a decision. Boogaard, the NHL's fiercest fighter, dead of a drug and alcohol overdose at 28, was going to be cremated.

There was little discussion.

The brain was carved out of his skull by a coroner in Minneapolis. It was placed in a plastic bucket and inside a series of plastic bags, then put in a cooler filled with a slurry of icy water. It was driven to the airport and placed in the cargo hold of a plane to Boston.

When it arrived at a laboratory at the Bedford VA Medical Center in Bedford, Massachusetts, the brain was vibrantly pink and weighed 1,580 grams, or about three and a half pounds. On a stainless-steel table in the basement morgue, Dr. Ann McKee cleaved it in half, front to back, with a large knife. Much of one half was sliced into sheets about the width of sandwich bread.

The pieces of Boogaard's brain were labeled as SLI-76. They were placed into large, deli-style refrigerators with glass doors, next to dozens of other brains.

The Boogaard family waited for results. One month. Two. Three. Two other NHL enforcers died, reportedly suicides, stoking a debate about the toll of their role in hockey.

Four months. Five. The news came in a conference call to the family in October.

Boogaard had chronic traumatic encephalopathy, commonly known as CTE, a close relative of Alzheimer's disease. It is believed to be caused by repeated blows to the head. It can be diagnosed only posthumously, but scientists say it shows itself in symptoms like memory loss, impulsiveness, mood swings, even addiction.

More than 20 dead former NFL players and many boxers have had CTE diagnosed. It generally hollowed out the final years of their lives into something unrecognizable to loved ones.

And now, the fourth hockey player, of four examined, was found to have had it too.

But this was different. The others were not in their twenties, not in the prime of their careers.

The scientists on the far end of the conference call told the Boogaard family that they were shocked to see so much damage in someone so young. It appeared to be spreading through his brain. Had Derek Boogaard lived, they said, his condition likely would have worsened into middle-age dementia.

And that was when Len Boogaard's own mind went numb.

REHAB, PILLS, AND A NEW TEAM

The Minnesota Wild prepared for the start of the 2009–2010 season. Derek Boogaard watched from a distance.

The team said that Boogaard, the preeminent enforcer in the NHL and a hugely popular Wild player, was sitting out a few weeks because of a concussion. Instead, he was at the Canyon treatment center in Malibu, California, being treated for addiction to prescription drugs.

Boogaard was embarrassed and worried that news of his addiction would shatter his reputation. He was also concerned that someone would take his role. From rehabilitation, he tracked the preseason fights of teammates and texted friends to gauge how badly he was missed.

He rejoined the team after missing the first five regular-season games and had his first fight on October 21, at home against the Colorado Avalanche's David Koci. Boogaard started with a left-hand jab to Koci's chin, then grabbed Koci's jersey and knocked him down with two right-hand punches.

Boogaard skated, expressionless, to the penalty box.

From the outside, everything seemed normal. It was not.

"His demeanor, his personality, it just left him," John Scott, a Wild teammate, said. "He didn't have a personality anymore. He just was kind of—a blank face."

Boogaard fell asleep while playing cards on the team plane, a teammate said. He passed out in corners of the team's dressing room. He was uncharacteristically late for meetings and workouts. Wild trainers and doctors warned Boogaard's teammates not to give him their prescription pills.

Most NHL teams have about 10 affiliated doctors—specialists and dentists with practices of their own. Boogaard had learned that there was no system to track who was prescribing what.

In one three-month stretch of the 2008–2009 season with the Wild, Boogaard received at least 11 prescriptions for painkillers from eight doctors—including at least one doctor for a different team, according to records gathered by his father, Len Boogaard. Combined, the prescriptions were for 370 tablets of painkillers containing hydrocodone, typically sold under brand names like Vicodin.

Derek Boogaard increasingly wanted more pills. He became adept at getting them.

In downtown Minneapolis, Boogaard's favorite hangout was Sneaky Pete's, a sports bar that becomes a raucous club on weekend nights. Stripper poles are erected on the dance floor, and a throbbing beat escapes beyond the velvet rope out front. Boogaard was a regular.

Young men fueled with alcohol begged Boogaard to punch them, so they could say they survived a shot from the Boogeyman. People bought him drinks. They took pictures of him and with him. They chanted his name. When the attention got overbearing, Boogaard escaped behind the bar, where his bobblehead likeness sat on a shelf.

"He was like Norm in *Cheers*," said Stewart Hafiz, whose family owns the bar.

And Boogaard often bought painkillers, thousands of dollars' worth at a time, from someone he knew there, according to Boogaard's brother Aaron.

He gobbled the pills by the handful—eight or more Oxy-Contins at a time, multiple people said, at a cost of around $60 each—chewing them to hasten their time-release effect. The line between needing drugs for pain and wanting them for celebration blurred.

"I didn't trust him to have that amount on him," said Aaron Boogaard, who lived with Derek in summer off-seasons. "He knew it too, so he would give them to me to hold, and I would hide them around the place, and he'd come to me when his back was hurt—or whatever was hurting him."

"What was I going to do?" he added.

Wild coaches saw the decline for a couple of seasons. Boogaard's admirable work ethic had faded, and no one could pinpoint why.

"I just said to him one day: 'What's up? What's up with you? Where is the guy I know?'" said Matt Shaw, who coached Boogaard as an assistant with the minor league Houston Aeros and, later, with the Wild. "Because he was not himself. And he didn't have an answer. He didn't want to look me in the eye."

Boogaard had been drafted by the Wild in 2001, a seventh-round pick given little chance of making the NHL. The Wild shepherded him through three seasons in the minor leagues and molded him into the most fearsome player in hockey. They saw how his gentle humility blossomed into fearless swagger. They felt how the game changed when he strode onto the ice.

But by the 2009–2010 season, Boogaard was 27, and his body carried a lot of mileage. He missed the start of the season while in rehabilitation, and his contract was to expire at season's end. He played 57 games, and had no goals and nine fights.

The Wild quietly dangled him as trade bait, then made a half-hearted attempt to re-sign him for about $1 million a year.

There were plenty of other suitors. The New York Rangers and the Edmonton Oilers each offered four-year contracts paying more than $1.5 million a season.

Boogaard's family wanted Edmonton. It was familiar and close to home in western Canada.

He chose New York. He signed a four-year, $6.5 million contract—a rather ordinary salary among his new Rangers teammates, but striking among the fraternity of enforcers who play only a few minutes a game.

"It's one of the great cities to be at and you're always on center stage when you're out there, so I'm excited," Boogaard told the *Star Tribune* of Minneapolis the night he signed.

The Rangers knew about Boogaard's substance abuse problem and time in rehabilitation, family members said. The team surely knew of his concussions and myriad other injuries.

But any concern the Rangers had was outweighed by their eagerness for his brand of toughness and intimidation. They needed an enforcer, and they wanted the best.

MANIC, SULLEN, AND LONELY

Boogaard had played 21 games for the Rangers when he took the ice in Ottawa on December 9, 2010. After leveling an opponent with a legal check, Boogaard was chased by Matt Carkner, a 30-year-old enforcer who had spent most of his career patrolling the minor leagues.

The two bickered as they glided across center ice. They barely stopped before Carkner cracked Boogaard's face with a right hand.

Boogaard usually responded to such shots with an angry flurry. This time, he turned his head away and held on to Carkner. He did not throw another punch.

All fall, Boogaard's family and friends had noticed an indifference in his fighting. Boogaard was listed at 260 pounds, but weighed nearly 300 when he joined the Rangers. Team officials expressed concern about his effectiveness on the ice, even his safety in a fight, his agent said.

But much of that was disguised by Boogaard's sound beating of Philadelphia's Jody Shelley on November 4 and a rare goal, the first since his rookie season, against Washington on November 9.

Days later, the Madison Square Garden crowd chanted Boogaard's name as he pounded Edmonton's Steve MacIntyre. During a rematch minutes later, few noticed a MacIntyre jab that broke Boogaard's nose and most likely gave him a concussion. Boogaard missed one game and played the next.

Then came Carkner. He lifted Boogaard and slammed him down. Boogaard landed on his right shoulder. The back of his head struck the ice. He rose slowly and went to the locker room.

"I noticed he kind of stopped fighting and I took him down and landed on top," Carkner told reporters. "Obviously, if you land a punch on a guy like that it feels good. It feels good to take down a big man like that."

The Rangers said Boogaard was out indefinitely with a shoulder injury. Ten days later, they revealed he was having headaches.

When Len Boogaard arrived in New York from Ottawa in January, he barely recognized his son. Several times over several days, the toughest man in hockey bawled in his arms.

"I had to hold him," Len Boogaard said of Derek. "It was like when he was younger, when he was a little kid growing up. He just sobbed away uncontrollably."

For weeks, Boogaard mostly shuttered himself inside his $7,000-a-month apartment on the 33rd floor of the Sheffield, on 57th Street near Columbus Circle in Manhattan. The view of Central Park was obscured by the blinds Boogaard kept closed.

The Rangers told him to avoid the rink because the commute, the movement, even watching hockey could bring nausea. The team delivered a healthy meal to his door every afternoon, but Boogaard usually threw it away. His kitchen counter overflowed with fast-food packages.

The fog of Boogaard's postconcussion syndrome slid into a hazy shade of loneliness. Early in the season, a stream of friends had gone to New York to see him play and take in the sights.

But with Boogaard out of the lineup, the number of visitors waned. Boogaard grew desperate for company. His January cellphone bill needed 167 pages to detail calls and text messages, some to people who had not heard from him in years. February's bill consumed 222 pages. It listed 13,724 text messages.

Those who went to New York noticed his memory lapses were growing worse. Boogaard joked about them, saying he had been hit on the head too many times. But they also came to worry about his darkening personality and impulsive behavior. His characteristic sweetness and easy manner, his endearing eagerness to please, had evaporated.

Friends said Boogaard was at turns manic and sullen. He went days without showering. He made grand and scattered plans. He talked about buying land in British Columbia and building one big house for himself and cabins for family members. He spent thousands on night-vision goggles, hundreds on walkie-talkies, and $150 on candy at a Duane Reade drugstore.

Len Boogaard, knowing that his son had been enrolled in a substance abuse program since September 2009, was surprised to see so many prescription bottles in the bathroom with the names of Rangers doctors. He was also surprised to hear from his son that he had been given four days' notice for his next drug test.

Len Boogaard played a DVD of family photos and home movies. He reminded his son of everything he went through to reach New York—the family moves, the bullying, the naysayers of youth hockey, the struggles through juniors and the minor leagues.

Boogaard cried, and his father held him.

Few knew that Derek, usually on Sunday evenings, carried thousands of dollars in cash and drove his Audi to Huntington, Long Island. He met a man in a parking lot there and bought Ziploc bags full of painkillers, according to Boogaard's best friend in New York, Devin Wilson.

Boogaard sorted the pills into pastel-colored plastic Easter eggs, which he stashed around his apartment, a one-man game of hide-and-seek. He carried one in a pocket whenever he left, the contents adjusted for how long he expected to be gone.

"You could tell he didn't trust himself," said Wilson, a teammate when they were teenagers who stayed with Boogaard many weekends last spring.

By March, Boogaard resumed light workouts with the Rangers, whose doctors continued to supply him with prescription drugs. Mark Messier, the team's Stanley Cup hero in 1994 and now a team executive, tried to motivate him with a pep talk.

A day or two later, a noodle-legged Boogaard fell during on-ice workouts. The Rangers recognized the symptoms.

It was early April, the last week of the regular season, and Boogaard was on his way back to drug rehabilitation in California.

Friends thought he was vacationing. He called and texted from his cell phone and ate in nice restaurants. After a couple of weeks, granted a recess from rehabilitation, he flew to New York and drove his car to Minneapolis. He dropped off more pills at his apartment and returned to rehabilitation in Los Angeles.

Boogaard rented a Porsche for $5,000 and spent $1,200 on one dinner that week, part of $32,000 he put on his Visa card over two weeks. Aaron Boogaard, four years younger, joined him in Los Angeles and stayed at a nearby hotel. The brothers exercised and boxed at a gym. They went to the beach every day.

"There'd be meetings going on and things like that, and he

wouldn't really be doing anything," Aaron Boogaard said. "I'd try to say: 'Dude, shouldn't you be doing that stuff? I think everybody else here is doing it. Why don't you?'"

Boogaard was under the guidance of the Substance Abuse and Behavioral Health Program, financed jointly by the NHL and its players union. They would not make the codirectors—David Lewis, a psychiatrist, and Brian Shaw, a clinical psychologist and professor at the University of Toronto—available for comment.

Cassidy Cousens, the founder and program administrator of the Authentic Recovery Center in Los Angeles, where Boogaard was assigned, would not discuss his case. Cousens said that patients generally go through a detoxification program and are subjected to random drug tests several times a week. Some are allowed to leave the grounds with an approved escort—a staff member for the first few weeks, a friend or a family member after.

"It might look odd to someone outside," Cousens said. "But integrity is not lacking on the ground."

On Thursday, May 12, about a month into his rehabilitation, Boogaard was granted a second extended recess. He left with Aaron to attend the graduation of their sister, Krysten, from the University of Kansas. The plan was to meet up with their other brother, Ryan, in Minneapolis for a few days first.

That morning, Derek Boogaard sent a message from the airport in Los Angeles to Wilson in New York. There was a picture of a drink in his hand.

"Bloody Mary No. 6," Boogaard wrote. "And we haven't even left the ground yet."

"HIS CHEST WASN'T MOVING"

The night of May 12 began with a painkiller, a 30-milligram Percocet that Aaron Boogaard later told the police he handed his brother at their two-bedroom apartment in Minneapolis. Derek, hours out of rehabilitation, was bent on a party.

He wore dark jeans, a blue-and-white checkered shirt, and Pumas. He had dinner with friends at a steak-and-sushi place, where he drank Jack Daniels and Cokes. The group shuffled among Sneaky Pete's and three other downtown Minneapolis bars. At some point, or several points, Derek fueled the buzz with more prescription painkillers.

Once home in his second-floor apartment on North First Street, he spent time in the bathroom. He went to his bedroom at the end of the hall.

Friends left. It was after 3:00 A.M. Aaron made pancakes in the kitchen. Derek called him back to the bedroom four or five times. Sitting at the end of the bed, he babbled and said the bed was spinning.

"He was miserable," Aaron said.

Eventually, the calls from the bedroom stopped.

Asleep at last, Aaron thought. He left to spend what remained of the night at a girlfriend's place. He returned at about 3:00 P.M. to shower and change. He poked his head into Derek's room. Still in bed. He shouted that he was leaving for the airport to get their brother Ryan and left again.

Nearly three hours later, Ryan and Aaron arrived and stepped into the back bedroom, expecting to find their older brother sleeping off a hangover. It was about 6:00 P.M. on Friday, May 13.

"I looked and it didn't look right," Ryan said. "Like, his chest wasn't moving."

Derek Boogaard's brothers stared at the giant body sprawled on the bed. On the dresser were framed photographs of their grandparents. There were pictures of former pets, including a bulldog named Trinity.

At the foot of the bed was a brown stain, where Derek had thrown up on the beige carpet.

"He was white," Ryan said. Like his father, he is a police officer, a member of the Royal Canadian Mounted Police in rural Saskatchewan. "And I touched his arm and I knew right away because rigor mortis had already set in."

Aaron began jumping up and down, screaming. Ryan told him to call 911, then took a couple of steps into the hallway and collapsed.

Lying on the floor, he called his father's house in Ottawa. Len Boogaard's wife, Jody, answered and heard nothing but unintelligible wails. She thought it was a prank call and nearly hung up. Finally, she made sense of the words contained in the screams.

Len was in the backyard. He grabbed the phone.

"I knew this was going to happen," he cried.

The Hennepin County medical examiner ruled it an accidental overdose of alcohol and oxycodone, the active ingredient in pain-killers like OxyContin and Percocet.

"The coroner said with that mixture, he probably died as soon as he closed his eyes," Aaron said.

RESEARCHERS' "WOW" MOMENT

It did not take long for Dr. Ann McKee to see the telltale brown spots near the outer surface of Boogaard's brain—the road signs of CTE. She did not know much about Boogaard other than that he was a 28-year-old hockey player. And the damage was obvious.

"That surprised me," she said.

A neuropathologist, McKee is one of four codirectors of Boston University's Center for the Study of Traumatic Encephalopathy and the director of the center's brain bank. She has examined nearly 80 brains of former athletes, mainly retired football players and boxers who spent their careers absorbing blows to the head. The center's peer-reviewed findings of CTE have been widely accepted by experts in the field. The National Football League, initially dismissive, has since donated money to help underwrite the research.

The group may now have its most sobering case: a young, high-profile athlete, dead in midcareer, with a surprisingly advanced degree of brain damage.

"To see this amount? That's a 'wow' moment," McKee said as she pointed to magnified images of Boogaard's brain tissue. "This is all going bad."

The degenerative disease was more advanced in Boogaard than it was in Bob Probert, a dominant enforcer of his generation, who played 16 NHL seasons, struggled with alcohol and drug addictions, and died of heart failure at age 45 in 2010.

In the past two years, CTE was also diagnosed in the brains of two other former NHL players: Reggie Fleming, 73, and Rick Martin, 59.

The condition of Boogaard's brain, however, suggests the possibility that other current NHL players have the disease, even if the symptoms have not surfaced.

The NHL is not convinced that there is a link between hockey and CTE.

"There isn't a lot of data, and the experts who we talked to, who consult with us, think that it's way premature to be drawing any conclusions at this point," NHL commissioner Gary Bettman said. "Because we're not sure that any, based on the data we have available, is valid."

The researchers at Boston University say that CTE is a nascent field of study, but that there is little debate that the disease is caused by repeated blows to the head. They said that the NHL was not taking the research seriously.

"We don't know why one person gets it more severely than another person, why one person has a course that is more quick than another person," said Dr. Robert A. Stern, a neuropsychologist and a codirector for the Center for the Study of Traumatic Encephalopathy. "But what we are pretty sure of is, once the disease starts, it continues to progress."

Linking CTE to Boogaard's rapid descent in his final years is complicated by his drug addiction.

"He had problems with abuse the last couple years of his life, and that coincided with some of the cognitive and behavioral and mood changes," Stern said. "What's the chicken? What's the egg?"

For years, the NHL has tiptoed between the allure of its fast-paced, hard-hitting action and the need to protect star players. Its best player, Sidney Crosby, returned to the Pittsburgh Penguins last month after sitting out since January following two hits to the head, four days apart. Several star players in recent years have been forced to retire early because of postconcussion symptoms.

The NHL formed a concussion prevention program in 1997. In 2010, it banned blindside hits to the head. In March, the league altered its treatment protocol, requiring teams to examine all suspected concussions in a "quiet" room, away from the bench.

But the league has shown little interest in ending on-ice fighting. The message is decidedly mixed: outlaw an elbow to the head during play, but allow two combatants to stop the game and try to knock each other out with bare-knuckle punches to the head.

"If you polled our fans, probably more would say they think it's a part of the game and should be retained," Bettman said. He noted that fights were down slightly this season.

"The issue is, do we increase the penalty?" Bettman added, referring to the five-minute punishment typically handed to both fighters. "Because it is penalized now. And there doesn't seem to be an overwhelming appetite or desire to go in that direction at this point in time."

Chris Nowinski, a former Harvard football player and professional wrestler who is another codirector of the Boston University center, is the one who usually makes the initial call to a grieving family to request the brain. He does not want to put an end to hockey. He wants leagues to take every possible precaution to ensure that athletes are both better protected and better informed.

In October, Nowinski attended a Bruins game in Boston. There was a fight, and he watched quietly as thousands of people stood and cheered while the players fought.

"They are trading money for brain cells," he said.

A FATHER HUNTS FOR ANSWERS

Len Boogaard, a cop and father, tries to make sense of it all. On leave from his desk job in Ottawa—a back injury years ago forced him off the streets—he patches together the remains of Derek's world.

Like a detective, he dials contacts in Derek's phone to ask who knows what. He explores hundreds of pages of phone records to reconstruct Derek's relationships, his moods, his sleep patterns. He follows paper trails, trying to link the history of his son's prescriptions to vague diagnoses in team medical reports.

Since the day of the funeral in May, Len Boogaard said, he has not heard from the Rangers.

The team refused to answer a detailed list of questions regarding their medical treatment of Boogaard during the season and his time in rehabilitation.

It also refused requests to speak to general manager Glen Sather and the team physician, Dr. Andrew Feldman, among others, about Boogaard. Instead, it e-mailed a four-sentence statement from Sather that read, in part, "We worked very closely with Derek on and off the ice to provide him with the very best possible care."

Boogaard's death took on added weight when, in August, two other NHL enforcers were found dead. Rick Rypien, 27, reportedly committed suicide after years of depression. Wade Belak, 35 and recently retired, reportedly hanged himself 16 days later. (The family has said it was an accident.)

Each bit of news, packed with a wallop, provided a backdrop for further debate about the role of fighting and the toll on enforcers. So did the start of the NHL season in October, as teams began the ritual of glossy video tributes and moments of silence. The eccentric former coach and current television commentator Don Cherry chastised former enforcers who second-guess their past roles as "pukes," "turncoats," and "hypocrites," and the debate flared.

Arguments enveloped Canada, in particular, where culture and tradition have collided with tragedy. No one quite knows what to make of it.

In Minnesota two Sundays ago, the Wild honored Boogaard with a pregame tribute. The team sold Boogaard jerseys, T-shirts, and autographed memorabilia that it had stored from two seasons ago. Fans crowded the team store. Some proceeds went to Boogaard's favorite charity.

Boogaard's parents and siblings were escorted onto the ice and presented with flowers, a painting of Derek, and a framed game-worn jersey of his. The arena was darkened. A 4-minute-45-second tribute was shown on the video boards.

The Wild had drafted Boogaard in 2001, groomed him to fight, and paid him several million dollars over five seasons to be the NHL's top enforcer. He punched his way to local adoration and leaguewide fear and respect.

The tribute showed Boogaard running over opponents, smiling with fans, and talking to children. It showed each of the three NHL goals he scored.

It did not show a single punch.

The Wild would not answer questions about the video. They also refused to address specific questions about Boogaard's medical care, concussions, addiction and rehabilitation, or the availability of drugs through team doctors. Requests to speak with general manager Chuck Fletcher and the medical director, Dr. Sheldon Burns, were refused.

For those who knew Derek Boogaard, there are questions that may never be resolved and regret that may never be relieved.

In July, Aaron Boogaard was charged with a felony for distributing a controlled substance—in this case, one pill to his brother the night of his death. The charge was dropped in October. He also told the police that he flushed pills down the toilet after placing the 911 call. He pleaded guilty to tampering with the scene of a death and received probation and 80 hours of community service.

He is trying to revive his own hockey career, and with his name has come the expectation to fight. Last season, in 53 games with the Laredo (Texas) Bucks of the Central Hockey League, Aaron Boogaard had two goals and 172 penalty minutes. He fought 20 times.

Now 25, he plays for the CHL's Rio Grande Valley Killer Bees in Hidalgo, Texas. He wears number 82, marking the year Derek was born. Aaron fought six times in a recent 10-game stretch. At the Wild tribute, he had a bruise under one eye and said he had knocked out an opponent with one punch the night before.

His mother has asked him to quit hockey. But he has no Plan B either.

"I mean, honestly, what else am I going to do?" Aaron said.

Between trips to Minneapolis to tend to Aaron and his legal issues, Joanne Boogaard distracted herself by gutting and rebuilding her kitchen in Regina. A corner of the refurbished family room is a sort of shrine to Derek. A thigh-high cabinet holds mementos, like photographs and jerseys. Two boxes hold his ashes.

As much as anything, Derek Boogaard always feared being alone.

"We weren't going to bury him somewhere and just leave him by himself," Joanne Boogaard said.

Len Boogaard tries to make his own peace. Several times during the summer, he drove back and forth between Ottawa and Minneapolis, about 20 hours each way. For company, he took two bulldogs—Trinity, one that Derek and a girlfriend bought in Louisiana, and a puppy Len Boogaard named Boogey. They stayed in the apartment where Derek died. The lease expired in October.

It was that month that the wait finally ended for the results from Boston. A conference call connected the scientists to Boogaard's parents and siblings.

The Boogaards learned of the surprising severity of the brain damage. And they heard about the prospects of middle-age dementia.

It was then that Len Boogaard stopped listening. Something occurred to him that he did not expect.

For months, he could not bear the thought of his son's death. Suddenly, he was forced to imagine the life his son might have been left to live.

The Ferocious Life and Tragic Death of a Super Bowl Star

FROM MEN'S JOURNAL

DAVE DUERSON SET the scene with a hangman's care before climbing into bed with the revolver. The former Pro Bowl safety for the Super Bowl–champion 1985 Chicago Bears drew the curtains of his beachfront Florida condo, laid a shrine of framed medals and an American flag to his father, a World War II vet, and pulled the top sheet up over his naked body, a kindness to whoever found him later. On the dining room table were notes and a typed letter that were alternately intimate and official, telling his former wife where his assets were and whom to get in touch with to settle affairs. He detailed his motives for ending his life, citing the rupture of his family and the collapse of his finances, a five-year cliff dive from multimillionaire to a man who couldn't pay his condo fees. Mostly, though, he talked about a raft of ailments that pained and depressed him past all tolerance: starburst headaches and blurred vision, maddening craters in his short-term memory, and his helplessness getting around the towns he knew. Once a man so acute he aced his finals at Notre Dame with little study time, he found himself now having to dash down memos about what he was doing and when. Names, simple words, what he'd eaten for dinner—it was all washing out in one long wave.

No one had to tell him what those symptoms implied or what lay in store if he stuck around. Once a savage hitter on the best defense the game has ever seen, Duerson filled the punch list for chronic traumatic encephalopathy (CTE), the neuron-killing condition so rampant these days among middle-aged veterans of the National Football League. Andre Waters and Terry Long, both dead by their own hands; John Mackey and Ralph Wenzel, hopelessly brain-broke in their fifties. It was a bad way to die and a worse way to live, warehoused for decades in a fog, unable, finally, to know your own kids when they came to see you at the home.

Among the personal effects Duerson arranged that night in February was the master clue to the act he'd soon commit, Exhibit A in a life turned sideways: his 1987 NFL Man of the Year trophy. It was a testimonial to a former colossus, a player whose brilliance on the football field was a taste of much grander things to come. Future meat-processing magnate and potential congressman, or successor to Gene Upshaw as director of the NFL Players Association—*that* Dave Duerson was all forward motion, the rarest amalgam of outsize smarts and inborn ambition. This version, though—the one slumped in bed with the .38 Special to his chest—this one had run into walls, head lowered, and he, not the walls, had buckled first.

Still, when someone turns a gun on himself, there are bound to be messy questions. Why, given the spate of concussions in the NFL season just past, would Duerson elect to keep silent about his suspected ailment at precisely the moment he should have spoken? Why would a man who knew as much about brain woes as anyone who's ever played the game, having served for six years and read thousands of case files as a trustee on the NFL's pension board, not have sought treatment and financial compensation from the very committee he sat on? And why, bizarrely, did he deny those very benefits to the men who needed them most, brain-dimmed veterans living in pain and squalor and seeking relief from the league?

Perhaps to stanch these questions, Duerson dispatched a blitz of texts in the last couple of hours of his life, some of them making an emphatic plea: get my brain to the NFL's brain bank in Boston. The meaning of the texts seems plain enough: I'm sick and my mind's failing from all the helmet-to-helmet collisions in 11 brutal seasons in the NFL. Please see to it that my cortex is studied by doctors seeking treatments for brain trauma—and inquire no further about my reasons. It was a grandiose gesture, killing himself at 50 so that current and future players might be spared this horror, and was italicized by a second theatrical stroke: he shot himself through the heart, not the head, to preserve his brain for science.

But the dramatics of the act didn't sanctify him or absolve him of blame for the part he'd played in the suffering of other ex-players. If anything, Duerson's death has become a referendum on his, and his sport's, brutality, a prism through which to finally take a look at the cost of all those hits.

If you're the kind of fan who keeps a mental lineup of ex-players headed for bad endings, Dave Duerson was the last name to make your list. Virtually from birth he'd been a special case, a gold-star guy who didn't bull through problems so much as soar above them. The youngest of four children born to Julia and Arthur Duerson Jr. in working-class Muncie, Indiana, he was as exceptional off the field as he was on it. A big, powerful kid with a nose for the ball and the long-stride speed to get there first, he dominated boys two and three years older in football from the time he hit sixth grade. (He excelled at baseball and basketball as well.) Even then, though, his dreams were broader than jock stardom. Among friends he talked brashly about owning his own factories and running for the Senate someday. Duerson made the National Honor Society in high school, learned the trumpet and tuba by the age of 15, and toured overseas in an ambassador's band while earning 10 varsity letters.

With his pick of football factories like Texas and USC, Duerson chose South Bend for its glorious campus and network of corporate contacts. "From when I met him in seventh grade, he was positioning himself for a career after football," says Dave Adams, Duerson's teammate at Northside High and his roommate at Notre Dame. He interned at a law firm, then for Indiana Senator Richard Lugar.

"Sports were the springboard," says his ex-wife Alicia, who met him at a bowl game his freshman year. "He made so many plans for such a young age and had the brains to pull it all off. He had a photographic memory, which used to make me mad, because he'd barely study and get A's, where I'd be up a week of nights and be happy to get a B." A four-year starter at Notre Dame and a team captain, Duerson was as proud of his degree in economics as of making All-American, which he did twice.

Duerson was nothing if not complicated. He had, besides ambition and swagger to burn, a deep well of kindness and soul. You could see it in the way he honored Muncie, returning each summer to run a camp for poor kids in memory of a high school friend who'd drowned, and you could hear it later from the teens he sent to college after making it big with the Bears. "Everything he did was a teaching tool," says Michael Gorin, a family friend and retired teacher from Muncie whose son Brandon attended Duerson's camp and went on to play nine years in the NFL. "He had the Super Bowl rings but kept harping on academics. My son says they talk about him at *Harvard*."

Harvard would come later, after Duerson got done playing and commuted to Cambridge for an executive program at the business school. Long before that, though, he got a brawler's education when he showed up at Bears training camp as a third-round pick. He should have gone higher in the '83 draft, but his talk about law school and political aspirations probably set him back a round or two. Buddy Ryan, the great, brutish coordinator of Chicago's 46 defense, loathed rookies, especially rookies with more on their mind than earholing Packers. "He knew I'd gone to Notre Dame and asked if I was one of those doctors or lawyers," Duerson said in an interview he gave last year for a book about Americans turning 50. "I said, 'Yes, sir.' He said, 'Well, you won't be here long, because I don't like smart niggers'"—a comment Ryan has denied making.

Dan Hampton, a Hall of Fame lineman on that absurdly dominant Bears defense, offers a different take. "Buddy didn't care if you were black, white, or green: He wanted smashmouth, and Duerson wouldn't nail guys. In practice, Buddy'd yell, 'That shit ain't cuttin' it! You dive on the ground again, I'm firing you!'"

Duerson submitted to doing it Ryan's way and became a ferocious hitter. He mostly covered kicks his first two seasons and backed up Pro Bowl safety Todd Bell. Then, in '85, Bell held out for more money, and Ryan had no choice but to start Duerson. "I played through that whole season with [Buddy] telling me that he was rooting for me to screw up," Duerson said in a 2005 interview. "So I became an All-Pro myself." On that banzai unit, which jammed the line with 10 men, Duerson came screaming off the edge on blitzes. In 1986, his second season as a starter, he had seven sacks, a record for defensive backs that stood till 2005. He made the Pro Bowl four years running, a breakout star on a squad of loud assassins. Tellingly, it was Duerson who, with linebacker Otis Wilson, developed the unit's calling card. After an especially vicious shot, they'd stand over their victim, barking and baying like junkyard dogs.

Of course, football has a way of evening things up between predators and prey. In his 11-year run with the Bears, Giants (where he won another Super Bowl, in 1990), and Cardinals, Duerson suffered multiple minor concussions, though he was never knocked out cold. Emerging after games in a pair of dark glasses and wincing against the dusk, he'd complain of nausea and ringing headaches, says his ex-wife Alicia. "Dave would get concussed on the first or second series and play the whole way through, or get a dinger in the second half and be back at practice Wednesday morning," she says. "Dave had one speed, and that was full-out."

In the years to come, he'd have cause to rethink that, at least when it came to his kids. His middle son, Tregg, now a bank analyst in Chicago, was a highly regarded prep-school running back who'd go on to play defensive back at Notre Dame. One game in high school, Tregg was dazed from a tackle and wobbled off the field. Watching from the stands, Duerson ran down to the sideline and snatched Tregg's helmet so he couldn't return; at halftime he whisked him off to the hospital to be checked out. Tregg had a concussion. "Just to be on the safe side," says Alicia, "Dave wouldn't let him play for three games."

As his playing days dwindled, Duerson weighed his options, beginning with politics. "Both the Republican and Democratic Parties in Chicago tabbed him to run for office," says Harold Rice, one of Duerson's oldest friends and the man who accompanied Alicia and Tregg to Florida after Duerson's death. "Dave wanted to be a difference maker, but realized pretty quick that it wasn't worth the scrutiny."

Rice, who owned a McDonald's, urged him to enter his business instead. Duerson opened a franchise in Louisville, Kentucky, his first year out of football, then got an attractive offer from a McDonald's supplier: there was an ownership opportunity in a meat-processing plant an hour outside Chicago. Duerson bought a controlling stake and, with his contacts and charm, promptly doubled the plant's revenue to more than $60 million a year. He bought himself a huge house in Highland Park, just up the road from Michael Jordan's place, engraved his jersey number, NFL 22, on the driveway pillars, and spent a bundle on exotic cars, including a midnight-blue Mercedes SL 600 with the vanity plate DD22. By then he'd had four kids with Alicia, had local sports talk shows on both radio and television, and was jetting off to Cambridge, Massachusetts, for months at a time for the executive program there. "Dave loved it at Harvard, getting to network with CEOs and bounce ideas off presidents of foreign companies," says Alicia. "When he took us to Europe, it was first-class all the way: stretch limos, four-star dining, and—his big dream—flying in the Concorde."

But friction eventually sparked between Duerson and his partner at the plant, who resented his comings and goings. In 2002, Duerson sold his interest to open his own processing plant nearby. It was the first big mistake in a life of shrewd decisions, and caught Duerson flat-footed, stunned by failure.

From the beginning, Duerson Foods had disaster written all over it. He shelled out millions to gut and double the factory's floor space, then borrowed heavily to buy state-of-the-art freezers from a company in the Netherlands. They were impressive to look at but so unsound that he had to postpone opening by six months. He fell behind on his schedule to supply Burger King and Olive Garden, and soon he was leveraged to the hilt. At his swank offices in Lincolnshire, Illinois, employees, some of them relatives, saw a change. His niece, Yvette Fuse, would call Rice in a panic to say that "Dave was berating people, acting mean." Duerson borrowed more, using his house as collateral, and sued the freezer maker. He won a $34 million judgment, but the company filed for bankruptcy and never paid him a dime. By 2006, creditors were raining down lawsuits, and Duerson, broke and heartsick, shut the plant. He'd lost his mother to a heart attack and his house to the finance company, and his father was ailing with Alzheimer's (he died in 2009). "The pressure on him was phenomenal," said Rice. "It would've taken Superman not to break."

As it turned out, Duerson *had* broken, if briefly. In February 2005, he and Alicia drove to South Bend for a meeting of Notre Dame's board of trustees, of which he was a member. During a small-hours argument at their hotel, he threw her out the door of their room into the hallway wall. Alicia suffered cuts to her head and went to the ER with dizziness and pain. Duerson was charged with several misdemeanor counts and later pleaded guilty to domestic battery. In an interview, he called that night "a three-second snap," but it was played up big in the Chicago papers and forced his resignation from Notre Dame's board of trustees. Alicia, looking back now through the prism of his death, sees a clear demarcation in his conduct. The old Dave, she says, "would never do that; he never showed violence toward me. It was the *changes*," she says of his new hair-trigger temper, sudden downshifts in mood, and lack of impulse control—all signs of brain trauma.

His missteps, meanwhile, were beginning to throw shade on his fine reputation in the game—a reputation he'd carefully nursed since the day he entered the league. As a rookie in Chicago, Duerson had been chosen by his teammates to be the Bears' union representative. He was the son of a strong labor man at General Motors and "wanted to make things better for the guys," says Alicia.

For more than 60 years, the owners had run roughshod over the players, shackling stars to teams and imposing whatever terms they liked in collective negotiations. Duerson deftly held the Bears together through the bitter 1987 strike and beyond, and became a key adviser to, and close friend of, Gene Upshaw, the union's chief executive. "The two of them traveled together, even during the season, to talk to players about their rights," says Alicia. "Dave believed in the cause with all his heart and set himself to learning about labor laws so he could explain it clearly to the guys."

In 1992 and 1993, the players finally turned the tables in a pair of historic trials in federal court. Duerson was a featured plaintiff in one, and his tour de force performance on the witness stand helped fray the owners' resolve to keep on fighting. "He was so knowledgeable on the facts and spoke them so beautifully that you could really feel the tide start to turn," says ESPN.com legal analyst Lester Munson, who covered the trial for *Sports Illustrated*.

The owners grudgingly cut a deal, awarding free agency and a broad slate of rights to players. Among the key gains was the creation of a board to hear the disability claims not only of active players but of retirees whose injuries prevented them from holding a job. The board was composed of six trustees (three each of management and union members, the latter being appointed by Upshaw), and the disability money, many hundreds of millions of dollars, was funded almost entirely by owners.

Right from its inception, though, an odd thing happened: in case after case before the board, former players were denied assistance or put through a maze of second opinions and paperwork. Men with bent spines and diced joints were told they could still hold a paying job and so were ineligible for aid. Then there were the veterans coming forward in their forties and fifties with the brain scans of aging boxers who also had their claims voted down by the board. "They made it real clear that they'd fight me to the death, like they did with Mike Webster," says Brent Boyd, a Vikings guard in the '80s who suffers from clinical depression related to brain trauma. (Webster, the Hall of Fame center of the Steelers, was profoundly impaired by CTE and lived out of his truck at times before he died at 50.) "They were supposed to push for us, but were in the owners' pockets. You had to live in a wheelchair to collect."

In 2006, a particularly fraught time in the struggles between veterans and the players union, Upshaw decided to name his old friend Duerson to the pension board. This seemed a peculiar choice at best: Duerson had been out of the sport for a decade, was tarnished by the recent incident in South Bend, and ran a company that was coming apart. Any doubts about Duerson—and Upshaw's critics had plenty—were quickly ratified by his demeanor. The man who'd been so eloquent in federal court under the grilling of NFL lawyers was barging around town like a pit bull on crank, attacking former players at every turn. At a congressional hearing in 2007 to investigate the ex-players' charges, Duerson started a shoving match with Sam Huff and Bernie Parrish, two former greats speaking out for injured vets. He maligned Brent Boyd to a Senate committee, questioning whether his documented brain woes were actually caused by football. He took to talk radio to disparage Mike Ditka, saying his old coach, who'd raised money for vets, had never cared about his players' health. The worst of it, though, was his sliming of Brian DeMarco, a crippled veteran with several crushed vertebrae who'd gone public about his rejection by the union. Duerson tore into him on a call-in radio show, deriding him as a liar and an insurance fraud, then appeared on a Chicago TV program to ambush DeMarco in person.

His mad-dog behavior was very much in line with the way he voted on claims. Says Cy Smith, the lawyer who won a landmark lawsuit on behalf of Mike Webster's estate: "I get dozens of these files coming across my desk—stark, sad cases of guys really banged up—and the vast majority of these judgments are 6–o against the players. That's a gross breach of practice by the board and a clear pattern of bias against paying." That Duerson was siding with management—and, apparently, Upshaw—is no surprise to his critics. Says Huff, the New York Giants Hall of Fame linebacker: "Dave wanted Gene's job when he finally stepped down, and was saying and doing whatever Gene wanted, or whatever he thought he wanted." Indeed, Duerson told people he'd been handpicked by Upshaw to succeed him as union chief, a position that paid nearly $7 million a year and was essentially a lifetime appointment. When Upshaw died in 2008, Duerson didn't get the post (attorney DeMaurice Smith did), though he retained his seat on the board.

Whatever Duerson's motives for voting against veterans, they ran counter to a life spent helping others. At Duerson Foods, he'd paid the health-care premiums for his factory-floor workers and footed the college tuition for kids from inner-city Chicago. That doesn't assuage the retired players he turned down, whose rancor isn't softened by his death. "He caused more suffering personally than all the other board members combined," says Boyd. Adds John Hogan, a lawyer who assists former players with their disability claims: "He really could've changed the story for vets, and done it from the inside without saying mea culpa. He didn't have to indict the system. All he had to do was say, publicly, 'I'm sick, and I need help like these other guys.'"

The last years of his life, Duerson knew he was in decline. He'd gotten divorced from Alicia in 2009 and fled to Florida in glum retreat, dropping out of sight for months on end. (He'd bought the condo, in the twin-tower Ocean One, in Sunny Isles Beach, as a winter house in 2000, but hadn't much used it until he moved in.) On his trips to Chicago to see his kids, he'd complain to Alicia about persistent headaches and frightening spells of blurred vision. "He thought at first he was getting old, but seemed more concerned as time went on," she says. His memory was shot, he wasn't sleeping much, and he had to ask her directions to get around Chicago—a town he'd known cold for 25 years. "He could hide the changes from friends and such, but he couldn't hide them from me. He'd say, 'Remember the time we did such and such?' as if to prove he wasn't fading, but he was."

He was a step above flat broke and trying to hide that too. He hocked his wedding ring and Rolex watch, unloaded a newer Mercedes and his beloved Harley, and borrowed heavily against the equity in his apartment, though he'd put the place in trust for his four children. Even so, he couldn't make his child support payments or keep up with his condo fees, and the stress and shame compounded his symptoms and began, it seemed, to derange him.

Says Ron Ben-David, who took over as building manager at the Ocean One towers in 2008: "I called Dave down and asked him politely why he hadn't paid his dues in almost a year. He told me someone had broken into his closet and stolen three paintings he'd bought in Cuba, and unless we reimbursed him the $7,000, he wasn't going to pay the arrears." But Duerson hadn't phoned the cops about his loss or filed an insurance claim, and ultimately paid his back maintenance fees via wire transfer. A year later, his checks stopped coming again, and again Ben-David called him down. "He said, 'Well, someone stole my paintings. Aren't you going to reimburse me?' And this time they were worth $30,000."

"He was definitely getting worse. I could hear it over the phone," says Alicia. "He was trying to reinvent who he was at 50, and that's hard even when you're thinking straight." Duerson talked a lot about having "irons in the fire"—some deals in the works with Costco and the USDA—but nothing ever seemed to pan out. When he filed for bankruptcy in Florida last year, he showed annual expenditures of $74,000, an income of less than $34,000, and a consulting business whose only assets were the furniture and equipment in his study. His one frail hope, a Hail Mary, was to get hired as a coach in the NFL. Last fall he phoned Steve Zucker, his former agent, and asked him to make some calls on his behalf. At the time, he had several ex-teammates running teams—Jeff Fisher, then with the Titans, Mike Singletary, then with the 49ers, and Leslie Frazier, who'd taken over in Minnesota—all three also proud alumni of that great Bears defense of the '80s. "His plan was to get a position-coach thing or a job in someone's front office," says Zucker, once a Chicago super-agent who is now in his seventies and mostly retired. "I talked to him all the time and had no idea. He sounded so positive on the phone."

With the exception of Alicia and a couple of his old cronies, Duerson told no one how grim things had gotten or how badly his symptoms had unhinged him. He holed up in Florida, where he avoided his neighbors. Beyond the occasional visit from one of his kids, the only break in the deepening gloom was a last-chance love affair. He'd met Antoinette Sykes in May 2010 at a business conference in Las Vegas, where he gave a talk to aspiring entrepreneurs about growing and selling a million-dollar company. By summer, he and Sykes, who owns her own PR and marketing firm in Washington, D.C., were speaking or texting 10 times a day and flying to each other's homes for weeklong stays. In the fall, he proudly showed her off to building manager Ben-David, calling her his "angel" and fiancée. They were scheduled to be married in April 2011, when his daughter, who would be on spring recess, could attend.

"What we shared was so sacred and joyful," Sykes said over the phone from D.C. "I knew he had headaches and—and a lump on his skull that he was worried about, but what I'm reading in the papers now about his brain, it's thrown me for such a loop. Maybe he wanted to shield me, but he seemed so excited about spending the rest of our lives together. On our last night, Valentine's, he joked that I owed him 29 more because we'd committed to 30 years of wedded bliss. And then I flew home to pack my things to move down there. . . ." She breaks off, convulsing.

On February 17, Sykes woke up in Washington to a text from Duerson. It began, "My dear Angel, I love you so much and I'm sorry for my past, but I think this knot on my head is the real deal." Sykes called him, heard nothing back, and became frantic as the morning passed. Sometime after two that afternoon, she called Ben-David and asked him to knock on Duerson's door. When no one answered, she faxed him her permission to use a spare key. "I got the door open, but there was a chair wedged against it. That's when I called 911," he says. Paramedics and cops arrived and pushed their way in. "I heard them in the bedroom, yelling 'Sir! Sir! Is everything all right?' Then they asked me to leave," says Ben-David. Duerson was found shortly after 3:00 P.M. He had shot himself about 12 hours earlier. Apart from the large patch of blood beneath him, the place was immaculate, said Miami-Dade police officers. Veteran detectives, they said they'd never seen a suicide planned and executed so meticulously.

In the months after his death, Duerson has become a wedge for practically anyone with a connection to the sport. The media has mostly lined up with *Time* magazine, which called him "football's first martyr." Ex-players have sourly mocked his sanctification, denying him any credit for calling attention to CTE in death when he could have worked for justice while alive. Even his Bears teammates are badly split: some are saddened and shocked by his death, while others deem him selfish and arrogant—"political to the end," groused a former lineman. The dissonance was put best by his son Tregg, now 25. "I just wish he'd played baseball," he told the *New York Times* five days after Duerson died. But, he added, sobbing, that his father "was looking for an answer and was hoping to be part of an answer."

At some point, it's hoped, Duerson's motives will matter less than the long-haul impact of his passing. A tremor has gone through the league, deep and wide; players are talking openly about football and brain cells and fretting over their own neural health. "Is it something that I think about? Yeah, absolutely," Baltimore Ravens center Matt Birk told the *Times*. He's one of more than a hundred current and former players who've signed over their brains for postmortem study at Boston University. You'd expect forward thinking from a Harvard grad like Birk, rated the sixth-smartest man in sports by *Sporting News* last year. But the message is getting across to less cerebral types too. Jim McMahon, the ex-passer and party monster who loved to celebrate touchdowns with ringing head butts, is battling serious memory problems and has also agreed to send his brain to Boston. "What the fuck do I need it for when I'm dead?" he says. That gesture, if not the sentiment, will be part of the answer to the questions Duerson lived and died to raise.

The People v. Football

FROM GQ

SHE HAD NO IDEA, back then, that he was sick. She had no idea he was losing his mind. Something neurological, the doctors are now saying, some kind of sludge blocking pathways in his brain. Would it have made a difference if she knew? Of course it would have. But you can't think like that. And you can't give a shit about people whispering behind your back. *You hear about Fred McNeill? Star linebacker for the Minnesota Vikings back in the '70s and '80s. Ended up going crazy, and his wife, Tia, couldn't handle it, so she walked out.* It's not like that, not even close, but whatever. People can think what they think.

She's double-parked outside his apartment in the Mid-Wilshire section of L.A., idiots honking as they veer. *Oh, forgodsakes. I'm in this world too, people.*

"Fred?" she says, calling him on her cell. "Are you coming down?" She has a sleepy, husky voice that announces her stance on just about everything these days: *I'm done.* Her face is round, still alive with curiosity, sturdy and pretty and framed by tight curls.

"Am I what?" Fred says.

"Are you coming down? I'm waiting."

"You're waiting?"

"Fred, I'm out here waiting!"

"Oh, okay, I'll come down."

"Don't forget the suitcase," she says.

"Suitcase?"

"Remember I need my suitcase back?"

He does not remember anything about a suitcase.

"Fred, I just told you ten minutes ago that I am outside waiting for you and to bring me the suitcase," she says.

"It's too early for karaoke," he says.

"Coffee," she says. "I am taking you out for coffee. Now, come on."

"Coffee. That sounds good."

"Please hurry, Fred."

"So what I'm going to do is, I'm going to put my shoes on, and I'm going to get my briefcase, and I am going to get you the suitcase, and I am going to come downstairs, and we are going to get coffee."

"Why are you bringing your briefcase?"

"I need to go to the office."

"No, you don't, Fred."

"Can we stop by the office?"

"Just come downstairs."

Five minutes go by. More honking. More idiots. No Fred. Her next call goes to voice mail: *"You've reached the law offices of Frederick Arnold McNeill. Please leave a brief message."* She hangs up. She reaches into a bag of trail mix, pops a handful, and chews. She stares forward and shakes her head slowly in that way that speaks of tragedy, of comedy, and the insidious fine line.

There was a time when Fred was brilliant. He started law school during his last year with the Vikings, studying on the plane to and from games while the other guys slept. He graduated from William Mitchell College of Law in St. Paul, top of his class. After he retired from the Vikings in 1985, he got recruited by a huge firm and then another one, where he was made partner. Then one day in 1996 a certified letter came while Fred and Tia were on vacation with the kids. *We voted you out,* it said. Fred was 44. It was devastating. How Tia hated those people. Fred was calm, though. He went into private practice, started doing workers' comp cases for athletes, including some injured Vikings—work that would later prove to be tragically ironic. But after two years, no money was coming in. "What is going on?" Tia asked. It's not like he wasn't trying. He worked all the time, gave it his all; you couldn't find a more honest, diligent man. But the family was going broke. Weird things started happening. Fred jumping out of bed in the middle of the night, panicked and ready to fight. *"They're here!"* he would shout, face hot with terror. "Fred, it's just me!" Tia would say. She would shake him until he snapped out of it. At the time you think he's just having a nightmare. You get used to things. You don't put it all together.

They have two sons, Gavin, now 23, and "Little Freddie," 26. Gavin shares the two-bedroom apartment with Fred, looks after him, cooks him pancakes in the morning. Freddie lives with Tia, about fifteen minutes away, both of them piled into her mother's house, a blessing, since it's paid for. The boys are good boys, trying to run a creative agency together, and they go to counseling to help deal with their dad, to help untangle all the craziness that was never understood.

Here now is Fred. Thank God. He knocks on the passenger window, flashes a wide, beautiful smile, does a little ta-dah! dance move. He's 58 years old, and he has a long, gentle face, a blocky brow, and sprouts of gray hair shooting this way and that. He's wearing a windbreaker, baggy jeans, sneakers. She thinks he looks terrible. He's carrying a white notepad, stained and smudged, and covered top to bottom with phone numbers. He forgot the suitcase.

"You need a haircut, Fred," Tia says. "You look like Bozo the Clown!"

"I don't want a haircut."

"All right, let's just go." She pulls out, and still, even now, listens as if there is going to be substance.

"I have to make some calls," Fred says, looking at the notepad. "One of the things you have to do is, people call you, you have to respond to them." He speaks softly, almost a purr. "You would do the same thing, Tia. Somebody called you, what would you do? Call them back. I take this, I put the number on a big sheet of paper, and I'm cool. I have to start now calling back, not just writing it down. That's next. And then when I call the person back, I have to respond to whatever it is they say. That's how it goes. You would do the same thing."

"Yup," she says.

"I need to go to the office," he says.

"Please, Fred."

There really is an office. He's not making it up. He's not delusional. One of the things that happens to people when they begin losing their minds is they fall prey to vultures. One such vulture swooped in on Fred about three years ago. An old-man paralegal offered Fred the dusty back room of his little green house over on Arlington. The man had use for a befuddled lawyer with a valid license, someone he could get to sign legal documents, do his bidding. Fred would show up each day, suit and tie, meticulous, a look befitting a partner in a big firm, and he would do what he was told to do.

Tia knew nothing about any of this. She'd left Fred in 2007. "I'm moving out with the boys, and you're not coming," she had said. She couldn't take it anymore. She thought he was severely depressed and refusing to get help. She kept up his car and phone payments but otherwise stepped out of his life. Gavin stayed in better touch, heard about the paralegal, which didn't sound quite right. He learned about a "girlfriend" who lived in a rented room Fred would sometimes share. He slept on people's couches or sometimes in his car. It was Gavin who first rallied the troops. He called Freddie home from college. "There is something seriously wrong with Dad," he said to Tia.

This was about a year ago, when all the lights went on. Tia met Fred outside his "office" and confronted him in the driveway of the little green house. She hadn't seen him in nearly a year.

"Fred!" she said. "What is *going on?*"

"Going on?" he asked. He was standing by his car, a silver Altima with fresh dents. It was filled with clothes and also dozens of Starbucks napkins and paper cups, which Tia instinctively began gathering.

"What are you *doing?*" he said.

"Throwing shit out."

"I need my cups!"

She let it go. "Gavin's taking you to a doctor, and I don't want you giving him any trouble," she told Fred. She felt like a one-woman ambulance with a big siren on top of her head. "Now, would you mind telling me what you are doing with this asshole paralegal?" she asked. "He's using your license and pimping you for rent!"

Fred stood in the driveway, taking in the sun and thinking about *asshole* and *pimping rent* for some time. There was still a vast intelligence beneath the fog. "That would be a *hustler,* not an asshole," he said to Tia.

"Oh, my God. Where did you meet this guy?" she asked. "He's crazy. Stay away from crazy people!"

"Okay," he said, and agreed to move out of the office.

He hasn't yet. He will. He has to pack it up first. There are materials in file folders. He has to open the file folders and read the materials and decide which box the file folder with those materials should go in. For example, he will open one file folder and read the materials and make a decision to put that file folder with those materials in this box, or that box, or some other box. That's how it works. That's how you would do it too. He's been packing up the office for about six months now.

Another former football player gone mad. This has been the story of the NFL, an $8 billion industry, over the past few years: players going crazy from concussions and head trauma sustained during their playing days. Crazy enough to kill themselves. One swallowed antifreeze, another shot himself, still another fled in a paranoid frenzy from police and crashed his car into an oncoming tanker. The tales have been tragic and dramatic, and the science, finally, has become undeniable.

Forensic pathologist Bennet Omalu was the first to figure it all out, to find microscopic changes in brain tissues of deceased players. The bodies were all found to have the same unusual formations of proteins, called tau, in the same regions of their brains, believed to be the result of repeated head trauma. Omalu first found the tau "threads" in the brain of former Steeler Mike Webster in 2002 and published his findings in 2005, in the journal *Neurosurgery*. The new disease was named chronic traumatic encephalopathy, and the NFL fervently and repeatedly denied that such a thing had anything to do with the league or its players.

But then, in September 2009, researchers at the University of Michigan's Institute for Social Research—in a telephone survey of retired players—found that Alzheimer's disease, or something very similar, was being diagnosed in former NFL players *nineteen times more often* than in the national population among men ages 30 through 49. Even worse for the NFL, the league had commissioned that survey, which was designed simply to gather data about retired players. It was like Big Tobacco ordering a study that ended up showing that smokers got cancer.

Last summer, before preseason games even started, the league began placing posters in locker rooms. "CONCUSSION. A Must

Read for NFL Players. Report It. Get Checked Out. Take Care of Your Brain." It spoke explicitly of personality changes, depression, and dementia. "Concussions and conditions resulting from repeated brain injury can change your life and your family's life forever."

The poster was heralded as a seismic shift in the NFL's handling of head trauma, and yet, at the same time, it was . . . a poster.

In mid-October of this season, after a weekend in which four players were knocked out with concussions, the league announced it would start handing out fines and suspending any player judged to be guilty of "devastating hits" and/or "head shots."

Discussion boards lit up:

This is not good. Freaking women organs running this league.

The NFL is turning into a touch football "Nancy Boy" League. Steer your kids that have talent into baseball, basketball or any other sport that will still have dignity left in 2 years. . . .

The pussyification of the NFL continues. Every single goddam year the rules get more and more VAGINIZED.

What Fred would do was sit in the apartment alone, and he would hold a blade to his wrist and look at it. That's when he would start thinking. It wasn't *Oh, everyone will be upset if I do this,* or, *I hate my life.* Nothing like that. Instead, he would feel the cool blade on his skin, and he would consider how thin and baby soft that skin was, and he would think, *This is going to hurt like hell. Now, how can I do this so it doesn't hurt?* It might actually have been quite simple if not for the pain part.

The pills the doctor gave him must be doing some good, because it's been two weeks since he sat there like that with the scissors or the knife. He plans to tell the doctor thank you for those pills. He wants to be positive, wants the doctors and nurses to feel positive about all their hard work.

Tia and Fred are sitting in the waiting room, and Fred is focused on positive thinking and how it's going to affect the memory test. He has a new line of attack. The last time he took the test, he thought he'd nailed it. He had it all worked out. He'd heard somewhere that a woman's memory is superior to a man's. Now, why would that be? Emotion, he reasoned. Women are more *emotional* than men, so they must attach *emotion* to their memories. Therefore, all he had to do was attach emotion to every answer and he would significantly boost his performance.

He tried. Oh, how he *tried*. The nurse would say a string of numbers and ask Fred to repeat them back. Fred tried caring, deep in his gut, *caring* about 4 and 16, 12 and 22. He opened his heart to the numbers and afterward he felt great.

"You did terrible," the doctor said. "Terrible." That put Fred into a whole new kind of funk.

Let it flow, that's his new memory strategy. It brings him a sense of calm. This is what he's explaining to the nurse who calls up the new memory test on the computer. "The way to improve memory is to not question but just go ahead and have the confidence to remember," he tells her. "I just have to allow myself to flow with it, knowing that if I just let go, that it's going to work."

"That's good, Fred," the nurse says. "That's good." She tells him she's going to read him a list of words and she wants him to repeat them, one by one, after her.

"Jazz," she says.

"Jazz," he says, enunciating.

"Bus," she says.

"Bus," he repeats, with a loud *b* and a loud *ssss*. It goes on like this: *lid, critic, dark, owner, guest, weather, peace, bass,* ten words in all. She then asks Fred to recall as many words as he can.

"Bass, peace, bus," he says. He sits there, biting his lip. In the long silence you can hear the lights buzz. "Bass, peace, bus, weather," he says. He sits a while longer, thumping his thumbs. "Interesting," he says. "Very, very interesting." The nurse repeats the test several times, and Fred never gets past remembering four of the ten words.

Let it flow is about as effective as emotional attachment was; the only difference is that now he's beginning to grasp the hopelessness.

"Oh, you did fine, Fred," the nurse says, and she ushers him to another office, where a doctor puts a tight white bonnet on Fred's head, an elastic cap dotted with sensors. She hooks wires into it and connects the wires to a computer, and then she tells Fred to stare at either the orchid or the bear, his choice. Fred chooses the bear, and for about ten minutes the computer reads his brain waves to determine, according to the doctor, the degree to which his "daydreaming" waves have hijacked his brain. Fred leans back in the chair and smiles slightly, fighting sleep.

"Fan-*tas*-tic, Fred!" the doctor says. She brings him to the next office, where Dr. Daniel Amen, a short, athletic, happy fellow, sits waiting. Tia is summoned into the room. Amen shuts the door.

"How's your mood?" Amen asks.

"My mood?" Fred asks. It takes him minutes of explanation to get out that he isn't suicidal, while Tia checks her phone, the time, her phone again, trying to keep herself calm.

Gavin was the one who first heard of Amen and the former football players who went to him for help with depression and strange symptoms. When he brought Fred here the first time, in 2009, Amen ran a standard battery of cognitive tests and afterward told Gavin that Fred had flunked spectacularly. He scored in just the first percentile on mental proficiency and less than 1 on information-processing speed. "I'm not going to sugarcoat it," Amen told Gavin. "It's bad." That's when Amen told him about football and brain injury and early-onset dementia and how Fred was not the only one.

Amen prescribed Wellbutrin for the depression and Namenda to help slow the dementia, and he gave Fred many bottles of his own special brain supplements to help him maybe get some of his brain back, and then Gavin went home to his mom and told her what he had learned. Fred was upset. He demanded that Tia and Gavin hand over the test results; he didn't want them getting into the wrong hands. Someone, he believed, was *after* him, and this might be the data they needed. Tia handed over the papers to Fred, called Amen for copies, said, "What the hell?" and made a follow-up appointment. Then she opened her laptop and searched "football" and "brain injury," and in the space of one hour, fifteen years' worth of history came crashing into place.

Right about the time the NFL started fining players for violent hits, it also quietly removed from its website the popular DVD *Moment of Impact,* which it sold for $14.99. The ad copy puts you on the scrimmage line:

First you hear the breathing, then you feel the wind coming through your helmet's ear hole. Suddenly you're down, and you're looking through your helmet's ear hole. Pain? That's for tomorrow morning.... *Moment of Impact* takes you ... into the huddle, up to the line, and under the pile with some of the game's roughest customers.

You don't have to be a brain surgeon to recognize the massive contradiction at the center of the NFL right now. Even sportscasters struggle to reconcile what football *is* versus what it's doing to its players.

The postgame commentary following *Monday Night Football* in mid-October got at the heart of the dilemma:

STEVE YOUNG: If you do something that's devastating—a big hit—you're going to probably be exposed to being suspended.

STUART SCOTT: But isn't that *football?* I mean, seriously. A devastating hit—isn't that, hasn't that been *football?*

MATT MILLEN: Listen, this bothers me, what we're talking about right here. It's wrong. You can't take the competition and the toughness and all the stuff that goes into making the game great—you can't take it out of the game.

YOUNG: What they're worried about is that Darryl Stingley hit. They're going to legislate it out.

MILLEN: That is stupid.

TRENT DILFER: This game was built—and people love it—because of the gladiatorial nature of it. Those are guys out there, and they're sacrificing their bodies and laying it all on the line, and that's what people enjoy. And the league is going to rob us all of that.... It's an absolute joke. First of all, every week we're talking about thousands of hits. Eventually the head is going to get hit. This is part of football.

MILLEN: It's the game. It's the way the game is played.

DILFER: It's just gonna happen! These guys are gonna get blown up. It's a physical game and you can't take it out of it.

YOUNG: A defenseless player, you're gonna have to take it easy on him.

MILLEN: You can't!

YOUNG: You're going to have to! Or you're going to sit out for a couple weeks.

SCOTT: That's not football!

*

Fred remembers the old days a lot better than anything you can throw at him in the new ones. Growing up, he figured he'd probably become a doctor someday, because that's what everybody said smart kids ended up being. Football was not even on his radar and might never have been, had some kids on his block in Baldwin Park, California, not invited him to the park to play when he was maybe nine years old. It was fun. Tackling was easy—wrap your arms around a kid and ride him down. No one could get past Fred.

He kept getting better at it, played in high school where the coaches pulled him aside. "Gifted!" they said.

UCLA recruited him, gave him a football scholarship, and when he got there, he signed up for premed. Then he went down to the field house to get his football stuff. The coaches said, "Premed? No, no, that's not how it works. You're here to *play football*."

So he postponed the doctor idea, switched to economics, figuring this was just a delay. He was, after all, going to school for free. He got his first concussion during college. "I got hit. I felt it—*zhz zhz zhz zhz*." He holds his hands up to his head, rocks back and forth. "I felt dizziness and just . . . I couldn't stand up, and I was like that for a week." He's sitting alone in the apartment, a stripped-down bachelor pad if ever there was one, couch, chair, TV, giant shoes strewn this way and that in the small foyer. The lights are out, and he's got *Monday Night Football* playing quietly on the TV, flickering the room bright and dim. Fred says he doesn't remember the play that resulted in that first big concussion, just the feeling, the *zhz zhz zhz*, a sharp, stinging static that would soon become as familiar as the smell of coffee announcing morning. Some things just go together. The brain static went with pounding your body into other bodies that came at you like stampeding elephants.

In 1974 the Minnesota Vikings recruited him in the first round with a $100,000 signing bonus. He helped take his team to two Super Bowls, including XI, when, scoreless and ten minutes into the game, he broke in clean on Oakland's Ray Guy and blocked a punt, recovered it at the Oakland 3. That felt good. There was plenty of good. And plenty of brain static.

"My thing was tackle. Bring him down. Stop him right here. Then a couple of smaller guys, defensive backs, they come up like a bullet . . . head down . . . just *boom! Zhz zhz zhz*. More and more it was like that, trying to be so aggressive with the intent to hurt. I didn't want to hurt anybody. But then I realized if they got a great running back and you hurt him, you might win the game, you know? So actually I started seeing that as a thing to do. To hurt them so they have to leave the game."

He pauses, stares for a moment at the TV, says nothing about the game, has no interest in the score or who anyone is.

"One time there was this guy, like a 280-pound guy, coming to block me, and I just turned and hit him with my head. I came up under his chin, knocked him up into the sky." He uses his fist to simulate his head, punches the air. "The guy flipped, *and he was hurt!* He wasn't totally out, but he was laying on the ground. After I did that to him, I made the tackle. If I ever saw that on TV, I would go, *Man* . . . I would be very proud that I did that."

Fred had been with the Vikings seven years when he met Tia and started talking about returning to school—not for medicine but for law. Tia encouraged him. She wasn't so big on the football thing, wasn't part of that world. The day Fred graduated law school in 1987 was the happiest day of his life. He was an emerging star attorney. He worked on huge cases, Dow breast implants, tobacco litigation. They built a five-bedroom house in Minnetonka. Fred was popular. A former Viking right there in the neighborhood! Fred coached youth football, taking Gavin's team through a season with zero—zero!—scores against it, which Gavin still thinks ought to be in the record books somewhere.

His memory started failing as early as the mid-'90s. He never told Tia; he didn't understand it himself. Even when he got voted out of Zimmerman Reed, and then the next firing, and the next. Everything was just taking so long. Something that should take an hour was taking him four. Reading a brief. The simplest tasks. He blamed his deteriorating eyesight. He went to an eye doctor—the only medical help he ever sought. He got glasses, then stronger ones, and stronger ones still. He kept forgetting things. He was supposed to pick up Freddie at school. Forgot. So many thoughts just—*poof!* He learned to compensate. He learned to say "Nice to see you" instead of "Nice to meet you." The latter was simply too risky. Apparently some of those people he had been saying that to were *friends.* But he had no memory of them. Blank. So it was "Nice to see you," always, just in case.

The boys were so young they thought their dad was just acting dumb when he would forget things. They thought he was being funny, and when he did that, they would punch him in the gut.

That was important information, the gut punch. That meant: *You just messed up, Fred. You messed up bad. Come on, get it together. Act like you know what the hell is going on.*

As for Tia, she would scream. She didn't have a lot of settings, just on or off.

"You think I'm stupid!" he would say to her.

"I don't think you're stupid!" she would say. She didn't. She thought he was depressed. She thought she understood. All that excitement being in the NFL, all that glory—the transition was hard for those guys. She urged him to get help. She would make the appointment herself, but the day would come and he would bail. "I have to work on my cases," he'd say.

They left Minnesota in 1999 at Tia's urging and headed home to her family in L.A. Fred managed to pass the California bar—remarkably he still had his intellect—and got a job with a general-practice firm but was fired after a year and a half. He got a job with another firm and was fired again. He was hired to do legal work for Farmers Insurance, but they fired him too. Within a year of moving to California, the family filed for bankruptcy.

After that, Tia gave up. It was all those years of urging Fred to go to a doctor, literally years of him promising and then not going, before she said, "I'm done," and walked out of the marriage. She didn't know that Fred's refusal to get help wasn't really a refusal. It was more about forgetting, about living in a fog and all the energy of trying not to show it. It was clutching for dignity and losing it, constantly losing it, feeling it dissolve.

In the spring of 2010, Tia, Fred, Freddie, and Gavin traveled to the Independent Retired Players Summit and Conference at the South Point Hotel just off the Vegas strip.

It was a full-on immersion into the world of football and dementia—a vast, confusing, seemingly infinite parallel universe. All this time Fred had been suffering, there were hundreds, maybe thousands, of other guys suffering, and scientists and lawyers and doctors and opportunists and all kinds of people getting into the brain trauma act for all kinds of reasons.

Bennet Omalu was there. He stood up to explain the science behind his discovery. He showed slides of tau threads, and told of dazzling advances, including the ability—soon, he believed—to diagnose CTE in a living person. Therein lay the key to finding a cure, he said, and he spoke of his devotion to finding it.

Chris Nowinski spoke, representing a team of researchers from Boston. He was a former WWE wrestler who'd gotten into the work because of his own bruised brain. He passed out paperwork. *Sign up to donate your brain to our group when you die. Sign up now!*

Fred sat next to Tia, listening to the speakers. Well, Fred always looks like he's listening, but the truth is, he's able to zoom in on only a few key points, and Tia hoped that brain donation wasn't one of them. Wasn't that sort of jumping the gun? She thought the brain donation guy sounded like a late-night infomercial barker and wanted no part of him.

Eleanor Perfetto got up to speak. She is the wife of retired Steelers and Chargers lineman Ralph Wenzel. Wenzel's dementia was the reason he had been institutionalized in 2007, no longer able to coordinate his body, to feed himself. Perfetto explained the NFL's "88 Plan," a bright spot of humanity. The 88 Plan was the result of a letter written to the league by Sylvia Mackey, wife of Hall of Famer John Mackey, who wore number 88 for the Colts. His existence, she wrote, had become a "deteriorating, ugly, care-giver-killing, degenerative, brain-destroying, tragic horror," and his monthly $2,450 pension didn't come close to covering the cost of the care he needed. The 88 Plan was created to help foot the bill for caregiving.

Since the plan's inception in 2007, 149 retired players suffering from dementia have been approved to receive benefits; 149 players sick enough in the head, by the NFL's own count. And those are the players who have come forward. There are about 16,000 retired players living here and living there, some—like Hall of Famer Rayfield Wright, a Cowboys tackle—too proud to get checked for dementia. There are players' wives waiting to apply for the plan, unwilling to do so while their husbands are still coherent enough to understand.

Tia drank up the information with the thirst of an exhausted mule. Could not get enough. So much to understand. Dementia. Brain injury. Class action. Forms to fill out. Brain scans and vitamin cocktails and don't forget fish oil. Who's who in neurosurgery, who's fake, whom to trust.

At one point, Tia went over to Omalu and thanked him for his work. She introduced him to Fred, to Gavin and Freddie, and Omalu smiled politely and called over Garrett Webster, the son of the great Mike Webster, whose brain was the first.

"Talk to Garrett," Omalu told Gavin and Freddie. "You have much in common." The three sons sat for a long time, straddling folding chairs. Garrett could tell them what it was like trying to care for his dad when things got bad. His dad pissing in the oven, his dad supergluing his teeth, his dad shooting himself with a Taser gun, his dad living out of his truck, and Gavin and Freddie nodded and nodded some more.

Other than obeying Tia and avoiding the dude who wanted to take his brain, Fred had fun at the conference. He likes people. He likes learning. Sometimes, seemingly out of nowhere, he would have moments of sparkling clarity and offer sharply defined opinions about workers' comp cases. Then he would get distracted wondering if the South Point Hotel had karaoke. He checked his BlackBerry a lot, worried about getting back to the office; he was thinking maybe he had to be in court or file a continuance or something, and it disturbed him that he could not remember. He understood he was unable to keep up with the rigors of a law practice. He understood he was sick and needed a hiatus. "I'll take a period of time," he said to Tia. "Ninety days, and then I can start all over as an attorney. That's if my brain is healed. I take a ninety-day break, and then I can choose to be a lawyer again."

So far, the youngest player to be diagnosed with CTE has been 21-year-old University of Pennsylvania defensive end Owen Thomas, who, in April 2010, hanged himself in his apartment.

His mother told reporters that her son had started playing football at age 9 or 10, had never been diagnosed with a concussion, had never shown any side effects normally associated with brain trauma.

Thomas's diagnosis shed light on a crucial fact that keeps getting lost in all the hoopla. *He never had a recorded concussion.* CTE is not about the big hit, or not only. It's the thousands of little hits, the sort that linemen constantly take and give; science suggests that it's these subconcussive collisions that cause permanent, cumulative brain damage.

It could, for all anyone knows, begin at the peewee level.

Gavin can hardly watch anymore, and Freddie, who played tight end through college, is even worse. "To me it's almost like modern-day slavery," he says. "They say it's America's sport, but like 95 percent of the players are African American, and they're all out there beating themselves up." He's home in the kitchen, making a tuna sandwich. He moves deliberately, like Fred, and has his father's smooth voice and gentle demeanor. "I mean, they're getting paid, but for a man who sacrifices his life, there's no number to put to that. I try to be there for my dad, get lunch with him. I do try. Having a conversation with him is probably the most difficult thing to do. You can tell he's still a brilliant dude. He'll break the information down for you, and then break it down again, and then break it down ten more times, and then start over."

As for Fred, he doesn't blame the NFL for making him sick.

"I mean, did anybody know?" he says, slouched on the couch. "Did the owners know? Did the players? I don't think you can get angry if no one could have anticipated that this was going to happen. The only thing is, okay, there is a problem now." He sits forward, brings his hands up parallel, like a trial lawyer moving blocks of logic into sequence. "You've got NFL football, and you've got quarterbacks, talented people, making millions of dollars. You've got a tough economy, and in a tough economy, sports are still popular. And still generating money. And so the owners are still making. . . . You can imagine! You're paying your employees millions of dollars. What kind of money are *you* making? And so how do you then look at something that wasn't anticipated? Your employees and your former employees are having difficulty living a normal life because of your business. So it's not looking at the owners and saying you're bad people. It's saying: 'Here's the situation—now take care of it. You can't say you can't afford it.'"

The boys know that the dad who can come out with coherent, reasoned thoughts like that is not likely to be around much longer. They know his condition is getting worse. Tia knows she will be taking care of Fred for the rest of her life. He has told her that the people chasing him in the middle of the night have largely been replaced by armies of insects, thousands of fat bugs crawling all over him. Tia doesn't know if that qualifies as improvement or deterioration.

One day, in the car on the way to a doctor's appointment, Fred asks Tia for a divorce.

"Why the hell do you want a divorce?"

"It's causing some tension," he says.

He means with his girlfriend, an adoring woman who goes to karaoke with him on Wednesdays, when it's not crowded, but also on Thursdays, when it is. She takes a bus to his apartment, and then he drives, which he most certainly shouldn't (Amen has suggested that Tia alert the DMV), while she tells him where to turn, and they get lost, deeply lost, in the hills of L.A., even though they go to the same place each week. Eventually they get there, and they clap for the other singers, because that is polite karaoke behavior, but really the whole point is waiting for Fred's turn, waiting for him to get up there and belt out some James Brown with his smooth, electric voice while the girlfriend dances, prances like a bopping reindeer around him. He tells her that singing relieves some of the stress that comes with being an attorney; it really helps.

Tia knows that the girlfriend may not be wrapped entirely tight. But she is not a vulture; she's a companion. For Tia, it's someone else looking out for Fred.

"Well, do you want to marry her?" Tia asks Fred.

He looks at her, squints. "Why would I want to marry her?"

She laughs. "Good Lord, Fred."

"She doesn't want me to be married to someone else, so it's causing problems."

"You can say I'm the bitch that won't divorce you," she says. "Blame it on me."

"I see. And then I don't marry her because I am already married to you," Fred says.

"Correct," she says.

"Cool," he says, and he repeats the strategy until he thinks he has it memorized.

"I need to go to the office," he says. "I am not making progress on the files."

"Do you have your keys with you?"

"Keys to what?"

"The office."

"For what?"

"You said you want to go to the office. Do you have your keys?"

"No. You say we're going to the office?"

"You just said you wanted to."

"To do what now?"

"Fred! Stop! You're making me nuts!"

"I'm making you nuts. I'm sorry."

He sits quietly awhile, watches the cars whiz along the 405.

"Tia, now, about my brain," he says, finally. "I don't want to give it away."

"Your brain? Is that what you're sitting here thinking about?"

"Well, I don't want to give it away to anybody."

"That's for after you die, Fred," she says. "Like I'm an organ donor on my driver's license. It's to *help* other people."

"The truth may be different from what people think," he says. "You don't know. A person still exists when the body stops working."

"Their spirit—"

"How long does that spirit sit there feeling the body, thinking 'What's going on around here?'" he says.

"Spirits don't have feelings, Fred."

"I don't want to be surprised. Like, 'Oh, God, I wasn't supposed to feel this! Oooh, owwww!'"

"You watch too many movies. You think your ghost is going to be, 'What the hell, they took my brain?'"

"No one gets to tell what happens. You don't get to say to the guy that buries you, 'Do you know what really happens down here?' You've lost all communication at that point, Tia."

"Okay, Fred. Okay." She understands. She understands that for most people there's living and then there's dying, but for Fred the whole gig has become more like being slowly buried alive.

"You can try, but there's no one who can *hear* you down there," he says.

She has nothing left on this one, jabs at the radio.

"Hello, it's me down here, ow, ow, ouch—"

S. L. PRICE

The Heart of Football
Beats in Aliquippa

FROM SPORTS ILLUSTRATED

THE FEAR CAME for Willie Walker that November. He was not expecting it. Evening had dropped early and hard, as it does in western Pennsylvania in the fall, but these were streets he had known forever. Hours had passed since the 2004 regional championship game had ended down in Pittsburgh; the adrenaline and bravado on the ride home had long since burned off, replaced by grief, then mere regret. They had lost. The Aliquippa High football team, for all its history of success, had been beaten. Now, in the backseat, Walker felt a numbness settling in. Losing happens. You move on. You start thinking about what's next.

Walker was a senior. Just seven months until graduation, and he'd be able to say it: he had survived. The town hadn't killed, hadn't crippled, hadn't defeated him, though God knows it had tried. His life had been a cliché of criminal pathology: father long dead, mother struggling with crack addiction, days of hunger, corners promising casual violence. Aliquippa's streets are, as one of Walker's coaches put it, "a spiderweb" capable of ensnaring the most innocent, and though Walker never lost sight of his prize—college somewhere, anywhere—he was hardly innocent. No, for a time he had leaped into the web, daring it to grab hold.

The year before, Willie "Silent But Violent" Walker had been a star lineman for Aliquippa's 2003 state championship team, a six-foot-one, 295-pound, 4.8-in-the-40 "monster," says Darrelle Revis, then Walker's teammate and now a Jets cornerback. But during the season, after Walker's mother was jailed on parole violation, the bottom had fallen out: Walker had gone to the coaching staff in tears, ready to quit. He was alone, 17, with a 13-year-old sister to care for and no money for food or rent. Coaches and boosters mobilized, had a refrigerator stocked with groceries delivered to Walker's apartment in the Valley Terrace housing project, got him odd jobs, handouts. It wasn't enough. His cousins were in the business. He began dealing cocaine and crack to make ends meet.

As the winter months unrolled, Walker found himself growing colder. He had no time to feel pity. He lived the predatory days of black-on-black crime, supplied the hollow-eyed with endless rock, saw one friend rob another at gunpoint. He avoided arrest when a SWAT team raided the operation's gun-and-drug-laden home base just minutes after he'd left. He watched as the mom of one of his associates came with cash in hand, and her son sold her a fix. Walker allowed himself a shiver, paused long enough to think, *Jesus*. Then he got back to business. "She came to him, he gave it to her," Walker says. "It was just normal."

His coaches and most teammates didn't know what he was doing. His sister, Kerrie, didn't know. Walker kept playing, going to practice when he could, consuming the free food laid out afterward: green tea, hoagies, kielbasa, barbecue. Since he had begun playing his freshman year, football had provided an identity, given his chaotic life its only frame. The field was the one place in Aliquippa where the spiderweb's strands couldn't get much purchase.

The season ended, spring came, Walker's mother was released. Nobody in the business hassled him when he decided to stop dealing; his cousins were notorious.

The next fall, the 2004 season, Walker studied, cut grass for coaches and teachers, prepped for the SATs. In the fall he had 82 tackles and four sacks at defensive tackle, blocked three kicks. He was just a player and student again, tooling around in a 1985 Dodge Diplomat he'd bought for $750. He had scraped the rust off, repainted the car blood red, and dubbed it the Red Baron. People still grin recalling Willie and that car, seemingly made for each other—both headed for the junkyard once, both proud and shining now. But Walker wasn't driving it that night in November, heading home from the game, when his heart started pounding as if to break through his chest.

For weeks he'd kept the thought at bay, but now it wouldn't be denied: *My last game. Football saved me, but now it's over.* The fear rushed through him, worse than on the worst days with his mom, worse than when a passing cop car slowed, worse than when he felt the weight of the Taurus .45 jammed in his pants. He had never been so scared. No practice, no workouts, nothing. College? He still had no offers. The van he was riding in took a left on Superior Avenue, engine gunning as the street rose under the wheels. He could see the lights of Valley Terrace looming when, without warning, he began to cry. Tears, silent sobs: he couldn't stop.

"Because going up that hill?" Walker says. "It was like driving into the mouth of a monster."

"It was your quintessential melting pot," says Don Yannessa, an Aliquippa High graduate and the coach of its football team from 1972 through '88. "Italians lived in [the] Plan 11 [neighborhood], Serbians in Logstown or Plan 7, Greeks downtown. We had a large Jewish community. And they all got along. There were 30,000 people and paychecks every two weeks, and the stores were thriving. What a great town it was."

What remains is a stadium, perched high above the near-dead downtown. To reach it you make a right off Franklin Avenue, climb roller-coaster-steep Main Street, and hook a right close to where, during the 2009 season, the team's brainy wideout escaped a drive-by shooting with two bullet holes in his pants leg. You walk toward the gates, seeing neither field nor grandstand. You wonder if you'll step off into an abyss, and, yes, you will. There's a reason they call it the Pit.

Carl A. Aschman Stadium, home of the Fighting Quips, was wedged into the hill's flank in the late 1930s, creating one of the nation's loveliest settings for football. But now, as you descend its ravaged wooden bleachers and crumbling concrete on a November game day, it provokes the dizzying fear that the whole ramshackle structure will at last release its grip and send hundreds of parents, coaches, and fans—not to mention the Indian mascot, his horse, and the flaming spear that quivers in the immaculate turf—hurtling to the street below.

Still, for opponents such disorientation, combined with the dungeonlike visitors' locker room, is a perversely welcome rite of passage. "You haven't played football in western Pennsylvania," says an adult accompanying the saucer-eyed preps from Pittsburgh's Shady Side Academy, Aliquippa's first-round victims in the 2010 playoffs, "until you've played the Pit."

What also remains is a coaching staff of 19, 11 unpaid, all ignited by the standards set by their fathers and uncles, all former Quips but one. Mike Zmijanac never played a down of organized football. This past season the 67-year-old son of an Aliquippa waitress and an absent Marine sergeant became the winningest coach of the best high school program in a region that unearths talent like so many chunks of coal. Zmijanac is quick to say that he inherited a machine built by his celebrated predecessor, Yannessa, and when reminded that he's the only high school coach to have won Pennsylvania state titles in football and basketball, his first impulse is to point out that he's the only one to have lost championship games in both too.

But if Zmijanac's default mode is self-puncturing, if he tends to forget his players' names—instead giving them indelible tags such as Pottymouth, Frankenstein, and Lunch—he also sets the tone of tough compassion used by assistant head coach Sherm McBride, defensive coordinator Dan "Peep" Short, and the rest of the staff. The Quips are efficient, disciplined. The offense is simple. There's no taunting. Each player learns to call elders "Sir."

"Tonight's the kind of night that I remember why I do this," Zmijanac says to his team just minutes before Aliquippa's final 2010 game at the Pit, the first-rounder against Shady Side. "You seniors: this is the last time you'll ever play on this field. This team: this is the last time you'll ever play together on this field. It's a special group of people that get to do this. Don't ever take it for granted. Make it special. Play Aliquippa football, play the game right, respect the people on the other side, and knock the crap out of 'em—and then help 'em up. Now for all those people who played here before and the ones who'll play here after: Our Father. . . ." And they all bow their heads to pray.

The Pit on Friday night is the one place where Aliquippa now feels closest to Aliquippa then. Those who moved away find their way back: The old millworkers in wool hats gather under blankets in the senior citizens' seats, people wary of the streets gather here to greet old friends. White and black, young and old sit together, taking swigs from tiny bottles, commenting on the cold. The starters run out arm-in-arm with a cheerleader. The smell of gyros and cheese fries fills the air, the gravelly voice of the PA announcer says, "First-and-10, *goooooo*, Quips!" and the masses softly answer, in less a cheer than a collective warning, "Yeeaaaah!"

"Did you get chills?" asks Sean Gilbert, a Pro Bowl defensive tackle and former Quip. "What football will do. Football's a religion sometimes."

They are cocky, this crowd, and why not? Few corners of the nation, certainly none as small as Aliquippa, have produced so many big names. A man will be shot and wounded tonight on a street in Plan 11, not far from where Gilbert, NFL Hall of Fame tight end and coach Mike Ditka, Hall of Fame running back Tony Dorsett, two-time Super Bowl champ Ty Law, and Revis, the 2009 AFC Defensive Player of the Year, grew up. But there's little danger of a shooting at a Quips game.

"There is no drug dealing at the Pit, and rarely any violence," Walker says. "It really is sacred ground; it's like a miracle. You've got guys that, any other time of the day, they're going to try and rip each other's throats out, but they just walk past each other in the Pit. They're there to watch those kids play."

What remains is the team. Aliquippa lost another 10 percent of its population in the last decade, down to 10,548 residents; there were only 32 males in the high school's 2010 graduating class. Yet the Quips—from the fifth-smallest high school in western Pennsylvania, a Single A team fighting well above its weight—have averaged 10 wins a year for three decades, dominating AA competition, beating richer schools and towns, producing so many Division I-A players that it beggars belief.

Some on today's roster are sure they're next in line. Maybe it will be senior defensive lineman Zach Hooks, six-foot-six and 286 pounds, whom Temple is looking at, or freshman running back Dravon Henry, who will romp for 177 yards and two touchdowns against Shady Side. Each season Zmijanac has to tell a few players, "You think you're next, but you're not. Someone lied to you."

Tonight, as always, they'll slap the plaque over the door that reads WE RULE OUR HOUSE as they spill out to the field. Then they'll destroy Shady Side 41–0. Next week it will be Beaver 34–0, then Ford City 26–7 before a 19–6 loss to South Fayette in Aliquippa's record 21st appearance in the Western Pennsylvania Interscholastic Athletic League final. Before all that, though, they will put on their pads and tape their wrists. Too many will take black markers and write carefully on the tape. *RIP,* it will say, on wrist after wrist. *RIP KLJ SR. BDB; RIP EAG; RIP WALL; RIP UNCLE CLYDE; RIP TDW; RIP TMG.*

Rest in Peace, Cousin. Brother. Friend. Father.

Then they won't look like boys anymore. Because what remains in Aliquippa, too, is a kind of war.

Football isn't kind. It wasn't invented to save men or to serve as a civic barrier against the ills unleashed by the end of an era. Fueled by obedience, reveling in brute force, dismissive of weakness, the game hardly seems nimble enough to withstand the social trends that made Aliquippa feel, over the past 40 years, like some corroding edge of the American Dream. Industrial collapse, race riots, massive layoffs, white flight, corporate greed, fatherless families, the scourge of crack: all battered this tiny town like a series of typhoons. It's as if the same mysterious alchemy that keeps producing Hall of Fame talent and a team with a record 13 WPIAL titles created an equally outsized appetite for destruction. Aliquippa takes everything to extremes.

But then, the tone was set early. "I was terrible," says Mike Ditka, who grew up in the 1940s and '50s. "I had to win, had to win when I played marbles, whatever I played. And I wasn't a good sport about losing." Ditka—Aliquippa's first college first-team All-America, first NFL first-round draft choice, first player to score a touchdown in the Super Bowl, first coach of a Super Bowl champion—established the template for commitment, the near-maniacal need to infuse mere games with life-and-death importance, which has only grown stronger with time. The mystery is why. Unlike today's players, Ditka grew up in an Aliquippa that had everything: jobs, community, a downtown complete with a soda shop, a sweet Main Street to cruise and the certainty that nothing would ever change.

After all, Aliquippa, about 20 miles northwest of Pittsburgh, was just one of many burgs built to process all that ore and coal wrested out of the hills, one more town full of people from eastern and southern Europe who kept the coke ovens fired and the stacks smoking 24 hours a day, 13,000 workers filling three daily shifts on the other side of the Aliquippa Tunnel. Jones & Laughlin Steel designed and built the town just after 1900 and divided it into 12 ethnically specific "plans," separating labor from management, hunkies from cake-eaters. But the soot still fell all over, dirtying your shirt collar even if you never set foot in the mill that stretched for seven miles along the Ohio River.

Ditka's parents, Mike and Charlotte, moved up from Carnegie, Pennsylvania, in 1941, but young Mike didn't see much of his dad until he was four. While the Aliquippa Works pumped out record tonnages of armor plate, shell forgings, bombs, landing craft, bullets, and mortar tubing, proudly shaping the weapons to beat back Hitler and Tojo, Mike Sr. served in the Marines at Camp Pendleton, California. He came home to a job as a "burner"—welding boxcars on the mill railroad, his hands scarred by daily scorchings—and ruled the cramped house in the Linmar neighborhood like a drill instructor. The four kids had to be in bed by 7:00 P.M., and any misbehavior brought out the Marine belt.

Young Mike never once fought back. In sports, though, he was a terror: his way was the only way. In one Little League game Mike was catching for his younger brother Ashton when Ashton surrendered a few walks. Mike stopped the game, and they switched positions. During an American Legion game, when Ashton, in center field, dropped what would have been a game-ending fly, Mike charged off the pitcher's mound, chased Ashton over the fence, and, Mike says, "whipped his ass." The Marine belt came out for that one. Word has it that Ashton, for being a bit lax in defending himself, also got a lash or two.

By the mid-1950s, football—relentless, down-the-throat running football—was the undisputed king of Aliquippa, a way to take on towns such as Ambridge and Beaver Falls in matchups that reflected the mills' blue-collar grind. Once coach Carl Aschman led Aliquippa to its first WPIAL title, in '52, the machine found its rhythm. "If you looked like a football player? The older people, the older athletes would get on your back: you're going out for football," says Frank Marocco, who was two years ahead of Ditka at Aliquippa High and was the Quips' coach from 1989 to '96. "They made you play whether you liked it or not."

Ditka, a scrawny 135 pounds as a sophomore at Aliquippa, struggled through the team's two-week training camp, starting off as fodder on the so-called "ghost battalion": Marocco and the rest of the seniors spent days running over him like so much dirt. Ditka would cry, wipe off the snot, and scream, "Come on, hit me again!" And so they did. Aschman finally pulled him out of prac-

tice for his own protection, sending him off to clean latrines. After
that Ditka tried quitting, but Aschman told him to wait. By the
following fall Ditka had grown into his meat-hook hands and done
enough push-ups to power a steam engine. Aschman would tutor him alone after practices: how to block, run patterns, catch
the ball. Ditka started at linebacker and tight end. The team went
undefeated and won the WPIAL title. When a teammate's leg was
broken on a clean hit, Ditka walked into the opposing team's
huddle and threatened to kill them all. Come winter Ditka would
play basketball for coach Press Maravich, whose eight-year-old son,
Pete—"A little s——!" says Ditka—could outshoot and outdribble
anyone. When the Quips lost four football games during his senior
year, Ditka set a team record for lockers trashed. After missing a
layup that basketball season, he broke his wrist punching a wall.

Aschman sold him hard to recruiters, and Ditka had his pick
of college football powers. The mill had been pumping for five
decades; two generations, uneducated immigrants and their
kids, had traded health and happiness for a decent house, three
squares, a foothold in the new world. But the third generation saw
the Aliquippa Works less as an opportunity than a cautionary tale.
Ditka toured the place once in high school and never got over its
filth. When he took the scholarship at Pitt in '57, it sent a message.

"Everybody in my family worked in the mill; that's what we
knew," Yannessa says. "It wasn't until I was a junior and Mike was a
senior that some people said, 'If you get your grades in order, you
can get a scholarship playing football.' So many of our guys did.
That's the first time the light came on: maybe I can escape."

Nights, Ditka would sit up late and tell his mother, "One of
these days I'm going to have four cars and a big house with a pool.
You'll be able to drive 'em, but Daddy can't."

"He always said he was going to make money," Charlotte says. "I
don't know where he got the idea." Ditka went to Pitt intending to
be a dentist, though the thought of that glowering face, enraged
by some stubborn molar, could make an ant swear off sugar. "Can
you see that big hand in your mouth?" Charlotte says. But he made
his money, all right, rattling teeth as an unstoppable tight end with
Chicago and Dallas, blossoming into a near cult figure as coach
of Da Bears and the Saints, and along the way gave some $80,000
back to the Quips' athletic program and raised another $250,000
in scholarships. Now, at 71, he owes no one, and his work con-

sists mostly of being Mike Ditka on ESPN and showing up once a month at his self-named steak houses to shake hands.

Charlotte, 89, still lives in the house in Linmar. Mike's image papers the walls, and a small crystal bear squats on the coffee table above her son's words, still quoted around town: TOUGH TIMES DON'T LAST. TOUGH PEOPLE DO. Charlotte, like some of Mike's old teammates and buddies still in Aliquippa, dresses up and makes the 15-minute trip to his restaurant near the Pittsburgh Airport when she hears he's coming. Before she arrived in November, Ditka took on all comers at a back table, fielding compliments, repeatedly thanking every customer he could.

"I *was* going to be a dentist, but that's because of Coach Aschman," Ditka said. "He thought it would be a good idea if I came back to Aliquippa and fixed teeth." He gave a little shrug. "But eventually there was nobody to work on. I would've went broke."

Late September, leaves starting to fall. It's a sparkling Friday morning in the neighboring township of Hopewell, and Tony Dorsett stands at the fence ringing the high school stadium. He has just finished saying that the christening of Hopewell High's home field as Tony Dorsett Stadium in 2001, with 100 relatives present and fireworks and parachutists filling the sky, is the greatest honor he has known. Greater than receiving the Heisman Trophy or winning a national championship with Pitt, greater than being enshrined in the college and pro football Halls of Fame. "This," he says, "is the ultimate."

Yet something about that moment, this field, unsettles him. Dorsett goes silent, his eyes reddening; 13 seconds pass before he can utter another word. Now he points to the spot where he saw it, the image of his dead brother smiling. Tony was a ninth-grader in the fall of 1969, just months after he'd watched Melvin, age 27, collapse and die of a heart attack at their home, which was in Aliquippa's Plan 11 but fell within the Hopewell school district. Tony couldn't sleep in the house after that, but he never expected to be spooked at a football game. Playing against his buddies at Aliquippa High was worry enough.

"My brother used to always sit in that one spot, back up in this corner there," Dorsett says. "I know people might think I'm crazy, but I made a great play, and I looked up to see my family, and I saw him. I saw a vision. Clear as could be. . . .

"Melvin dropped out of school. But when I was a kid, we used to watch him. Talk about speed? My brothers all had speed, but he was the one I'd watch at the park on Fourth of July, everybody playing softball, and it was amazing the stuff he'd do. He ran from left field to right field and caught a fly ball—the most unbelievable thing I've ever seen in my damn life."

Dorsett—and Hopewell—won that game, and he went on to win plenty more in high school, at Pitt and with the Cowboys, the only one of Wes and Myrtle Dorsett's five boys to make it out. The couple had moved to Aliquippa from Pittsboro, North Carolina, in 1944 amid the Great Migration's second wave, a rural-to-urban odyssey that transformed African American culture and every northern city. Wes never spent a day in school, but his every lesson was a variation of the one he gave while racing his boys, switch in hand, whipping their hams as they fled: *move.* Tony visited his dad once outside the mill's open-hearth department and didn't recognize him under a mask of grime. "Come in the mill, you don't know if you're coming out," Wes said. "And if you do, you might be missing an arm or eye or leg. Do something better with your life."

When, at 16, Tony's friends took summer jobs at the mill, he refused. He never did go inside, not once. Eventually all four older brothers—each quicksilver fast, each eyed by coaches—made that ride through the Aliquippa Tunnel. Drink, drugs, or dwindling motivation proved too hard to fight, and only Tony, the scared mama's boy with eyes so wide that Wes dubbed him "Hawk," proved strong enough. So, yes, Dorsett feels pride when he sees his name on the sign at his old school, but it's diluted by guilt and mystery. At 56 years old he still asks, *Why me?*

Another reason the christening ceremony felt so miraculous is that Dorsett was sure it couldn't happen. Rename a stadium in Hopewell after a black kid from Aliquippa? Never. Because Hopewell, the wealthy, spacious Pittsburgh suburb that borders Aliquippa, had, by the time Dorsett came along, become a haven for whites bolting the town—and many looked down their noses at all they'd left behind.

By 1970, Aliquippa's population was 25 percent African American and had shrunk to 22,277. An explosion of racial strife, the tail end of nearly three years of nationwide integration battles and civil rights protests, only fueled the exodus. In May 1970, Aliquippa schools were shuttered after confrontations between white and black teenagers resulted in the suspension of 54 students. According to a state report, eight white students said, when questioned, that "they would be willing to get killed fighting blacks." Three weeks later racial clashes spilled from the junior high to the streets, leaving 11 students injured and dozens arrested. That night 250 whites clashed with police after demanding the release of four white youths. More than 30 gunshots were fired; tear gas filled the air. Whites and blacks divvied up territory.

"You were only allowed up in the school [area], where the white people lived, during school," says Sherm McBride, the assistant head coach. "If you ran into a certain type, you were getting jumped on. Vice versa for whites: if they were downtown, they were getting jumped on by black guys. And in the school, from what my brothers say, there wasn't a day you didn't have guys carrying switchblades."

The state report also relates stories of "battles between police and alleged snipers" in Aliquippa, an "angry charging mob of chanting whites" confronting blacks in Plan 11, blacks and whites arming themselves, and whites organizing neighborhood protective groups. Ditka's dad, Big Mike, was one of the patrol leaders, his house but a minute's drive from the mostly black housing project Linmar Terrace. "They were going to clean out the white people," Charlotte says.

Yannessa, who had left Aliquippa in '68 to teach and coach at nearby Ambridge, spent free periods listening to reports over the police scanner. By then the Quips' football program had been gutted. Aschman had a heart attack and stopped coaching after winning his last WPIAL title in '65, and soon whites and blacks wouldn't play together; the '70 team fielded just 16 players. Aliquippa won 12 games over the next seven years, losing seven of eight to Hopewell, before Yannessa, a teammate of Ditka's and disciple of Aschman's, came home to take over in 1972.

"I had never seen a community change so dramatically in a negative sense," Yannessa says of Aliquippa. "It was all racism, white flight. They wouldn't even let the kids play nighttime football. You're getting your ass kicked, and by the third quarter you're playing in front of 18 people? It was ugly."

Meanwhile, a zoning fluke—the line drawn just 30 yards from the front door—had placed the Dorsetts' home in the Hopewell district. While the boosters at Aliquippa might have finagled a way to keep him, Tony's parents took one look at the stable, peaceful halls of Hopewell High and put him on the bus headed there. Within two years Vikings coach Butch Ross had the most spectacular running back yet seen in western Pennsylvania.

It wasn't easy for Dorsett, though. He was one of only a handful of blacks among more than 1,500 Hopewell students, living "in two worlds," as he puts it: by night a resident of the Hill, hardscrabble and all black, by day a student in what he and his friends called Whiteyland. But Dorsett had football to insulate him, and he says the two-world split prepared him to deal with just about any social situation. In fact, the only thing Hopewell didn't prepare him for was the notion that his school, state—hell, entire country—could evolve, that white and black kids would someday date without inciting comment, that a black man could see his name raised on the most revered structure in town.

Of course, change didn't come overnight. At Aliquippa High, Yannessa walked into the gym his first day as coach, saw his prospective team self-segregated by race, and demanded that they mix—or else. It didn't help that even the booster club had separated into black and white factions. But within a year the Quips began to win. A black steelworker named Charlie Lay served as a goodwill conduit to the white community, setting up mixed meetings of parents, boosters, and players in white and black homes, buying drinks in white bars and black, and the battle lines began to soften. Yannessa, along with Zmijanac, his defensive coordinator, had been cocky enough to think he could calm the waters, bring back the old days, and he felt even cockier now. Then, in the fall of 1977, the town cracked again.

A fight between a black and a white student outside the school cafeteria ended with the white student stabbed, and all the tamped-down tensions erupted. Aliquippa High closed for three days. After that police roamed the halls, and every day brought another fight with a knife or chain. Teachers locked their doors and hid. For the first time Yannessa felt the football program, and the town, were surely lost.

He was wrong. Although town and school were savagely split, the team's core was not. Short, McBride, and five other players, a mix of juniors and seniors, black and white, met the weekend before the '78 season opener and heard Short demand, "This has got to stop somewhere." The next day, after the team entered the gym and, for the first time in years, divided itself into white and black factions, the seven players walked together to the center of the floor. "You're either with us," they announced, "or you're out."

"No one left that gym," McBride says. "Everybody came together as one." Not long after, some felt a shift in Aliquippa's air. Black and white players were seen double-dating, sometimes interracially. The crowds at games began to mix. In the off-season Yannessa insisted that the annual banquets for the black and white booster clubs be combined, and it happened.

"Football brought the families, the community, everything back together," McBride says, walking behind the Pit's grandstand. "You'd go down to the mill where everybody's mother or father was working and hear, 'You going to the game this week?' If you wanted to rob a bank in Aliquippa? Friday night at eight o'clock was the best time."

Tony Dorsett is walking downtown. A car passes, slows: *Why would anyone be walking . . . wait. Was that Hawk?* It has been years since he's been down to Franklin Avenue. Most storefronts are empty now, mocking like a toothless grin the spiffy red banners on the light posts that plead, TAKE PRIDE IN ALIQUIPPA. Two men, their clothing loose and fraying, appear and head Dorsett's way. They stop, shake hands, chat. "Man," Dorsett says. "Everything's shut down."

"Only one thing that ain't shut down, Tony," one replies. "The bullets."

Aliquippa is, in one sense, like a big city: people warn you away from certain spots. There's a safe stretch along Brodhead Road, but the occasional burglary keeps residents edgy. You don't want to be on Franklin Avenue at night, and places that used to be crime-free, like Main Street just outside the high school, have grown grimmer. "You can be anywhere," says Revis. "Every time somebody gets killed, I'm getting a call: 'Stephen died.' 'This guy died.' I have been home and talked to somebody, and two weeks later I'm getting a call like, 'He's dead.' It's not safe. You can die just like that."

It's not rare to hear someone declare Aliquippa dead too. The streets give off a postapocalyptic feel, at once simmering and still. You can't be sure that what you see is a mercilessly dismantled past or a nightmare vision of the future—a vivid preview of what can happen when a nation ships its manufacturing work, the kind that once offered blue-collar security, overseas.

The J&L mill, battered by cheap, inventive Japanese products and taken over by the Ohio-based LTV Corporation, began shutting down nearly 30 years ago, and closed for good in 2000. Pittsburgh has made a successful transition to the new economy, but "Aliquippa's in a weird place," says Pitt labor economist Chris Briem. "It's not the center of the region, it's not the city, it's not quite rural. What is the competitiveness of towns that used to have a reason for being—and don't anymore?"

Yet others insist that a molten stream of the old immigrant sensibility, alloyed with the hard-won unity forged in the '70s, still courses through the town. Aliquippans say hard times weeded out the weak, and only the strong remain. They see a drive among the youngest, especially the athletes who've lived entire lives amid the ruins, that keeps pushing them to win against ridiculous odds.

"My sister was murdered," says 35-year-old Dwan Walker, a former receiver for Aliquippa who intends to run for mayor this spring. Standing behind the Aliquippa stands during a September game, Walker describes how his sister, Deirdre, 33, was killed in the fall of 2009 by James Moon, a 24-year-old former Quips running back who, the Aliquippa police say, was jealous of Deirdre's relationship with another man. "She was shot and killed in front of my nephew, shot three times," Walker says. Moon then turned the gun on himself. Afterward, Walker says, "I wanted to leave. I'm mad at this place every day. But I have never felt so much love in my life as I felt from [Aliquippans] when my sister was murdered. My Facebook page exploded; I had to shut it down, there were so many messages.

"All in all, I wouldn't trade Aliquippa for nothing in the world. We're going to keep fighting. You'll read the paper tomorrow: 'Aliquippa won.' That's all we need. Because it's heart, man. It's pride. It's a mystery, how you keep wanting to come back."

"Aliquippa will never die," says Aileen Gilbert, Sean Gilbert's mom and Revis's grandmother. "On the surface it looks like a ghost town. It looks desolate. But I don't see desolation."

What she does see is spirit, handed down from parent to son, that can be best summed up in four words: no track, no problem. Because the story that best illustrates the town's mix of triumph and tragedy is only tangentially related to football. It involves Mc-

Bride, who doubles as the Quips' track coach; four football players who ran sprints; and a long jumper named Byron Wilson.

With no running track, the Quips practice in the school parking lot, spikes on asphalt. Before 2005 an Aliquippa team had never won a state title. Yet at that spring's state championships, against schools fielding up to 20 boys, Aliquippa won its first team title with just those five.

The sprinters finished one-five-eight in the 100 meters, took second in the 200, and won the 4 × 100 relay. But to claim the title the team would need points from Wilson, who rarely worked hard at practice and was seeded 21st of 24 competitors. After he fouled on his first two jumps, there wasn't much hope. "It wasn't like Byron had technique," says Michael Washington, one of the football player–sprinters. On his third jump, however, Wilson stuck it: 22' 3¼", good for first place and 43 team points. Aliquippa won the championship by two points.

"When he called, you could hear it in his voice; it was really gratifying," says Andre Davis, Wilson's stepfather, who had raised him from age three. "To me and his mother, it meant, Thank God. Now he knows that he has a talent. He realizes if you put your mind to something, you can accomplish something." His parents hung the medals on their bedroom mirror so they could see them every day when they woke. They hang there still.

It was, all admit, the kind of Hollywood finish capable of changing a life. Ask McBride what happened to Wilson, though, and his eyes drop. Wilson had a scholarship to run track at California (Pennsylvania) University under Olympic great Roger Kingdom. "Guess what," McBride says. "He shot a guy. Here at Aliquippa you can be top dog one day and in the wrong place at the wrong time the next." McBride pauses. "Great kid. Father is a chief of police here."

Andre Davis is, indeed, Aliquippa's assistant chief of police, a member of the department for 24 years. He has battled rising gang activity in the housing projects and now in Plan 12. His stepson's case was different. Drugs or turf weren't the issue so much as personality: soon after high school Wilson's hot temper, sharp tongue, and inability to back down inflamed the boys from Linmar Terrace, and word spread. "A lot of guys wanted to kill him," Revis says. "You'd hear that all the time."

Revis saw it too. On a visit home during his sophomore year at

Pitt he went to Curenton's Mini Market on the Hill to buy the latest Air Jordans. Wilson showed up talking to a friend, Revis's half-brother Jaquay. Revis exchanged pleasantries with a male standing by the door, a Linmar lookout guy who complimented Revis on his college career. Minutes later, as Revis walked out, shoes in hand, a white car pulled up and a man jumped out shooting. Wilson and Jaquay hit the pavement. Revis dived behind a car, where he ended up face-to-face with the now-panicked lookout. They stared at each other as the bullets flew.

"My heart is beating so fast, and you just hear the gunshots: *boom, boom, boom!*" Revis says. "I'm like, Yo, my brother might be shot, then I heard the car pull off. Nobody got shot. Byron got up and started shooting. I'm shaking. My car was shot up; it had a couple bullets in it."

Still, Revis loves Aliquippa. He feels a need whenever he's in town to get back to the Hill, to the street he grew up on. The always crowded 13-room family home on Seventh Avenue is where Ty Law would stop by when Darrelle was in elementary school, where his uncle Sean Gilbert's teammates would congregate laughing, where Darrelle would step out to stare up at the stars and dream of flying to outer space. When he was three years old, his mother, Diana, would find him waiting summer nights on the step out front; she was puzzled until one evening Sean, doing his preseason training, came chugging up the hill. He'd reach the top, tap Darrelle, and then turn and jog back down. "Let him stay right here," Sean said. "I'm going to keep touching him."

Revis ran some with a junior Griffin Heights crew and backed out when they started flashing guns. But these days he doesn't want to seem stuck-up. In Aliquippa he makes a point of talking to everyone who stops him, even crackheads, "just to let them know I still know where home is, and I still come back."

He knows this might not be wise. But Revis believes that Aliquippa's lunacy helped make him one of the best cornerbacks alive, and besides, he's one of many who say that the end of the town's biggest menace has brought a measure of calm. In August 2009, Anthony "Ali" Dorsett, 34, the son of Tony's brother Keith, pleaded guilty to charges of dealing crack and powder cocaine in a joint federal, county, and local crackdown on a drug ring that had operated out of Linmar Terrace from '03 to '08. Twelve other men, described by federal prosecutors as sellers or gun-toting "shooters," have been sentenced; Dorsett, the acknowledged ring-leader, is scheduled to be sentenced on March 17. He could face life in prison.

When the arrests were announced in December 2008, Tony Dorsett was appalled by the coverage. He has lived in Texas since joining the Cowboys in 1977, but seemingly every news story labeled Ali as "Tony Dorsett's nephew." His own son, Anthony Jr., a former NFL player also living in Dallas, was at first mistakenly reported to be the drug dealer, and Tony had to quell rumors that the feds had seized some of his property, including the house he bought for his mother with his first signing bonus. All untrue, Tony says, though his son had been involved with Ali in a real estate venture.

Davis was involved in the sweep, which was dubbed Operation Enough Is Enough. Since then Aliquippa has indeed seen "a big change for the better," he says, with fewer reports of shots fired and far less loitering at the Linmar projects. But any satisfaction he feels about it is tempered by the fact that in 2006 Byron Wilson plea-bargained a 15-month sentence after pulling up next to his Linmar enemies in a car and opening fire. Two years later he wounded two men in a bar shootout, for which he has just begun serving a one- to two-year prison sentence.

Since then Davis has gotten job offers outside Aliquippa. He won't leave. He played football for the Quips, and on fall Saturdays he referees for the WPIAL and the Beaver County Youth League, which includes the Little Quips—four levels of junior teams from ages five to 12—who play to crowds even more jacked than Friday night's. Davis thinks he's figured out why Aliquippa, in spite of everything, keeps producing greatness.

"You get through here and the hard times? Everything else is easy," Davis says. "They've survived not eating at night, or went through watching a brother or sister get killed. I personally had to see my son arrested and prosecuted and put in jail. So what could be harder? Playing football? That is nothing."

Sirens? They almost don't hear the sirens anymore. But when, early in the evening of October 7, Quips players and coaches saw the helicopter flying in low, its blades *whap-whap-whapping* over the Pit and beyond, the usually smooth rhythm of practice began to stutter. A chopper is never good news. Dread spread, and soon running backs coach Timmie Patrick, a Beaver County detective, had learned the latest awful news. Medevac: man stabbed at Curenton's Mini Market, and one of their own.

Art "Rooster" Motton, 47, with multiple wounds to his neck and trunk, was flown to a Pittsburgh hospital and pronounced dead, and 16-year-old Aliquippa High student James D. Motton, a nephew whom Art had raised as a son, was charged with the murder. (His trial is pending.) Word was that the two had argued over damage to Art's car, but the motive almost didn't matter. Up at the football field, shock leaped from face to face.

Art Motton had been one of the hardest hitters in Quips history, a 170-pound cornerback whose ferocity had been a legend for 30 years. The hit Rooster put on Belle Vernon tailback Marlon McIntyre—all 220 pounds of him laid out, unconscious—on the first play of Aliquippa's 1980 playoff win was almost as devastating as the line Motton delivered walking away. "Call the ambulance," Rooster said. "He'll be here for a while." Motton had had his troubles—a crack addiction, since kicked, an unsteady marriage—but lately seemed to have found his footing. For the next week Zmijanac found himself fighting back tears.

It has been a particularly grueling year for the Quips. Not so much the football: Aliquippa finished 12–1 and lost the WPIAL final largely because it fumbled three times inside South Fayette's 20-yard line. Of its 45 players, a couple have a shot at a D-I scholarship and 35 to 40 will be back next fall. But last May former Aliquippa defensive end Kevin Johnson, father of the senior who had escaped with bullet holes in his pants leg in 2009, took six bullets and died in Beaver, police say, after he forced his way into the home of a former girlfriend. Then, a month before Motton's death, assistant chief Davis and volunteers called the Council of Men and Fathers found it necessary to patrol outside the home game against Beaver Falls, defusing any possible violence in retaliation for the August shooting death in Beaver Falls of Stephen Hardy Jr., 22, a law-abiding former Quips quarterback about to graduate from Robert Morris University with a degree in mechanical engineering.

There's no pattern. Kids who study hard and avoid trouble have been destroyed; kids once immersed in crime have grown into caring citizens. "Half of them make it, and half of them don't—and you never know which half it's going to be," says Zmijanac, who took over the Quips' football program in 1997. "It's joyful, and then it breaks your heart—all in the same day."

Zmijanac estimates that he loses a half-dozen players to the street each year, and he has a long record of suspending stars. But the team has an open-door policy: "If he wants to come back, we'll always bring him in," McBride says. "No matter how many times they fail. Our job is not to give up on them."

That's why you'll hear Zmijanac call a kid like Willie Walker, former crack dealer, "wonderful." Because maybe, just maybe, Walker beat the spiderweb. He negotiated the final seven months of school without football, weathered the disappointment of 2005 Signing Day coming and going without one offer. A day later a coach from California (Pennsylvania) University came to Aliquippa with a full scholarship for him. It wasn't until the fall of '06, after he'd moved to the campus 60 miles away, bought books, and been brutally sandwiched by a pair of massive twins on his first collegiate snap, that Walker allowed himself to believe: *I'm here. I finally made it.*

Four years later Walker, a defensive lineman, led the Vulcans to the semifinals of the NCAA Division II tournament and was named to the AP's Little All-America first team. There were bumps: his girlfriend in Aliquippa had a baby his freshman year, and he wanted to be involved, but two of his cousins and an uncle were indicted in the roundup of Ali Dorsett's crew, and Willie's mom—stepping up at last—told him to stay at school, away from the trouble. She helped out with the baby in Aliquippa and brought her on game days to watch Willie play. Sometimes some of his former confederates would come up to cheer him on too. He intends to graduate. He still keeps the Red Baron immaculate.

This, of course, isn't a picture of conventional mores, but Aliquippa rarely allows for black-and-white assertions of right and wrong. The town is small, the lines blurred and ever shifting; it is, indeed, a web in which everyone knows or is related to everyone else. Ty Law grew up in the house once occupied by Sean Gilbert's mother. Willie Walker stayed good friends with Byron Wilson, even though it was his own kin who wanted to kill him. "And are you ready for this?" says Short, the Quips' defensive coordinator, one day in November. "Ali Dorsett is married to my daughter."

When he first learned about the relationship, years ago, Short tried warning the drug dealer off. The next time he saw the couple together, he punched Dorsett in the face. "But he's actually a pretty good guy," Short says, shrugging. "Just trying to get that easy money—and now he's going to pay for it."

People often describe the Aliquippa football program as an oasis in the desert. It's not that tidy. When asked if he'd like his two-year-old son, Jayden, who lives with his mother in Beaver Falls, to be a Quip, Revis hesitates, then says, "I don't want him in Aliquippa. If Aliquippa can pick their school up, and their coaches, and move somewhere else? Yes." But that's impossible. The team is the town, its pride and pain.

In July, Tony Dorsett returned for the funeral of his 61-year-old brother, Tyrone, a longtime drug user whom Tony could never pry away from Aliquippa. As he drove the broken streets, past the weeds creeping down out of wood structures as if to consume the place whole, past the monument to the workers of Jones & Laughlin Steel, he was hit by a force hard to understand. For the first time he told his wife, Janet, "Let's look at some houses." He wants to move back, maybe to Pittsburgh, maybe somewhere closer. "Every time I come back, the feeling's there, more and more," Dorsett said in September, steering his Chrysler 300 up Monaca Road. "It hurts me to see it, but this is Aliquippa. This is me. This is where I got everything."

He hits the gas going up Kennedy Boulevard, takes a right on Brodhead Road, crosses the border into Center Township, and veers onto Chapel Road. His mother is up there now, waiting. Dementia has been a patient thief, but Myrtle still thrills to Tony's voice. He pulls into the driveway. She's sitting by the door and looks up blankly—face so youthful under the cottony hair—at the man by the black car now standing and waving. She wiggles her fingers back. "She's wondering who I am," Tony says. "She sits on the porch a lot these days."

Dorsett walks up the little path, shoulders squared, the usual roll gone out of his step. He leans down and hugs her, not too hard. The front door is wide open. Soon they'll have lunch, mother and son, in a dimmer light, survivors holding fast to all that's left of home.

JOHN BRANT

Frank's Story

FROM RUNNER'S WORLD

BY PAINFUL BUT UNEQUIVOCAL choice, Frank Shorter possesses no photographs of the late Dr. Samuel Shorter, even though, of the 11 children in the Shorter family—five boys, six girls—Frank, the second eldest, looked most like his father. They had the same inquisitive eyes, thick shock of hair, and fine-boned, patrician profile. Throughout Frank's childhood, the people of Middletown, New York, frequently noted the resemblance. They meant it as a compliment, but like everything else connected with his father, the comment aroused a wild, secret fear in the boy.

Dr. Shorter served the 22,000 residents of this Hudson River Valley town, about 60 miles northwest of New York City, as a general practitioner. During the 1950s, when Frank was growing up, house calls still formed a staple of Dr. Shorter's practice, and sometimes he brought Frank along on his calls in town. Dr. Shorter would pack up his black bag in his ground-floor office of the family home, a grand Victorian, with a mansard roof and a wraparound porch, two doors down from the armory castle on Highland Avenue. Frank would follow him out to the family's Buick station wagon. There was a lot of foot traffic on Highland in those days. The YMCA stood a few blocks away, and a 10-minute walk along East Main Street delivered pedestrians to the bustling heart of downtown.

Everybody in Middletown admired Dr. Shorter. During a fearsome polio epidemic in 1952, he'd worked tirelessly to control the spread of the disease, and thus spared Middletown the worst of the scourge. Dr. Shorter had delivered a high percentage of the children in the area's postwar baby boom, and was venerated for "forgetting" to send bills to financially struggling patients. His standing was such that years later, when Middletown staged a welcome-home celebration for Frank after he'd won the gold medal in the marathon at the 1972 Olympic Games in Munich, the party honored the father as much as the son. Louis Mills, the emcee of the event, called Dr. Shorter "one of the greatest humanitarians I have ever known." A headline in the local paper proclaimed "Dr. Sam: Father of the Olympian" above a lengthy and glowing profile of the man.

The doctor's popularity, however, led to some acutely difficult moments for his son. One day when Frank and his father were heading out on house calls, for instance, a woman on a shopping errand stopped to greet them. "Why, Dr. Shorter, this young man looks just like you!" she said, and then turned to Frank. "And I bet you're smart like your daddy too! When you grow up, you're going to be a doctor just like him, aren't you?"

Frank remained silent. The woman smiled encouragingly, thinking that the boy was perhaps shy, that the cat had got his tongue, but in fact he didn't know how to answer. He certainly couldn't tell the woman the truth, which he knew she'd never believe, and which Frank was just beginning to admit to himself: that the man whom the community knew as a devoted healer transformed into a violent, abusive sociopath at home, capable of inflicting the most horrible of crimes upon his children; that Frank and his family lived in perpetual, suffocating fear of his father and his sadistic, incestuous proclivities; and that, even at age nine, the boy had resolved to live his life by *not* emulating Dr. Samuel Shorter.

As the silence wore on, the woman's smile grew strained. Feeling his father looming over him, Frank panicked. Maybe his moment's hesitation had already earned him a beating. Some night soon, as Dr. Shorter climbed the stairs toward his children's bedrooms, belt in hand, it would be Frank's name that he'd call.

"Yes!" the boy finally blurted to the woman, praying that he hadn't spoken too late. "Yes! I want to be a doctor too!"

Today, more than 50 years later, the memory still staggers Frank Shorter. He rises from his kitchen table and moves to the window, staring out at the Flatirons standing sentinel over Boulder, Colorado, his home of nearly 40 years. Blinding January sunshine shatters off Wonderland Lake, and a steady stream of runners works the trail around it. Spotting Shorter in the window, one runner waves to him excitedly. A storm is forecast for later, but at midmorning the sky is cerulean above the Rocky Mountain snow peaks.

"I can imagine what a wonderful picture we made," Shorter says, turning back to the table. His tousled hair is mostly gray now, but just as thick as in the iconic photos of him from the 1970s. "Everybody in Middletown loved my father. They probably thought I was the luckiest little boy in the world to be able to tag along with him." Another pause. "But those house calls were like all the other times I spent around him. I was terrified. I was on red-alert every minute. You never could tell what was going to set him off. A lot of times, it didn't take anything." Shorter's voice thickens. He speaks with a Yale man's precision, avoiding profanity and cliché. "He wasn't going to hit me in the car. He'd wait until later, at home, where no one could see him."

A heavy silence descends. As the ghost of Dr. Samuel Shorter rises, Frank's eyes fill. He begins to tell a story of his father, then stops. He starts again, and stops once more. He can tell you the exact date of his first significant running injury—February 19, 1976, a hairline fracture in his foot at an indoor meet here in Boulder at the University of Colorado—but he struggles to conjure fragmentary memories of his traumatic early family life; a life that, until now, he has never fully revealed.

The silence between these pauses seems all the more wrenching because, normally, the stories flow out of Shorter: the story of his Olympic gold medal run in '72, which is generally regarded as the precipitating event of the modern running movement; of his silver medal marathon performance at the '76 Games in Montreal, where Waldemar Cierpinski, an East German who was later documented to be part of that nation's doping system, beat Shorter out for the gold; of Shorter being the last person to see Steve Prefontaine alive on the night of his fatal car crash in May 1975; and of Shorter's seminal work as the first chairman of the board of the U.S. Anti-Doping Agency. Shorter fluently recounts these stories and others, weaving them into a narrative that he delivers to audiences around the nation in his enduring role as the father of the running boom.

"Frank's contributions crossed over—they affected the whole

culture," says the novelist John L. Parker, the author of *Once a Runner* and Shorter's roommate and training partner during their days with the Florida Track Club in Gainesville during the 1970s. "Alongside figures like Prefontaine, Bill Rodgers, and Roger Bannister, Shorter was the quintessential runner."

But the story that Shorter only recently has come to acknowledge as the genesis for all others emerges in agonized fits and starts. He tried to tell it before, first in 1991. He'd been invited to a race in Florida that was benefiting a center for abused children. He mentioned to a reporter from the *Fort Lauderdale Sun Sentinel* that the cause was dear to him because his father had abused him as a child. The reporter wrote an article based on that claim, and the *New York Times* later ran a brief item. But Shorter didn't go into detail about the abuse, his father denied any wrongdoing, and the story soon died. "There was less awareness of child abuse in that era, and more willingness to deny the extent of the problem, especially when it involved a successful man like my father," Shorter says. "Also, my father was still alive, and I was still afraid of him."

Another reason Shorter refrained from elaborating at the time had to do with his deeply ingrained stoicism and an instinct for understatement. He had long been known, even by his peers, as a bit of a loner and as someone willing to stand apart from the pack. Back in 1972 at the Munich Olympics, Shorter had watched the swimmer Mark Spitz rack up an unprecedented seven gold medals. With each race that he won, the number of handlers and marketers around Spitz grew. Shorter didn't begrudge Spitz his self-promotion; like all Olympians in that rigidly amateur era, Spitz had toiled for years without making a dime, and was only seeking to leverage his moment. But on the day of the Olympic Marathon, as he waited to run, Shorter resolved that if and when his moment came, he'd handle it differently—no entourage, no image, not even an agent.

His moment soon arrived. "I threw a 4:33 surge between miles nine and 10, and from that point on I was out of sight of the guys trailing me—Mamo Wolde [of Ethiopia], Derek Clayton [of Australia], and Kenny [Moore of the United States]," Shorter says, recalling the Munich marathon. "The whole second half, I kept hitting my pace. I had the talent to go out fast, by myself, and ride the pain. I learned that from watching Clayton and Ron Clarke, but it was also something I internalized from my childhood."

Shorter's masterful gold medal performance, run in a time of 2:12:19, made him a household name across America, and soon thousands of his previously sedentary countrymen were taking to the roads, running in his footsteps. In the years since, in all his various roles, Shorter has upheld his resolution, operating with consistent integrity and good taste. As a track and road-race commentator for network TV, for instance, he avoided sensationalism in favor of thoughtful analysis. During U.S. distance runners' battle to gain professional status in the 1970s, Shorter rejected confrontation, capitalizing on his relationship with the sport's leaders to broker a compromise in which athletes' prize winnings were placed in trust. During his tenure as the first head of USADA, Shorter deemphasized outing individual dopers in favor of building an overall system of deterrence. In his present public speaking career, he employs no agency to arrange his appearances—"People are amazed when they call me and I pick up the phone myself," he says—and prefers to stay in the homes of local runners when he travels to events rather than in hotels.

In his reluctance to build a brand, paradoxically, Shorter has done just that. Combining his Olympic fame with a bachelor's degree from Yale and a law degree from the University of Florida, he has established a reputation for dignity and decorum that resembles the status that Joe DiMaggio achieved in his postbaseball career. "Working with Frank sort of ruined me for working with other professional athletes," says Steve Bosley, the founder of the Bolder Boulder 10-K, the nation's second-largest road race, whose course features a statue of Shorter. "I would compare their style to the way that Frank does business, and I was always disappointed."

Accordingly, Shorter has avoided jumping on any bandwagon—including that of abuse victim. "To fuse my identity with what has become a trendy syndrome, to get lumped in with the confessions of fading rock stars and politicians looking to boost their careers, is against everything I stand for," he says.

And yet, here he is on this winter morning, 63 years old, renowned and respected, with three happy adult children of his own and his first grandchild on the way, with the runners who are his heirs flowing past his sun-filled house on the edge of the Rocky Mountains, suffering to recall the crimes his father committed more than a half-century ago. Recent, pivotal events, Shorter explains, have prompted him to speak out.

The first was his father's death, in June 2008, in Middletown, on the same day that Shorter was in town for the city's annual Classic 10-K, a race he has come home to run nearly every year since 1981. The evening before the race, Shorter went to see his father, who was 86 and under hospice care due to renal failure, for the final time. "What I felt, looking into his eyes, was an enormous sense of relief," Shorter says. "Now he couldn't hurt me anymore. He couldn't hurt my mother [Katherine, who died two years later, in 2010], and he couldn't hurt my sisters or brothers. He couldn't hurt anyone. I would never have to think about him again." Or so he thought. Instead, the death started to move things around inside Shorter. Old hauntings began to stir, quietly simmering until they found expression two years later at a road race and expo in Springfield, Missouri.

At the event, which took place last November, Shorter came to speak, along with fellow distance-running legends Bill Rodgers and Dick Beardsley. While there the three men were taken to the venue the charity-race was benefiting, a residential high school for children who were in the juvenile justice system. "Our host asked us to meet some of the kids and give a brief motivational talk in the auditorium," Shorter says. "I looked out at the audience, at all those damaged young people, and realized that I belonged to the same veterans' organization that they did."

Rodgers and Beardsley each talked about perseverance, goal-setting, and overcoming obstacles. Then it was Shorter's turn. Rather than delivering his standard motivational rap, he started remembering. "I talked about lying in bed as a child and hearing my father's footstep on the stairs," he says. "I explained how I tried to anticipate my father's moods and movements, and about the enormous daily effort it took us kids to keep out of his way. I talked about searching for an outlet for my fear and anger, and finding it in running. I admitted that I ran to escape. I described the guilt I felt for not being able to save the rest of my family."

"The entire room was rapt, silent," Beardsley recalls. "I was stunned. I've known Frank for years, and I'd never heard any of this. None of us had. Bill always looks sort of dazed, but as Frank spoke he looked even more dazed than usual. Suddenly things about Frank clicked into focus. I'd always felt this sense of aloofness and distance from him—sometimes he would look at me like he didn't even know me. I thought it was something I'd done to offend him, or it was just who I was, an average guy, when Frank is just so cotton-pickin' smart. I talked to friends, and they said, 'Don't take it personally, that's just Frank.' Sitting there at that center, listening to him talk about his father coming up the stairs and deciding which of his kids he was going to hammer that night, I understood where Frank's distance came from."

After his talk, Shorter says, a girl, who appeared to be about 14 or 15, approached him. "'That story you told, that's my story,'" he recalls her saying. "'All of those things happened to me. The way you tried to keep one step ahead of your father, and tried to protect your sisters and brothers, and hated yourself for not being able to—that was me you were talking about.'"

At that moment the dime dropped for Shorter. He realized that his responsibility to share his story outweighed the risk of appearing trendy or self-serving. "There was a purpose to it beyond feeding my ego or joining the therapeutic age," he says. "I saw that my story could be of use to people like this girl."

There was one more reason for speaking out. For his entire adult life Shorter had been explaining things to people. He explained the power and allure of the marathon to uncomprehending journalists. He explained to an exercise-adverse public that the benefits of distance running were available to anybody. He explained the pervasiveness and danger of performance-enhancing drugs. All that explaining, and yet he'd never explained the central fact driving his life and career—to others, or to himself.

"People deserve the truth," Shorter says. "I think I deserve the truth. And my father? Well, I've come to the conclusion that he deserves mercy, but he also deserves justice. It's not right for him to get away with what he did."

That Buick station wagon. A 1953 Chrysler limousine. A 1960 Chevrolet Carryall, the ancestor of today's Suburban. A 1958 Citroën, the only one in Middletown. Shorter associates these cars with his father because, even though his office was on the ground floor of the family home, Dr. Shorter was rarely present in the living quarters. Other than Thanksgiving and Christmas dinners, Shorter can't recall sharing a meal with him. "He was always out ministering to patients and saving the world," Shorter says, adding that the source of his father's extraordinary altruistic drive remains a mystery. Although Dr. Shorter later worked on medical missions sponsored by the Presbyterian Church, Frank doesn't remember him being especially religious, nor does he recall him having strong political convictions. By the same token, Shorter can only speculate regarding the source of his father's rage.

"Serving others—carrying the Hippocratic Oath to an extreme—was his way of proving and defining himself," Shorter says. "His entire identity was wrapped up with being this heroically selfless healer. But somehow he developed this Jekyll-and-Hyde personality. He showered care and love on the community, and terror and abuse on his wife and children."

Samuel Shorter grew up in Middletown, a member of the city's professional elite. His father, Harry Sanford Shorter, was a prominent optometrist known for his practice's catchy motto: "See Longer, See Shorter." Samuel Shorter graduated from Hobart College and married Katherine Chappel, his hometown sweetheart. In 1943, he entered an accelerated wartime program at Temple University School of Medicine in Philadelphia, receiving his MD in 1945. That year, Samuel Jr., the couple's first child, was born. Soon thereafter Dr. Shorter was stationed at an Army hospital in Germany. While they were in Munich in 1947, Katherine gave birth to Frank. (Twenty-five years later, Frank would return to his birthplace to win the Olympic Marathon.) In 1948, Dr. Shorter left the Army and returned to the States with his young family.

In his first U.S. practice, he served coal miners and their families in a hamlet called Cow Hollow, West Virginia. The Shorters' house had a train track to the mine running through the backyard. Around that time, during a visit to Florida, Shorter says he received his first beating from his father. "I'm running, screaming, across a hot asphalt road," he recalls. "My father has taken his belt to me because I've soiled my diapers."

Shorter says he has repressed the memories of many of the subsequent beatings that he received from his father, but he can clearly remember four or five especially violent episodes. "They tended to happen often enough, both to me and my siblings," he says, "that I came to think of them as almost routine."

The charges of beatings and abuse are supported by the five Shorter sisters who agreed to be interviewed for this story. "It was a horror show," Barbara duPlessis, Frank's 52-year-old sister, says of her childhood. "I remember my mother dressing a cut in my groin area when I was six years old. The wound was in the shape of my father's belt buckle." Another sister, who requested anonymity, says, "The first whipping I remember from my father happened when I was four years old, when some water from my bath sloshed out of the tub, and he came at me with the belt."

Along with the physical abuse, according to his children, Dr. Shorter also practiced a form of psychological cruelty. "He was a master at singling out each kid's insecurity or flaw and probing them to the point where you lost all feelings of confidence or self-worth," says duPlessis. "I was slightly cross-eyed as a kid, and he'd ridicule me for that without mercy. He took huge chunks out of my life that I'll never get back."

Frank agrees that the deepest cuts may have been emotional. "We could never relax in his presence. The only attention he ever gave me was when 'disciplining' me. During my career, he only saw two of my races."

But then there were times when the father's rage and cruelty escalated to a level unconscionably beyond the belt-whippings and mind games. According to two of the Shorter sisters, their father raped them.

Nanette Shorter, 60, says that Dr. Shorter raped her once, when she was 13, in the midst of a prolonged, savage physical beating that ensued after Nanette came home from a date. "It changed me forever," she says of the attack. "My father said he'd kill me if I ever told anybody, and I believed him."

Mary Shorter-King, 55, says she can remember being raped by her father when she was six years old. "I believe rape was part of my father's desire to dominate," she says. "I felt like I lived under a giant thumb. The sexual abuse was part of an overall program of oppression, of keeping kids under that thumb."

Shorter's fragmentary memories of his father's attacks, along with the fear and shame that prevented him and his siblings from revealing the abuse when it was occurring, could lead to the conclusion that he and his sisters are exaggerating or distorting their late father's behavior. But Elizabeth Loftus, PhD, a professor at the University of California–Irvine and an expert on human memory, says genuine victims of abuse sometimes do not think about their experiences for a long time and not until reminded of them later. "Just because memories of abuse are fragmentary, or were not talked about for a long time," Loftus says, "doesn't rule them out."

Indeed, the Shorter sisters' memories form searing testimony.

"Did my father's behavior constitute abuse? Yes. Beyond the shadow of a doubt," says duPlessis, a registered nurse by profession, who works with abused and delinquent youths for the state of New Mexico. "Today, he'd be arrested in a minute. I would invite doubters of my father's crimes to have lived one day in my shoes. A six-year-old kid with belt wounds in her groin is not a sign of 'discipline,' even back in the 1960s."

"My father's abusive violence was unquestionably over the deep end," says Nanette Shorter. "I'd say it was psychotic. The terror we lived under is indescribable."

(Calls for comment made to a number listed for Ruth Shorter, Frank's 58-year-old sister, were not returned. Sam Jr. declined to comment for this story when contacted. Chris Shorter, 57, and Michael Shorter, 44, were not contacted due to their health and at the behest of their siblings. Another brother, Thomas, was born with severe health problems and died in the '60s.)

For his part, Frank insists his father's "discipline" constituted criminal abuse. "I'm not making this up," he says. "Why would I? I'd much rather have happy memories."

In 1950, the family left West Virginia and returned to Middletown, where Dr. Shorter hung out his GP's shingle. He made house calls. He delivered babies. He volunteered to cover other doctors' rounds on weekends and holidays. His work is still remembered in Middletown. If you go to the public library downtown, housed in the old passenger railroad station, Gail Myker, one of the reference librarians, will recall that Dr. Shorter treated her case of poison ivy. Ed Diana, a boyhood friend of Frank's who now serves as an Orange County executive, proclaimed a "Dr. Samuel Shorter Day" when the GP retired from practice in 1996.

"Dr. Shorter was a wonderful man," recalls Bill Bright, a 59-year-old Middletown resident. "He delivered my twin brother and me. Years later, when I heard he was dying, I went to visit him. I went into his room and just said a few words of thanks for all that he'd done for this town. His eyes were closed, and I didn't think he could hear me. But just as I was leaving, he opened his eyes and said, 'Bill, your coming here means a lot to me.' Then he started talking a blue streak about Middletown in the old days. I'll never forget that. Dr. Shorter was a great man."

By all evidence, the community never suspected that the great man showed a different face to his family. According to Shorter, his father carefully hid his ferocity. Another of Shorter's sisters, who also requested anonymity, corroborates her brother's claim. "The violence and abuse remained a secret because of our father's standing in the community," she says. "We children felt a lot of shame and guilt, and we never talked about it, even among ourselves."

"It's my opinion that my father had a profound narcissistic personality disorder," says duPlessis. "He was also brilliant and charismatic. It was a full-time job for him to pull off his double life, but he was a master at it."

Car trips and vacations, some of them coinciding with Dr. Shorter's save-the-world expeditions, formed the principal sustained periods that he spent with his children. They also served as an arena for the devastating psychological cruelty he inflicted. For instance, in 1959, when Frank was 12, Dr. Shorter decided to go to Cuba and serve as a missionary doctor. He piled his family into the Chevy Carryall, hooked up a 26-foot Airstream trailer, and started driving south. While the family was traveling, Fidel Castro and his revolutionaries took over Havana, and Americans could no longer travel freely to the island nation. So Dr. Shorter instead drove the family to Mexico for a vacation. Frank missed an entire quarter of school.

"From the outside, that trip seemed like a wonderful family adventure, but the reality was that it passed in an atmosphere of anxiety and fear," Shorter recalls. "At any moment my father might combust. He would carry road rage to ludicrous extremes."

On one occasion, Shorter remembers, a driver abruptly swerved back into the right lane after passing the Shorters' vehicle. His father grew enraged. He pulled out into the passing lane, floored the gas pedal, and pulled abreast of the offending driver. Then, employing the trailer as a battering ram, he tried to run the other car off the road. "All of this with his wife and children in the car with him," Shorter says. "It was like a scene from a bad Hollywood thriller. We were terrified."

Such car trips, though, couldn't match the torture of the seemingly innocuous house calls around Middletown Shorter often had to go on with his father. These outings were especially disturbing because, unlike family trips, the boy would be alone with his father. While in the car, Shorter says, his father would drive a wedge between Frank and his siblings. "My father would say how disappointed he was that his children were so lazy and selfish, and weren't honoring the sacrifices that he was making on their behalf. He knew that if he turned us against one another, it would strengthen his hold over us."

Shorter would go rigid with anxiety during his father's monologues. "I just tried to be quiet and compliant, to not disagree with him, to not say or do anything that might set him off. As I mentioned, he wasn't going to hit me in the car, where somebody from the town might see him."

Finally they'd arrive at the house of the patient, often a modest house in one of the working-class neighborhoods south of downtown. There, Shorter says, his father would affect his transformation from manipulative bully to beneficent healer. "He would take his bag and go into the house, leaving me in the car," Shorter says. "I would pass the time dreaming about the afternoon, when I could get away from my father."

Apart from the house and his family, the boy felt happy and free. Middletown was still small enough to explore on foot or bicycle, but large enough to remain fascinating, especially to a boy of Shorter's energy and intellect. He liked going to the public library, playing Little League baseball, and fishing on the lake, and he especially enjoyed trotting a few blocks up Highland Avenue to the YMCA, where he swam in the pool and battled to the top of the ping-pong ladder.

Due to his secret feelings of fear and shame, Shorter says, he never hosted friends in his house. Instead he became a fixture in their homes, where a prevailing atmosphere of affection and respect proved to the boy that a functional family life was possible. "I was especially close friends with a boy named Alec Preston, whose father was also a doctor," Shorter says. "A few times I drove up to Martha's Vineyard with the Prestons on their family vacations, and the contrast between those trips and riding with my father couldn't have been greater. Like my father, Dr. Preston did a great deal of pro bono work. Unlike my father, Dr. Preston didn't serve others to hide the shadow in his character."

Soon enough, though, Frank would have to return to the grand

Victorian that his mother could never control, and yet couldn't escape. Shorter remembers his mother as a quiet, intelligent woman and an accomplished painter who was bullied into near-total submission by her husband. "She almost never left the house," Shorter says. "She didn't have any friends and never socialized."

His mother's seclusion reached the point where it fell on Frank, when he was just nine, to do the family's grocery shopping. He would walk down East Main to the A&P, and then push the loaded cart uphill toward the house. Years later, his mother confided to Shorter that her social anxieties arose from fear rather than neurosis. "She told me that every time she left us alone in the house with our father, 'something bad' would happen to us," Shorter says. "My mother was so scared of my father, and so much in denial of his violence toward her children, that she couldn't say what those bad things were. She just stopped leaving us alone with him. Eventually, except on rare occasions, she stopped going out altogether." (One sister remembers Katherine in a less charitable light. "My mother was frightened of my father, but she also took a lot of pleasure in being a doctor's wife," she says. "I still feel anger toward her. Why didn't she do a better job protecting us?")

But home was bearable, Shorter says, as long as his father was absent. Dr. Shorter often worked late, making house calls or rounds at the hospital, and usually came home late in the evening. It was then, Shorter says, that his father would routinely administer the beatings that continued until he was about 10 years old.

Shorter says the beatings followed a similar pattern. Downstairs his father wouldn't so much converse with Frank's mother as cross-examine her. Listening in his bedroom above, Frank would hear his father's increasingly strident accusations and his mother's increasingly frantic demurrals as she vainly tried to protect her children. "He didn't really need a reason to attack," Shorter says. "All he required was the hint of a transgression, which he'd twist into justification."

At that point, Frank would typically hear his father's footsteps on the stairs. "I would listen to him running through our names as he decided which one of us he was going to whip," Shorter remembers. He would tense and wait. If Frank was that night's victim, he says, his bedroom door would fly open and his father would stand framed by the light of the hallway. If he came at Frank, it would almost be a relief. It was more excruciating to lie in bed and listen to one of his siblings absorb a beating, Shorter says, than to bear the blows himself.

"Frank felt responsible for us younger children," one sister says. "He was always trying to protect us."

Another sister, who recalls Dr. Shorter pulling her out of bed one night when she was 14 or 15, says that Frank tried to intervene on her behalf. "Frank was pulling on my father's arm, begging him to stop," she says.

When it was the boy's turn, Dr. Shorter would throw back the covers, pull Frank out of bed, and tear away his pajama pants to expose his bottom. Often Frank could smell liquor on his breath, which was both good news and bad. The bad news was that alcohol would juice his father's fury. The good news was that, if he were sufficiently enraged, he might grow befuddled and use the strap end of his belt instead of the buckle end.

But most often, Shorter says, his father employed the buckle end. Holding his second child with an outstretched left hand, he would apply the belt with the right, lashing Frank repeatedly. "He would hit me so hard that he grunted like a power-lifter," Shorter recalls. "I can still hear the *uh-huhh* of his voice as he got his weight behind each blow."

Shorter says that his father hit him with such anger, hatred, and pent-up rage that, even as he delivered the blows, Frank understood, in some small, dispassionate sector of his mind, that he wasn't responsible. "I realized that no crime I'd committed could possibly deserve this," Shorter says. "I also understood that this beating went far beyond the spankings that my friends occasionally endured from their parents. This was something much bigger and darker."

Shorter says that his father would whip him until his strength gave out. If he wept too loudly, Shorter remembers, his father would often mutter the bully's cliché: "Quit your blubbering or I'll really give you something to cry about."

"So I tried not to cry," Shorter says. "I isolated my pain where I could watch it and control it. That way I could keep it secret, and eventually I could forget it—or at least seem to forget it. The whippings were extremely painful, but my father was a doctor. He knew not to leave bruises that would show."

"He focused on our backs, bottoms, and the backs of our

thighs," duPlessis says. "And remember, our father was also our family doctor. We didn't see another pediatrician."

Another sister recalls suffering all day when, as a six-year-old, she wore a wool sweater to school: the fabric scratched the scabs off the welts on her back raised by her father's belt. Then there's Nanette, who remembers when, in junior high school, a concerned PE teacher asked about the bruises on her back and thighs. The girl was too ashamed and terrified to reply.

A piercing wind carries down from the Front Range above Boulder, driving storm clouds onto the plain; the weather has turned during Shorter's long, draining morning of remembering. Still recovering from hip-resurfacing surgery a year ago, and carefully rationing his running mileage, he breaks from the house for a brisk walk. As the years and aches accrue, Shorter says, he increasingly works out in the gym, building muscle mass and bone density against the leeching of age. But he appears sanguine about his years.

"I'm happy to be in my 60s and part of the redefinition of aging," he says, lacing up his shoes at the door. "For some reason I always seem to be locked in on the main theme of the baby boom generation. When our parents hit their sixties, they were old. We're not buying into that. I think it's an exciting age, and an interesting time."

Shorter hopes to run more marathons. (He has run approximately 60 over his career; the 1980 Olympic Marathon Trials, in which he finished in 2:23:24, was his final elite effort at the distance.) But for now his goals are more modest: to maintain his signature hauteur while running 10-minute miles, or in his words, "to slow down as gracefully as possible." One race, however, is circled in red on his calendar: the Classic 10-K in Middletown. The annual summer race is months away, but Shorter vows to toe the starting line this year after missing last year's with his hip injury.

Outside his front door, the Flatirons soar, appearing close enough to touch. You can taste the looming snow in the air. Shorter punches his watch and sets off, wearing a Russian-style hat with furry earflaps, his feet dancing lightly over snow crusted from earlier storms. As he moves he describes his daily routine: e-mail and phone calls early in the morning, some of it involving his continuing work on anti-doping issues, followed by a vigorous physical

workout at midmorning. Then more desk work, followed by another workout. "I consider myself embarked on a 40-year, ongoing
experiment in self-coaching," he says. "My goal has always been
to simplify my training to the point where it becomes absolutely
consistent."

He moves quietly for a moment, his breath chuffing in the
frigid air. "Now you know where that hunger for consistency
comes from," he says in a low voice. "What my childhood taught
me was to be eternally vigilant. Vigilance evolves into consistency.
I learned the solace of routine. I developed a way to ride my pain."
He gives a thin smile. "I guess you could say that's the perfect
background for a marathoner."

In the early 1960s, however, the marathon remained virtually
unthinkable; Frank Shorter had not yet given birth to the running boom. As Frank entered his upper-elementary-school years,
his mother spent increasing time sequestered in her attic studio.
In her way, however, she tried to help her children escape. She
arranged for Sam Jr. to audition for the choir at the Cathedral
School of St. John the Divine in New York City, a boarding school
that drew students from around the country. Frank tagged along
for the session. The school director listened to Sam sing, and then
asked his little brother if he wanted to try out. Frank nailed the
audition, exhibiting a high soprano voice, and thus Shorter spent
his sixth-grade year in Manhattan. At the end of the spring term,
however, Shorter decided to leave. He liked singing (later, at Yale,
he was a member of one of the singing groups on campus), but
not enough to give himself to it completely. He sensed that music
wouldn't form his true avenue of escape. So Shorter returned to
Middletown, still in search of it.

Little had changed at the big house on Highland Avenue. Now,
however, Frank was spared the beatings—at least the physical ones.
"I had gotten too big," he explains. "I represented too much of a
challenge for my father. There was the chance that I'd resist or
fight back. It was easier for him to beat on the younger children."

That fall Shorter started seventh grade at Middletown Junior
High School, two miles across town. At around the same time, he
got interested in ski racing. Reading up on the elite European
racers, he learned that they trained in the off-season by running
long distances. So Shorter started running the hilly two-mile route

back and forth from school. As he ran his father disappeared from his consciousness. The miles vanished with a similar dreamlike quality. Running was just as structured as music, and yet it had a fierce, unfettered, physical dimension. Also, he was good at it. On any day that the weather allowed, he covered the distance to and from school faster than the previous run. As the autumn wore on, Shorter kept running, but he forgot about ski racing. "I was already following my escape route," he says.

Two years later, again hoping to get Sam Jr. away from the house, Katherine Shorter arranged for him to take the entrance exam at Northfield Mount Hermon Academy, an elite prep school in western Massachusetts. As was the case at choir school, Frank tagged along to the admissions interview, and again school officials were more impressed by him than his brother. Frank, not Sam Jr., enrolled at Mount Hermon, which boasted one of the top cross-country programs in the Northeast. The following year, as a 10th-grader, he won the New England prep cross-country championship. Through his prep school years, he continued to excel as a student and athlete. In 1965, he enrolled at Yale, where he mostly employed running as a relief from studying. During his senior year, as academic pressure eased, Shorter intensified his training. A four-year series of dramatic breakthroughs followed, beginning with an NCAA championship in the six-mile and culminating, in 1972, with the Olympic gold medal.

"I was blessed to have outstanding coaches, Samuel Greene at Mount Hermon and, later, Bob Geigengack at Yale," Shorter says. "Both men believed in laying down a solid fundamental training program, and then letting the runner develop at his own pace. That was perfect for me. By my junior year at Yale, I was essentially coaching myself, which I continued doing postcollege."

Shorter adds that, besides using running to escape his childhood trauma and, later, academic pressure, he used the sport as a means of self-discovery. "I never went into a race focused on winning," he says. "I went in wanting to find out. That was even how I approached the marathon at the Munich Games. When I ran into the stadium and crossed the finish line, my first thought wasn't, *My God, I just won an Olympic gold medal!* And I didn't feel like I was taking revenge on my father. That was the whole point of running for me, to pursue to my utmost something that maybe he couldn't touch and couldn't beat out of me. Crossing that finish line in Munich, I told myself, *Yes! I got this one right.*"

A few weeks after our interview in Boulder, Shorter flies to Indiana to speak at the annual banquet of the Fort Wayne Track Club. His host picks him up at the airport and drives him not to the Marriott or Sheraton, but to the home of Brett Hess, a local runner. You might expect that the father of the running boom would find such small-market gigs tiresome, but Shorter swings into it with gusto.

First comes a supper with a small group of baby boomers and their kids. The boomers are Shorter's core audience, men around his age or a few years younger, who remember watching on TV as Shorter, in his drooping hippie mustache, powered to his Munich gold medal. These are the fans that thrilled to Shorter's friendly rivalry with Steve Prefontaine on the track. They remember that on a night in May 1975, after a track meet at Hayward Field in Eugene, Oregon, Prefontaine had dropped off Shorter at the house where he was staying and then sped away in his MGB convertible. Minutes later Prefontaine crashed into a rock outcropping and died under his overturned car.

These mostly graying men scarfing macaroni casserole with Shorter might've had a photo of the great marathoner up on their college dorm walls. Maybe that black-and-white shot of Shorter gliding through the streets of Munich, running all alone for the final nine miles, or the picture of him on the medal platform, standing proudly yet circumspectly as the gold medal was laid around his neck, mute proof that in 1972, during all the clamor and doubt of the Vietnam War era, an American man could prevail in a race of supreme difficulty.

This mythic figure, Frank Shorter, sits rumple-haired across the kitchen table from them, unreeling one of his greatest hits. He tells the story of the Munich Massacre at the '72 Games, of waking up on the dorm balcony because his roommate, the 800-meter runner Dave Wottle, was honeymooning with his bride in their bedroom. Shorter describes staring across the courtyard at a hooded terrorist holding an Uzi. Shorter tells of following the events on local TV in those pre-CNN days, with Prefontaine translating because he grew up speaking German. Shorter tells of agonizing with Kenny Moore about how to approach the Olympic Marathon, Moore choosing to dedicate his race to the 11 murdered Israeli athletes, Shorter saying no, the thing is to not give the horror a thought, to shut the pain away in a small, still spot inside of you, to block it out with discipline and order, and to channel your anger, guilt, and fear into the unforgiving yet redemptive act of running, one foot in front of the other.

Shorter did not tell his good friends Kenny Moore or Steve Prefontaine, nor does he tell the starstruck men in this bright kitchen on a dark winter night nearly 40 years later, the true source of his discipline, the silent boyhood suffering that taught Frank Shorter how to ride his pain.

In 1967, when Frank was at Yale, Dr. Shorter left Middletown to work at a medical mission hospital in Taos, New Mexico, and father and son were basically estranged for the rest of Dr. Shorter's life. In New Mexico, according to Frank and his sisters, Katherine rebelled at her husband's violent abuse of the couple's youngest child, a son who is developmentally disabled. The couple separated and divorced around 1978. By then, Dr. Shorter had returned to Middletown, where he resumed his medical practice and later remarried. (His second wife, Marianne Shoemaker Shorter, still lives in Middletown. During an attempt to contact Mrs. Shorter by phone, a woman who identified herself as Mrs. Shorter's caretaker said that the abuse cited by Dr. Shorter's children "never happened"; the woman declined further comment.)

In 1972, after Shorter won his gold medal in Munich, Middletown staged a welcome-home party for its native son. The town fathers sent a limousine down to JFK Airport to pick him up. Back in Middletown, Frank was presented with an additional surprise—his father had driven 2,000 miles across the country to attend the event. That was the occasion when the emcee called Dr. Shorter a great humanitarian. A newspaper photo of the event shows Frank hugging his father with apparent affection. In fact, Shorter says, he was only feeling awkward. "My father turned away from me just as I started to greet him," Frank remembers. "He made a big show out of being proud of me. But he was really there to grab as much of the limelight as he could. In fact, he said he didn't even watch my Olympic Marathon on TV. He said it made him too nervous."

"Frank had barely crossed the finish line in Munich when my father started criticizing him," says duPlessis, who still lived with her parents in New Mexico at the time. "'Oh boy, Frank's going to get a big head now,' he said. My father competed against his own children. He didn't want to see any of us succeed—and that applied to Frank even after he won the gold medal. Instead of being proud, or simply letting us be proud of him, my father did everything he could to undermine Frank's accomplishment."

In 1982, Dr. Shorter made a brief visit to Frank's home in Boulder after his second child was born. (Each of Shorter's two 13-year marriages ended in divorce; he has two children by his first wife and one by his second.) At the time, Shorter owned a dog named Smokey. One morning his father stepped outside to pick up the newspaper, and Smokey tried to follow him. Frank says Dr. Shorter slammed the door on the dog, breaking one of its ribs. "That'll teach you to try and escape," Shorter recalls his father saying.

Shorter decided at that moment to never allow his father around his children, and they grew up with no relationship with their grandfather. "I just told them that it wasn't good for him to be around children," Shorter says. "And my kids never questioned that. I think they sensed something was wrong about him. And because of my experience with my father, I never raised a finger against my children. Privately, my purpose in life has always been to stop the cycle of violence."

With the publication of this story, Shorter says, he'll begin to state that purpose in detail and in public. Already, he says, ventilating old secrets has had a healing effect. "My father's violence, and his complete lack of love and respect, profoundly affected all of us," Shorter says, referring to himself and his siblings. "Several of us have struggled with issues ranging from substance abuse to the inability to trust or maintain relationships." The most severe instance involves Sam Jr., who was convicted in 1989 by the Orange County Court of the State of New York for felony sexual abuse and sentenced to one to three years at Downstate Correctional Facility.

"There's been a tragic waste of potential," Shorter continues. "Most of us haven't kept in contact with one another because we don't have many happy memories to share. Now, as word of this story gets out among us, I see lines of communication opening."

At times, however, the communication has proved painful. For instance, Frank was unaware of his sisters' claims of rape before they discussed them for this article. "I believe it," he says, his voice shaking with anger.

"I still don't intend to jump on any bandwagon," he adds. "I'm not going to suddenly bill myself as a spokesman on this issue. But at the same time, in certain situations, in front of certain audiences, I think I have something to offer. For a big chunk of my life, I felt like the only way I could contribute—the only way I could survive—was by burying the memories of my father. Now I feel just as strongly that the best way I can contribute is by talking about what he did. In the end, I'll likely approach the issue of my father's abuse just like I have my running. I want to find out. I want to get it right."

In mid-June, Frank Shorter hits the road again, traveling to Middletown for the 2011 Classic 10-K. He drives up from Newark Airport two hours behind schedule on the night before the race, thus missing the Orange County Runners Club dinner at a downtown restaurant. During the meal a woman named Valerie Kilcoin comes up to the bar. "Frank's going to be exhausted when he finally makes it in," she says.

Kilcoin explains that she and her husband have hosted Shorter for the last five or six years when he's returned for the Classic. "Frank's great," she says. "He's no trouble at all. He loves coming home to Middletown."

There's no hint of irony in Kilcoin's voice, no sign that, during his visits over the years, Shorter might have confided to her about his father's abuse. "He doesn't talk too much about his childhood," she says, adding that she grew up in the same neighborhood as the Shorter family and went to school with one of Frank's sisters. "I didn't really know him then, but I remember watching him run past our place when he came home from prep school and college. He was such a beautiful runner. He lived in that big beautiful house with his doctor father. He seemed like the happiest, luckiest guy in the world."

Other townspeople, however, know about the shadow. "The real story of Frank Shorter lies right here in Middletown with his relationship with his family," says Frank Giannino, a codirector of the Classic. "We know that the relationship wasn't all good. We learned that back in '91 when Frank first talked about it to the press. The consensus around town is that Dr. Shorter carried normal corporal punishment—normal for the time anyway—to an extreme. Today we might consider that child abuse." Giannino pauses, choosing his words carefully. "This area, this part of New

York State, is a little bit different," he says. "A lot of families go way back to the Dutch settlers. Middletown has a lot of stories, and a lot of secrets."

Many residents, clearly, prefer that the secrets remain sealed. "No way could Dr. Shorter have done those things to his kids," says Bill Bright, the man whom Dr. Shorter delivered. "In my opinion it's just not possible."

Kevin Gleason, a sportswriter for the *Times Herald-Record* in Middletown, wrote a column about Frank Shorter's appearance at the 2008 Classic, which fell on the day of Dr. Shorter's death. "I debated whether to mention the trouble between Frank and his father, and finally put in one sentence about it," Gleason says. "Some readers called to complain. They thought I'd been disrespectful of Dr. Shorter. They have so much respect, pride, and gratitude for Frank, but they have an equal affection for his father."

Race morning in Middletown breaks cool and overcast. "A no-excuse morning," Shorter tells the field of about 60 at the start of the 5-K. He's decided that he's not up to the 10-K, but can handle this shorter distance. At the starting line, as he's done here for the last 30 years, he welcomes the field of runners. He tells the story of running to school as a seventh-grader, carrying his books in his left arm in those prebackpack days. "Even today I hardly move my left arm when I run," he says, and the crowd laughs appreciatively, basking in the presence of a man who is both legend and local hero. You wonder how Shorter will be received at the start of next year's race, when his relationship with his father will be more widely known.

And then the race is on. Shorter runs once more through Middletown, along the streets he covered as a boy. He moves with a light, tentative stride, mindful of his hip, but manages to look graceful logging 10-minute miles. When runners pass him, they give a shy, respectful greeting, careful not to intrude on his privacy, or to violate that odd sense of distance that Dick Beardsley talked about, that ineffable but unmistakable cone of dignity and loneliness that has always enclosed the father of the running boom.

"Way to go, Frank!" the guys in front of the firehouse yell to him. "Thanks for coming back!" hollers a man at the water station.

Over the last mile, with the crowd at the finish at the high school stadium within earshot, Shorter breaks his race-long silence. "See that house with the van in the driveway?" he says, pointing. "That's the house where I last saw my father, the day before the 2008 Classic. He was dying from kidney failure. He was in a sort of semiconscious daze by then, but when I saw him his eyes were opened wide and staring at me. And while he couldn't talk, I could see the pathological anger was still there. I said what I had to say and left pretty quickly. The next day, after the race, I flew back to Boulder. When I landed, I found out that he'd died while I was in flight. I didn't come back for the funeral service. I didn't see the need."

The noise from the stadium grows louder. "I've thought about what this story will mean for the people of Middletown," Shorter continues. "I'm aware that it might make people uncomfortable. But the story isn't about them—it's about my father. I love the people here. Why else would I keep coming back each year? I wouldn't have survived without my friends in this town. I'm not trying to hurt them. The truth can only help. Maybe some kid going through the same thing will get counseling. I wish my sisters and brothers and I had gotten help. I wish all the tools and awareness that are available now were around when we were growing up.

"I wish my father had gotten help," Frank Shorter says finally, making the course's last turn and, to the rising, enduring cheers of his old hometown crowd, running alone into the stadium.

BILL DONAHUE

Fixing Diane's Brain

FROM RUNNER'S WORLD

EVERY FEW SECONDS, there's another flash in the darkness, and for an instant you see them—the jubilant Chinese ultramarathon runners, lit up, posing for photographs. At 5:00 A.M. on this day last May, roughly 200 of them are gathered in the chill that envelops Juyongguan, China, where the ancient Great Wall lures millions of tourists annually from nearby Beijing. And never mind that the North Face 100, the exasperating 62-mile race that awaits them, offers some 2,100 feet of vertical climbing. Nearly all of them are spritzing around as though they're about to embark on a champagne cruise.

Everyone is taking digital photos of everyone else. One wizened 58-year-old racer, Bian Jinghai, is wearing an orange bandanna pirate-style and inexplicably shouting, "Mao Zedong is up there, and I am down here," as he dances about like a prizefighter poised to enter the ring. Another older runner vows to race barefoot, in homage to Mother Earth, and tiny, 92-pound Xu Yuan Shan, who claims to have once run a 2:45 marathon, is raging around Nixon-like, flashing the victory sign at myriad cameramen.

Amid this morning's starting line mayhem, though, one athlete, an American, is almost totally still. Diane Van Deren is standing off to the side, by the shuttered Great Wall souvenir stands, wearing sunglasses and a fresh, glistening coat of sunscreen as her husband, Scott, holds her close, quietly offering counsel.

Van Deren is 50, and she's traveled from her Colorado home as an athlete sponsored by the North Face, the race organizer. In the days before the race, Van Deren has proven a sprightly and winning spokesperson for the outdoor apparel company. Five feet nine inches tall, and blond with blue eyes, she exudes a windblown good cheer and a certain renegade spark. She's promoted running in near-religious terms. "When I run in the mountains, that's my medicine," she told the Chinese journalists during a press conference. "That's my heart." She's also told the story of how she once ran up 14,110-foot Pikes Peak in Colorado, and then hitched a ride down on the back of a stranger's Harley. She's a jaunty jock who travels nearly everywhere in pastel-bright running togs, and she's a sentimental mother of three 20-something kids. Back in Beijing, she brought a roomful of reporters to their feet by singing, a cappella, a song she'd written herself about her son, a Marine who until recently was driving a Humvee through the battlefields of Iraq.

Now, however, Van Deren is silent. Her face is impassive behind her wraparound shades. This race—every race—looms large for her. Her running career is the culmination of a long and trying saga.

For nearly 17 years, until she was 37, Van Deren suffered from epilepsy, enduring hundreds of seizures, sometimes as often as two or three times in a week. With each seizure, she lost consciousness for about a minute. Usually, her body just went limp as she stared off into space. But there were also the two dozen or so grand mal seizures she suffered, when her muscles radically contracted and her legs and arms flailed uncontrollably. With each seizure came the distinct chance that she could die. Rather than risk death, she did the next best thing: she let doctors drill a hole into her skull.

In 1997, Van Deren underwent a partial right temporal lobectomy. Doctors removed a portion of her brain that was the focal point of her seizures. The surgery ended her epilepsy; Van Deren hasn't seized once since the operation. But the surgeon's work created a blind spot in the upper left part of her vision. And there is also the residual neural damage from the seizures. She cannot track time well; she is always running late, and she has almost no sense of direction. Her memory is weak—she can't recall where, exactly, she took her honeymoon—and when she's confronted with excessive sensory noise, as she is now, at this clamorous starting line, she gets weary and irritable. Sometimes Van Deren needs to lie down and nap for hours.

She is an ultra-marathoner with extraordinary limitations. In races she must cover hundreds of miles, and yet often has no idea how long she has been running—or where she is going.

Still, Van Deren's surgery may actually have aided her distance running. "The right side of the brain, where Diane had surgery, is involved in processing emotion," says one of her doctors, Don Gerber, a clinical neuropsychologist at Craig Hospital in Denver. "The surgery affected the way she processes her emotional reaction to pain. I'm not saying Diane doesn't *feel* pain, but pain is a complex process. You have a sensory input, and then the question is: how does the brain interpret that? Diane's brain interprets pain differently than yours or mine does."

Gerber's assessment is controversial among neurologists, and all that's certain, really, is that Van Deren has almost primordial gifts of endurance. In February 2008, in the Canadian Yukon, she won the Yukon Arctic Ultra, spending nearly eight days pulling a 50-pound supplies sled 300 miles and through temperatures that plunged to around 50 below. The next winter she covered 430 miles. And once, in Alaska, she trudged 85 miles through snow on a sprained ankle after stepping in a moose hole.

This race in China will be, relatively speaking, a cakewalk. Still, it begins by scrambling up about 1,000 steep steps carved into the Great Wall itself. "Dear runners," says the race starter, speaking in stiff, stilted English as she summons the runners to the line. "Dear runners."

When the race starts, the field erupts with hoots of applause. Van Deren moves forward, quietly, her head down.

Diane Van Deren first experienced brain trauma when she was 16 months old. Otherwise healthy, she came down one day with a high fever. She was rushed to a hospital near her childhood home in Omaha, Nebraska. Nurses packed her quivering body in ice, but still she trembled for almost an hour. The seizure was not extraordinary. About 5 percent of American children endure a fever-induced seizure before age five. Most never seize again. For many years, it seemed Van Deren would end up in that lucky majority.

As a kid, she played catcher on a boys' baseball team, going by the name Dan and shoving her pigtails under her cap. As a teenager, she was a Colorado state champion in tennis and golf. She left high school early to spend four years touring the United States and Europe as a professional tennis player. She also ran a bit to keep fit. In 1982, at the age of 22 and on a whim, she entered a marathon in southwest Texas and won the women's division.

Her infantile seizure had scarred a small portion of her right brain, though, and the cells there were vulnerable to reinjury. In her twenties, without even being aware of it, Van Deren began having tiny seizures. They didn't manifest as convulsions, but rather as subtle perceptual shifts. Out on the tennis court, or while relaxing at home, she had what she calls "funny sensations. It was like a déjà vu feeling," she says, "like you're in a dream, and you're thinking, *Oh, what's happening right now has happened to me before.* You feel like you're floating; it's an out-of-body experience."

Lasting just seconds, these mini-seizures were "auras," in neurological parlance. Auras are the first stage of a full-blown epileptic attack. Dr. Mark Spitz, the University of Colorado neurologist who would later order Van Deren's surgery, describes them as an electrical phenomenon. The brain, he explains, consists of millions of cells that are "wired" to one another to transmit sensory, motor, and processing data. "When an aura occurs," he says, "it's like the beginning of a fire in the brain. That fire can grow so that the person is increasingly vulnerable to stronger seizures."

None of this was evident, though, when Diane and Scott Van Deren met in 1982. The two were recent college graduates, and he was taken by her larksome spirit and drive. At the time Diane was training for the Ironman World Championship. She was a novelty—Ironwomen were still rare then—and Scott was smitten. "She seemed spontaneous," he says. "She seemed fun."

The Van Derens married when they were both 23. A few years later Scott went to work for Mountain Steel & Supply, founded by Diane's father. Diane worked there herself, in sales, but lasted only six months—and never pursued another desk job. "Office work has never been my thing," she says. She taught aerobics instead, and kept running, sometimes five miles, sometimes 20, a day. When the mood struck, she entered a local triathlon.

By the time Diane was 28, she was pregnant with her third child. Her brain was at the mercy of hormonal shifts. One night, as he lay in bed, sleeping, Scott awoke to the sound of his wife having a grand mal seizure. "She was violently shaking," Scott says. "I'd never seen a [grand mal] before." Diane had been diagnosed with epilepsy due to an attack earlier in that pregnancy, and now, Scott says, "I thought to myself, *Here we go.* I knew that we were entering a new chapter in our lives. I moved a lamp, so she wouldn't knock it over, and then I called 911."

For years afterward, Scott would lie awake in bed, intently listening. "I got very in tune with Diane's breathing," he says. "Snoring was a good thing; it meant she was getting some peaceful rest." But there were more seizures, and when their children were small, says Scott, the household "revolved around how Diane was feeling. There was constant worry over when she'd have her next seizure." Each one crushed her. "I'd feel like I'd been run over by a truck," Diane recalls. Depending on the severity of the seizure, she'd take to bed for two or three days. Nannies were hired to drive the children and to clean the house.

Throughout all the trauma, though, Diane evolved a rare trick: she learned to abort her seizures by running.

She had noticed that her attacks usually occurred when she was resting—at the movie theater, say, or in a quiet restaurant. Her brain cells were "idle" then, as Dr. Spitz explains it, and as such more prone to "catch fire" when an abnormal seizure discharge occurred. What she needed to do was to activate brain cells quickly, the instant she felt an aura come on. Few people can do this, Spitz says, but Van Deren kept her running shoes by the door, and whenever that eerie déjà vu feeling settled upon her, she stood up and rushed toward those shoes. "I knew that I only had a few seconds," she says. "I had to get moving."

Dr. Spitz says Van Deren's seizures always began in her right hippocampus, a small sea horse–shaped ridge that sits deep within the brain, storing and retrieving memories. "Running," he says, "probably activated the part of the hippocampus where seizures started. When the cells there were active, they didn't accept the abnormal electrical activity, and the seizure fizzled out."

She laced up her shoes and started running—out her driveway and then over ranchers' tawny, fenced rangeland in the rural area outside of Denver. "I'd go right out into a forest," she says. "I'd be anxious, but there was a softness to being outdoors. I felt the pine needles underfoot on the trail, and listened to the birds. It calmed me. I kept running. The point was to just keep my mind going, my body moving. I'd run until I'd broken the cycle of the seizure. Sometimes I'd run for two or three hours."

*

After climbing up the Great Wall, the race course rolls onto back roads. Then, roughly 12 kilometers into the race, it climbs to its highest point, at 2,477 feet, offering a hazy view of Beijing 30 miles away. From the ridgetop, it's a steep, pounding descent into Tiger Valley, where, near the 19-K mark, race officials have festooned several desolate cliffs with 20-foot-high red-and-white banners.

Scott Van Deren and I are standing beside these banners, on the bank of a river, in the morning coolness, waiting. Van Deren is a big man—six-four and quite fit, thanks to a weight-room regimen and a heavy cycling habit. His voice is deep, and his manner toward his wife protective and steady. In 1995, when Diane was suffering frequent seizures, he moved the family to their current home on a 35-acre windswept property in Sedalia, Colorado, in part so that Diane could be around horses. "There's something therapeutic about brushing horses," he says.

Scott now owns the family steel business. He has the confident air of a man accustomed to getting things done, but at this moment he can only peer with hope up the mountain path as the runners start trickling down toward us, their voices echoing in the narrow canyon. First comes a boyish-looking Chinese student, 23-year-old Yun Yan Qiao, bounding through in one hour, 39 minutes. The first woman—43-year-old Zhang Huiji—comes through at 1:57. More than 20 minutes later, Scott Van Deren is still waiting. "I expect her any moment," he says.

Scott has waited helplessly like this before. In 2008, at the North Face Ultra-Trail du Mont-Blanc, Diane started the 103-mile race with a fever and began shaking as she ran. Twice she stopped to sleep for an hour—something she'd never done before. It took her more than 40 hours to finish. Today, after two hours and 22 minutes, she finally comes through the 19-K mark, in eighth place in the women's race, running at a 12-minute, 15-second pace. She's not far off from where she should be, really. By her standards this race is a sprint—it doesn't play to her strengths—and at 50, she's older than all but one woman beating her. Still, Scott is worried. "My instinct is this isn't her day," he says. "She looks tight."

Indeed, Van Deren's face is a tense mask, her stride slightly halting and choppy. She strained her Achilles a few months earlier during a predawn run. It's been stiff ever since. But it's impossible to discern if Van Deren's in pain, for she's dialed into the race.

When she comes to the aid station at 26-K, now in seventh place, Scott can only try to get through to her by delivering one clear message that he's carefully rehearsed in his mind. "Get your pace," he says. "You've got three big climbs ahead."

Scott isn't a coach. He's never been a runner. His advice isn't necessarily astute. It's chivalrous. For a few seconds he runs beside Diane. "You look great, babe," he shouts as she gulps down some water.

"I'm outta here," says Diane. She tosses the water bottle and then breaks into a trot.

When Van Deren first began having grand mal seizures in 1988, she refused to give in to them. Unable to drive, she walked to the supermarket, three miles away, pregnant, and pushing her two infant children in a stroller. Then she walked home, with the groceries in a backpack. Once her kids grew, she went downhill skiing—and wrapped her arms around the back of the chairlift each time she boarded, so she wouldn't fall out if she seized.

The auras kept coming, though, and sometimes Van Deren didn't grab her running shoes fast enough. She seized, and more cells in her brain died, and more rewired, and as a result her prelude-like auras shortened and shortened. "The seizures," she says, "overtook my body and my confidence. I tried to dig deep and hide my confusion. I didn't want my kids to feed off my fear."

Nonetheless, Michael Van Deren, the Marine, says that his mom's illness permeated his childhood. He remembers his mother once having a grand mal attack in the living room when he was seven and his dad was away for the weekend. "It was full-blown," says Michael, who is now 24. "She was clenching her teeth. I yelled at Robin and Matt"—his younger siblings—"to leave the room. I didn't want them to see that."

Scott Van Deren adds, "Diane's epilepsy absolutely dominated the relational pattern of the family. The second I walked in from work, I'd ask, 'How's Mom? What's she doing?' I couldn't rest." The next seizure was always a threat. Once, when Scott was treating customers to dinner at a restaurant in Vail, Diane seized at the table. "It was a casual meeting on a summer day," he says, "and we hadn't discussed Diane's epilepsy with those people."

But the seizure that pains Diane most, in hindsight, happened when her daughter, Robin, now 22, was in grade school. Diane was coaching Robin's basketball team, and at a game, before hundreds of spectators, Diane says, "I had this aura and the next thing I knew the other coach was standing over me, saying, 'Diane, is everything okay?'" The gym went silent. "I was out of control," Diane says, woefully re-creating the moment. "I couldn't control myself, and I hurt for my children: they had to see their mom having a grand mal seizure right on the gym floor."

Dr. Spitz wanted to send Van Deren to surgery, but he could operate only if he could identify the source of her seizures. To do so, he brought her into the hospital, deprived her of meds, and then attached electrodes to her scalp to measure electrical activity. She proceeded to have three seizures over the next four days. A videotape of one, a grand mal, shows Diane biting her tongue and then gurgling audibly on the bloody saliva in her throat.

Dr. Spitz isolated Diane's problems to her right hippocampus. She'd be seizure-free, probably, if the damaged tissue there was excised. Spitz saw surgery as Van Deren's safest path. Without it, her seizures were likely to become more severe and more frequent, he explained, and she faced about a 10 percent chance of dying from a seizure over the next 10 years. The surgery, in contrast, delivered just a 3 percent chance of a stroke. "I was calling Spitz's office over and over, trying to get into surgery right away," says Diane. "I was in fear of dying of a seizure."

Scott was more measured. He insisted they seek a second opinion. Again, surgery was recommended. So in February 1997, in Denver, a neurological team operated on Diane's brain. Using a high-speed drill, the surgeon removed an outer section of bone from her skull. He cut deeper, into the brain's dura, or protective membrane, and then focused a microscope on the exposed temporal lobe. Using an aspirator, he excised part of the lobe along with the affected portion of the hippocampus.

A few hours after Van Deren awoke, she felt "horrific pain." And it seems that her innate stubbornness kicked in. There was a shunt lodged in her skull, to drain blood, and she tried to tear it out. According to Scott, "She tried to get out of the room. A doctor and two nurses had to strap her into the bed, and she tried to bite one of them. Then she kicked a nurse."

The doctors had to remove the partially dislodged shunt, exacerbating the pressure in Van Deren's head. "When I went in to see her," Scott says, "she was like a combative animal. She said, 'Get me out of here. Why are you letting them do this to me? I hate you.' She called me every name in the book—f'ing this, f'ing that."

"The brain is very personal," Diane would explain later. "It doesn't like be messed with."

By the time Van Deren reaches the aid station at 32-K, she remains in seventh place. She has blood on her arms and her shins. While running on rubbly dirt a few miles back, and staring downward in search of good footing, she couldn't see the low branches surrounding the narrow trail due to her poor peripheral vision. A couple of times she had tripped and fallen down. But she continued to press on. "I just listen to my feet when I run," she had told me earlier, "and I try to get a rhythm going. I breathe in two steps. I breathe out two steps."

At one point, Scott Van Deren and I ride in a van alongside Diane. We're so close to her that we can hear her footfalls. "Get mad," Scott yells out the window. "Get mad now!"

"You got any gels?" Diane asks. "Got any gels?"

We don't. There'll be nothing for her to eat until the 44-K mark. She sucks at her energy drink and keeps running.

What Diane Van Deren remembers most from the weeks following the surgery is the pain. "Every time I'd bend down, it hurt," she says. "Even tying my shoes, I felt like my head was going to explode from the pressure. I played golf, and when I put the tee in, my head just throbbed." She was eager to run again, however, and roughly a month after the operation, she did, covering 10 miles, gingerly. "I tried to hold my head as steady as possible," she says. Still, she kept running every day. "The mountains were my safe zone. I was at peace there."

Having worked with many patients who had undergone surgeries similar to Van Deren's, Dr. Spitz says the weeks, months, and even years after such an operation can be as emotionally challenging as they are physically. "You need to figure out what your future in this world is without having seizures," Spitz explains. "And that can be harder than you might think. I've seen many divorces take place after the surgery. In the years before her surgery, Diane had pretty much stopped competing because of the seizures. She had become very dependent on her family. Now she had to figure out what to do with her new life."

For a while, Van Deren seemed content to live in the moment. When she ran, her husband says, it wasn't about competing; it was about "being free and outside." Van Deren could cover 20 miles on the trails, and when she was done feel invigorated versus being exhausted. And then she would run a little farther.

Finally, in 2002, roughly five years after her surgery, she entered a low-key race—a 50-mile Colorado trail run in which there was only one other entrant. "The race director had to run along with them through the first few miles," Scott says, "to show them the route." Diane finished, in a tie with the other runner, and soon she was dreaming big. Later that year she signed up for the Hardrock 100, which climbs more than 30,000 feet in the Colorado Rockies. "If I could get through years of seizures and then brain surgery," she says, "I could take this baby on. I could do it."

Hardrock's race director stifled Van Deren's race plan, though—she previously needed to have finished at least one 100-mile ultra. Undeterred, she jumped into another 100-miler, this one starting in Leadville, Colorado, elevation 12,600 feet. She ran for about 70 miles, twisted her knee, and continued to hobble on. When Van Deren finally dropped out at the 72-mile mark, her desire to run, and to compete, had only intensified.

She began planning for her next 100-mile race, and, Van Deren told a friend, Kathy Pidcock, "I expect to win it." Pidcock, who was then an elite ultrarunner, crafted for Van Deren a rugged training program—a 100-mile-per-week regimen heavy on high-altitude training and back-to-back 25-mile outings. "Whatever I told her to do, she did," says Pidcock. "She never questioned me, and she was so strong. I knew she would make it." She did. In June 2003, Van Deren completed the Bighorn Trail 100 Mile Run, in Wyoming, in 31 hours, 54 minutes, finishing sixth in the women's race. She figured, "I've done it. That's my last one."

Two days later, though, she talked to a roomful of grade-schoolers with epilepsy at a camp in Colorado. "These were kids who had 20 or 30 seizures a day," she says. "They were having seizures right in front of me, and one of them, a girl named Mandy, asked, 'Are you going to run another 100-mile race?'"

Van Deren's feet were still swollen; her shins were bruised from postholing in snowfields. But Mandy persisted: "Will you run your next 100-miler for me? I can't run. I have seizures."

"I felt guilty," Van Deren says. "I thought, *If I could only give them a piece of what I've felt overcoming my epilepsy. . . .*"

Soon, Van Deren was the first woman finisher in the San Diego 100-Mile Endurance Run, placing second overall. Then in 2004, over a six-month period, she ran seven ultras, including three longer than 95 miles. In 2004, after finally being accepted into the race, she was the ninth-place woman at the Hardrock 100.

How did Van Deren rise so suddenly from obscurity? Granted, she'd already proven herself a world-class athlete, but that was in tennis, a very different sport. And she'd run some, sure. But what enabled her to knock off so many ultras, so speedily, with so little recovery time? Each year, thousands of Americans have epilepsy surgery. Can we expect some of them to start flourishing in endurance sports with new and magical pain tolerance?

Dr. Gerber credits her endurance in part to her brain limitations. He says runners who can better track time and map where they are can be distracted by the details. But Van Deren has a special facility for what he calls "flow" that lets her transcend the anguish of running long. "It's a mental state," Gerber says. "You become enmeshed in what you're doing. It's almost Zen. She can run for hours and not know how long she's been going."

But Dr. William Theodore, chief of the clinical epilepsy division at the National Institutes of Health, says no evidence exists that epilepsy surgery will cause a change in pain tolerance. "Certain parts of the brain are related to pain, but they're very deep structures. They're almost never involved in epilepsy surgery."

Another expert, Dr. Jerome Engel, director of the UCLA Seizure Disorder Center, says the majority of epilepsy patients who undergo partial lobectomies do not experience either diminished brain function or changes in character. Still, Engel calls Van Deren an "atypical case." While he has never examined her, he's struck by reports of her unusual postsurgical cognitive problems—of her trouble with getting lost, for instance. To him, such symptoms suggest that her brain bears "bilateral damage"; in other words, her presurgical seizures could have scarred both lobes of her brain. If that is the case, Engel suggests, "it could affect her pain tolerance." He explains that the electrical shocks involved in a seizure cause the brain to release its own opioids, or pain relievers. When both sides of the brain have endured seizures, the opioids' effect is, Engel says, "more powerful."

One medical professional who worked directly with Van Deren thinks the equation is simpler. "Diane was a great athlete before surgery, and she's still a great athlete," says Mark Spitz, her original doctor. "The surgery didn't change that."

Van Deren herself disagrees, slightly. "The surgery helped," she says, "because it was painful. I learned how to endure pain. But I've always been superfocused and stubborn." Van Deren argues that her gift lies in keeping up the fight—in refusing to wallow in sadness, even amid the trials of epilepsy and her current impairments. During a recent 50-mile race, she says, "a guy knocked me off the trail in the first mile. I rolled my ankle all the way over and just kept running, for 49 miles more, even though a PT thought it was broken. Here's why I'm good: I don't give up."

At about 45-K, the North Face 100 cuts through a small village, and the course markers are nowhere to be seen. Several runners get lost, and our guide—Sky Song, a young North Face marketing rep—gets a call: the top 10 runners are stalled at a country store. We begin flying toward them. En route, we see diminutive Xu Yuan Shan, the 2:45 marathoner, churning along, just off the lead pack. "Get in the van," Sky cries out the window. "You're lost!"

Xu climbs in, sweaty and winded, and then Song keeps rolling. The leaders elude him, though. Some, but not all, catch a ride back to the course from a policeman, and soon there's another snafu. When leader Yun Yan Qiao hits the 50-K aid station, he looks for the drop bag he packed the night before with extra socks and snacks. Race organizers were supposed to bring each runner's bag to this station, but Yun's isn't here. In exasperation, he drops out. Later, when Van Deren learns that Yun quit, she's disgusted. "He could have finished," she hisses. "So many people in ultras lose it when one thing crumbles. You just can't do that."

Van Deren doesn't. In 2008, in the Yukon Arctic Ultra, her water bottles froze solid—for 20 miles, she ran without a drop. A few days later, she reached the Yukon River in 70-mile-per-hour winds and didn't know which way to go. As the wind tossed her to her knees, she began marking her way with red tape. She went in one direction for an hour. When it appeared that was the wrong way, she doubled back, patiently. She kept at it for four hours and eventually found her way.

Now, in China, Van Deren's caught in another long struggle. All day, there's been a phenom running ahead of her—a chipper young Chinese woman in navy knee-length pants, a red collared shirt, and cheap gray running sneakers. Zheng Rufang, 28, is primarily a cyclist. She trains with the Chinese national team, and she's dressed, she'll say later, to signal, "I am not a runner. I know nothing about running." About 75 kilometers into the race, her inexperience starts to show. Climbing a small mountain, up hundreds of concrete steps, past little Buddhist shrines carved into the cliffs of the Yinshan Pagoda Forest, she's worn out—dragging. There's another Chinese woman just ahead of her. And when Van Deren chugs up behind them, out of sight but closing, it's as though she can smell the roadkill.

"How far ahead are they?" she asks as she passes me on the stairs. Her cool reserve is gone now, more than 11 hours into the race. Her face is sunburned, and there's an edge of wild hunger to her voice.

"About three minutes," I say.

Van Deren cranes her neck skyward, looking for them.

For all her ambition, Diane Van Deren can seem very vulnerable. On a trip to Beijing in 2009, she got lost for two hours after leaving her hotel for a run. It was the sort of misadventure that could befall any tourist, but the incident still looms for Van Deren as terrifying: worrisome proof of her limitations. She remembers being on the verge of tears and desperately beseeching directions, in shouted English, from the white-gloved soldiers who stand on small pedestals all over Beijing, stock still, at attention. The Chinese businessman who eventually saved her, leading her by the hand for more than a mile, back to her hotel, still shines for her as a saint.

Van Deren's general disorientation could prove fatal in competition—what if she took a wrong turn in the Arctic?—but she insists that it is also an anguishing impediment at home, in day-to-day life. She forgets appointments, she says, and cannot remember people's faces. Once at a family gathering, when everyone was asked to name their favorite Christmas, she drew a blank. "So many emotions were packed into those 10 seconds," she says, "Sadness, frustration, embarrassment. You don't know how much pain these disabilities have brought me. It's challenged my relationships with my family and friends."

Donald Gerber, the neuropsychologist, has provided her counsel over the past six years. He meets informally with Van Deren before each of her races. He tries to anticipate the trouble she might encounter, given her brain injury, and then devises coping strategies. "You want to minimize distraction and dangers," he says, "and make everything as routine as possible."

It was Dr. Gerber who advised Van Deren to take red tape to the Arctic, so she could mark her path if she got lost. Before she ran the snowy course of Alaska's Iditarod on foot, he likewise advised her to stop if suddenly the snow underfoot seemed soft and untrammeled by dogs. "That could be a sign you're off the Iditarod Trail," he advised.

As Dr. Gerber himself admits, his tips are "not rocket science." But they give Van Deren a certain assurance. "When I go out to race," she says, "I feel confident. And that's because Don and I had put together a game plan. I'm prepared. I'm always prepared."

On Yinshan Mountain, Van Deren keeps climbing past the treeline, and on up to where the mountain is just a windswept exposed rock looking out onto a succession of other slabs of basalt speckled with small, green, scrubby trees. Then she guts past Zheng Rufang and the other Chinese woman. At the 90-K checkpoint, she's intent on burying them. "That girl in red," she shouts to Scott, "she's on my ass."

Scott Van Deren is now riding in Sky Song's van. "Babe, she *isn't* on your ass," he shouts out the window, a bit wearily. It's been a long day for him too, and in fact, neither Chinese woman is anywhere in sight now. They're fading.

"She's on my ass. Where is that girl? Is she walking behind me?"

Genially, Scott ignores the question. "You look good, honey," he says. The van revs away from Diane, and then, with a smirk, he says to me, "Sometimes you have to lie."

The course rolls onto a mostly flat paved road, and between 90-K and 98-K, Van Deren passes 14 men. At about the 99-K mark, in the darkness, Scott is anxious again as we sit in the idling van, by a fork in the road. "Wait here," he says to Sky Song. "She could miss this turn." She doesn't. Scott guides her in and she finishes in 13:16, good for fifth among 10 women.

From the finish area, we ride away in the van. Diane is in the back, with her feet up, resting her Achilles, which bears a swollen, grape-sized bulge. It's dark out. She's taken her sunglasses off, and it's as though all her armor has melted. She's woozy and mushy—happily delirious, like a society dowager high on martinis. "Sky," she calls out to our guide, "you've been so sweet. Let me buy you a glass of wine. Sky, come to Colorado. Bring your wife."

Scott fixes a jacket into a pillow for Diane. She moans a little, in pain. They are middle-aged warriors, both of them, and Diane, who hopes to write a memoir some day, has admitted she may be nearing the end. "When I finished the 430-miler in the Yukon," she told me, "I thought, *There's a great chapter for my book*. There comes a time and a place where the odds just get slimmer and slimmer."

The van swoops over hills, and through little villages. Eventually, we're on the outskirts of Beijing, rolling through traffic for a few minutes before cutting north, back to our hotel by the Wall. It's a warm Saturday night. People are out taking strolls and drinking at sidewalk tables outside cafés. Inside the van, there's tranquillity: the deep satisfaction that comes after a long race.

At this stage in her life, Diane Van Deren says her days are happy, mostly. She is grateful for her surgery—"without it," she says, "I'd probably be dead." And her older son, Michael, has returned safely from Iraq and begun working at the family steel business. He calls his mother before races, wishing her well. "There's laughter in our house now," Diane says, "and there wasn't before."

Weeks after we return from China, though, I give her a call. During our conversation I ask what she remembers of her trip and of the 100-K race, and for a second there's a weird silence. "I'm sitting here panicking a little," she says. "My heart's pounding. It's almost like I'm drawing a blank. I remember the big picture. I remember landing at the airport. I remember being on the Great Wall, and I can always remember things that are traumatic, like falling on the trail. But other things?" There's a long pause.

We soon hang up, and when we speak a couple of days later, she says, "You know, when I went running today, I was like, 'Okay, Diane, *think*. What do you really remember of China?'" She goes on to recite her memories. They are essentially the same memories she's already told me about, and soon she seems to recognize that once again a small part of her has been lost, irretrievably. For maybe half a second, there's a blue silence.

But then Van Deren muscles past it, and back into good cheer. "Hey, you know, I just went to the doctor's yesterday," she says, "and I got an MRI done on my Achilles. There's nothing wrong with it. It's just tender and swollen. I can keep training, which is good. The Hardrock 100 is only four weeks away. Four weeks, baby. It's coming right up. I'm there."

MICHAEL MOONEY

He Do What He Do

FROM D MAGAZINE

RON WASHINGTON IS not happy to see me. I wasn't supposed to come here. Not to New Orleans, the place where he was born, the place he has called home his entire life. Not to his neighborhood in the notorious Ninth Ward, where he and his wife, Gerry, have lived for more than 25 years. And certainly not to his front door, which, after a knock, is opened wide enough for him to peer out, but not so wide that I can see in. The usually jubilant, smiling Texas Rangers manager looks tired, worn down. Behind his wireframed glasses, his normally bright brown eyes appear sunken, shot with flecks of yellow. His hair—the ring of what's left of it—is disheveled, his mustache ruffled.

He doesn't give interviews in New Orleans, I was told. This is his safe zone, his off time, a respite from the game he's been a part of for all but a few of his 58 years on this planet. But I'm here to learn about Ron Washington. About the man. About what created the force that propelled the Rangers to the greatest season in franchise history. So I had to come to this neighborhood. And I had to knock on his door.

He looks like a grandfather just roused from a postprandial Thanksgiving Day nap. I tell him who I am and ask if he has a few minutes to talk.

"I'm not interested," he says. His tone is apologetic but firm. He looks around to see if there's anyone with me, and he squints in the sunlight. He sees I'm alone.

"Can I at least ask about what's carved into the sidewalk over there?" I ask.

In front of Ron Washington's house, in capital letters that span three or four squares of the sidewalk, someone has etched into the concrete NIGGERS. You can tell it wasn't written when the concrete was wet, either. No, someone had to take a sharp object and cut into the concrete with so much persistence and pressure that the gashed letters would remain visible for years.

"Oh, that," he says. "That's some ugliness. It was done before I got the house."

Tax records show he bought this house in 1986. He was a backup infielder for the Minnesota Twins then. That means that a man who's been coaching or managing—and before that, playing—in the major leagues for three decades has seen this racial slur every time he stepped out into his own front yard. And he has never paid the couple hundred dollars it would take to replace the concrete. And he's never moved out of this modest single-story brick-and-brown-shingle house—valued by the Orleans Parish tax assessor's office at $110,000—even after it was flooded and gutted and uninhabitable for more than a year.

A lot of people with money have left New Orleans. Anne Rice is gone. So are Brad and Angelina. Harry Anderson, the judge from *Night Court,* left too. Even Sean Payton, head coach of the Saints, recently moved his family out of New Orleans and into the Dallas suburb of Westlake.

But Ron Washington has stayed. Though he's certainly not among the highest-paid managers in the game—the hosts on 1310 The Ticket joke that he lives in a cardboard box by the ballpark—he has still earned millions of dollars over his career. He could live in a six-bedroom mansion in a pleasant suburb somewhere, behind a wall and gate and a guard who calls him "sir."

But he rebuilt his house here, in an area my hotel concierge and cab driver both told me not to visit at night. I want to ask the man why he came back. Why he stays.

Standing in his doorway, in his wind pants and gray sweatshirt, Ron Washington looks like a regular guy on his day off. He could be a cable repairman maybe, or an airline employee. This man didn't ask to be famous. He didn't ask to have his ungrammatical utterances quoted and printed on shirts, or to have children dress like him for Halloween.

"I promise I don't mean to bother you," I tell him. "I just came all this way, and I figured I'd try."

"I'm sorry you made the trip all the way out here," he says. "I'm just really not interested."

From the outside, the house that Ron Washington rebuilt seems pleasant enough: a modest 2,000 square feet or so, windows with new white shutters, a brick mailbox out front, a two-car garage in the back. The lawn has been mowed and edged. His is certainly one of the nicer houses on the block.

This neighborhood is full of houses that never got fixed, empty tombstones for families and friends who never came back. Just a few hundred yards from the salty waters of Lake Pontchartrain, these blocks were under five feet of murky sludge for more than six weeks. There are reminders of the storm everywhere. The house directly behind Washington's has been completely gutted. The address is spelled out in scripted iron letters mounted to the front wall, and green floral-print drapes still hang over the glass behind the open front door—small remnants of a life that no longer exists—but the rest of the house has been stripped, barred, and abandoned. The rotted furniture, warped photos, useless appliances, even the copper wiring in the walls—are all gone.

The uninhabited house across the street to the west has newspapers from 2005 taped over the inside of the windows and a brown, smudgy water line that never washed off. The empty shell of a house across the street to the north still has bright orange spray paint on the brick wall: a giant "X" and a "9/6," disaster-response shorthand for "On September 6, 2005, there were no dead bodies inside this house."

About half the houses in Washington's neighborhood have been rebuilt or repaired enough to be repopulated. So this is also a place for survivors, for people who have endured. This is a city that has for centuries buried its dead one on top of the other. The people here continue to endure, plodding through life one day at a time, because it's the only way they know.

At the last Rangers press conference before spring training, an event in Round Rock, Texas, celebrating the acquisition of the new Triple A affiliate, a reporter asked Ron Washington if he planned to go back to New Orleans when he was done in Texas.

"I haven't left New Orleans," he responded. "I still make New Orleans my home. I still go back there in the wintertime. I was grown there. I was born there. It's part of my heritage. It's slow coming back, but I want to be there and be a part of it when it do come back."

That's how Ron Washington talks, with a very particular syntax acquired in the Ninth Ward.

The team provides him with a house in Arlington worth a little more than $200,000—still quite modest by the standards of professional sports. But any time he gets off, he comes back here.

One thing is certain: it isn't because he's a neighborhood hero —or even close to his neighbors. His only adjacent neighbor, Esha McDougle, a 31-year-old hairstylist, has never exchanged more than a friendly honk and a wave with him or Gerry. McDougle moved in a few months ago. Before I knocked on her door earlier today, she had not only never heard of Ron Washington, she wasn't sure what sport the Texas Rangers play.

"I had no idea there was someone like that around here," she tells me. "They seem so down to earth."

Sonja Rollins, who lives across the street, had never heard of Ron Washington either. She figured maybe the guy in the corner house was a traveling salesman. "They don't be home too much," she says.

Adam Owens, a firefighter in his twenties who lives a few doors down, follows baseball and has known who lives in the corner house for a few years now. Owens sees them outside every once in a while when he walks his dogs. The two men usually exchange a smile and a nod and nothing more. "He's a quiet dude," Owens says. "Most people around here have no clue who he is."

So much of baseball is about failure. The best sluggers in the game fail to get a hit in two-thirds of their at-bats. The best pitchers still let in an average of two runs a game. Everyone makes errors. Everyone strikes out. The sport is about dealing with disappointments and pain and moving forward to another day. And Ron Washington has had more than his share of disappointment and pain: from growing up in the projects, one of 10 kids in a family that sometimes didn't have enough to eat, to losing a brother in Vietnam, to losing his house in a giant hurricane, to slowly losing his mother to Alzheimer's. He's had his share of failures too, with only 10 major league games played in the first 11 years of his pro career and more than two decades spent pining for a big league manager position. But even in the cynical world of sports, his biggest failure was shocking.

In front of a line of cameras and reporters, last season Ron Washington desperately asked the public to believe that, at 57 years old, the one and only time he'd ever tried cocaine just happened to be a few days before the one time that year he was scheduled to be tested. He said he was sorry, that what he'd done was stupid, that he'd gone to counseling, that he promised he'd help young people.

He summed up the situation like only Ron Washington could: "Challenges are what you make of life that makes it interesting," he said. "Overcoming those challenges is what makes life meaningful. And I do want to make a difference. And I do want to put something meaningful in everybody's life." Then he looked directly into the cameras. "That's just been the way Ron Washington has been."

Despite the support of his players, there were immediate calls for his firing. "Now that the story of Washington's failed drug test is public, the question is how long the Rangers can afford to stand behind their man," Tim Cowlishaw wrote in the *Dallas Morning News*. "My guess? Not very long."

The next day, Jean-Jacques Taylor wrote, "The Rangers should've fired Ron Washington the day he admitted using cocaine during last year's All-Star break. No questions asked."

But Jon Daniels, the wunderkind who'd gone from intern to general manager in under five years, was less inclined to give up on the man he hired. "My emotions were all over the place," Daniels told reporters at the time. "I was shocked. I was disappointed. I was angry. I felt all those things that probably our fans are going to feel. We decided to work through it. You hope at some point some good will come out of this."

No honest Rangers fan could have imagined what good could come of this. Even Nolan Ryan, the greatest Ranger of all time and a model of austerity and sobriety (he swears he's never taken an illegal drug in his life), admits he had backup plans if Washington didn't work out.

"We went into last year with a lot of questions," Ryan says now. Looking back, he's obviously pleased with his decision to stick with his manager, though he says so with the modesty of a lifelong

Texan who, no matter where he went, always came home to Texas. "With Ron, I think that he has probably been the right person in the right place for the way that this organization has come together."

That's Ryan's way of saying the Rangers needed someone like Ron Washington. They needed a survivor, someone who could rebuild. In so many ways, Washington's entire life had been preparing him for this moment.

The first time he moved away from New Orleans was 1970, when he was 18. It was also his first time to fly in a plane. He had just signed his first baseball contract, for $1,000 with the Kansas City Royals, and he was heading for the team's new baseball academy in Sarasota, Florida, where he knew no one. He would later say that when he looked out the window of the plane, he couldn't help but tear up.

He grew up in the Desire Housing Project, one of the city's most crime-ridden developments, working hard to stretch a three-dollar-a-week allowance into five days of lunch money and bus fare. A wiry kid with glasses, he couldn't always outrun the bullies who wanted his money. But he found refuge in baseball. He played catcher, and, as a boy, he slept with the mitt his father—a truck driver—gave him. After high school, he learned about a series of tryouts the Royals were holding all over the country, the franchise's attempt to cultivate talented minority kids from places other teams wouldn't even send scouts. Of the 156 players at the tryouts in New Orleans, Washington was the only one invited to the academy.

That's where he met a quiet, thoughtful middle infielder from Mississippi named Frank White. "He was one of the most rambunctious guys I'd ever met," remembers White, who recently resigned from the Royals front office to pursue broadcasting. "He'd sit there behind home plate and just talk nonstop. He never let things get boring."

The two of them—the chatter-mouth catcher and the pensive second baseman—became fast friends. They were also the star pupils. The academy drilled the importance of fundamentals and technique, and the young ballplayers took direction well. When coaches told the confident catcher there was no chance he would ever make it to the big leagues squatting behind the plate at

140 pounds, he agreed to switch to the infield. He loved playing catcher because he felt he could control the whole game, but he was dedicated to playing in the majors and he did what he was told.

"He had this great ability to adapt to any situation," White tells me. "And he could always take the lemons and make lemonade."

Both men worked their way up into the Royals farm system. White went on to play 18 seasons in the majors, all with Kansas City. He made five All-Star Games, won eight Gold Gloves, and, in 1985, he was a key part of the team that won the World Series.

That's not what happened to Washington, though. After six years, he still couldn't break into the big leagues—at least partially because White was so consistent at second base—and he was traded to the Dodgers for a guy who never played in the majors. After nearly two full years in the Dodgers organization, he finally got called up at the end of the 1977 season. In the 10 games he played, he batted .368 and stole one base, but the Dodgers in the late '70s had one of the all-time great infields. The promising 25-year-old started the next season back in Triple A.

He was trying to beat out a grounder in a freezing ballpark in Utah early that next year—"He was never one to slack off," White says—when he tore up his knee. And because this was before the days of laparoscopic surgery, it would take four more years and another team before he'd make it back to the show.

When he finally made the Twins roster as a utility infielder in 1981, he was nearly in his thirties. He'd play second base one night, pinch-hit the next, then not see any action for a week. But he had a reputation as a hard worker. "If he messed up, or even if he dropped a ball in practice, he'd take responsibility immediately," says Randy Bush, a teammate from '82 to '86 and a fellow New Orleanian. Bush was primarily a pinch hitter in those days and spent plenty of nights in the dugout next to his friend. Day after day, no matter how long he'd been sitting on that bench, Washington would never miss the chance to stand up and congratulate his teammates as they returned to the dugout.

"Ron was always intense," Bush says. "He wasn't about to take anything for granted."

The two of them used to go to the ballpark early and play pepper to make sure they were fresh. They'd also train together back in New Orleans in the off-season. They used to meet in the morning and run for miles. Then they'd throw each other batting practice. Then they'd lift weights. Five days a week, like factory workers. If it was raining too hard, they'd spend the day running sprints inside a gym.

Ron Maestri was the head coach of the baseball team at the University of New Orleans at the time, and he let the two pros work out in the school facilities. "I used to get my players together and tell them to watch those guys," Maestri says. "I'd say, 'This is what it takes to make it in the big leagues.'"

These days Maestri is an executive with the New Orleans Zephyrs minor league club, but he still talks to both men often. "He always had this great ability to just be the same every day," Maestri says. "When things are hard, Wash doesn't change. When things are good, Wash doesn't change."

Most of his career has been long bus trips and strange beds, a long-distance call home every night and a life in a suitcase. He lived in the shadows of the game. Even when he eventually made it to the majors, not even the most dedicated stats geeks knew the name Ron Washington. He was a .261 batter who never hit more than five homers in a season.

"Ron and I weren't superstars," says Bush, now the assistant general manager of the Chicago Cubs. "We didn't have the natural talent or size some of those guys had. We were never guaranteed a spot. We had to go into spring training ready to play."

One year, Bush led the American League in pinch hits and twice more he finished in the top three. He went on to win two World Series rings with the Twins.

That's not what happened to Washington, though. He was released in spring training before the '87 season, the year the Twins won their first World Series. He watched his buddies—the men he'd congratulated from the dugout for six years—win a championship without him. He spent a year with the Baltimore Orioles, a year with the Cleveland Indians, and seven final games with the Houston Astros in 1989—where he was briefly a teammate of Nolan Ryan's.

When no more major league teams wanted him, he spent another year in the minors, finishing his career the way he started it, as a catcher. And when no more minor league teams had room for him, he played in a seniors' league in Daytona Beach until the league folded in December of 1990.

Years later, on rare occasions when the mood got serious, Bush would ask his friend about 1987, about getting cut the year the team won the World Series. "I know I would have been so mad, but I never heard him complain," Bush says. "He said he truly has no bitterness over it. He told me, 'It is what it is. You just gotta let it go and turn the page. You gotta keep working. What else can you do?' That's always stayed with me."

His managing career began the same way his playing career did, with several years spent moving up and down through minor leagues. He didn't get a chance to coach on a major league staff until a former Twins teammate, Billy Beane, became the Oakland A's general manager. Beane, too, had spent nights in the dugout with Ron Washington, listening to him chatter. He knew his scrappy history and he remembered the positive attitude and focus on fundamentals. He brought him on as the first-base coach.

The new coach brought the creeds he'd been taught so many years ago at the academy: footwork, situational awareness, practicing hard even if you probably won't play, playing today like yesterday never happened. He also brought the infectious smile of a man who loves his job.

Within a few years, he'd garnered a reputation as a man who could make a professional infielder out of anyone. Author Michael Lewis took note of him when he wrote the 2003 book *Moneyball: The Art of Winning an Unfair Game.* "Wash's job was to take the mess Billy Beane sent him during spring training and make sure it didn't embarrass anyone by opening day," Lewis wrote. "He had a gift for making players want to be better than they were—though he would never allow himself such a pretentious thought." He also noted how wonderfully quotable the entertaining coach can be, writing, "Ron Washington can't open his mouth without saying something that belongs in Bartlett's."

Despite Washington's fine work as a coach, nobody wanted to give him a chance to manage. And that included Billy Beane, who interviewed him—and passed him over—several times.

"That definitely hurt him," Maestri says. "He felt like he would make a good manager, and he wanted people to believe him."

Though they were longtime friends, Beane was, at heart, a stats man. And Washington was, statistically speaking, 100 percent heart. Even if he wasn't beloved by management, his players adored him. A's third baseman Eric Chavez actually gave the coach one of his Gold Glove trophies. And when the trophy was destroyed in the hurricane, Chavez asked Rawlings to commission another one and gave him that.

Washington was in Baltimore the night the storm hit. His wife and family had driven to Atlanta. What the storm itself spared, the floods did not.

"He lost everything," Maestri says. "Every room in the house was destroyed."

He had good insurance, but both past and present players wanted to help him, to chip in. Jason Giambi, by then in the middle of his $120 million contract with the Yankees, slipped him a check for $25,000 before a game one night.

It was one more thing to endure for Washington. But when the insurance company finally got around to checking out the damage, and the supplies and construction crews eventually became available, they got to work rebuilding the house one room at a time. All told, it took nearly five years to rebuild Washington's house, but he never complained. Instead, he went to the ballpark every day and did his job.

"For Ron, baseball is an escape," Maestri says. "When he's at the ballpark with all his friends, that's like a personal heaven for him."

His house was still under repair in November 2006, when he finally got his big league managing job—not from his A's, but from their rival Texas Rangers—reportedly sealing the deal a few days earlier by impressing Jon Daniels and Tom Hicks at a backyard barbecue. He promised that the Rangers would no longer rely on a power-hitting offense alone. He announced the team would finally learn to play small ball. They'd work the counts, take the extra bases, never stop applying pressure. He said the Ron Washington era would include a focus on defense, which would, in turn, help out the pitching.

It sounded good in theory—even if it sounded strange coming out of his mouth. But it was slow going at first. There were reports that certain veterans were feuding with the new manager. In 2007, his first season with the Rangers, the team went 75–87, but a few of those veterans weren't around by the end of the year.

In the 2008 season, they continued to struggle but finished the year in second place in the division. In 2009, the team was in play-off contention—and in first place for short stretches—late in the summer. Rangers fans had something to believe in for the first time in years. Then came that infamous All-Star break.

He's never discussed the details in public. He said he met up with old friends in Anaheim. They were out drinking. One thing led to another. A few days later, there was a knock on the door, a urine sample, a phone call to the league's employee assistance number. There was the tense conversation with Jon Daniels and Nolan Ryan, an offer to resign—if that's what they wanted. He'd do anything to save his career. He couldn't bear the thought that, after 39 years of giving everything to the game of baseball, this would be what he'd be known for.

They told him he could stay if he agreed to counseling and regular tests. But they warned that if the news got out, nobody would believe a 57-year-old manager just decided to try cocaine for the first time in his life.

Then the news broke. The national sports media descended upon Surprise, Arizona, for what was one of the more bizarre stories of the year. After all he'd been through in life, Ron Washington had never felt shame like this. This, he did to himself.

He called his old friend from the academy, but the old chatter-box catcher could barely get his words out. "He said he felt like he let me down," White says. "I assured him he hadn't. I said, 'You've been accountable. You admitted to what you did. You've taken the right steps. You didn't let me down, Ron.'"

He placed a similar call to Ron Maestri, back in New Orleans. "He said, 'Maes, I feel like I really let you down.' I said, 'Wash, you made a mistake, but you handled this like a man. I'm proud of you.'"

The season started slowly, and it looked like the prediction that he would be fired was coming true. But then something happened. Daniels and Ryan noticed it. The players noticed it too. Elvis Andrus started showing up early for extra fielding practice. Josh Hamilton became a more vocal leader. The Texas Rangers became grinders. They worked the count to wear opposing pitchers down. They took the extra base any chance they got. The entire team began to take on the personality of Ron Washington. They even started repeating his quirky, Yogi Berra–esque pearls of wisdom such as: "This team do what it does, it do what it do" and "I just think that's the way my hair grow" and, of course, the slogan that launched a thousand T-shirts, "That's the way baseball go."

By the middle of June, they were in first place. Then the team added Cliff Lee and never looked back. And as the team won more and more, it seemed like people liked those funny things he said more and more. There were T-shirts, radio montages, songs on YouTube, a seven-year-old who, with the help of a shaved head and stick-on mustache, looked hilariously like the manager. These were strange days indeed.

In September, the team clinched first place in Oakland, right in front of Billy Beane. The Rangers entered the postseason as underdogs. First, they took down the Tampa Bay Rays—the team that had finished the regular season with the best record in baseball—in five dramatic games. Next up were the Yankees, the defending champions who had ended so many Rangers seasons in the past.

Game 1, in Arlington, started well, but the team blew a five-run lead and lost. Washington got a chance at redemption the very next night, in the bottom of the first inning. Andrus beat out a grounder to lead off, then took second on a wild pitch. He stole third on a curveball in the dirt. With two outs and runners at the corners, the manager called for a rare double steal.

As the pitcher went into his windup, Josh Hamilton broke for second base. When the catcher tried to pick him off, Andrus sprinted for home. The throw back to home came in wide and—safe! Just like that, a one-run lead, momentum, the Ron Washington way.

After the amazing play, the manager stood smiling at the top of his dugout, ready to high-five each of his players. The Rangers won the game 7–2, won the series in six games—the clinching moment of game 6 coming with a symbolic Alex Rodriguez strikeout. And for the first time in franchise history, the Texas Rangers were going to the World Series.

"October was one of those magical months that you see in baseball," Nolan Ryan says. "I can honestly say that when we clinched against the Yankees that night, it was truly one of the highlights of my baseball career and probably one of the most exciting times on a personal basis that I've ever had."

And of course we know how this story ends. No, Ron Washington didn't win the World Series. In football and basketball, they measure greatness only in rings. But in baseball, sometimes championships aren't the most important thing. Sometimes it's just about who finds a way to keep showing up. Sometimes it's about surviving.

About half an hour after he sends me away from his door, I see Ron Washington in his driveway next to his white Infiniti SUV. He has a bottle of Armor All next to him and a rag in his hand. I approach one more time and hand him a piece of paper with my number on it. I apologize again and tell him I'll be in town for a day, and if he changes his mind to please give me a call.

"I probably won't," he says.

If you ask Washington's neighbors why they think he comes back here, they say it's because the neighborhood is a nice place to live. Kids can ride their bikes and play outside after school, they say, and a lot of neighborhoods nearby aren't like that. There's even a local security guard who circles the blocks in an old Crown Victoria. Sure, there are empty houses, but that means it's quiet.

And the truth is, he likes the anonymity. It's nice to get recognized by a baggage handler every once in a while, but most of his life has been in the shadows of baseball. And the more people who know who he is, the weirder things get. He likes coming back here because this place reminds him who he is. The winter is his. He gets to spend time with his wife. He likes to keep the grass cut and the cars clean.

Before I go, I take another look at the house Ron Washington rebuilt. You could fit three, maybe four of this house into some homes in Southlake, where his players live. I can't help it.

"Mr. Washington," I say, "after the storm, why didn't you buy a bigger house?"

He thinks about it and smiles. "One day," he says, "we will. Right now, all the mansions in this town are destroyed. You do that, you just taking on someone else's problems. But someday."

He has said before that he hopes he can be a part of baseball until his brain no longer functions. After the wonder that was last year, 2011 seems destined to be a failure by comparison. There are injury worries and trade demands and some big names not coming back. As always, there are concerns about pitching. But for now, Ron Washington is content here, at home, washing his car as the sun goes down in New Orleans.

The Forgotten Hero

FROM SPORTS ILLUSTRATED

ON THE LAST DAY of his short life Mike Reily awoke in a hospital bed at Touro Infirmary in his native New Orleans, barely a mile from the house in which he was raised. It was Saturday, July 25, 1964, and the temperature outside would climb to a sticky 91 degrees. A single intravenous fluid line was connected to Reily's body, which had been a sinewy six-foot-three and 215 pounds before being withered by Hodgkin's disease and by the primitive treatments that couldn't slow its progress. Mike's mother, Lee, had been in the spartan room with him almost every minute of the four days since he had been brought in to die.

Three months short of his 22nd birthday and recently graduated from college, Reily must have known the end was near. This day had stalked him for 17 months. His childhood friend John Gage, who was heading into his second year at Tulane's medical school, had visited him in the hospital. "He was lucid, but he was beaten to death," says Gage. "People who are terminal eventually have a look. The life is gone. That's the way Michael looked. He told me that when I became a doctor, [I should] find a cure for this miserable disease."

Maybe as he lay there, Michael Meredith Reily also thought about things he would never see again: The flat, brackish waters of Bayou Liberty, where as a boy he had water-skied all day and never grown tired. The cold, green football field in faraway New England, where one November afternoon Williams College had upset Amherst and the rangy linebacker from New Orleans had been the best player on the field. The tall, blond girl from Skidmore College with blue-green eyes, the kind of girl you never forget whether you live one more year or 100.

But Reily could not have imagined the ways he would endure in memory. He could not have known what older men learn: that friends and teammates are never really forgotten, and those who live largest and die soonest are remembered in the most poignant way. He could not have known that nearly half a century after his death, those who knew him best would still be haunted by his absence. He could not have known that men who served in combat would recall his courage in the face of death and compare it to bravery in battle.

And Reily surely did not know that on a late fall afternoon in the Berkshire Mountains of northwest Massachusetts, seven months before he graduated and went home to die, his young football coach and the college's equipment manager had made an impulsive decision to put away the purple, white, and gold number 50 jerseys that he had worn on the field, and that over the next 47 football seasons five more coaches and six more equipment managers would quietly honor that decision, most without knowing why. They would leave the jerseys packed away, unofficially retiring number 50 at a college where numbers were not retired. And one day, quite by accident, the story of Mike Reily's jerseys would be unearthed, and the young man who inspired so many others would come back to life.

Fall 2010: The Box

Early in October of last year, Ben Wagner was at home in Portsmouth, New Hampshire, perusing the website of Williams, a small, highly selective Division III school in Williamstown, Massachusetts. Calling up the football page, he found a section titled "Eph Legends." (Williams teams are nicknamed the Ephs or Ephmen after the school's founder, Col. Ephraim Williams, who was killed in 1755 during the French and Indian War.) Wagner, 69, had been an Ephs baseball player and cocaptain of the 1963 football team, a six-foot-four, 235-pound offensive and defensive tackle whom everyone of course called "Big Ben." The other cocaptain was Mike Reily. Over the years Wagner had been disappointed that Reily was not listed among the Eph legends, not only for his dominant play but also for his courage as he faced death.

Wagner finally e-mailed the college's football coach, Aaron Kelton, to inquire about adding Reily to the list, and he encouraged his teammates to do the same. Wagner also got in touch with Dick Quinn, Williams's sports information director. Quinn, 60, had been raised in Williamstown and had begun working at the school in 1989. He recognized both Reily's and Wagner's names. Back in the 1960s kids in town attended Williams games in all sports; Quinn had been present when Wagner hit a baseball into the distant football bleachers, which had rarely been done. Quinn also remembered attending football games at which the public address announcer kept saying, *Tackle by Reily. Tackle by Reily.*

"You could not go to a game Reily played in and not hear his name over and over," says Quinn. "I remember hearing that Mike died the summer I was 13, and I was stunned. I knew he didn't play his senior year because he was sick, but I had no clue that meant terminal." Quinn asked the college's assistant archivist, Linda Hall, to dig up some photos of Reily, so that he could add Reily to the web page. He told Wagner he was on the case.

Around the same time, Williams assistant offensive line coach Joe Doyle made one of his routine prepractice visits to the school's equipment room in Cole Field House, a three-story brick building that sits atop a steep hill overlooking a broad expanse of practice fields. Doyle, then 69, was a five-foot-ten, 230-pound inside linebacker at UMass in the 1960s and later a high school coach in Cheshire, Massachusetts. When he became an assistant principal in the mid-'80s, he was no longer allowed to coach high school football, but then–Williams coach Bob Odell made Doyle a volunteer assistant. Odell couldn't pay him, but he did get him a gift. "A nice sideline parka from the college," says Doyle. "I could wear it when it was cold." He picked number 50, his number at UMass.

Now, on an October afternoon in 2010, Doyle sat with Williams equipment manager Glenn Boyer next to the washers and dryers and cleats and jockstraps and noticed an old cardboard football box on a shelf. The box was red on top, white in the middle, and yellow on the bottom, with a Wilson logo on the side and the top. The cardboard was torn in a couple of spots, stained by water and sealed with six strips of deteriorating tape.

What caught Doyle's attention was a faded message written on the side of the box, in felt-tip marker:

FOOTBALL
#50 DO NOT ISSUE

The same words were written on the top of the box. Doyle asked Boyer what that was all about. The equipment man said, "We don't give out number 50."

"Why not?"

"I don't know," Boyer said. "We just don't." Boyer, then 50, had been working in the equipment room since November 1987 and had looked at the battered box nearly every day without ever opening it to see what was inside. He just left it alone and went about his business.

Curious, Doyle sought out Dick Farley, who had been Williams's football coach from 1987 through 2003 and still helped coach the track team. If anybody knew the story behind number 50, it would be Farley. Except he didn't. "I just knew we didn't give it out," Farley recalls telling Doyle. "When we ordered jerseys every year, number 50 would be on the list, and I'd just put a line through it. I assumed it was a fallen player, maybe in the military."

Not long afterward Williams played Wesleyan on Homecoming day on Weston Field. Quinn was filming Flip video of the game while standing on the sideline. Doyle approached him and said, "Do you know there's a retired number in Williams football?"

"Williams doesn't retire numbers," Quinn replied.

"Apparently it does," Doyle said.

On the Monday after that game Quinn called Boyer and asked, "Williams has a retired football number?"

"I don't know about retired," Boyer said, "but there's this box down here."

Quinn walked across the campus from his office in Hopkins Hall to Boyer's equipment room. Boyer showed him the box, and Quinn opened it. Inside were three tightly rolled football jerseys, stiff but otherwise well preserved. Two were white and one was purple. All were number 50. By the time Quinn arrived back in his office, the photos he had requested had been e-mailed from the archives: black-and-white portraits of a handsome kid wearing jersey number 50. In one of them Mike Reily smiled back at him.

The jersey trim seemed to match that of the ones Quinn had just pulled from the old, tattered box. Quinn thought: *Number 50 is Mike Reily.*

Fall 1960: The Big Cat

A freshman class of 288 students entered Williams in the fall of 1960. They were all males (the college would not accept women for 10 more years but is now 52 percent female), almost all white and largely from privilege. They arrived in a time of fading innocence, still tethered to the Elvis and Buddy Holly '50s but very much on the precipice of change. "I spent four years at Williams and never heard anybody mention marijuana," says Chris Hagy, 69, who graduated in the class of '64 and is a federal judge in Atlanta. "I came back to visit the next year and everybody was talking about marijuana." The civil rights movement was nascent. Vietnam was a distant rumble that had not yet affected most U.S. campuses.

Like most of his classmates Reily was rich, white, and clean-cut, but in some ways he stood out: not just tall but also broad-shouldered and narrow-waisted, with a Southern drawl and an easy confidence. "He had a big cat's physical serenity, with a big cat's action, not just athletically but every day too," recalls Joel Reingold, then a hockey goalie from Newton (Massachusetts) High. "He was sophisticated, with that New Orleans thing. His voice sounded like burnt sugar, man, like burnt sugar. All the girls who came to the campus wanted to date him, and that made him a quasi-magical figure. All the guys wanted to be in his circle, and it was a big circle. He was the alpha male."

Yet to a Southern kid about to turn 18, Williams must have seemed a cold, distant, and isolated place, dominated by boys from prep schools such as Exeter, Andover, and Choate. Reily was born in 1942 into the upper crust of New Orleans society, the second son of James Weaks Reily Jr. and Leila Manning. James, whom everybody called Jimbo, ran the family's lucrative coffee firm, Wm. B. Reily & Co., for a number of years and rebuilt a flagging electrical supply company after that. He and Leila, who was known as Lee, had four boys: Patrick in 1941, Michael a year later, and, seven years after that, twins Tim and Jonathan. The Reilys lived in a big white Victorian on Valmont Street in Uptown and shared the family's 200-acre vacation compound an hour north of the city on

Bayou Liberty. All the kids water-skied like mad, and most of them could balance on a wooden disk, spinning it while holding a tow rope. "But Michael was the only one who would put a chair on the disk," says Tim Reily. "He'd stand up on the chair, on the disk, and ride by. That's the kind of athlete he was. He was the star of the show."

In New Orleans, Patrick and Mike lived hard, fast, and generally beyond their years. By their midteens they were regulars at Pat O'Brien's bar in the French Quarter and Bruno's Tavern in Uptown, near Tulane. "Both my mother and father tended to drink and party a little bit too much, and we were probably an impediment to that, so we had a lot of freedom," says Patrick, 70, a retired lawyer in Miramar Beach, Florida. "We were in the French Quarter at 14. The legitimate drinking age was 18, but nobody was carding anybody." Family photos capture the moments, boys playing dress-up in dark suits with skinny ties, beers in hand and pretty girls nearby.

They called themselves and their friends the Krescent City Krewe, and while Mike was not the oldest in the group, he was the leader. On a crazy weekend in 1958, Mike rode with 18-year-old Joe Carroll in Carroll's '51 Ford Victoria from a party in Pass Christian, Mississippi, to Key West and then took the ferry to pre-Castro Cuba. "You had to be 18 to get on that ferry, and Michael was only 16," says Reily's cousin Larry Eustis III. "But Michael looked older and acted older, and he just talked them into it."

In the fall of 1955, Mike had been shipped off to Woodberry Forest (Virginia) School, where he became a star football player, wrestler, and track athlete and prefect of the senior class, the highest honor bestowed on a student. Woodberry's big football rival was Episcopal High School, and by the autumn of '59, when Mike was a senior, Woodberry hadn't beaten Episcopal in 13 years. That streak ended when Mike, playing tight end, caught a game-winning 67-yard touchdown pass from quarterback Charlie Shaffer. It's a famous play in Woodberry history but not the play that Shaffer remembers best. Early in the game Episcopal ran a sweep to Mike's side. "Mike delivered the most bone-crushing tackle I'd ever seen or heard," says Shaffer. "It was a play that made all the young guys on our team feel like we could compete."

In the spring of their senior year Shaffer and Reily were offered Morehead Scholarships, academic-based grants that would

pay four years' room, board, and tuition at North Carolina. Both
young men were also recruited to play football for the Tar Heels.
Shaffer accepted, but Reily declined, having decided to attend
Williams. His siblings are still flummoxed by the decision. North
Carolina was big and Southern, with Division I sports. Williams was
Northern and stodgy, with small-time sports. "Maybe he wanted to
get away from all the partying and drinking," says Patrick Reily,
"but he could have gone to Chapel Hill for free. Our father had a
lot of money, but he held on to it. He would have taken it all with
him when he died, if he could have."

Shaffer blew out his knee as a freshman quarterback but was
such a skilled athlete that he switched to basketball; he played on
Dean Smith's first three teams and was the Tar Heels' cocaptain in
1963–64. "I so wish that Mike had accepted the Morehead," says
Shaffer, 69, who spent 36 years as a trial lawyer in Atlanta. "He
would have been a great football player at North Carolina, there's
no doubt. He could have played at a much higher level than Williams. But I think he wanted to reach for the stars in sports *and*
academics."

Reily was surely the best player at Williams. He became the
starting center and inside linebacker in 1961 on the first day of
sophomore practice. (Freshmen were ineligible for the varsity.)
Assistant coach Frank Navarro, 31, ran the defense for Len Watters, who was 63 and would retire after the following season. Navarro installed a 5–2 "monster" defense, modeled on Oklahoma's
52 scheme. Vital to the defense was the strong-side linebacker,
Reily's position. "That linebacker ran free," says Navarro, now 81
and retired. "He had to call the defense, read the play, and make
a hit in the backfield."

Reily filled the role brilliantly. In a preseason scrimmage the
Ephs battled Dartmouth on even terms for more than two quarters, and afterward Big Green coach Bob Blackman expressed disappointment that an athlete as talented as Reily didn't wind up in
Hanover, New Hampshire. Reily would finish his sophomore season with 89 tackles in eight games, then a school record, but it was
the force of those tackles that teammates would remember. Bill
Holmes, a junior end in '61, recalls that in the Amherst game he
grabbed a running back around the ankles and hung on to a foot.
"Then there was this tremendous force transmitted down the guy's
body, and it was Mike Reily just clobbering him," says Holmes, 70

and a recently retired physician. "As we're getting up, Mike says, 'Nice tackle, Willie.'"

Reily and those '61 Ephmen were never better than on that day against Amherst, which was not only Williams's rival but also unbeaten and ranked the number-one small college team in the East. The annual Williams-Amherst game, which will be held for the 126th time on November 12, is as vital to the players and alumni of both schools as Auburn-Alabama or Harvard-Yale is to theirs. ("Sixty minutes to play, a lifetime to remember," Farley would tell his players years later.) On this day Williams, 5–2 going in, upset Amherst and its cutting-edge Delaware wing T offense 12–0, holding the visitors to just 63 yards on the ground and three pass completions.

Film of the game reveals Reily as a dominant force, easily flowing to the ball, making nine tackles, intercepting two passes—one inside the Williams 10-yard line—and recovering a fumble. Reporting on the game for the *Berkshire Eagle,* Williams senior Dave Goldberg wrote, "Reily, who in a year of varsity play looks like one of the best linemen in Williams history, was all over the field."

In a snapshot after the victory all 32 Williams players stand in front of the school bus that would transport them from Weston Field to Cole Field House. Reily, the defensive star of the game, is hiding in the back row, far to the right, giving seniors the moment. Surely he would have his time.

Winter 1963: "Incurable"

After the 1961 season Reily was named to the Associated Press All–New England Team and was a third-team small-college All-American. A year later Williams again went 6–2, and it allowed just 25 points in eight games. Again Reily was All–New England, though years later his teammates would recall ominously that while he was good, he wasn't quite as good as he had been in '61. On campus he had moved into a room in the Alpha Delta Phi house; Williams was dominated by fraternities, and AD was the jock house. As a freshman and sophomore Reily had driven around on a Triumph motorcycle that everyone remembers as his but in fact he'd bought together with classmate John Winfield. "We used to ride on it together up to Bennington, looking for dates," says Winfield, 69, a practicing physician and retired professor of medicine. As a junior and senior Reily had a '63 Jaguar XKE. Often he took Navarro's nine-year-old son, Damon, for rides in the countryside. Once, on a whim, he hopped into the Jag in Williamstown on a Friday afternoon, drove to New York City, and flew with roommate Bill O'Brien to St. Croix for the weekend. And Reily did not retire his drinking shoes. "He liked to party," says Bruce Grinnell, 71, senior quarterback of the Williams '61 team, "but he was always under control. He was the Big Kahuna." Friends say Reily also excelled in the classroom as an English major and planned on a future in banking.

He embraced his popularity without flaunting it. "Handsome and gregarious, yet humble and charming," says Winfield. Once, in the sitting room of the AD house, a regal three-story yellow-brick building in the middle of the campus (with a Coke machine that served up beers), junior Max Gail was emotionally arguing a point that he now can't recall. When the discussion broke up for dinner, Reily, by then the president of the fraternity, said to Gail, "You make up your own mind, don't you? I really respect that."

"Mike had a kind of depth to him," says Gail, 68, who later achieved pop-culture fame as Detective Stan "Wojo" Wojciehowicz on the TV comedy series *Barney Miller* (1975 through '82). "Knowing him was one of the most powerful experiences of my life."

One morning in the winter of 1963, Williams junior and AD member Jack Beecham was awakened by violent coughing in Reily's room. Reily didn't come to breakfast and wasn't seen for a few days after that. Soon after developing the cough he went home to New Orleans.

Patrick Reily was there when his brother came home. "He went to the doctor here, they did a chest X-ray, and they found a growth of some sort," says Patrick. Mike's chest had to be cracked open so the mass could be biopsied. "He started getting treatment," Patrick continues, "and then one day he came home and opened up this encyclopedia we had on the coffee table. He tapped his finger on the book and said, 'That's what I've got.' I asked him how he knew for sure, and he said, 'Nobody told me, but I looked at my chart at the treatment center.' He was pointing to Hodgkin's disease. I remember it said, *Incurable. Life expectancy one to two years.* Then I remember Michael just walked up the stairs."

Hodgkin's disease, a cancer of the lymphatic system discovered in 1832, has become one of the most curable of cancers, with five-year disease-free survival rates as high as 98 percent. Had Reily developed Hodgkin's as little as four years later, his chances for survival would have been much better. But in the winter of 1963 he was facing a deadly illness.

He was treated with radiation—"They just cooked him," says Gage, 69, a surgeon in Pensacola, Florida. "That's what radiation was at that time"—and then with intravenous nitrogen mustard, a chemical warfare agent that is regarded as the first chemotherapy agent. It was very effective at killing cells but brutal on the infected individual. As soon as treatment started, Reily began to deteriorate.

He also made the last important decision of his young life: he would spend his final months as he had spent the previous two and a half years. "I asked him what he was going to do," says Patrick. "I would have gotten drunk in every bar on earth. Michael said, 'I'm going back to Williams for the rest of my junior year, and then I'm going to graduate. I'm going to spend time with my friends and my family. Those are the most important things in my life.'"

A little more than a month later he returned to Williams and told O'Brien the same thing. "I asked him if he was tempted to just get in the Jaguar, take off, and have some fun," says O'Brien, 71, who would spend most of his adult life as a lawyer. "We all think of that, right? What would we do if we had a year to live? He said, 'What would I accomplish by doing that? I owe it to a lot of people to finish this out.'"

Reily gathered up a bunch of AD buddies in the house kitchen one night and told them he was sick but never said he was dying. They figured that out on their own. "He would show up in class wearing shirts with 18-inch necks," says Dan Aloisi, 68, a football teammate and later a successful entrepreneur, "except his neck was only 15 inches."

There was a girl. In Reily's life there had always been girls. "They could have filled the church at his funeral," says his younger brother Tim. But this one was special. Sandra Isabella Skinker, who had been a cheerleading cocaptain at Summit (New Jersey) High, was tall and blond and smart. She was in the class of 1963 at Skidmore, then an all-women's college, an hour away from Williams in Saratoga Springs, New York. Skinker, now 70 and living in Vermont as Sandy Bennett (her married name, though she is divorced), had dated O'Brien, but they drifted apart in the spring of '62, and that fall she and Reily, who were already close friends, began dating. (She was with Reily the morning he awoke coughing, and she watched him spit mouthfuls of blood into a frat-house sink.)

"Football players could be so full of themselves, but Mike was such a warm and caring person," says Bennett. "And he had this irreverence about himself. I had never known anyone like him." In the spring of 1963, even as Reily began to suffer the effects of treatment, they met up in the Bahamas, where Sandy had gone with her parents and Mike with his mother and some AD guys. "We all had great fun," says Bennett, "but we all wore rose-colored glasses. Mike was already beginning to look tired, his eyes were sunken." He and Sandy danced together to "Autumn Leaves," and as they swayed to the music Mike said, "I hope I live to see another fall." They had talked about a life together, but shortly before her graduation from Skidmore that spring he sent her away. "He told me, 'I wish it could work out for us,'" says Bennett, "and he told me he loved me. But he said, 'I don't want you to watch me disintegrate.'" They cried together. They would never see each other again.

In the summer of '63, Reily visited Chapel Hill. After a party there, a woman named Bonnie Hoyle spoke to Reily and expressed her sympathy for his condition, but Reily told her not to feel sorry, saying he had experienced more in his short life than many people who live much longer. "I will always remember that night," she says, "and the peaceful look on Mike's face." Nearly a year later, in the spring of 1964, Shaffer would ask Reily to be in his wedding that summer. Reily said yes, but surely knew he wouldn't make it.

Reily had two goals left that fall: to help captain the Williams football team and to graduate. He returned to the Berkshires in the late summer of '63, gaunt and burned by radiation, unable to put on pads. Watters had retired, and Navarro, at 33, had been named coach. After an early practice Navarro gathered the team on the Cole Field practice grass and told them, "Mike won't be able to practice, but he'll be here every day with us." Reily wore gray sweats and a helmet every afternoon, the best athlete on the field helping to lead calisthenics drills and hold tackling dummies.

It was a Williams tradition for players to sprint up the steep hill to Cole Field House after practice, and Reily would join his teammates in that effort. "He'd get to the top of the hill, snap his helmet off, and start coughing and spitting," says Aloisi. "He just couldn't take it." Aloisi would later do a tour in Vietnam with the Marines and says, "Mike faced a terminal illness the same way my buddies faced combat. He faced it head-on, never looked for sympathy, and led the team to the best of his ability. It was incredibly inspiring." Every Saturday, Reily would join Wagner at midfield for the pregame coin toss and then take a spot on the bench, where he would listen for the coaches' defensive signals on headphones.

During that senior year, in which the Ephs went 2–6 and lost to Amherst 19–13, Reily was a ghost among his peers, often spending long stretches in the college infirmary. He would wear a parka in class because he was frail and cold. His roommate on the third floor of the AD house was Dave Johnston, now 69 and a general surgeon in Jacksonville. Late at night, alone in their room, Reily would ask Johnston, "Johnny, what do you think about dying?" It was a difficult topic for Johnston to discuss. "I'm 21 years, I'm omnipotent," recalls Johnston. "I didn't want to talk about dying."

On Sunday, June 14, 1964, Reily put a cap and gown over a white dress shirt and tie for graduation in a field called Mission Park, behind the Williams Hall dormitory where he had lived so large as a freshman. He sat in a folding wooden chair as U.S. Secretary of State Dean Rusk delivered the commencement address, warning of a military escalation in Vietnam. Reily's parents, divorced by then, sat in the audience.

Joel Reingold, who had so worshiped Reily four years earlier, sat next to him at graduation. "He coughed throughout the ceremony," says Reingold. "This magnificent specimen, reduced to almost nothing. He kept saying, 'I just want to graduate, I just want to graduate.' Then he walked up there and got his diploma, and when he got back to his seat he was exhausted. It was so heroic. We were all young, and we felt strong. We didn't know the war was coming, we didn't know the world was about to change. And here was Reily, the best of us, doing this one beau geste. It was incredible."

When the ceremony ended, the graduates marched joyously out of the makeshift stadium. Jack Beecham looked off to the side and saw Reily standing in a grove of pine trees. "He was looking at all of us parading past, smiling and happy," says Beecham. "He looked to be alone. And he had this sadness on his face, that I think only an awareness of impending death can bring."

On a late spring afternoon nearly five decades later, Big Ben Wagner sipped an iced tea on the porch of a seafood shack on the New Hampshire coast. "After that day, we scattered to the wind to make our mark on the world," he said. "Mike went home to die."

November 1963: The Jersey

At the end of each football season the Ephs' coach would meet with his equipment manager, and they would go through the jerseys and make a list of those that needed replacing. The coach would then place the order with visiting Champion salespeople and later walk the list down to a store on Spring Street. So it was that after the season-ending loss to Amherst in '63, Navarro stood in Cole Field House as the jerseys were laid out one by one, in numerical order. When Reily's number 50 was spread on the counter, Navarro recalls, the equipment man asked, "What should we do here?"

"We decided, let's put this thing away for a while," says Navarro. "Let's just put it away and not order it." The equipment man rolled up Reily's three jerseys and put them in an empty red, yellow, and white football box and wrote on two sides the imperative that Joe Doyle would notice 47 years later.

It will probably never be known for certain *which* equipment man wrote the message that endured so long. When first interviewed by *SI* last spring, Navarro said it was Jimmy MacArthur, who had started work at Williams in 1937. MacArthur, born in 1892, was a courtly gentleman with a full head of silvery hair and just a thumb and index finger on his right hand. He was closer to the players than the coaches were, recalls Navarro, who would occasionally ask, "Jimmy, how are the boys doing today?" MacArthur died at 72 in July 1964, the same month as Reily. His obituary in *The Transcript* of North Adams, Massachusetts, noted that he had retired two years earlier, which means that he shouldn't have been the man who put away Reily's jerseys (though members of the Williams teams of '62 and '63 recall frequently seeing MacArthur around the equipment cage after his retirement). Navarro, on being told this, backed off on his assertion that it was MacArthur who put the jerseys away. "Maybe we shouldn't say for sure," said Navarro, who would be a college head coach for 22 years and raise eight children with his wife, Jill. "Maybe it was Charlie."

That would be Charlie Hurley, who joined MacArthur in the cage in 1958, at age 50, and worked at Williams until 1973. Hurley served as a corporal in the U.S. Air Force in World War II and worked at clothing stores in North Adams and Williamstown before coming to the college. If he didn't put Reily's jerseys away, he surely protected them from 1964 to '73, as the Williams coaching reins were passed from Navarro to Larry Catuzzi in 1968 and from Catuzzi to former Maxwell Award winner Bob Odell in '71. With Hurley, the pattern was established, and a succession of equipment managers—most of them working-class men arriving at Williams from other jobs and other careers—simply read the writing on the box and obeyed it.

Hurley, who died in 1978, was succeeded by John Murphy, who had retired from a job at Sprague Electric, five miles up Route 2 in North Adams. "My father loved to work," said Murphy's son, also named John, "and he was terribly disappointed that he had to retire. He was elated when Williams brought him on." He would be known to a generation of Williams athletes as "Murph," and the standard-issue white cotton shorts and gray T-shirt would come to be known as "Murph Wear." Murphy worked at Williams until the early 1980s and died in 2000. He never gave out number 50.

But he did something else. In 1977, when his North Adams neighbor Joe Janiga was out of work after many years as a salesman on the floor of a furniture store, Murphy arranged for Janiga to become his assistant at Williams. Murphy was quiet, and Janiga was a ballbuster. "My father loved working for that college," says Janiga's daughter, Diane Simpson. "He loved the students." They loved him too. For many years Bill Keville and Bill Haylon, Williams athletes in the class of 1981, would conference-call Janiga at his home around the Christmas holidays, and that call would make Janiga's day. He died in 2007. He never gave out number 50.

Dick Cummings was a local legend, a man-among-boys running back at Williamstown's Mount Greylock High in the late 1960s and a 250-pound fullback at UMass after that. He spent a decade in Colorado working underground in mines and then came home and was hired by Williams to work with Janiga. He found a small, empty, gray metal recipe file with Mike Reily's picture taped to the top, except that he didn't know who it was. Cummings still works at Williams, in the basement of the gymnasium, back underground. He never gave out number 50. He still has the recipe file on his desk, with Reily's photo still taped to the lid.

Dave Walsh came aboard after Janiga retired. He had been a Marine on Guadalcanal in World War II and then a police sergeant in Florida before moving with his family to New England in 1967 and taking a job as a Williams security officer. Two years shy of 65, Walsh was transferred to the athletic equipment room in 1985 and finished up there. Diminished in later years by Alzheimer's disease, he would still attend Williams football games, where alumni of a certain age would remember him fondly, even if he didn't remember them. Walsh died in 2009. He never issued number 50.

Finally there was Boyer. He was a baseball star at Drury High in North Adams and went to work on the assembly line at Sprague in 1979. He spent nine years on the soul-sucking job, but it was a paycheck. When Williams called after Walsh retired in '87, it wasn't an easy decision. "My wife was pregnant with our first child, and I'd be losing 50 cents an hour and a week's vacation," Boyer says. But he took the job and saw the cardboard box early on. In 2004 first-year coach Mike Whalen, who succeeded Farley, offered number 50 to a hot recruit. "He wore 50 in high school, so I thought he might want it at Williams," says Whalen, who in '10 left to become coach at Wesleyan, his alma mater, and was replaced by Aaron Kelton. "I went to Glenn, and he said, 'Sorry, we don't use number 50.' And that was it."

Boyer was there through a major renovation of Cole Field House in the winter of 1996, when everything was moved into a storage facility. The box came back out, battered but intact. "I looked at it all the time, but I never looked inside," says Boyer, 23 years on the job. "It just seemed like maybe there was something special inside."

November 2011: Homecoming

Mike Reily lived just 41 days after his graduation from Williams. He went home to a bachelor pad on Danneel Street in New Orleans, where he lived with his brother Patrick but was mostly confined to a bed and doted on by his mom. On Tuesday, July 21, 1964, Mike was transferred to Touro Infirmary, and four days later, at 1:40 on that hot Saturday afternoon, he passed away. The coroner would write on Reily's death certificate that his illness had "disseminated," meaning it was throughout his body. His remains were shipped to Houston for cremation, but there was a funeral, and the church was full of mourners.

Nearly 47 years later Patrick and Tim Reily are sitting with their cousin Larry Eustis at the kitchen table in Eustis's New Orleans home, telling stories about Mike, recalling the euphoric and the tragic, sometimes in the same sentence. There is a pause in the conversation, and Eustis removes his glasses to wipe tears from his eyes. "We've never talked about this," he says. "We just submerged it."

Tim Reily says, "When Michael died, he was never spoken about in our family. It was like he never existed. I think it was just too much, too painful." Jimbo is gone, having died in 1988. Lee went five years later. Patrick battled alcoholism (he's been sober for 19 years); Tim lost a teenage son named after Jimbo, a good young football player who reminded his father of Michael and died of a drug overdose far from home. In all of this, memories of Michael drifted away.

This was also true among many of the young men—now old—who knew Reily. He was frozen in their minds, forever young, and there was no closure, only an inexorable moving forward. Dave Johnston went through life wishing he had been more willing to talk about death when that's what Reily needed. (He was in Europe when Reily died, and Reily was supposed to have gone on the trip. Jimbo had been given orders by Mike to wait a week before calling Johnston, so he wouldn't ruin his vacation by rushing home for the funeral.)

Chris Hagy beat himself up for not visiting Reily in the infirmary during that long senior year. "I was young and selfish," he says. "Maybe I was scared that Mike's illness was the first time I learned I wasn't invincible."

Jack Beecham wished he had comforted Reily when he stood alone in that grove of trees after graduation, something he would do for dying patients many times in later years. "Of course I didn't know to do that," he says. "It took me years to learn how."

Sandy Bennett kicks herself for not staying with Reily when he told her to leave. "But 50 years ago," she says, "women just didn't do that."

Big Ben Wagner got cut late by the Kansas City Chiefs, went to Vietnam and captained a swift boat, came back and got his MBA, made some money, and then went home to New Hampshire to help his dad and brothers run their apple orchard. Always he felt a nagging sense of incompleteness. "I was Mike's cocaptain," says Wagner. "I felt like I had unfinished business with him."

So there is now a humbling power in a pummeled old box of jerseys and a photograph snapped so long ago. On November 12, on Homecoming weekend, Williams will formally make Reily's 50 its first retired number, and it will also establish the annual Michael Meredith Reily '64 Award, to be given to the football player who, in the estimation of his teammates and the equipment manager, best exemplifies the qualities of performance, leadership, and character. Teammates will be there, and family members too. Estranged for decades, the Reilys were brought together by a writer's query, and finally talking about Mike has helped them to heal. They drove together through New Orleans on a warm spring afternoon, past the hospital, the cemetery, and the home where they once lived. There was laughter and silence too. Now, on one night in the Berkshires, stories will flow again. And tears.

There had been another ceremony, after Mike's funeral. His ashes were returned from the crematorium in a cardboard container, and his family gathered on a wooden footbridge on the bayou that Mike loved so much. Somebody said a quick prayer, and then Jimbo poured Mike's ashes into the water and weeds. "Nobody said anything about Michael," says Patrick. "My father just sort of threw the ashes out there, and we all walked off the bridge." This awkward, joyless image was all that was left for many years.

Now there will be much more: a celebration of spirit, a recognition of courage, and sweet, full memories of a short life fully lived.

ALEX BELTH

The Two-Fisted, One-Eyed Misadventures of Sportswriting's Last Badass

FROM DEADSPIN.COM

GEORGE KIMBALL HUNG upside down some 70 feet in the cold Manhattan air, still in need of a cigarette. Well, the doctors had said smoking would kill him, hadn't they? The previous autumn, they had found an inoperable cancerous tumor the size of a golf ball in his throat and given him six months to live. Five months had passed. He'd finished his latest round of chemotherapy, and now George, 62 years old and recently retired from the *Boston Herald,* was at the Manhattan Center Grand Ballroom in 2006, to cover a night of boxing for a website called The Sweet Science.

He'd never set foot in the place before. He didn't even know what floor he was on when he went for a smoke between fights. There was a long line at the elevator so he went looking for a back-stage exit and stepped out into the winter night, onto a tiny plat-form seven stories over the sidewalk. And then, as George would later tell the story, he plunged into darkness.

His leg caught between the fire ladder and the wall. He knew right away it was broken. He dangled from the fire escape like a bat—except bats can let go. He tried calling for help but his voice was too weak from the cancer treatments; he could barely whisper. Also, he wanted that fucking cigarette. A security guard, ducking out for his own smoke, found him, and it took another 20 minutes before the paramedics could get George on his feet. They wanted him to go to the hospital for X-rays but George talked them out of it. His wife was a doctor, he explained, and with all the chemo, he had more than enough painkillers at home.

He went back to his seat to watch the last two fights. Afterward, he hobbled to a drugstore and bought a knee brace, an ice pack, a large quantity of bandages, and a lighter to replace the Zippo he lost in the fall. Two days later George would go to a hospital to set his broken leg. But that night, he went home. His wife Marge cleaned the scrapes on George's arms, and he took a big hit of OxyContin. Then he filed his story on the fight.

George was a large man with one good eye, a red beard, a gap between his two front teeth, and a huge gut. He was a literate, two-fisted drinker who never missed a deadline and never passed up an argument. One night, when he was 21 and partying in Beacon Hill, he was struck on the side of the face with a beer bottle. That's how George got his glass eye.

It became his favorite prop. "You'd be amazed," he said, "by how many people ask you to keep an eye on their drink."

George began his career when Red Smith and Dick Young were the lords of the press box. On the night he fell out of the Manhattan sky, he had been a sports columnist for close to 40 years, "the last of his kind," according to Michael Katz, the longtime boxing reporter for the *New York Times*. He drank one-eyed with Pete Hamill and Frank McCourt, smoked dope with Abbie Hoffman and Jerry Rubin, and did with William Burroughs and Hunter S. Thompson whatever was in their heads to do at the time. George covered Wimbledon and the Masters, the World Series and the Super Bowl, and more than 300 championship fights. He golfed with Michael Jordan and sat in a sauna with Joe DiMaggio. "He'd show up with Neil Young," Katz said, "and get drugs from the Allman Brothers. Mention a name and he'd somehow know the person."

He loved being around celebrities. The walls of his home office were covered with framed pictures: George with Marvin Hagler and Mike Tyson, George with Muhammad Ali, George with Phil Mickelson, George with Bo Derek. His daughter, Darcy, remembered all the times her father would approach someone famous: "I would brace myself for an awkward moment, and the celebrity would call out to him first: 'George! Long time no see.'"

It might look like an enviable life; then again it might also look empty. For all the drinking and drugs and Hunter Thompson–style wild times, the Hunter Thompson–style best-sellers were never there. Nothing but soft pornography (*Only Skin Deep,* 1968) and a sports book (*Sunday's Fools,* 1974), cowritten with Patriots tight end Tom Beer. A single poem in the *Paris Review.* He drank, he smoked, he ate sticks of butter with mashed potatoes in a river of ketchup, slept in a coffin over McSorley's tavern, and fretted that he'd never written a meaningful book. It wasn't just the booze and drugs that got in the way; it was life on the road: the next fight, the next deadline, the next bar, the next party. "He was always impatient to get to the next thing," said Jenny Dorn, the wife of the poet Ed Dorn, an old friend of George's, "which is why a newspaper was the ideal place for him. Maybe he felt safer in that realm to avoid something else."

George didn't think he'd live past 40 and nobody who knew him ever got the feeling that his work had his full attention. "He was never ambitious," remembered his friend Bill Lee, the pitcher for the Boston Red Sox. "He was just there for the moment."

But he lived beyond his wild years, and when his time grew short, it turned out that George had more than a trace of ambition left. He burned to leave something that would last.

By the time I met George he had lost his famous gut. I saw him at a reading for his book *Four Kings,* George's account of the middleweight rivalry between Roberto Duran, Marvin Hagler, Tommy Hearns, and Sugar Ray Leonard. It was the fall of 2008. Not long after, he invited me to a screening of *Fat City,* John Huston's movie adaptation of Leonard Gardner's peerless boxing novel. He was in good company, joined by his old friend Pete Hamill. They stood on the sidewalk before the movie started and smoked cigarettes. George didn't wait more than a minute after finishing a Lucky before he lit another one. Someone said to him, "George, don't you think you should quit?"

He looked up at them with a crooked smile. "Why?" he asked. "Is it going to fucking give me cancer?"

When I edited a book of essays about Yankee Stadium, George contributed a gem about a brawl between the Yankees and Red Sox in 1977. Bill Lee got body-slammed to the ground by Yankees third baseman Graig Nettles and then made the mistake of getting up.

"In Nettles' defense," George wrote, "what he probably saw was just a crazy man charging at him. In any case, when Lee got close enough, Nettles cut loose with a right cross, and when Lee tried to block it with his left, he discovered that he couldn't lift his arm above his waist. The punch caught Spaceman flush in the face and dropped him in his tracks.

"A few months later, Ali and Ken Norton fought in almost exactly the same spot, and in fifteen rounds neither one of them landed a punch as hard as that one."

George and I started a correspondence. I can't pose as a close friend because I only got to know him in the last few years of his life. I had heard stories about him—about how he was buddies with Thompson and how he got in a screaming match with Norman Mailer; about how he once called former New York mayor John Lindsay a tight-assed WASP to his face (and then smudged cigar ash on Lindsay's forehead); about Kimball's fourth marriage ceremony, at which George Foreman officiated. But mostly, I was intrigued that George was still writing despite suffering from cancer. What was behind this uncharacteristic burst of ambition?

George Kimball III was born on December 20, 1943, the son of an Army officer whose career took his family to Taiwan, Germany, Kentucky, Maryland, Texas, and Kansas. He was the oldest of seven children, and his parents doted on him. When he was two, his father took out a set of cards with national flags on them and taught him to name all the countries. He was always willing to perform the feat for guests.

George was a tall, thin boy, a natural athlete. He ran track and played football and basketball in high school. He was also a voracious reader who spent most of his time in the library and seemed to retain everything he'd read. "I expected him to be a writer," his mother said. "In first grade, he signed his papers, 'George Edward Kimball, the Third.'"

But George was a lousy student. One year he was at Kansas University on an ROTC scholarship, the next at a community college outside of Boston, then back to Kansas, then to jail after an arrest in 1965 at an antiwar demonstration for carrying a FUCK THE DRAFT sign.

"George was one of the first hippies," said his brother, Rocky. "He was listening to folk music, hanging around beatniks, and involved in radical politics." FUCK THE DRAFT didn't reflect well on his father, a colonel with ambitions of retiring as a general. By this time, sports were all father and son could discuss without arguing. His mother, however, was unreserved in her affection—no matter where he was, she sent cartons of Lucky Strikes as care packages.

George moved to New York and got a job working as a junior assistant for the Scott Meredith Literary Agency, where he met Hunter Thompson. He became a regular at the Lion's Head Tavern in Greenwich Village, the walls there covered with the jackets of books by regulars like Pete Hamill, Joe Flaherty, and Leonard Shecter. But writing was hard and drinking wasn't. "You didn't go to the Head at night to improve your work habits," Hamill said.

George moved out of his sublet above McSorley's in August 1968. "Nothing really promising loomed on the horizon," he said. Ted Berrigan, an accomplished poet in the New York scene and a friend, "was headed out to Iowa to teach," said George. "After receiving encouragement from the people in charge of the Iowa Writers' Workshop they assured me that I'd be not only welcomed there but would have funding too. Big mistake. I should have gotten that in writing."

He worked on a second novel. Robert Coover was his thesis adviser, but George told me he didn't consult Coover much because they didn't see eye to eye. During the holiday break, George drove back to New York to talk about the book with Maurice Girodias, the owner of Olympia Press (which had published *Only Skin Deep*). Girodias "thought it wasn't dirty enough but grudgingly gave me a few hundred up front," George said. "In the end I junked the book."

He stayed at Iowa for a few semesters then left and never talked about it. His sister, Jenny Kimball, was blunt about that opportunity. "He squandered it."

Soon, George was back in Lawrence, Kansas, this time with the idea of running for sheriff. It was "high camp and theater," he recalled. He'd spoken to Jerry Rubin about it in New York without knowing that Hunter Thompson would run for office in Aspen, Colorado, that summer. In spring 1970, George announced that he would run as the Youth International Party candidate against the incumbent, Rex Johnson, a Republican who had run unopposed for years and who had arrested him back in '65. George waited until a half-hour before the deadline and filed as a Democrat; if he'd done it any sooner the party would have found somebody else.

He wore a tin badge and carried a rusty old six-shooter. He declared that the only laws he'd enforce regarding the "drug problem" would be "fraud, truth in packaging, and price-fixing conspiracy statutes against unscrupulous dealers." He announced he'd appoint African Americans to half the deputyships and said that the state attorney general "harbored a predilection for engaging in unusual activity with livestock."

"You can never be sure you know when George Kimball is taking himself seriously," Bill Moyers, LBJ's White House press secretary and later a journalist, wrote in *Listening to America: A Traveler Rediscovers His Country*. "You are not even sure he knows. But enough townspeople take him seriously to give him stature with the street community."

During his campaign, George made the local papers when he was arrested at a demonstration in Topeka for obscenity, one of several times he found himself in jail. He was even featured in *Time*. His parents displayed a copy of the magazine without shame. "They appreciated the attention he got," said his sister, Becky, "if not the reasons for it."

Johnson had a withered right hand and George's slogan was, "Douglas County needs a two-fisted sheriff." Johnson won by a landslide and George lit out for Boston. The sheriff's assessment: "He wasn't the worst son of a bitch I ran against."

Hunter Thompson lobbied Jann Wenner, the publisher of *Rolling Stone*, to hire George, who had been writing freelance music reviews. In a letter to George, Thompson wrote, "I want Wenner to have the experience of dealing with someone more demonstrably crazy than I am—so that he'll understand that I am, in context, a very reasonable person."

Wenner apparently felt one Hunter Thompson was all he needed, so George headed instead to the *Boston Phoenix,* that town's version of the *Village Voice*. It was the ideal place for his freewheeling reviews of poetry, books, and music. His passion, however, was sports.

"At least once a week someone asks me why I write about sports," George wrote in a column. "My friends on the Left persistently refer to the 'pig mentality' which governs organized sports and want to know how I can fathom sharing the delectations of Richard Nixon. On the other side of the spectrum—people I run into in bars, and not a few brethren sportswriters (many of whom have closer ties to the management and/or ownership of various teams than I) are wont to ask, 'If you *hate* sports so much, why the hell do you write about it?'"

There were other young Turks on the scene, the *Globe*'s Leigh Montville, Peter Gammons, and Bob Ryan among them, but none as worldly as George. His reputation preceded him and he played on it, unnerving the management of the local teams, particularly the Red Sox, because he was getting stoned with players like Bernie Carbo, Fergie Jenkins, and Bill Lee. Bob Sales, the editor of the *Phoenix* in the late '70s, remembers coming into his office to find George passed out on one couch and Lee on another.

"My favorite story about him came to me secondhand from *Phoenix* vets," said the writer Charlie Pierce, who worked with George at the paper. "One week, George came in and typed up his piece, dropped it at the editor's desk, and went off into the night. The editor looked at the copy and it was utter gibberish. Lots of consonants. Remembering that George was a touch-typist, the editor took the piece, put his hands on the keyboard, but moved them *one key to the side*. The piece was perfect, except George had started one key over."

The story became legend, and George later confirmed it—sort of. Loath as he was to let the facts stand in the way of a good yarn, he allowed as how it might've been one paragraph he mistyped, not the whole story.

Though away from his typewriter he was a maverick, George's prose style was clear, full of mordant observation, almost traditional, not at all like that of his gonzo friend Thompson. "He was a tremendous reporter," said Michael Katz, "not only one of the best, one of the fastest."

George once wrote a story for the *Phoenix* about opening day at Fenway Park. He sat in the now-fashionable bleachers, no longer the intimate place he'd known in the early '60s. When George returned to his seat from a beer run, "the guy who'd been keeping my scorecard wanted to know what the funny little illegibly-scrawled notes in the margin were all about," he wrote. "I briefly considered a number of spectacular fabrications, but finally admitted that I wrote for the *Phoenix* and planned to do a story of some sort about Opening Day.

"'Oh, yeah?' He eyed me strangely. 'If you're a sportswriter why the fuck are you sittin' *here*,' he gestured toward the press box. 'Instead of up there?' The fact of the matter was that the Red Sox had declined to provide the paper with press tickets, but for some reason I mumbled that I liked it better in the bleachers. At one time that would've been true; today it made me twice a liar."

By the early '80s, George had moved to the daily *Herald American* (later just the *Herald*) to cover sports. He latched onto boxing when Marvin Hagler, who lived in Brockton, Massachusetts, won the middleweight championship. "I jumped on Marvin's coattails," George said. Away he went, covering boxing's last golden age, when Hagler was pitted against Tommy Hearns, Roberto Duran, and his nemesis, Sugar Ray Leonard.

He encouraged younger writers like Pierce and Mike Lupica who went on to become better known than he ever was. The more prestigious *Boston Globe* passed him over and he never got a call from *Sports Illustrated*. When Lee wrote a book that went on to become a runaway best-seller, he tapped another collaborator. One reporter who was with George in Boston said, "I always had a feeling that he kind of wanted more to happen."

"I think the drinking and drug use was exaggerated by some over the years," George said. "It wasn't like I was walking around drunk or stoned while I was at the *Herald*. But there are people who know me well, or think they do, who think I spend all kinds of time boozing in saloons to this day, and I haven't had a drink in almost 20 years." He quit drinking cold turkey and when someone asked him if he wanted a drink, George would reply, "No, thanks. I've had enough."

"I think that the alcohol is too easy an answer for why George never became the writer that he and his friends thought he should be," Pierce said. "I look at him and I see a guy raised by a father who was distant and a mother who worshiped him. This left him trying (a) to play a game he could never win, and (b) playing a game he'd won just by being born. That is a helluva bind, and I think it created in him a dreadful insecurity. Something deeper in him made him coast."

Montville remembers going to the Lion's Head with George when they were in New York. George introduced him to all of his high-profile friends. "In his heart, George thought he was good as any of them," Montville said, "and he probably was but he never put it together. Anybody who works at a paper thinks, 'I'll get it all together and write the book tomorrow,' but tomorrow you're covering the Patriots game, so when you do have free time, you say I'd rather dig a hole on my day off than write. As a working newspaper reporter it's hard to get that focus."

George picked up golf and played with an enthusiasm that bordered on obsession. It was on the golf course that he could spend time with his father, who was diagnosed with lymphoma in the early '80s. The old man had never made general, and George was bothered by the possibility that his arrests and his FBI file had derailed his father's career. It wasn't just his politics. It was the porn novel; it was the expulsion from school; it was the arrest; it was the eye he lost in a fight.

His father was given less than a year to live and lasted two. He visited George at spring training where he was introduced to Johnny Pesky and Dom DiMaggio. They even played golf with the old Red Sox stars. Mostly, though, it was father and son: no heart-to-heart confessions, no pat sentimentality, just peace.

Benn Schulberg paced on the worn carpet in George's living room. The Final Four was on TV, and Benn, the youngest son of George's late and much-loved boxing pal, writer Budd Schulberg, had money on a game and his team was losing. It was spring 2011. George lay on the couch, a blanket covering his legs. He'd recently returned from Lawrence, where he had visited old friends and did three book signings to promote two boxing anthologies: *At the Fights* and *Manly Art*. It had been five and a half years since doctors had given him six months to live. George hadn't wasted his time. Four books carrying his name had been published since 2009, an atonement for a career of half-measures and disappointments.

"It was as if I woke up one morning and realized that however good or bad it might have been, well over 95 percent of what I'd written in my life had been used to wrap fish," George told me. "If I wanted to leave something more permanent, write things I'd always planned to write, and leave a worthwhile body of work behind, I needed to get off my ass and do it."

George lit a Lucky and studied the Final Four on TV. His gaunt face was covered with a choppy gray beard; his clothes hung loosely off his emaciated frame. He didn't talk much, not because his throat hurt but because it was his nature. "He's more intimate as a writer than he is in person now," his brother Rocky wrote in an e-mail. "George builds relationships by being side by side with people, at a barstool or at the fights." When George did say something, he spoke in bullet points about poor shooting and rebounding, about not selling enough books at a recent signing.

At halftime, he went upstairs to feed himself through a tube. Schulberg watched him go. "I knew George from the fights that my dad took me to as a kid," he said. "George had such a big gut, he'd knock over everything as he moved down the press row. When dad died, George had me over all the time. He wanted to make sure I was okay and looked after."

And now Schulberg, whom Marge called the Saintly Benn Schulberg, was returning the favor. His father was dead, and there were sad reports coming in from George's old friends. Pete Hamill told George, "Now they're shooting at *our* regiment."

George returned from upstairs. Schulberg had gone to the store on an errand, and now it was just George and me. He looked at the TV, and I asked him if he was afraid to die. "No," he said in a soft voice that I hadn't heard from him before. He looked at the ceiling and said that he was preoccupied with the idea of not being there to provide for Marge and his kids. "I worry about things that won't get done."

George filed hundreds of stories after he retired from the *Herald,* mostly on boxing, for the *Irish Times* and websites like The Sweet Science. The boxing pieces were collected in *Manly Art,* and his *Irish Times* work was published as *American at Large.* They are the work of a historian as raconteur, an insider, written in an easy, conversational style.

"He'd be the first to tell you he made his share of mistakes in the sixty-four years he'd spent on this earth," George wrote about Vin Vecchione, "but rescuing Peter McNeeley that night in Vegas wasn't one of them."

Vecchione threw in the white towel on McNeeley's behalf 89 seconds into a 1995 fight against Mike Tyson, saving him from a sure beating. Customers who shelled out 50 bucks to see the fight on pay-per-view were furious, but George thought Vecchione deserved to be named manager of the year; after all, McNeeley collected almost $10,000 per second for his effort.

"Vinnie was a boxing guy through and through," George wrote, "a Runyonesque character who looked as if he'd modeled his image on that of Joe Palooka's manager, Knobby Walsh. It was as if he'd been born in that white cap he wore into the ring when he saved McNeeley, and for all I know he slept in it too; I don't think I ever saw him without it. The other constant was the stubby remains of a cigar he kept clenched between his teeth. You never saw him light up a new cigar, and I always wondered whether Vinnie had found a good deal somewhere on half-smoked stogies."

George also cowrote a book with Eamonn Coghlin, the Irish miler, and coedited a compilation of boxing poetry, *The Fighter Still Remains. Four Kings,* the story of Hagler, Hearns, Duran, and Leonard, however, is perhaps his finest work.

"*Four Kings* was George's last best shot at a great book," said John Schulian, a sports columnist and screenwriter. "Some of us think it is great, others think it is very good. Either way, in these lean times for the sport, there are precious few books about boxing that deserve anything close to legitimate praise of that magnitude. It was as honest and heartfelt as a book can be. And smart too, in the way George at his best was smart—incisive, irreverent, unyielding."

George had covered all nine fights between the fighters. "I do feel fortunate to have staked a claim to the subject matter," George said in an interview with British sportswriter James Lawton. "I'd love to see *Four Kings* take its place in the pantheon of sports literature." Then George remembered what a sports editor once said to a sportswriter after the writer had won an award. "Well, that certainly makes you a tall midget."

It was *At the Fights,* which he coedited with his old pal Schulian, that cemented his legacy. A compilation of great American boxing reporting and commentary, it was published by the Library of America, "that distinguished arbiter of durable literature," according to the *New York Times.* For George it was a merging of his own literary aspirations and his great affection for, and pride in, the writers whose world he shared and understood.

"Trying to do justice to a great 12-round fight when you've got 28 minutes to make an edition is the most excruciating exercise imaginable," George said in an interview on the Library of America's website. "You just get it done and send it and hope it comes out in English. Of course the real test comes when you have to write a deadline story about a stinking fight. I remember the old AP fight scribe Eddie Schuyler sending his [story] after [one of those stinkers] and turning to me to sigh, 'If they want me to write better, they're just going to have to fight better.'"

With *At the Fights,* George had found a way to make all those nights, all those deadlines, all those seemingly ephemeral pieces take on a kind of permanence and purpose. Here was a chance to show that he belonged in the same collection as Mencken, Liebling, and Mailer. He wasn't leaving it for fate or history to decide. He would anthologize himself. He would help select America's finest boxing writing, and he would put himself in there too, alongside Hamill and Schulberg and W. C. Heinz. If he wasn't going to be elected to a hall of fame, well, fuck it—he would build one himself, right over his head.

Nobody was sure if George would live long enough to attend the publication party for *At the Fights.* His friends didn't know if they'd be celebrating with George or eulogizing him. "He was self-destructive," said Rocky, "but he's a hard one to kill."

The party was held in a large banquet room on the 11th floor of the New York Athletic Club, and unlike most parties hosted by the Library of America, more than 150 people crowded the room—Gay Talese, Larry Merchant, Jeremy Schaap, Schulian, in from L.A., George's mother, and most of his siblings. Friends from the Lion's Head and Lawrence, friends from the fights.

George and Schulian made short, earnest speeches, then let Robert Lipsyte and Schaap do the crowd-pleasing. George signed copies of the book with his 90-year-old mother sitting next to him. Jenny Kimball, standing nearby, admired her big brother's newfound discipline. For most of her life she saw him having a good time, working hard on his column but rarely pushing beyond that. "What he did these last years," she said, "he had that capability all of his life."

The morning after the party, George was back in front of his computer. "Writers write," he said. "It's who I am and what I do. It's really only been the last month or two that I've felt truly debilitated, and mostly tired. I haven't tried to make a secret of it but I haven't written about my illness and have rejected several invitations to do so. When you start defining yourself as a 'cancer victim,' you start thinking like a victim, and that in no sense defines who I am or what I do.

"Even after he'd had his larynx removed, Damon Runyon continued to work and write, communicated by notes—he carried a notepad that said 'Damon Runyon says'—so he certainly wasn't trying to hide his illness, but he never wrote about it and when he died most people in New York were actually surprised to learn he'd had cancer at all. *My* kind of guy."

"George was always looking ahead to the next project," Schulian said. "He couldn't have stopped if he wanted to. As long as he was working, he was alive." A line from George's *Paris Review* poem comes to mind: "[T]here is no rest for the other living. Too much real in the light of day."

Three days before George died, on July 6, 2011, he wrote a story for the *Herald* in which he fondly remembered two old friends, a reporter and a boxer who had died of cancer. He didn't mention that it was also killing him.

TOMMY TOMLINSON

Something Went Very Wrong at Toomer's Corner

FROM SPORTS ILLUSTRATED

ON A FEBRUARY AFTERNOON, they found out it was true. So many times they had filled up the place because the place filled them up. But now they went for a different reason.

Toni Rich raises money for scholarships through Auburn University's alumni office. She got the phone call on the way back from an Auburn Club meeting in north Georgia. She drove into town and picked up her five-year-old son, Gabriel, from day care. They went straight to Toomer's Corner.

Along the way she told the boy what had happened. *There was this bad man who came. He poured some poison on the ground. It got in the trees. We might not be able to stop it.*

They were among the first ones to arrive. But then Toni Rich saw the people coming from every direction, across the lawns of the campus, up Magnolia Avenue and down College Street, to the spot where the two 30-foot-tall oak trees have framed Auburn's main entrance for 130 years. Sheldon Toomer, a halfback on the Tigers' first football team, in 1892, built a drugstore diagonally across the street in 1896. Because of Toomer's Drugs the intersection is Toomer's Corner, and because of that, the trees are Toomer's Oaks.

About five weeks before, when Auburn beat Oregon 22–19 for the national championship, thousands of people came to cry and holler and whoop War Eagle. Fans have crowded Toomer's Corner after big Auburn wins for more than 50 years. At some point they started to bring rolls of toilet paper. One story traces it to 1972 when Auburn running back Terry Henley promised to "beat the number two" out of second-ranked Alabama, and the Tigers ran back two blocked punts for touchdowns in the last six minutes to win 17–16. Fans used to drape toilet paper over the power lines. After the city buried the lines, fans flung the TP into the trees. And on that championship night, January 10, they rolled Toomer's Oaks until the trees streamed white.

But on this February day, people laid offerings at the roots. A roll of toilet paper with *Get Well* drawn in Sharpie. A memo to God on a diner receipt. A hand-drawn card with a painting of a tree and a quote from Alabama native Helen Keller: "What we have once enjoyed, we can never lose. All that we love deeply becomes a part of us."

That quote is both truth and a lie.

Toomer's Oaks stand for Auburn, and they will live as long as memory. But they are also trees, and they can be killed. The dying had begun.

Toni Rich and her boy lingered in the crowd for three hours, staring at the poisoned oaks. Gabriel had many questions, but this one most of all:

Why would somebody do that?

Harvey Updyke wears Alabama colors every day. Last year he had a favorite T-shirt for game days. On the front, Calvin from *Calvin and Hobbes* pees on the Auburn logo. On the back it says, *If You See Me in a Turban & Sandals AU Is Playing Iraq!!*

"I saw that on a bumper sticker and told him about it," says Wayne Barnes, an old high school friend of Updyke's. "He went on the Internet and found somebody to make it into a shirt. I think he bought two."

Harvey Updyke didn't always hate Auburn, but for half a century he has loved Alabama. He was born in 1948 and grew up in Milton, Florida, in the panhandle near Pensacola. A drunk driver killed his dad when Harvey was three. When he was 10, he was watching a TV station out of Mobile one Sunday afternoon when *The Bear Bryant Show* came on. Bryant had arrived in Tuscaloosa from Texas A&M. Here was a strong man with a deep voice who announced to the world, "I ain't nothing but a winner." Harvey latched on.

He played offensive line at Milton High. One year he went
to watch the Senior Bowl in Mobile, and the story he later told
friends was that he walked right up to the Bear and declared, "I'm
going to play for you." The coach supposedly replied, "I hope so,
son." But Updyke didn't. After graduating from Milton in 1967,
he went to junior college, then headed for Texas believing there
were better job opportunities for him there. He went to his first
Crimson Tide game in 1970, when Alabama played Oklahoma in
the Astro-Bluebonnet Bowl in Houston. He ran onto the field in
the third quarter, carrying two rolls of toilet paper on a broom
handle and a box of Tide detergent. Roll Tide.

In 1976 he got a job as a Texas state trooper. He got married
and had a daughter he named Crimson Tyde. He remarried and
had two more children; he named his son Bear Bryant. (His second daughter is named Jennifer Lynn.) He married a third time,
to his current wife, Elva. He pushed to call their daughter Ally
Bama. His wife pushed back. They named her Megan instead.

Updyke hurt his neck in a crash that occurred as he was rushing to help another officer, and things got tough after that. He
retired in 1988 on disability. In 1996 he was arrested in Texas and
charged with criminal mischief. (Updyke says it was a family quar-
rel; he spent three days in jail, and the case was eventually dismissed.) He was also charged twice for theft, in 2003 and '06, for
passing hot checks. (Both charges were dismissed after he paid the
money back.) He had two bulging disks in his neck as a result of
the crash and money problems. He and Wayne Barnes had drifted
apart after high school but renewed their friendship after a high
school class reunion in 1997. Updyke knew Barnes had a house
in Alabama, a little cinder-block place on Lake Martin near Dadeville. Barnes offered to rent it to him for $300 a month. Harvey
and Elva moved into the lake house in the winter of 2009. He
lived just 130 miles from Tuscaloosa and the Alabama campus. He
also lived just 30 miles from Auburn.

To understand the Alabama-Auburn rivalry, think of those Russian nesting dolls. College football has the most intense fans of
any American sport. The SEC has the most intense fans in college
football. The Auburn-Alabama rivalry has the most intense fans
in the SEC. And the teams' annual game—the Iron Bowl—is the

most intense three hours of the sports calendar. It's the hard, hot ember of a feud that burns all year long.

Michigan–Ohio State, Oklahoma-Texas: those fans live across borders. Alabama people and Auburn people grow up together, go to church together, shop at the same malls, eat at the same catfish joints. They share one state with no pro teams and not a square foot of neutral ground.

The rivalry flows deep into the class divide among Southern whites. Alabama used to be where the children of doctors and lawyers went to school. Auburn was for the sons and daughters of farmers and factory workers. Auburn people saw Alabama people as phonies. Bryant himself dismissed Auburn as a "cow college." As the state modernized and the campuses integrated, the differences leveled off. But troll an Alabama or Auburn message board and it won't take long to find somebody calling a Tigers fan Jethro, or somebody referring to a Tide fan as Forrest Gump. The old resentments itch like a phantom limb.

"Everybody searches for some kind of group identity," says Wayne Flynt, a professor emeritus in history at Auburn. "In a [state] like Alabama, which was so poor and so looked down upon for so long . . . all year long you can put on the jersey and belong to something. And part of that identity is who you are not."

Going into last year's Iron Bowl, the rivalry was just about even. Alabama led 40–33–1, and Auburn had won seven of the previous 10. But while Auburn had won plenty of games, Alabama had won trophies. The Crimson Tide claimed 13 national titles, including several from the days when four or five polls might've picked different champions. Auburn owned one outright title, from 1957, and listed two more from the undefeated seasons in '93 and '04. That's how things stood, with an 11–0 and number two–ranked Auburn team led by star quarterback Cam Newton coming to Tuscaloosa.

While both programs have been in trouble with the NCAA over the years, the 2010 season was largely dominated by allegations that Newton's father, Cecil, tried to sell his son's services when Cam was coming out of junior college. The NCAA cleared Newton, but legions of Alabama fans believe that one day Auburn will have to give back the 2010 national title.

Harvey Updyke and Wayne Barnes had tickets to the Iron Bowl.

Before the game they went by the Bear Bryant statue outside Bryant-Denny Stadium. Someone had put a Newton jersey on it.

Alabama still had most of its best players from the '09 title team, and the game started like a 'Bama fan's wildest wish. It was 21–0 Tide after the first quarter, 24–0 halfway through the second. What's better: winning your own title, or denying your worst enemy theirs?

Then Tide running back Mark Ingram broke loose on a 41-yard reception down the right sideline, headed for another six—but Auburn defensive end Antoine Carter caught him from behind and punched the ball out. If it had gone out of bounds, Alabama ball. If it had kicked to the left, there'd have been a scramble. But it tightroped the sideline, rolled into the end zone, and Auburn fell on it for a touchback.

And right there, everything tilted—the game, the season, all those nesting worlds pressure-sealed into four quarters played once a year. Alabama led 24–7 at the half, but you could feel the Tigers coming, and it was almost no surprise early in the fourth when Auburn went up for good 28–27. Newton threw for three touchdowns and ran for another. Updyke and Barnes had booked a room for the night but drove back instead. They didn't say 10 words all the way to Dadeville. Barnes let Updyke out at the lake house and went on home to Florida.

The Iron Bowl took place on the day after Thanksgiving. Two months later, on the afternoon of January 27, Updyke called the Paul Finebaum sports-talk radio show out of Birmingham.

The Finebaum show gets monster ratings in Alabama, mainly because it keeps Auburn-Alabama boiling four hours a day, five days a week, all year long. Auburn fans had owned the show since the Iron Bowl. It had taken the Tigers just one year to unseat Alabama as the best in the nation—and, more important, the best in the state. Auburn fans called every day to crow. Updyke listened until he could no longer stand it. He called in and identified himself as Al from Dadeville. (His middle name is Almorn.) Finebaum put him on.

"Al" talked about seeing the Newton jersey on the Bryant statue. He added that a friend had sent him a newspaper clipping that said Auburn students rolled Toomer's Corner after Bryant died in 1983. Finebaum disputed this, and he was right. It didn't happen. This is what followed:

AL: Let me tell you what I did. The weekend after the Iron Bowl,
I went to Auburn, Alabama, 'cause I live 30 miles away, and I
poisoned the two Toomer's trees.

FINEBAUM (*nervous laugh*): Okay, well, that's fair.

AL: I put Spike 80DF in 'em.

FINEBAUM: Did they die?

AL: Do what?

FINEBAUM: Did. They. Die?

AL: They're not dead yet, but they definitely will die.

FINEBAUM: Is that against the law, to poison a tree?

AL: Well, do you think I care?

In April, Gary Keever, a horticulture professor at Auburn, stopped
by Toomer's Corner on his bike to check on the trees. Normally,
in spring, Southern live oaks are budding. Instead, Toomer's
Oaks were shedding. Keever called a guy from landscaping, and
together they scooped leaves into a five-gallon bucket. Keever
wanted a few to analyze at the lab. But even more, he didn't want
the leaves to blow down the street because they could potentially
damage other plants.

Spike 80DF blocks photosynthesis. When it gets into the leaves
of a tree, the chlorophyll can't absorb the energy already in the
leaves. The loose energy then destroys the leaves from the inside.
They yellow around the edges and eventually fall off. The tree
goes into survival mode. It puts out another set of leaves, then another—every three to five weeks—until the tree runs out of stored
energy. Most times, once the poison is in deep, there's not much
anyone can do. Eventually the tree gives up.

Spike 80DF has little or no effect on people and animals. It
is manufactured to murder plants. Ranchers use it to clear fence
lines; road crews use it to clear highway shoulders. A four-pound
bag can kill an acre of brush. Keever thinks Updyke dumped a
whole bag into the soil around Toomer's Oaks. When the initial
lab tests came back on February 9, the level of Spike in one soil
sample was 500 times what it takes to kill a tree.

Auburn's schools of agriculture and forestry are full of authorities on trees and soil and herbicides. Almost immediately after the
poison was discovered, a group of more than a dozen professors,
plus some outside experts, decided to soak the ground with liquid
charcoal, hoping it would bind to the poison. Then they put down

tarps to keep the roots from taking in Spike with rainwater. Next
they decided to change out the soil. Crews dug as deep as four feet
down, washed the roots as clean as they could and sucked up the
slurry. They repacked the holes with fresh soil. Not long after, the
tree on the College Street side started turning yellow.

Toomer's Oaks weren't in great shape to begin with, because
fans have just about loved them to death. Over the years, fans have
expanded the Toomer's Corner party from big road victories to
any football win, plus big wins in other sports. The toilet paper
has to be pressure-washed out of the trees. The branches still bear
marks from a couple of times when the TP caught fire. By the standards of live oaks—the most majestic trees of the South—Toomer's Oaks are gap-toothed and scraggly.

"If they were in my yard, I'd be hard-pressed to keep them,"
Keever said in April. "But these aren't trees; these are symbols.
People cherish that."

As he talked, a tour group came through. A student was showing off the campus to some prospective Auburn students and parents. They stopped under the trees, at the edge of the shade where
the boughs touch overhead.

The tour guide talked about Toomer's Corner, rolling the oaks,
and the poison in the trees. "The trees are doing okay, but we
don't know if they're going to make it," she said. "Even if they
don't, we'll continue the tradition."

She paused.

"I'm not sure how."

Updyke showed up for a preliminary hearing in April wearing a
crimson tie. Glennon Threatt, who is taking the case pro bono, is
Updyke's fourth lawyer. The first three quit; two of them cited Auburn connections. The Alabama state seal behind the judge's desk
in Opelika is painted orange and blue. Auburn colors.

Police haven't said how they figured out Al from Dadeville was
Updyke. But Updyke has admitted to making the call, and they
arrested him, and now he's charged with four felonies—he could
get up to 10 years in prison for each—and two misdemeanors.
A special agent from the Environmental Protection Agency also
came to the hearing. The EPA is considering federal charges.

The court session was quick. Threatt waived the preliminary
hearing and got permission for Updyke to relocate to Louisiana

until the trial, now set to begin in late October. Threatt did all the talking at the news conference outside the courthouse.

About an hour later, Updyke ended up in the emergency room.

He said somebody whacked him in the face outside a convenience store when he stopped to buy a bottle of green tea. No one stepped forward as a witness. The staff said they didn't know anything had happened until the Opelika police showed up.

The next day Updyke went back on the Finebaum show, this time under his own name. Threatt was on the air with him. At one point Updyke walked right up to the edge of admitting that he poisoned the trees. Threatt interrupted him. "Let me make clear to listeners that you are not confessing on the Paul Finebaum show," he said. So all Updyke copped to was making the call. He called himself a "crap stirrer." He wished his friend Barnes a happy birthday, talked about his 40 Alabama hats, apologized to his old high school coach.

Finebaum started taking callers, and the callers ripped Threatt for letting Updyke on the air.

"I don't know what you do for a living," Threatt answered one caller. "I doubt I'd get on the radio and criticize your work. But I can say that my intention was for Harvey to be humanized."

A few weeks later, Threatt filed a plea for Updyke: not guilty by reason of mental disease or defect.

Let me tell you the true story," Harvey Updyke says.

He was sitting there at the Iron Bowl, he says, watching Auburn rapidly fill in that 24–0 hole, when he started talking to a stranger next to him. "A kid, 30 years old at the oldest." The stranger said he was going to poison Toomer's Oaks with Spike. Harvey says he had never heard of Spike and had barely heard of the oaks.

"I swear on a Bible, all that is true," he says.

This is how, Updyke explains, he knew enough to call the Finebaum show and describe exactly what happened to the trees. Barnes, who was sitting on the other side of Updyke, says he never saw or heard that conversation. But, he says, he and Updyke didn't pay much attention to each other. They both had headphones on so they could follow the game on the radio.

Updyke is not thrilled with the mental defect plea. He says Threatt and his other lawyer believe it's the best chance at keeping him out of prison. He's 62 years old, and his neurosurgeon says he needs neck surgery to fix his bulging disks and lower-back problems. He's worried that prison would kill him.

"But if we stay [for the trial] in Lee County [Alabama], I would bet the farm that they're gonna put me in jail," he says. "Auburn wants me to pay for it."

He has lost 24 pounds and now weighs 209. He grew a beard, shaved it off, and then grew a mustache. But people still recognize him. On June 10, driving back through Alabama after another pretrial hearing, he stopped at a sporting goods store to get one more Alabama decal for his car. A Crimson Tide fan pestered him until Updyke agreed to let him take a picture. He told the guy not to post it on the Internet. He expects to see it there any day now.

His lawyer got the judge to approve his move to Louisiana so he could be close to his youngest daughter and her six-month-old girl, Updyke's 18th grandchild.

He loves Alabama football as much as ever. The only thing different is that he knows he can't go back for home games; he'd be too much of a distraction. But the Tide plays at Ole Miss on October 15. That game's not too far from his house in Louisiana. Updyke plans to be there. He wants the court date to hurry up and arrive. He hates what he has brought upon his family. Crimson, he says, is a wreck. Everybody else is worried too. He talks on the phone with Bear a lot. After all these months, Bear still doesn't understand why his father might go to prison over this.

"He keeps telling me, 'These people are acting like this is a tragedy,'" Updyke says. "And I just say, 'Well, yeah, it is.'"

Bear Bryant Updyke says other kids never made fun of his name. He grew up in Texas, and just went by Bear Updyke, and nobody made the connection. Sometimes a kid would growl at him, but that was about it.

Bear's 30 now and just got out of the Air Force. He tries to explain his dad. Harvey loves to talk trash, but he gets annoyed if you trash-talk him. He plays a lot of cards and haunts the Tider Insider message board. He once let a woman and her daughter stay at their house in Texas one night because the woman was driving drunk. He gave his son a clock inscribed with a Bear Bryant quote, and Bear can recite it from memory: *If you believe in yourself and have dedication and pride—and never quit, you'll be a winner. The price of victory is high but so are the rewards.*

Bear reads all the stories, absorbs all the Facebook comments, tangles online with an Auburn fan who wishes the whole Updyke family would die. He understands the meaning of Toomer's Oaks. He respects tradition. But still.

"I've been in the military," Bear says. "I've seen people die. If the trees die, I will feel bad, yes, but I'm gonna get sleep. If he is rightly convicted in a court of law . . . punishment fits the crime, that's all I'm asking for."

Greg Britt was a first-grader at the tail end of the 1960s. His dad was getting his PhD at Auburn, and his grandmother was the house mom for a fraternity. It was safer to leave kids alone back then. The oaks were Greg's playground. He romped around on the trees while his dad studied and his grandmother worked. Britt lives in Mexico City now. On football Saturdays he put the Auburn game on the TV and a Toomer's Corner webcam on his computer, and when the Tigers won, he watched fans roll the oaks from 1,200 miles away.

Kristi and Dennis Barker stopped by Toomer's Corner after their wedding in 1994. They hadn't planned the visit, but the oaks were on the way to the reception, and a friend had left them a spare roll of TP after decorating their car. So the Auburn grads rolled the oaks on their wedding day.

In 2002 Auburn's forestry department started culling acorns from the oaks and growing them as seedlings. Now children of the oaks grow all over the country. In May, Dennis Ross, an Auburn grad who's now a Florida congressman, planted a sapling on the grounds of the U.S. Capitol. By the next day, somebody had rolled it.

The trees won't die: they live in their descendants and in the stories.

The trees will die: Spike 80DF has nearly made its cruel climb into the last of the leaves.

We should be used to this dual existence. Sports, so often, make two out of one.

Put a broken-down trooper far from his childhood and he's harmless. Set him near the team he's always loved — and even nearer to the team he hates — and he becomes a villain.

What hurts Updyke most is that Alabama turned on him. Tide coach Nick Saban said whoever poisoned the trees "does not represent our institution, our program, or our fans in any way." Alabama fans raised $50,000 to help save the oaks. Auburn fans later raised money for April's tornado victims in Tuscaloosa. The feuding families have found a bit of common ground.

Then again, football season hasn't started yet.

Trees die slowly. Auburn will allow people to roll the oaks this fall, but the TP will be removed by hand. The trees are surrounded by guardrails. You can't touch them.

Right now, in the midst of a green Southern summer, the trees are nearly as brown as November. The Magnolia Avenue tree leans to one side. The College Street tree bears an old wound from a drunk driver. The oaks look as if you could just about pull them out with your hands.

But it's a hard thing to take 130 years, and all that comes with it, and rip it from the ground.

The roots go down so deep.

TAYLOR BRANCH

The Shame of College Sports

FROM THE ATLANTIC

"I'M NOT HIDING," Sonny Vaccaro told a closed hearing at the Willard Hotel in Washington, D.C., in 2001. "We want to put our materials on the bodies of your athletes, and the best way to do that is buy your school. Or buy your coach."

Vaccaro's audience, the members of the Knight Commission on Intercollegiate Athletics, bristled. These were eminent reformers—among them the president of the National Collegiate Athletic Association, two former heads of the U.S. Olympic Committee, and several university presidents and chancellors. The Knight Foundation, a nonprofit that takes an interest in college athletics as part of its concern with civic life, had tasked them with saving college sports from runaway commercialism as embodied by the likes of Vaccaro, who, since signing his pioneering shoe contract with Michael Jordan in 1984, had built sponsorship empires successively at Nike, Adidas, and Reebok. Not all the members could hide their scorn for the "sneaker pimp" of schoolyard hustle, who boasted of writing checks for millions to everybody in higher education.

"Why," asked Bryce Jordan, the president emeritus of Penn State, "should a university be an advertising medium for your industry?"

Vaccaro did not blink. "They shouldn't, sir," he replied. "You sold your souls, and you're going to continue selling them. You can be very moral and righteous in asking me that question, sir," Vaccaro added with irrepressible good cheer, "but there's not one of you in this room that's going to turn down any of our money. You're going to take it. I can only offer it."

William Friday, a former president of North Carolina's university system, still winces at the memory. "Boy, the silence that fell in that room," he recalled recently. "I never will forget it." Friday, who founded and cochaired two of the three Knight Foundation sports initiatives over the past 20 years, called Vaccaro "the worst of all" the witnesses ever to come before the panel.

But what Vaccaro said in 2001 was true then, and it's true now: corporations offer money so they can profit from the glory of college athletes, and the universities grab it. In 2010, despite the faltering economy, a single college athletic league, the football-crazed Southeastern Conference (SEC), became the first to crack the billion-dollar barrier in athletic receipts. The Big 10 pursued closely at $905 million. That money comes from a combination of ticket sales, concession sales, merchandise, licensing fees, and other sources—but the great bulk of it comes from television contracts.

Educators are in thrall to their athletic departments because of these television riches and because they respect the political furies that can burst from a locker room. "There's fear," Friday told me when I visited him on the University of North Carolina campus in Chapel Hill last fall. As we spoke, two giant construction cranes towered nearby over the university's Kenan Stadium, working on the latest $77 million renovation. (The University of Michigan spent almost four times that much to expand its Big House.) Friday insisted that for the networks, paying huge sums to universities was a bargain. "We do every little thing for them," he said. "We furnish the theater, the actors, the lights, the music, and the audience for a drama measured neatly in time slots. They bring the camera and turn it on." Friday, a weathered idealist at 91, laments the control universities have ceded in pursuit of this money. If television wants to broadcast football from here on a Thursday night, he said, "we shut down the university at three o'clock to accommodate the crowds." He longed for a campus identity more centered in an academic mission.

The United States is the only country in the world that hosts big-time sports at institutions of higher learning. This should not, in and of itself, be controversial. College athletics are rooted in the classical ideal of *Mens sana in corpore sano*—a sound mind in a sound body—and who would argue with that? College sports are deeply inscribed in the culture of our nation. Half a million young men and women play competitive intercollegiate sports each year. Millions of spectators flock into football stadiums each Saturday in the fall, and tens of millions more watch on television. The March Madness basketball tournament each spring has become a major national event, with upwards of 80 million watching it on television and talking about the games around the office water cooler. ESPN has spawned ESPNU, a channel dedicated to college sports, and Fox Sports and other cable outlets are developing channels exclusively to cover sports from specific regions or divisions.

With so many people paying for tickets and watching on television, college sports has become Very Big Business. According to various reports, the football teams at Texas, Florida, Georgia, Michigan, and Penn State—to name just a few big-revenue football schools—each earn between $40 million and $80 million in profits a year, even after paying coaches multimillion-dollar salaries. When you combine so much money with such high, almost tribal, stakes—football boosters are famously rabid in their zeal to have their alma mater win—corruption is likely to follow.

Scandal after scandal has rocked college sports. In 2010, the NCAA sanctioned the University of Southern California after determining that star running back Reggie Bush and his family had received "improper benefits" while he played for the Trojans. (Among other charges, Bush and members of his family were alleged to have received free airfare and limousine rides, a car, and a rent-free home in San Diego, from sports agents who wanted Bush as a client.) The Bowl Championship Series stripped USC of its 2004 national title, and Bush returned the Heisman Trophy he had won in 2005. Last fall, as Auburn University football stormed its way to an undefeated season and a national championship, the team's star quarterback, Cam Newton, was dogged by allegations that his father had used a recruiter to solicit up to $180,000 from Mississippi State in exchange for his son's matriculation there after junior college in 2010. Jim Tressel, the highly successful head football coach of the Ohio State Buckeyes, resigned last spring after the NCAA alleged he had feigned ignorance of rules violations by players on his team. At least 28 players over the course of the previous nine seasons, according to *Sports Illustrated,* had traded autographs, jerseys, and other team memorabilia in exchange for tattoos or cash at a tattoo parlor in Columbus, in violation of NCAA rules. Late this summer, Yahoo Sports reported that the NCAA was investigating allegations that a University of Miami booster had given millions of dollars in illicit cash and services to more than 70 Hurricanes football players over eight years.

The list of scandals goes on. With each revelation, there is much wringing of hands. Critics scold schools for breaking faith with their educational mission, and for failing to enforce the sanctity of "amateurism." Sportswriters denounce the NCAA for both tyranny and impotence in its quest to "clean up" college sports. Observers on all sides express jumbled emotions about youth and innocence, venting against professional mores or greedy amateurs.

For all the outrage, the real scandal is not that students are getting illegally paid or recruited, it's that two of the noble principles on which the NCAA justifies its existence—"amateurism" and the "student-athlete"—are cynical hoaxes, legalistic confections propagated by the universities so they can exploit the skills and fame of young athletes. The tragedy at the heart of college sports is not that some college athletes are getting paid, but that more of them are not.

Don Curtis, a UNC trustee, told me that impoverished football players cannot afford movie tickets or bus fare home. Curtis is a rarity among those in higher education today, in that he dares to violate the signal taboo: "I think we should pay these guys something."

Fans and educators alike recoil from this proposal as though from original sin. Amateurism is the whole point, they say. Paid athletes would destroy the integrity and appeal of college sports. Many former college athletes object that money would have spoiled the sanctity of the bond they enjoyed with their teammates. I, too, once shuddered instinctively at the notion of paid college athletes.

But after an inquiry that took me into locker rooms and ivory towers across the country, I have come to believe that sentiment blinds us to what's before our eyes. Big-time college sports are fully commercialized. Billions of dollars flow through them each year. The NCAA makes money, and enables universities and corporations to make money, from the unpaid labor of young athletes.

Slavery analogies should be used carefully. College athletes are not slaves. Yet to survey the scene—corporations and universities enriching themselves on the backs of uncompensated young men, whose status as "student-athletes" deprives them of the right to due process guaranteed by the Constitution—is to catch an unmistakable whiff of the plantation. Perhaps a more apt metaphor is colonialism: college sports, as overseen by the NCAA, is a system imposed by well-meaning paternalists and rationalized with hoary sentiments about caring for the well-being of the colonized. But it is, nonetheless, unjust. The NCAA, in its zealous defense of bogus principles, sometimes destroys the dreams of innocent young athletes.

The NCAA today is in many ways a classic cartel. Efforts to reform it—most notably by the three Knight Commissions over the course of 20 years—have, while making changes around the edges, been largely fruitless. The time has come for a major overhaul. And whether the powers that be like it or not, big changes are coming. Threats loom on multiple fronts: in Congress, the courts, breakaway athletic conferences, student rebellion, and public disgust. Swaddled in gauzy clichés, the NCAA presides over a vast, teetering glory.

Founding Myths

From the start, amateurism in college sports has been honored more often in principle than in fact; the NCAA was built of a mixture of noble and venal impulses. In the late 19th century, intellectuals believed that the sporting arena simulated an impending age of Darwinian struggle. Because the United States did not hold a global empire like England's, leaders warned of national softness once railroads conquered the last continental frontier. As though heeding this warning, ingenious students turned variations on rugby into a toughening agent. Today a plaque in New Brunswick, New Jersey, commemorates the first college game, on November 6, 1869, when Rutgers beat Princeton 6–4.

Walter Camp graduated from Yale in 1880 so intoxicated by the sport that he devoted his life to it without pay, becoming "the father of American football." He persuaded other schools to reduce the chaos on the field by trimming each side from 15 players to 11, and it was his idea to paint measuring lines on the field. He conceived functional designations for players, coining terms such as *quarterback*. His game remained violent by design. Crawlers could push the ball forward beneath piles of flying elbows without pause until they cried "Down!" in submission.

In an 1892 game against its archrival, Yale, the Harvard football team was the first to deploy a "flying wedge," based on Napoleon's surprise concentrations of military force. In an editorial calling for the abolition of the play, the *New York Times* described it as "half a ton of bone and muscle coming into collision with a man weighing 160 or 170 pounds," noting that surgeons often had to be called onto the field. Three years later, the continuing mayhem prompted the Harvard faculty to take the first of two votes to abolish football. Charles Eliot, the university's president, brought up other concerns. "Deaths and injuries are not the strongest argument against football," declared Eliot. "That cheating and brutality are profitable is the main evil." Still, Harvard football persisted. In 1903, fervent alumni built Harvard Stadium with zero college funds. The team's first paid head coach, Bill Reid, started in 1905 at nearly twice the average salary for a full professor.

A newspaper story from that year, illustrated with the Grim Reaper laughing on a goalpost, counted 25 college players killed during football season. A fairy-tale version of the founding of the NCAA holds that President Theodore Roosevelt, upset by a photograph of a bloodied Swarthmore College player, vowed to civilize or destroy football. The real story is that Roosevelt maneuvered shrewdly to preserve the sport—and give a boost to his beloved Harvard. After *McClure's* magazine published a story on corrupt teams with phantom students, a muckraker exposed Walter Camp's $100,000 slush fund at Yale. In response to mounting outrage, Roosevelt summoned leaders from Harvard, Princeton, and Yale to the White House, where Camp parried mounting criticism and conceded nothing irresponsible in the college football rules he'd established. At Roosevelt's behest, the three schools issued a public statement that college sports must reform to survive, and representatives from 68 colleges founded a new organization that would soon be called the National Collegiate Athletic Association. A Haverford College official was confirmed as secretary but then promptly resigned in favor of Bill Reid, the new Harvard coach, who instituted new rules that benefited Harvard's playing style at the expense of Yale's. At a stroke, Roosevelt saved football and dethroned Yale.

For nearly 50 years, the NCAA, with no real authority and no staff to speak of, enshrined amateur ideals that it was helpless to enforce. (Not until 1939 did it gain the power even to mandate helmets.) In 1929, the Carnegie Foundation made headlines with a report, "American College Athletics," which concluded that the scramble for players had "reached the proportions of nationwide commerce." Of the 112 schools surveyed, 81 flouted NCAA recommendations with inducements to students ranging from open payrolls and disguised booster funds to no-show jobs at movie studios. Fans ignored the uproar, and two-thirds of the colleges mentioned told the *New York Times* that they planned no changes. In 1939, freshman players at the University of Pittsburgh went on strike because they were getting paid less than their upperclassman teammates.

Embarrassed, the NCAA in 1948 enacted a "Sanity Code," which was supposed to prohibit all concealed and indirect benefits for college athletes; any money for athletes was to be limited to transparent scholarships awarded solely on financial need. Schools that violated this code would be expelled from NCAA membership and thus exiled from competitive sports.

This bold effort flopped. Colleges balked at imposing such a drastic penalty on each other, and the Sanity Code was repealed within a few years. The University of Virginia went so far as to call a press conference to say that if its athletes were ever accused of being paid, they should be forgiven, because their studies at Thomas Jefferson's university were so rigorous.

The Big Bluff

In 1951, the NCAA seized upon a serendipitous set of events to gain control of intercollegiate sports. First, the organization hired a young college dropout named Walter Byers as executive director. A journalist who was not yet 30 years old, he was an appropriately inauspicious choice for the vaguely defined new post. He wore cowboy boots and a toupee. He shunned personal contact, obsessed over details, and proved himself a bureaucratic master of pervasive, anonymous intimidation. Although discharged from the Army during World War II for defective vision, Byers was able to see an opportunity in two contemporaneous scandals. In one, the tiny College of William and Mary, aspiring to challenge football powers Oklahoma and Ohio State, was found to be counterfeiting grades to keep conspicuously pampered players eligible. In the other, a basketball point-shaving conspiracy (in which gamblers paid players to perform poorly) had spread from five New York colleges to the University of Kentucky, the reigning national champion, generating tabloid "perp" photos of gangsters and handcuffed basketball players. The scandals posed a crisis of credibility for collegiate athletics, and nothing in the NCAA's feeble record would have led anyone to expect real reform.

But Byers managed to impanel a small infractions board to set penalties without waiting for a full convention of NCAA schools, which would have been inclined toward forgiveness. Then he lobbied a University of Kentucky dean—A. D. Kirwan, a former football coach and future university president—not to contest the NCAA's dubious legal position (the association had no actual authority to penalize the university), pleading that college sports must do something to restore public support. His gambit succeeded when Kirwan reluctantly accepted a landmark precedent: the Kentucky basketball team would be suspended for the entire 1952–53 season. Its legendary coach, Adolph Rupp, fumed for a year in limbo.

The Kentucky case created an aura of centralized command for an NCAA office that barely existed. At the same time, a colossal misperception gave Byers leverage to mine gold. Amazingly in retrospect, most colleges and marketing experts considered the advent of television a dire threat to sports. Studies found that broadcasts reduced live attendance, and therefore gate receipts, because some customers preferred to watch at home for free. Nobody could yet imagine the revenue bonanza that television represented. With clunky new TV sets proliferating, the 1951 NCAA convention voted 161–7 to outlaw televised games except for a specific few licensed by the NCAA staff.

All but two schools quickly complied. The University of Pennsylvania and Notre Dame protested the order to break contracts for home-game television broadcasts, claiming the right to make their own decisions. Byers objected that such exceptions would invite disaster. The conflict escalated. Byers brandished penalties for games televised without approval. Penn contemplated seeking antitrust protection through the courts. Byers issued a contamination notice, informing any opponent scheduled to play Penn that it would be punished for showing up to compete. In effect, Byers mobilized the college world to isolate the two holdouts in what one sportswriter later called "the Big Bluff."

Byers won. Penn folded in part because its president, the perennial White House contender Harold Stassen, wanted to mend relations with fellow schools in the emerging Ivy League, which would be formalized in 1954. When Notre Dame also surrendered, Byers conducted exclusive negotiations with the new television networks on behalf of every college team. Joe Rauh Jr., a prominent civil rights attorney, helped him devise a rationing system to permit only 11 broadcasts a year—the fabled *Game of the Week*. Byers and Rauh selected a few teams for television exposure, excluding the rest. On June 6, 1952, NBC signed a one-year deal to pay the NCAA $1.14 million for a carefully restricted football package. Byers routed all contractual proceeds through his office. He floated the idea that, to fund an NCAA infrastructure, his organization should take a 60 percent cut; he accepted 12 percent that season. (For later contracts, as the size of television revenues grew exponentially, he backed down to 5 percent.) Proceeds from the first NBC contract were enough to rent an NCAA headquarters, in Kansas City.

Only one year into his job, Byers had secured enough power and money to regulate all of college sports. Over the next decade, the NCAA's power grew along with television revenues. Through the efforts of Byers's deputy and chief lobbyist, Chuck Neinas, the NCAA won an important concession in the Sports Broadcasting Act of 1961, in which Congress made its granting of a precious antitrust exemption to the National Football League contingent upon the blackout of professional football on Saturdays. Deftly, without even mentioning the NCAA, a rider on the bill carved each weekend into protected broadcast markets: Saturday for college, Sunday for the NFL. The NFL got its antitrust exemption. Byers, having negotiated the NCAA's television package up to $3.1 million per football season—which was higher than the NFL's figure in those early years—had made the NCAA into a spectacularly profitable cartel.

"We Eat What We Kill"

The NCAA's control of college sports still rested on a fragile base, however: the consent of the colleges and universities it governed.

For a time, the vast sums of television money delivered to these institutions through Byers's deals made them willing to submit. But the big football powers grumbled about the portion of the television revenue diverted to nearly a thousand NCAA member schools that lacked major athletic programs. They chafed against cost-cutting measures—such as restrictions on team size—designed to help smaller schools. "I don't want Hofstra telling Texas how to play football," Darrell Royal, the Longhorns coach, griped. By the 1970s and '80s, as college football games delivered bonanza ratings—and advertising revenue—to the networks, some of the big football schools began to wonder: Why do we need to have our television coverage brokered through the NCAA? Couldn't we get a bigger cut of that TV money by dealing directly with the networks?

Byers faced a rude internal revolt. The NCAA's strongest legions, its big football schools, defected en masse. Calling the NCAA a price-fixing cartel that siphoned every television dollar through its coffers, in 1981 a rogue consortium of 61 major football schools threatened to sign an independent contract with NBC for $180 million over four years.

With a huge chunk of the NCAA's treasury walking out the door, Byers threatened sanctions, as he had against Penn and Notre Dame three decades earlier. But this time the Universities of Georgia and Oklahoma responded with an antitrust suit. "It is virtually impossible to overstate the degree of our resentment . . . of the NCAA," said William Banowsky, the president of the University of Oklahoma. In the landmark 1984 *NCAA v. Board of Regents of the University of Oklahoma* decision, the U.S. Supreme Court struck down the NCAA's latest football contracts with television—and any future ones—as an illegal restraint of trade that harmed colleges and viewers. Overnight, the NCAA's control of the television market for football vanished. Upholding Banowsky's challenge to the NCAA's authority, the *Regents* decision freed the football schools to sell any and all games the markets would bear. Coaches and administrators no longer had to share the revenue generated by their athletes with smaller schools outside the football consortium. "We eat what we kill," one official at the University of Texas bragged.

A few years earlier, this blow might have financially crippled the NCAA—but a rising tide of money from basketball concealed the structural damage of the *Regents* decision. During the 1980s, income from the March Madness college basketball tournament, paid directly by the television networks to the NCAA, grew 10-fold. The windfall covered—and then far exceeded—what the organization had lost from football.

Still, Byers never forgave his former deputy Chuck Neinas for leading the rebel consortium. He knew that Neinas had seen from the inside how tenuous the NCAA's control really was, and how diligently Byers had worked to prop up its Oz-like facade. During Byers's tenure, the rule book for Division I athletes grew to 427 pages of scholastic detail. His NCAA personnel manual banned conversations around water coolers, and coffee cups on desks, while specifying exactly when drapes must be drawn at the NCAA's 27,000-square-foot headquarters near Kansas City (built in 1973 from the proceeds of a 1 percent surtax on football contracts). It was as though, having lost control where it mattered, Byers pedantically exerted more control where it didn't.

After retiring in 1987, Byers let slip his suppressed fury that the ingrate football conferences, having robbed the NCAA of television revenue, still expected it to enforce amateurism rules and police every leak of funds to college players. A lethal greed was "gnawing at the innards of college athletics," he wrote in his memoir. When Byers renounced the NCAA's pretense of amateurism, his former colleagues would stare blankly, as though he had gone senile or, as he wrote, "desecrated my sacred vows." But Byers was better positioned than anyone else to argue that college football's claim to amateurism was unfounded. Years later, as we will see, lawyers would seize upon his words to do battle with the NCAA.

Meanwhile, reformers fretted that commercialism was hurting college sports, and that higher education's historical balance between academics and athletics had been distorted by all the money sloshing around. News stories revealed that schools went to extraordinary measures to keep academically incompetent athletes eligible for competition, and would vie for the most-sought-after high school players by proffering under-the-table payments. In 1991, the first Knight Commission report, "Keeping Faith with the Student Athlete," was published; the commission's "bedrock conviction" was that university presidents must seize control of the NCAA from athletic directors in order to restore the preeminence of academic values over athletic or commercial ones. In response, college presidents did take over the NCAA's governance. But by 2001, when the second Knight Commission report ("A Call to Action: Reconnecting College Sports and Higher Education") was issued, a new generation of reformers was admitting that problems of corruption and commercialism had "grown rather than diminished" since the first report. Meanwhile the NCAA itself, revenues rising, had moved into a $50 million, 116,000-square-foot headquarters in Indianapolis. By 2010, as the size of NCAA headquarters increased yet again with a 130,000-square-foot expansion, a third Knight Commission was groping blindly for a hold on independent college-athletic conferences that were behaving more like sovereign pro leagues than confederations of universities. And still more money continued to flow into NCAA coffers. With the basketball tournament's 2011 television deal, annual March Madness broadcast revenues had skyrocketed 50-fold in less than 30 years.

The Myth of the "Student-Athlete"

Today, much of the NCAA's moral authority—indeed much of the justification for its existence—is vested in its claim to protect what it calls the "student-athlete." The term is meant to conjure the nobility of amateurism, and the precedence of scholarship over athletic endeavor. But the origins of the "student-athlete" lie not in a disinterested ideal but in a sophistic formulation designed, as the sports economist Andrew Zimbalist has written, to help the NCAA in its "fight against workmen's compensation insurance claims for injured football players."

"We crafted the term *student-athlete*," Walter Byers himself wrote, "and soon it was embedded in all NCAA rules and interpretations." The term came into play in the 1950s, when the widow of Ray Dennison, who had died from a head injury received while playing football in Colorado for the Fort Lewis A&M Aggies, filed for workmen's compensation death benefits. Did his football scholarship make the fatal collision a "work-related" accident? Was he a school employee, like his peers who worked part-time as teaching assistants and bookstore cashiers? Or was he a fluke victim of extracurricular pursuits? Given the hundreds of incapacitating injuries to college athletes each year, the answers to these questions had enormous consequences. The Colorado Supreme Court ultimately agreed with the school's contention that he was not eligible for benefits, since the college was "not in the football business."

The term *student-athlete* was deliberately ambiguous. College players were not students at play (which might understate their athletic obligations), nor were they just athletes in college (which might imply they were professionals). That they were high-performance athletes meant they could be forgiven for not meeting the academic standards of their peers; that they were students meant they did not have to be compensated, ever, for anything more than the cost of their studies. *Student-athlete* became the NCAA's signature term, repeated constantly in and out of courtrooms.

Using the "student-athlete" defense, colleges have compiled a string of victories in liability cases. On the afternoon of October 26, 1974, the Texas Christian University Horned Frogs were playing the Alabama Crimson Tide in Birmingham, Alabama. Kent Waldrep, a TCU running back, carried the ball on a "Red Right 28" sweep toward the Crimson Tide's sideline, where he was met by a swarm of tacklers. When Waldrep regained consciousness, Bear Bryant, the storied Crimson Tide coach, was standing over his hospital bed. "It was like talking to God, if you're a young football player," Waldrep recalled.

Waldrep was paralyzed: he had lost all movement and feeling below his neck. After nine months of paying his medical bills, Texas Christian refused to pay any more, so the Waldrep family coped for years on dwindling charity.

Through the 1990s, from his wheelchair, Waldrep pressed a lawsuit for workers' compensation. (He also, through heroic rehabilitation efforts, recovered feeling in his arms, and eventually learned to drive a specially rigged van. "I can brush my teeth," he told me last year, "but I still need help to bathe and dress.") His attorneys haggled with TCU and the state worker compensation fund over what constituted employment. Clearly, TCU had provided football players with equipment for the job, as a typical employer would—but did the university pay wages, withhold income taxes on his financial aid, or control work conditions and performance? The appeals court finally rejected Waldrep's claim in June of 2000, ruling that he was not an employee because he had not paid taxes on financial aid that he could have kept even if he quit football. (Waldrep told me school officials "said they recruited me as a student, not an athlete," which he says was absurd.)

The long saga vindicated the power of the NCAA's "student-athlete" formulation as a shield, and the organization continues to invoke it as both a legalistic defense and a noble ideal. Indeed, such is the term's rhetorical power that it is increasingly used as a sort of reflexive mantra against charges of rabid hypocrisy.

Last Thanksgiving weekend, with both the FBI and the NCAA investigating whether Cam Newton had been lured onto his team with illegal payments, Newton's Auburn Tigers and the Alabama Crimson Tide came together for their annual game, known as the Iron Bowl, before 101,821 fans at Bryant-Denny Stadium. This game is always a highlight of the football season because of the historic rivalry between the two schools, and the 2010 edition had enormous significance, pitting the defending national champion Crimson Tide against the undefeated Tigers, who were aiming for their first championship since 1957. I expected excited fans; what I encountered was the throbbing heart of college sports. As I drove before daybreak toward the stadium, a sleepless caller babbled over WJOX, the local fan radio station, that he "couldn't stop thinking about the coin toss." In the parking lot, ticketless fans were puzzled that anyone need ask why they had tailgated for days just to watch their satellite-fed flat screens within earshot of the roar. All that morning, pilgrims packed the Bear Bryant museum, where displays elaborated the misery of Alabama's 4–24 run before the glorious Bryant era dawned in 1958.

Finally, as Auburn took the field for warm-ups, one of Alabama's public-address system operators played "Take the Money and Run" (an act for which he would be fired). A sea of signs reading $CAM taunted Newton. The game, perhaps the most exciting of the season, was unbearably tense, with Auburn coming from way behind to win 28–27, all but assuring that it would go on to play for the national championship. Days later, Auburn suspended Newton after the NCAA found that a rules violation had occurred: his father was alleged to have marketed his son in a pay-for-play scheme; a day after that, the NCAA reinstated Newton's eligibility because investigators had not found evidence that Newton or Auburn officials had known of his father's actions. This left Newton conveniently eligible for the Southeastern Conference championship game and for the postseason BCS championship bowl. For the NCAA, prudence meant honoring public demand.

"Our championships," NCAA president Mark Emmert has declared, "are one of the primary tools we have to enhance the student-athlete experience."

"Whoremasters"

NCAA v. Regents left the NCAA devoid of television football revenue and almost wholly dependent on March Madness basketball. It is rich but insecure. Last year, CBS Sports and Turner Broadcasting paid $771 million to the NCAA for television rights to the 2011 men's basketball tournament alone. That's three-quarters of a billion dollars built on the backs of amateurs—on unpaid labor. The whole edifice depends on the players' willingness to perform what is effectively volunteer work. The athletes, and the league officials, are acutely aware of this extraordinary arrangement. William Friday, the former North Carolina president, recalls being yanked from one Knight Commission meeting and sworn to secrecy about what might happen if a certain team made the NCAA championship basketball game. "They were going to dress and go out on the floor," Friday told me, "but refuse to play," in a wildcat student strike. Skeptics doubted such a diabolical plot. These were college kids—unlikely to second-guess their coaches, let alone forfeit the dream of a championship. Still, it was unnerving to contemplate what hung on the consent of a few young volunteers: several hundred million dollars in television revenue, countless livelihoods, the NCAA budget, and subsidies for sports at more than 1,000 schools. Friday's informants exhaled when the suspect team lost before the finals.

Cognizant of its precarious financial base, the NCAA has in recent years begun to pursue new sources of revenue. Taking its cue from member schools such as Ohio State (which in 2009 bundled all its promotional rights—souvenirs, stadium ads, shoe deals—and outsourced them to the international sports marketer IMG College for a guaranteed $11 million a year), the NCAA began to exploit its vault of college sports on film. For $29.99 apiece, NCAA On Demand offers DVDs of more than 200 memorable contests in men's ice hockey alone. Video game technology also allows nostalgic fans to relive and even participate in classic moments of "NCAA Basketball." "NCAA Football," licensed by the NCAA through IMG College to Electronic Arts, one of the world's largest video game manufacturers, reportedly sold 2.5 million copies in 2008. Brit Kirwan, the chancellor of the Maryland university system and a former president at Ohio State, says there were "terrible fights" between the third Knight Commission and the NCAA over the ethics of generating this revenue.

All of this money ultimately derives from the college athletes whose likenesses are shown in the films or video games. But none of the profits go to them. Last year, Electronic Arts paid more than $35 million in royalties to the NFL players union for the underlying value of names and images in its pro football series—but neither the NCAA nor its affiliated companies paid former college players a nickel. Naturally, as they have become more of a profit center for the NCAA, some of the vaunted "student-athletes" have begun to clamor that they deserve a share of those profits. You "see everybody getting richer and richer," Desmond Howard, who won the 1991 Heisman Trophy while playing for the Michigan Wolverines, told *USA Today* recently. "And you walk around and you can't put gas in your car? You can't even fly home to see your parents?"

Some athletes have gone beyond talk. A series of lawsuits quietly making their way through the courts cast a harsh light on the absurdity of the system—and threaten to dislodge the foundations on which the NCAA rests. On July 21, 2009, lawyers for Ed O'Bannon filed a class-action antitrust suit against the NCAA at the U.S. District Court in San Francisco. "Once you leave your university," says O'Bannon, who won the John Wooden Award for Player of the Year in 1995 on UCLA's national championship basketball team, "one would think your likeness belongs to you." The NCAA and UCLA continue to collect money from the sales of videos of him playing. But by NCAA rules, O'Bannon, who today works at a Toyota dealership near Las Vegas, alleges he is still not allowed to share the revenue the NCAA generates from his own image as a college athlete. His suit quickly gathered coplaintiffs from basketball and football, ex-players featured in NCAA videos and other products. "The NCAA does not license student-athlete likenesses," NCAA spokesperson Erik Christianson told the *New York Times* in response to the suit, "or prevent former student-athletes from attempting to do so. Likewise, to claim the NCAA profits off student-athlete likenesses is also pure fiction."

The legal contention centers on part IV of the NCAA's "Student-Athlete Statement" for Division I, which requires every athlete to authorize use of "your name or picture . . . to promote NCAA championships or other NCAA events, activities or programs." Does this clause mean that athletes clearly renounce personal interest forever? If so, does it actually undermine the NCAA by implicitly recognizing that athletes have a property right in their own performance? Jon King, a lawyer for the plaintiffs, expects the NCAA's core mission of amateurism to be its "last defense standing."

In theory, the NCAA's passion to protect the noble amateurism of college athletes should prompt it to focus on head coaches in the high-revenue sports—basketball and football—since holding the top official accountable should most efficiently discourage corruption. The problem is that the coaches' growing power has rendered them, unlike their players, ever more immune to oversight. According to research by Charles Clotfelter, an economist at Duke, the average compensation for head football coaches at public universities, now more than $2 million, has grown 750 percent (adjusted for inflation) since the *Regents* decision in 1984; that's more than 20 times the cumulative 32 percent raise for college professors. For top basketball coaches, annual contracts now exceed $4 million, augmented by assorted bonuses, endorsements, country club memberships, the occasional private plane, and in some cases a negotiated percentage of ticket receipts. (Oregon's ticket concessions netted former football coach Mike Bellotti an additional $631,000 in 2005.)

The NCAA rarely tangles with such people, who are apt to fight back and win. When Rick Neuheisel, the head football coach of the Washington Huskies, was punished for petty gambling (in a March Madness pool, as it happened), he sued the NCAA and the university for wrongful termination, collected $4.5 million, and later moved on to UCLA. When the NCAA tried to cap assistant coaches' entering salary at a mere $16,000, nearly 2,000 of them brought an antitrust suit, *Law v. NCAA*, and in 1999 settled for $54.5 million. Since then, salaries for assistant coaches have commonly exceeded $200,000, with the top assistants in the SEC averaging $700,000. In 2009, Monte Kiffin, then at the University of Tennessee, became the first assistant coach to reach $1 million, plus benefits.

The late Myles Brand, who led the NCAA from 2003 to 2009, defended the economics of college sports by claiming that they were simply the result of a smoothly functioning free market. He and his colleagues deflected criticism about the money saturating big-time college sports by focusing attention on scapegoats; in 2010, outrage targeted sports agents. Last year *Sports Illustrated* published "Confessions of an Agent," a firsthand account of dealing with high-strung future pros whom the agent and his peers courted with flattery, cash, and tawdry favors. Nick Saban, Alabama's head football coach, mobilized his peers to denounce agents as a public scourge. "I hate to say this," he said, "but how are they any better than a pimp? I have no respect for people who do that to young people. None."

Saban's raw condescension contrasts sharply with the lonely penitence from Dale Brown, the retired longtime basketball coach at LSU. "Look at the money we make off predominantly poor black kids," Brown once reflected. "We're the whoremasters."

"Picayune Rules"

NCAA officials have tried to assert their dominion—and distract attention from the larger issues—by chasing frantically after petty violations. Tom McMillen, a former member of the Knight Commission who was an All-American basketball player at the University of Maryland, likens these officials to traffic cops in a speed trap, who could flag down almost any passing motorist for prosecution in kangaroo court under a "maze of picayune rules." The publicized cases have become convoluted soap operas. At the start of the 2010 football season, A. J. Green, a wide receiver at Georgia, confessed that he'd sold his own jersey from the Independence Bowl the year before, to raise cash for a spring break vacation. The NCAA sentenced Green to a four-game suspension for violating his amateur status with the illicit profit generated by selling the shirt off his own back. While he served the suspension, the Georgia Bulldogs store continued legally selling replicas of Green's number 8 jersey for $39.95 and up.

A few months later, the NCAA investigated rumors that Ohio State football players had benefited from "hook-ups on tatts"—that is, that they'd gotten free or underpriced tattoos at an Ohio tattoo parlor in exchange for autographs and memorabilia—a violation of the NCAA's rule against discounts linked to athletic personae. The NCAA Committee on Infractions imposed five-game suspensions on Terrelle Pryor, Ohio State's tattooed quarterback, and four other players (some of whom had been found to have sold their Big 10 championship rings and other gear), but did permit them to finish the season and play in the Sugar Bowl. (This summer, in an attempt to satisfy NCAA investigators, Ohio State voluntarily vacated its football wins from last season, as well as its Sugar Bowl victory.) A different NCAA committee promulgated a rule banning symbols and messages in players' eye black—reportedly aimed at Pryor's controversial gesture of support for the pro quarterback Michael Vick, and at Bible verses inscribed in the eye black of the former Florida quarterback Tim Tebow.

The moral logic is hard to fathom: the NCAA bans personal messages on the bodies of the players, and penalizes players for trading their celebrity status for discounted tattoos—but it codifies precisely how and where commercial insignia from multinational corporations can be displayed on college players, for the financial benefit of the colleges. Last season, while the NCAA investigated him and his father for the recruiting fees they'd allegedly sought, Cam Newton compliantly wore at least 15 corporate logos—one on his jersey, four on his helmet visor, one on each wristband, one on his pants, six on his shoes, and one on the headband he wears under his helmet—as part of Auburn's $10.6 million deal with Under Armour.

"Restitution"

Obscure NCAA rules have bedeviled Scott Boras, the preeminent sports agent for Major League Baseball stars, in cases that may ultimately prove more threatening to the NCAA than Ed O'Bannon's antitrust suit. In 2008, Andrew Oliver, a sophomore pitcher for the Oklahoma State Cowboys, had been listed as the 12th-best professional prospect among sophomore players nationally. He decided to dismiss the two attorneys who had represented him out of high school, Robert and Tim Baratta, and retain Boras instead. Infuriated, the Barattas sent a spiteful letter to the NCAA. Oliver didn't learn about this until the night before he was scheduled to pitch in the regional final for a place in the College World Series, when an NCAA investigator showed up to question him in the presence of lawyers for Oklahoma State. The investigator also questioned his father, Dave, a truck driver.

Had Tim Baratta been present in their home when the Minnesota Twins offered $390,000 for Oliver to sign out of high school? A *yes* would mean trouble. While the NCAA did not forbid all professional advice—indeed, *Baseball America* used to publish the names of agents representing draft-likely underclassmen—NCAA bylaw 12.3.2.1 prohibited actual negotiation with any professional team by an adviser, on pain of disqualification for the college athlete. The questioning lasted past midnight.

Just hours before the game was to start the next day, Oklahoma State officials summoned Oliver to tell him he would not be pitching. Only later did he learn that the university feared that by letting him play while the NCAA adjudicated his case, the university would open not only the baseball team but all other Oklahoma State teams to broad punishment under the NCAA's "restitution rule" (bylaw 19.7), under which the NCAA threatens schools with sanctions if they obey any temporary court order benefiting a college athlete, should that order eventually be modified or removed. The baseball coach did not even let his ace tell his teammates the sad news in person. "He said, 'It's probably not a good idea for you to be at the game,'" Oliver recalls.

The Olivers went home to Ohio to find a lawyer. Rick Johnson, a solo practitioner specializing in legal ethics, was aghast that the Baratta brothers had turned in their own client to the NCAA, divulging attorney-client details likely to invite wrath upon Oliver. But for the next 15 months, Johnson directed his litigation against the two NCAA bylaws at issue. Judge Tygh M. Tone, of Erie County, came to share his outrage. On February 12, 2009, Tone struck down the ban on lawyers negotiating for student-athletes as a capricious, exploitative attempt by a private association to "dictate to an attorney where, what, how, or when he should represent his client," violating accepted legal practice in every state. He also struck down the NCAA's restitution rule as an intimidation that attempted to supersede the judicial system. Finally, Judge Tone ordered the NCAA to reinstate Oliver's eligibility at Oklahoma State for his junior season, which started several days later.

The NCAA sought to disqualify Oliver again, with several appellate motions to stay "an unprecedented Order purporting to void a fundamental Bylaw." Oliver did get to pitch that season, but he dropped into the second round of the June 2009 draft, signing for considerably less than if he'd been picked earlier. Now 23,

Oliver says sadly that the whole experience "made me grow up a little quicker." His lawyer claimed victory. "Andy Oliver is the first college athlete ever to win against the NCAA in court," said Rick Johnson.

Yet the victory was only temporary. Wounded, the NCAA fought back with a vengeance. Its battery of lawyers prepared for a damages trial, ultimately overwhelming Oliver's side eight months later with an offer to resolve the dispute for $750,000. When Oliver and Johnson accepted, to extricate themselves ahead of burgeoning legal costs, Judge Tone was compelled to vacate his orders as part of the final settlement. This freed NCAA officials to reassert the two bylaws that Judge Tone had so forcefully overturned, and they moved swiftly to ramp up rather than curtail enforcement. First, the NCAA's Eligibility Center devised a survey for every drafted undergraduate athlete who sought to stay in college another year. The survey asked whether an agent had conducted negotiations. It also requested a signed release waiving privacy rights and authorizing professional teams to disclose details of any interaction to the NCAA Eligibility Center. Second, NCAA enforcement officials went after another Scott Boras client.

The Toronto Blue Jays had made the left-handed pitcher James Paxton, of the University of Kentucky, the 37th pick in the 2009 draft. Paxton decided to reject a reported $1 million offer and return to school for his senior year, pursuing a dream to pitch for his team in the College World Series. But then he ran into the new NCAA survey. Had Boras negotiated with the Blue Jays? Boras has denied that he did, but it would have made sense that he had—that was his job, to test the market for his client. But saying so would get Paxton banished under the same NCAA bylaw that had derailed Andrew Oliver's career. Since Paxton was planning to go back to school and not accept their draft offer, the Blue Jays no longer had any incentive to protect him—indeed, they had every incentive to turn him in. The Blue Jays' president, by telling reporters that Boras had negotiated on Paxton's behalf, demonstrated to future recruits and other teams that they could use the NCAA's rules to punish college players who wasted their draft picks by returning to college. The NCAA's enforcement staff raised the pressure by requesting to interview Paxton.

Though Paxton had no legal obligation to talk to an investigator, NCAA bylaw 10.1(j) specified that anything short of complete

cooperation could be interpreted as unethical conduct, affect-
ing his amateur status. Under its restitution rule, the NCAA had
leverage to compel the University of Kentucky to ensure obedience.

As the 2010 season approached, Gary Henderson, the Kentucky coach, sorely wanted Paxton, one of *Baseball America*'s top-
ranked players, to return. Rick Johnson, Andrew Oliver's lawyer,
filed for a declaratory judgment on Paxton's behalf, arguing that
the state constitution—plus the university's code of student conduct—barred arbitrary discipline at the request of a third party.
Kentucky courts deferred to the university, however, and Paxton
was suspended from the team. "Due to the possibility of future
penalties, including forfeiture of games," the university stated, it
"could not put the other 32 players of the team and the entire
UK 22-sport intercollegiate athletics department at risk by having
James compete." The NCAA appraised the result with satisfaction.
"When negotiations occur on behalf of student-athletes," Erik
Christianson, the NCAA spokesperson, told the *New York Times* in
reference to the Oliver case, "those negotiations indicate that the
student-athlete intends to become a professional athlete and no
longer remain an amateur."

Paxton was stranded. Not only could he not play for Kentucky,
but his draft rights with the Blue Jays had lapsed for the year,
meaning he could not play for any minor league affiliate of Major
League Baseball. Boras wrangled a holdover job for him in Texas
with the independent Grand Prairie AirHogs, pitching against the
Pensacola Pelicans and Wichita Wingnuts. Once projected to be
a first-round draft pick, Paxton saw his stock plummet into the
fourth round. He remained unsigned until late in spring training,
when he signed with the Seattle Mariners and reported to their
minor league camp in Peoria, Arizona.

"You Might as Well Shoot Them in the Head"

"When you dream about playing in college," Joseph Agnew told
me not long ago, "you don't ever think about being in a lawsuit."
Agnew, a student at Rice University in Houston, had been cut from
the football team and had his scholarship revoked by Rice before
his senior year, meaning that he faced at least $35,000 in tuition
and other bills if he wanted to complete his degree in sociology.

Bereft of his scholarship, he was flailing about for help when he discovered the National College Players Association, which claims 7,000 active members and seeks modest reforms such as safety guidelines and better death benefits for college athletes. Agnew was struck by the NCPA scholarship data on players from top Division I basketball teams, which showed that 22 percent were not renewed from 2008 to 2009 — the same fate he had suffered.

In October 2010, Agnew filed a class-action antitrust suit over the cancellation of his scholarship and to remove the cap on the total number of scholarships that can be awarded by NCAA schools. In his suit, Agnew did not claim the right to free tuition. He merely asked the federal court to strike down an NCAA rule, dating to 1973, that prohibited colleges and universities from offering any athletic scholarship longer than a one-year commitment, to be renewed or not, unilaterally, by the school — which in practice means that coaches get to decide each year whose scholarships to renew or cancel. (After the coach who had recruited Agnew had moved on to Tulsa, the new Rice coach switched Agnew's scholarship to a recruit of his own.) Agnew argued that without the one-year rule, he would have been free to bargain with all eight colleges that had recruited him, and each college could have decided how long to guarantee his scholarship.

Agnew's suit rested on a claim of an NCAA antitrust violation combined with a laudable academic goal — making it possible for students to finish their educations. Around the same time, lawyers from President Obama's Justice Department initiated a series of meetings with NCAA officials and universities in which they asked what possible educational rationale there was for allowing the NCAA — an organization that did not itself pay for scholarships — to impose a blanket restriction on the length of scholarships offered by colleges. Tidbits leaked into the press. In response, the NCAA contended that an athletic scholarship was a "merit award" that should be reviewed annually, presumably because the degree of "merit" could change. Justice Department lawyers reportedly suggested that a free market in scholarships would expand learning opportunities in accord with the stated rationale for the NCAA's tax-exempt status — that it promotes education through athletics. The one-year rule effectively allows colleges to cut underperforming "student-athletes," just as pro sports teams cut their players. "Plenty of them don't stay in school," said one of Agnew's lawyers,

Stuart Paynter. "They're just gone. You might as well shoot them in the head."

Agnew's lawsuit has made him a pariah to former friends in the athletic department at Rice, where everyone identified so thoroughly with the NCAA that they seemed to feel he was attacking them personally. But if the premise of Agnew's case is upheld by the courts, it will make a sham of the NCAA's claim that its highest priority is protecting education.

"They Want to Crush These Kids"

Academic performance has always been difficult for the NCAA to address. Any detailed regulation would intrude upon the free choice of widely varying schools, and any academic standard broad enough to fit both MIT and Ole Miss would have little force. From time to time, a scandal will expose extreme lapses. In 1989, Dexter Manley, by then the famous "Secretary of Defense" for the NFL's Washington Redskins, teared up before the U.S. Senate Subcommittee on Education, Arts, and Humanities, when admitting that he had been functionally illiterate in college.

Within big-time college athletic departments, the financial pressure to disregard obvious academic shortcomings and shortcuts is just too strong. In the 1980s, Jan Kemp, an English instructor at the University of Georgia, publicly alleged that university officials had demoted and then fired her because she refused to inflate grades in her remedial English courses. Documents showed that administrators replaced the grades she'd given athletes with higher ones, providing fake passing grades on one notable occasion to nine Bulldog football players who otherwise would have been ineligible to compete in the 1982 Sugar Bowl. (Georgia lost anyway, 24–20, to a University of Pittsburgh team led by the future Hall of Fame quarterback Dan Marino.) When Kemp filed a lawsuit against the university, she was publicly vilified as a troublemaker, but she persisted bravely in her testimony. Once, Kemp said, a supervisor demanding that she fix a grade had bellowed, "Who do you think is more important to this university, you or Dominique Wilkins?" (Wilkins was a star on the basketball team.) Traumatized, Kemp twice attempted suicide.

In trying to defend themselves, Georgia officials portrayed Kemp as naive about sports. "We have to compete on a level playing field," said Fred Davison, the university president. During the Kemp civil trial, in 1986, Hale Almand, Georgia's defense lawyer, explained the university's patronizing aspirations for its typical less-than-scholarly athlete. "We may not make a university student out of him," Almand told the court, "but if we can teach him to read and write, maybe he can work at the post office rather than as a garbage man when he gets through with his athletic career." This argument backfired with the jurors: finding in favor of Kemp, they rejected her polite request for $100,000, and awarded her $2.6 million in damages instead. (This was later reduced to $1.08 million.) Jan Kemp embodied what is ostensibly the NCAA's reason for being—to enforce standards fairly and put studies above sports—but no one from the organization ever spoke up on her behalf.

The NCAA body charged with identifying violations of any of the Division I league rules, the Committee on Infractions, operates in the shadows. Josephine Potuto, a professor of law at the University of Nebraska and a longtime committee member who was then serving as its vice chair, told Congress in 2004 that one reason her group worked in secret was that it hoped to avoid a "media circus." The committee preferred to deliberate in private, she said, guiding member schools to punish themselves. "The enforcement process is cooperative, not adversarial," Potuto testified. The committee consisted of an elite coterie of judges, athletic directors, and authors of legal treatises. "The committee also is savvy about intercollegiate athletics," she added. "They cannot be conned."

In 2009, a series of unlikely circumstances peeled back the veil of secrecy to reveal NCAA procedures so contorted that even victims marveled at their comical wonder. The saga began in March of 2007, shortly after the Florida State Seminoles basketball team was knocked out of the NIT basketball tournament, which each spring invites the best teams not selected for the March Madness tournament. At an athletic department study hall, Al Thornton, a star forward for the team, completed a sports psychology quiz but then abandoned it without posting his written answers electronically by computer. Brenda Monk, an academic tutor for the Seminoles, says she noticed the error and asked a teammate to finish entering Thornton's answers onscreen and hit Submit, as required for credit. The teammate complied, steaming silently, and then complained at the athletic office about getting stuck with cleanup chores for the superstar Thornton (who was soon to be selected by the Los Angeles Clippers in the first round of the NBA draft). Monk promptly resigned when questioned by FSU officials, saying her fatigue at the time could not excuse her asking the teammate to submit the answers to another student's completed test.

Monk's act of guileless responsibility set off a chain reaction. First, FSU had to give the NCAA preliminary notice of a confessed academic fraud. Second, because this would be its seventh major infraction case since 1968, FSU mounted a vigorous self-investigation to demonstrate compliance with NCAA academic rules. Third, interviews with 129 Seminoles athletes unleashed a nightmare of matter-of-fact replies about absentee professors who allowed group consultations and unlimited retakes of open-computer assignments and tests. Fourth, FSU suspended 61 of its athletes in 10 sports. Fifth, the infractions committee applied the byzantine NCAA bylaws to FSU's violations. Sixth, one of the penalties announced in March of 2009 caused a howl of protest across the sports universe.

Twenty-seven news organizations filed a lawsuit in hopes of finding out how and why the NCAA proposed to invalidate 14 prior victories in FSU football. Such a penalty, if upheld, would doom coach Bobby Bowden's chance of overtaking Joe Paterno of Penn State for the most football wins in Division I history. This was sacrosanct territory. Sports reporters followed the litigation for six months, reporting that 25 of the 61 suspended FSU athletes were football players, some of whom were ruled ineligible retroactively from the time they had heard or yelled out answers to online test questions in, of all things, a music appreciation course.

When reporters sought access to the transcript of the infractions committee's hearing in Indianapolis, NCAA lawyers said the 695-page document was private. (The NCAA claimed it was entitled to keep all such records secret because of a landmark Supreme Court ruling that it had won in 1988, in *NCAA v. Tarkanian,* which exempted the organization from any due-process obligations because it was not a government organization.) Media outlets pressed the judge to let Florida State share its own copy of the hearing transcript, whereupon NCAA lawyers objected that the school had never actually "possessed" the document; it had only seen the transcript via a defendant's guest access to the carefully restricted NCAA website. This claim, in turn, prompted intercession on the side of the media by Florida's attorney general, arguing that letting the NCAA use a technical loophole like this would undermine the state's sunshine law mandating open public records. After tumultuous appeals, the Florida courts agreed and ordered the NCAA transcript released in October of 2009.

News interest quickly evaporated when the sports media found nothing in the record about Coach Bowden or the canceled football victories. But the transcript revealed plenty about the NCAA. On page 37, T. K. Wetherell, the bewildered Florida State president, lamented that his university had hurt itself by cooperating with the investigation. "We self-reported this case," he said during the hearing, and he later complained that the most ingenuous athletes—those who asked, "What's the big deal, this happens all the time?"—received the harshest suspensions, while those who clammed up on the advice of lawyers went free. The music appreciation professor was apparently never questioned. Brenda Monk, the only instructor who consistently cooperated with the investigation, appeared voluntarily to explain her work with learning-disabled athletes, only to be grilled about her credentials by Potuto in a pettifogging inquisition of remarkable stamina.

In January of last year, the NCAA's Infractions Appeals Committee sustained all the sanctions imposed on FSU except the number of vacated football victories, which it dropped, ex cathedra, from 14 to 12. The final penalty locked Bobby Bowden's official win total on retirement at 377 instead of 389, behind Joe Paterno's 401 (and counting). This carried stinging symbolism for fans, without bringing down on the NCAA the harsh repercussions it would have risked if it had issued a television ban or substantial fine.

Cruelly, but typically, the NCAA concentrated public censure on powerless scapegoats. A dreaded "show cause" order rendered Brenda Monk, the tutor, effectively unhirable at any college in the United States. Cloaking an old-fashioned blackball in the stately language of law, the order gave notice that any school hiring Monk before a specified date in 2013 "shall, pursuant to the provisions of Bylaw 19.5.2.2(l), show cause why it should not be penalized if it does not restrict the former learning specialist [Monk] from having any contact with student-athletes." Today she works as an education supervisor at a prison in Florida.

*

The Florida State verdict hardly surprised Rick Johnson, the law-yer who had represented the college pitchers Andrew Oliver and James Paxton. "All the NCAA's enforcements are random and se-lective," he told me, calling the organization's appeals process a travesty. (Johnson says the NCAA has never admitted to having wrongly suspended an athlete.) Johnson's scalding experience prompted him to undertake a law review article on the subject, which in turn sent him trawling through NCAA archives. From the summary tax forms required of nonprofits, he found out that the NCAA had spent nearly $1 million chartering private jets in 2006. "What kind of nonprofit organization leases private jets?" Johnson asks. It's hard to determine from tax returns what money goes where, but it looks as if the NCAA spent less than 1 percent of its budget on enforcement that year. Even after its plump cut for its own overhead, the NCAA dispersed huge sums to its 1,200 member schools, in the manner of a professional sports league. These annual payments are universal—every college gets some-thing—but widely uneven. They keep the disparate shareholders (barely) united and speaking for all of college sports. The pay-ments coerce unity within the structure of a private association that is unincorporated and unregulated, exercising amorphous powers not delegated by any government.

Searching through the archives, Johnson came across a 1973 memo from the NCAA general counsel recommending the adop-tion of a due-process procedure for athletes in disciplinary cases. Without it, warned the organization's lawyer, the association risked big liability claims for deprivation of rights. His proposal went no-where. Instead, apparently to limit costs to the universities, Wal-ter Byers had implemented the year-by-year scholarship rule that Joseph Agnew would challenge in court 37 years later. Moreover, the NCAA's 1975 convention adopted a second recommendation "to discourage legal actions against the NCAA," according to the minutes. The members voted to create bylaw 19.7, Restitution, to intimidate college athletes in disputes with the NCAA. Johnson recognized this provision all too well, having won the temporary court judgment that the rule was illegal if not downright despotic. It made him nearly apoplectic to learn that the NCAA had delib-erately drawn up the restitution rule as an obstacle to due process, contrary to the recommendation of its own lawyer. "They want to crush these kids," he says.

The NCAA, of course, has never expressed such a desire, and its public comments on due process tend to be anodyne. At a congressional hearing in 2004, the infractions committee vice chair, Josephine Potuto, repeatedly argued that although the NCAA is "not bound by any judicial due process standards," its enforcement, infractions, and hearing procedures meet and "very likely exceed" those of other public institutions. Yet when pressed, Potuto declared that athletes would have no standing for due process even if the Supreme Court had not exempted the NCAA in the 1988 *Tarkanian* decision. "In order to reach due-process issues as a legal Constitutional principle, the individual challenging has to have a substantive property or liberty interest," she testified. "The opportunity to play intercollegiate athletics does not rise to that level."

To translate this from the legal jargon, Potuto used a circular argument to confine college athletes beneath any right to freedom or property in their own athletic effort. They have no stake to seek their rights, she claimed, because they have no rights at stake.

Potuto's assertion might be judged preposterous, an heir of the *Dred Scott* dictum that slaves possessed no rights a white person was bound to respect. But she was merely being honest, articulating assumptions almost everyone shares without question. Whether motivated by hostility for students (as critics like Johnson allege), or by noble and paternalistic tough love (as the NCAA professes), the denial of fundamental due process for college athletes has stood unchallenged in public discourse. Like other NCAA rules, it emanates naturally from the premise that college athletes own no interest in sports beyond exercise, character-building, and good fun. Who represents these young men and women? No one asks.

The debates and commissions about reforming college sports nibble around the edges—trying to reduce corruption, to prevent the "contamination" of athletes by lucre, and to maintain at least a pretense of concern for academic integrity. Everything stands on the implicit presumption that preserving amateurism is necessary for the well-being of college athletes. But while amateurism—and the free labor it provides—may be necessary to the preservation of the NCAA, and perhaps to the profit margins of various interested corporations and educational institutions, what if it doesn't benefit the athletes? What if it hurts them?

"The Plantation Mentality"

"Ninety percent of the NCAA revenue is produced by 1 percent of the athletes," Sonny Vaccaro says. "Go to the skill positions"—the stars. "Ninety percent African Americans." The NCAA made its money off those kids, and so did he. They were not all bad people, the NCAA officials, but they were blind, Vaccaro believes. "Their organization is a fraud."

Vaccaro retired from Reebok in 2007 to make a clean break for a crusade. "The kids and their parents gave me a good life," he says in his peppery staccato. "I want to give something back." Call it redemption, he told me. Call it education or a good cause. "Here's what I preach," said Vaccaro. "This goes beyond race, to human rights. The least educated are the most exploited. I'm probably closer to the kids than anyone else, and I'm 71 years old."

Vaccaro is officially an unpaid consultant to the plaintiffs in *O'Bannon v. NCAA*. He connected Ed O'Bannon with the attorneys who now represent him, and he talked to some of the additional coplaintiffs who have joined the suit, among them Oscar Robertson, a basketball Hall of Famer who was incensed that the NCAA was still selling his image on playing cards 50 years after he left the University of Cincinnati.

Jon King, an antitrust lawyer at Hausfeld LLP in San Francisco, told me that Vaccaro "opened our eyes to massive revenue streams hidden in college sports." King and his colleagues have drawn on Vaccaro's vast knowledge of athletic department finances, which include off-budget accounts for shoe contracts. Sonny Vaccaro and his wife, Pam, "had a mountain of documents," he said. The outcome of the 1984 *Regents* decision validated an antitrust approach for O'Bannon, King argues, as well as for Joseph Agnew in his continuing case against the one-year scholarship rule. Lawyers for Sam Keller—a former quarterback for the University of Nebraska who is featured in video games—are pursuing a parallel "right of publicity" track based on the First Amendment. Still other lawyers could revive Rick Johnson's case against NCAA bylaws on a larger scale, and King thinks claims for the rights of college players may be viable also under laws pertaining to contracts, employment, and civil rights.

Vaccaro had sought a law firm for O'Bannon with pockets deep enough to withstand an expensive war of attrition, fearing that NCAA officials would fight discovery to the end. So far, though, they have been forthcoming. "The numbers are off the wall," Vaccaro says. "The public will see for the first time how all the money is distributed."

Vaccaro has been traveling the after-dinner circuit, proselytizing against what he sees as the NCAA's exploitation of young athletes. Late in 2008, someone who heard his stump speech at Howard University mentioned it to Michael Hausfeld, a prominent antitrust and human rights lawyer, whose firm had won suits against Exxon for Native Alaskans and against Union Bank of Switzerland for Holocaust victims' families. Someone tracked down Vaccaro on vacation in Athens, Greece, and he flew back directly to meet Hausfeld. The shoe salesman and the white-shoe lawyer made common cause.

Hausfeld LLP has offices in San Francisco, Philadelphia, and London. Its headquarters are on K Street in Washington, D.C., about three blocks from the White House. When I talked with Hausfeld there not long ago, he sat in a cavernous conference room, tidy in pinstripes, hands folded on a spotless table that reflected the skyline. He spoke softly, without pause, condensing the complex fugue of antitrust litigation into simple sentences. "Let's start with the basic question," he said, noting that the NCAA claims that student-athletes have no property rights in their own athletic accomplishments. Yet, in order to be eligible to play, college athletes have to waive their rights to proceeds from any sales based on their athletic performance.

"What right is it that they're waiving?" Hausfeld asked. "You can't waive something you don't have. So they had a right that they gave up in consideration to the principle of amateurism, if there be such." (At an April hearing in a U.S. District Court in California, Gregory Curtner, a representative for the NCAA, stunned O'Bannon's lawyers by saying: "There is no document, there is no substance, that the NCAA ever takes from the student-athletes their rights of publicity or their rights of likeness. They are at all times owned by the student-athlete." Jon King says this is "like telling someone they have the winning lottery ticket, but by the way, it can only be cashed in on Mars." The court denied for a second time an NCAA motion to dismiss the O'Bannon complaint.)

The waiver clause is nestled among the paragraphs of the "Student-Athlete Statement" that NCAA rules require be collected yearly from every college athlete. In signing the statement, the athletes attest that they have amateur status, that their stated SAT scores are valid, that they are willing to disclose any educational documents requested, and so forth. Already, Hausfeld said, the defendants in the Ed O'Bannon case have said in court filings that college athletes thereby transferred their promotional rights forever. He paused. "That's ludicrous," he said. "Nobody assigns rights like that. Nobody can assert rights like that." He said the pattern demonstrated clear abuse by the collective power of the schools and all their conferences under the NCAA umbrella—"a most effective cartel."

The faux ideal of amateurism is "the elephant in the room," Hausfeld said, sending for a book. "You can't get to the bottom of our case without exposing the hypocrisy of amateurism, and Walter Byers says it eloquently." An assistant brought in Byers's memoir. It looked garish on the shiny table because dozens of pink Post-its protruded from the text. Hausfeld read to me from page 390:

> The college player cannot sell his own feet (the coach does that) nor can he sell his own name (the college will do that). This is the plantation mentality resurrected and blessed by today's campus executives.

He looked up. "That wasn't me," he said. "That was the NCAA's architect." He found a key recommendation on page 388:

> Prosecutors and the courts, with the support of the public, should use antitrust laws to break up the collegiate cartel—not just in athletics but possibly in other aspects of collegiate life as well.

Could the book become evidence? Might the aged Byers testify? (He is now 89.) Was that part of the plaintiffs' strategy for the O'Bannon trial? Hausfeld smiled faintly. "I'd rather the NCAA lawyers not fully understand the strategy," he said.

He put the spiny book away and previewed what lies ahead. The court soon would qualify his clients as a class. Then the Sherman Antitrust Act would provide for thorough discovery to break down exactly what the NCAA receives on everything from video clips to jerseys, contract by contract. "And we want to know what they're carrying on their books as the value of their archival footage," he concluded. "They say it's a lot of money. We agree. How much?"

The work will be hard, but Hausfeld said he will win in the courts, unless the NCAA folds first. "Why?" Hausfeld asked rhetorically. "We know our clients are foreclosed: neither the NCAA nor its members will permit them to participate in any of that licensing revenue. Under the law, it's up to them [the defendants] to give a pro-competitive justification. They can't. End of story."

In 2010 the third Knight Commission, complementing a previous commission's recommendation for published reports on academic progress, called for the finances of college sports to be made transparent and public—television contracts, conference budgets, shoe deals, coaches' salaries, stadium bonds, everything. The recommendation was based on the worthy truism that sunlight is a proven disinfectant. But in practice, it has not been applied at all. Conferences, coaches, and other stakeholders resisted disclosure; college players still have no way of determining their value to the university.

"Money surrounds college sports," says Domonique Foxworth, who is a cornerback for the NFL's Baltimore Ravens and an executive committee member for the NFL Players Association, and played for the University of Maryland. "And every player knows those millions are floating around only because of the 18-to-22-year-olds." Yes, he told me, even the second-string punter believes a miracle might lift him into the NFL, and why not? In all the many pages of the three voluminous Knight Commission reports, there is but one paragraph that addresses the real-life choices for college athletes. "Approximately 1 percent of NCAA men's basketball players and 2 percent of NCAA football players are drafted by NBA or NFL teams," stated the 2001 report, basing its figures on a review of the previous 10 years, "and just being drafted is no assurance of a successful professional career." Warning that the odds against professional athletic success are "astronomically high," the Knight Commission counsels college athletes to avoid a "rude surprise" and to stick to regular studies. This is sound advice as far as it goes, but it's a bromide that pinches off discussion. Nothing in the typical college curriculum teaches a sweat-stained guard at Clemson or Purdue what his monetary value to the university is.

Nothing prods students to think independently about amateurism—because the universities themselves have too much invested in its preservation. Stifling thought, the universities, in league with the NCAA, have failed their own primary mission by providing an empty, cynical education on college sports.

The most basic reform would treat the students as what they are—adults, with rights and reason of their own—and grant them a meaningful voice in NCAA deliberations. A restoration of full citizenship to "student-athletes" would facilitate open governance, making it possible to enforce pledges of transparency in both academic standards and athletic finances. Without that, the NCAA has no effective checks and balances, no way for the students to provide informed consent regarding the way they are governed. A thousand questions lie willfully silenced because the NCAA is naturally afraid of giving "student-athletes" a true voice. Would college players be content with the augmented scholarship or allowance now requested by the National College Players Association? If a player's worth to the university is greater than the value of his scholarship (as it clearly is in some cases), should he be paid a salary? If so, would teammates in revenue sports want to be paid equally, or in salaries stratified according to talent or value on the field? What would the athletes want in Division III, where athletic budgets keep rising without scholarships or substantial sports revenue? Would athletes seek more or less variance in admissions standards? Should non-athletes also have a voice, especially where involuntary student fees support more and more of college sports? Might some schools choose to specialize, paying players only in elite leagues for football, or lacrosse? In athletic councils, how much would high-revenue athletes value a simple *thank you* from the tennis or field hockey players for the newly specified subsidies to their facilities?

University administrators, already besieged from all sides, do not want to even think about such questions. Most cringe at the thought of bargaining with athletes as a general manager does in professional sports, with untold effects on the budgets for coaches and every other sports item. "I would not want to be part of it," North Carolina athletic director Dick Baddour told me flatly. After 44 years at UNC, he could scarcely contemplate a world without amateur rules. "We would have to think long and hard," Baddour added gravely, "about whether this university would continue those sports at all."

I, too, once reflexively recoiled at the idea of paying college athletes and treating them like employees or professionals. It feels abhorrent—but for reasons having to do more with sentiment than with practicality or law. Not just fans and university presidents but judges have often found cursory, nonstatutory excuses to leave amateur traditions intact. "Even in the increasingly commercial modern world," said a federal court judge in *Gaines v. NCAA* in 1990, "this Court believes there is still validity to the Athenian concept of a complete education derived from fostering the full growth of both mind and body." The fact that "the NCAA has not distilled amateurism to its purest form," said the Fifth Circuit Court of Appeals in 1988, "does not mean its attempts to maintain a mixture containing some amateur elements are unreasonable."

But one way or another, the smokescreen of amateurism may soon be swept away. For one thing, a victory by the plaintiffs in O'Bannon's case would radically transform college sports. Colleges would likely have to either stop profiting from students or start paying them. The NCAA could also be forced to pay tens, if not hundreds, of millions of dollars in damages. If O'Bannon and Vaccaro and company win, "it will turn college sports on its ear," said Richard Lapchick, the president of the National Consortium for Academics and Sports, in a recent interview with the *New York Times*.

Though the O'Bannon case may take several years yet to reach resolution, developments on other fronts are chipping away at amateurism, and at the NCAA. This past summer, *Sports Illustrated* editorialized in favor of allowing college athletes to be paid by non-university sources without jeopardizing their eligibility. At a press conference last June, Steve Spurrier, the coach of the South Carolina Gamecocks football team (and the winner of the 1966 Heisman Trophy as a Florida Gator), proposed that coaches start paying players $300 a game out of their own pockets. The coaches at six other SEC schools (Alabama, Florida, Ole Miss, Mississippi State, LSU, and Tennessee) all endorsed Spurrier's proposal. And Mark Emmert, the NCAA president, recently conceded that big changes must come. "The integrity of collegiate athletics is seriously challenged today by rapidly growing pressures coming from many directions," Emmert said in July. "We have reached a point where incremental change is not sufficient to meet these challenges. I want us to act more aggressively and in a more comprehensive way than we have in the past. A few new tweaks of the rules won't get the job done."

Threats to NCAA dominion also percolate in Congress. Aggrieved legislators have sponsored numerous bills. Senator Orrin Hatch, citing mistreatment of his Utah Utes, has called witnesses to discuss possible antitrust remedies for the Bowl Championship Series. Congressional committees have already held hearings critical of the NCAA's refusal to follow due process in disciplinary matters; other committees have explored a rise in football concussions. Last January, calls went up to investigate "informal" football workouts at the University of Iowa just after the season-ending bowl games—workouts so grueling that 41 of the 56 amateur student-athletes collapsed, and 13 were hospitalized with rhabdomyolysis, a life-threatening kidney condition often caused by excessive exercise.

The greatest threat to the viability of the NCAA may come from its member universities. Many experts believe that the churning instability within college football will drive the next major change. President Obama himself has endorsed the drumbeat cry for a national playoff in college football. This past spring, the Justice Department questioned the BCS about its adherence to antitrust standards. Jim Delany, the commissioner of the Big 10, has estimated that a national playoff system could produce three or four times as much money as the existing bowl system does. If a significant band of football schools were to demonstrate that they could orchestrate a true national playoff, without the NCAA's assistance, the association would be terrified—and with good reason. Because if the big sports colleges don't need the NCAA to administer a national playoff in football, then they don't need it to do so in basketball. In which case, they could cut out the middleman in March Madness and run the tournament themselves. Which would deprive the NCAA of close to $1 billion a year, more than 95 percent of its revenue. The organization would be reduced to a rule book without money—an organization aspiring to enforce its rules but without the financial authority to enforce anything.

Thus the playoff dreamed of and hankered for by millions of football fans haunts the NCAA. "There will be some kind of playoff in college football, and it will not be run by the NCAA," says Todd Turner, a former athletic director in four conferences (Big East, ACC, SEC, and Pac-10). "If I'm at the NCAA, I have to worry that the playoff group can get basketball to break away too."

This danger helps explain why the NCAA steps gingerly in enforcements against powerful colleges. To alienate member colleges would be to jeopardize its own existence. Long gone are television bans and the "death penalty" sentences (commanding season-long shutdowns of offending teams) once meted out to Kentucky (1952), Southwestern Louisiana (1973), and Southern Methodist University (1987). Institutions receive mostly symbolic slaps nowadays. Real punishments fall heavily on players and on scapegoats like literacy tutors.

A deeper reason explains why, in its predicament, the NCAA has no recourse to any principle or law that can justify amateurism. There is no such thing. Scholars and sportswriters yearn for grand juries to ferret out every forbidden bauble that reaches a college athlete, but the NCAA's ersatz courts can only masquerade as public authority. How could any statute impose amateur status on college athletes, or on anyone else? No legal definition of *amateur* exists, and any attempt to create one in enforceable law would expose its repulsive and unconstitutional nature—a bill of attainder, stripping from college athletes the rights of American citizenship.

For all our queasiness about what would happen if some athletes were to get paid, there is a successful precedent for the professionalization of an amateur sports system: the Olympics. For years, Walter Byers waged war with the NCAA's older and more powerful nemesis, the Amateur Athletic Union, which since 1894 had overseen U.S. Olympic athletes. Run in high-handed fashion, the AAU had infamously banned Jesse Owens for life in 1936—weeks after his four heroic gold medals punctured the Nazi claim of Aryan supremacy—because instead of using his sudden fame to tour and make money for the AAU at track meets across Europe, he came home early. In the early 1960s, the fights between the NCAA and the AAU over who should manage Olympic athletes become so bitter that President Kennedy called in General Douglas MacArthur to try to mediate a truce before the Tokyo Olympic Games.

Ultimately, Byers prevailed and effectively neutered the AAU.

In November 1978, President Jimmy Carter signed the biparti-
san Amateur Sports Act. Amateurism in the Olympics soon dis-
solved—and the world did not end. Athletes, granted a 20 percent
voting stake on every Olympic sport's governing body, tipped balances in the United States and then inexorably around the world.
First in marathon races, then in tennis tournaments, players soon
were allowed to accept prize money and keep their Olympic eligibility. Athletes profited from sponsorships and endorsements.
The International Olympic Committee expunged the word *amateur* from its charter in 1986. Olympic officials, who had once
disdained the NCAA for offering scholarships in exchange for
athletic performance, came to welcome millionaire athletes from
every quarter, while the NCAA still refused to let the pro Olympian Michael Phelps swim for his college team at Michigan.

This sweeping shift left the Olympic reputation intact, and perhaps improved. Only hardened romantics mourned the amateur
code. "Hey, come on," said Anne Audain, a track-and-field star
who once held the world record for the 5,000 meters. "It's like
losing your virginity. You're a little misty for awhile, but then you
realize, *Wow, there's a whole new world out there!*"

Without logic or practicality or fairness to support amateurism,
the NCAA's final retreat is to sentiment. The Knight Commission
endorsed its heartfelt cry that to pay college athletes would be "an
unacceptable surrender to despair." Many of the people I spoke
with while reporting this article felt the same way. "I don't want to
pay college players," said Wade Smith, a tough criminal lawyer and
former star running back at North Carolina. "I just don't want to
do it. We'd lose something precious."

"Scholarship athletes are already paid," declared the Knight
Commission members, "in the most meaningful way possible: with
a free education." This evasion by prominent educators severed
my last reluctant, emotional tie with imposed amateurism. I found
it worse than self-serving. It echoes masters who once claimed that
heavenly salvation would outweigh earthly injustice to slaves. In
the era when our college sports first arose, colonial powers were
turning the whole world upside down to define their own interests
as all-inclusive and benevolent. Just so, the NCAA calls it heinous
exploitation to pay college athletes a fair portion of what they
earn.

S. L. PRICE

Staring Down History

FROM SPORTS ILLUSTRATED

LATE ON THE AFTERNOON that the 2011 Serbia Open began in Belgrade, Novak Djokovic sat down in a large tent for his opening press conference. He had driven onto the grounds of what will soon be his own tennis academy in a cockatoo-white $90,000 Mercedes, wearing natty brown suede shoes with tassels that dangled like stemmed cherries. He showed not the slightest sign of strain.

This was strange, because Djokovic, the former clown act of tennis who has transformed himself into the most dominant athlete of the year, had every reason to feel the world bearing down on his once-suspect psyche. Unbeaten in 2011, riding a streak that would soon have him surpass runs by greats Ivan Lendl and Björn Borg and current number one Rafael Nadal (and on Sunday would reach 39 since December 5), the second-ranked Djokovic was starting his clay-court season before hometown fans who expected—no, demanded—that he keep on winning. Not only that, but as the omnipresent face of a tournament owned by his 150-employee company, Family Sport, the 23-year-old Serb known nationally by his nickname, Nole, also bore almost sole responsibility for filling the seats in a country with almost 20 percent unemployment.

Yet in a week marked by cold and rain, by Nadal's admission that Djokovic's rise was unstoppable, and by a parade of Fellini-esque characters that would faze even the most jaded New York City bouncer, Djokovic never so much as rolled an eyeball. No player can prepare for all the energy-draining nonsense that gravitates, like filings to a magnet, to the newest man who would be king, but Djokovic brushed off a nagging chest cold and played to his sellout crowds, gave every minispeech with feeling, greeted each sponsor with a smile, took each question as if hearing it for the first time. In the final, against Feliciano López on May 1, he shook off the scariest fall a player has taken on court this year—and won. Seconds later a courtside wall collapsed, sending fans sprawling onto the court. Djokovic barely blinked.

In fact there was only one moment when he visibly stiffened. It came early in the pretournament press conference, on Monday, April 25, when a Dutch reporter said, "It's a lot easier to represent, say, Switzerland than Serbia. How do you see that?"

Djokovic stared. "Can you repeat the question?"

It was clear what the reporter meant: Unlike Switzerland—Roger Federer's dull bastion of clocks and discreet banking—Serbia was reviled in the 1990s as a nation of gangsters; it engaged in attacks on Slovenia, Bosnia, and Croatia; and it committed atrocities against Albanian Muslims in Kosovo under President Slobodan Milosevic's policy of ethnic cleansing. Unlike, say, Zurich, Belgrade was bombed for 78 days in 1999 by a U.S.-led NATO coalition, and the towering, empty-faced wreckage of those bombs still flanks its downtown streets 12 years later. Nor has Switzerland been accused of lax pursuit of an accused war criminal, as Serbia has with Ratko Mladic, its military commander in Bosnia in the early '90s.

"How do you see that?" the Dutch reporter repeated.

Djokovic didn't say what he could have: that Serbia has now had three consecutive national democratic elections; that last year its president, Boris Tadic, increased the reward for Mladic's capture 10-fold, to 10 million euros ($14 million); and that Serbia's legislature had voted to officially apologize for the 1995 massacre of 8,000 people in the Bosnian town of Srebrenica. Nor did Djokovic say that, earlier that day, he had taken some fellow players to Belgrade's 671-foot-tall Avala Tower—destroyed in the '99 attacks and rebuilt last year—and scrawled in the guest book, *The symbol of Belgrade: We'll be back.*

Djokovic fingered the microphone. "Well," he began, "I don't think that. . . ."

Then he hesitated. How to describe the terror and rage he felt as a 12-year-old when the air raid sirens wailed and explosions thundered across Belgrade? How to describe the way it all got balled together, the tennis and the bombing, because tennis is what kept his family sane? The way his life, his future career, became the prime focus of his parents' attention and his success became his family's goal and salvation? "He is something special," says Novak's mother, Dijana. "I always say he is the child of God."

Easier to represent Switzerland?

How to explain what it meant to his country when, at 19, he rocketed up the rankings? With each big win, everyone—his family, his fellow Serbs, even his government—believed more deeply that he, more than any tower, could be the symbol of Serbia's rebirth. Overnight his words had the power to inspire or inflame. In February 2008, fresh off winning the Australian Open, his first Grand Slam title, in Melbourne, Djokovic addressed by video link more than 150,000 people gathered in Belgrade to protest Kosovo's U.S.-backed declaration of independence. "We are united and ready to defend what is ours," Djokovic told the crowd, his face as big as a billboard. "Kosovo is Serbia." The night ended in rioting and looting, with dozens hurt; the Croatian and Bosnian embassies were vandalized; and the U.S. embassy was ransacked and set on fire.

How do you see that?

The reporter waited. "That's not a simple question," Djokovic said finally. "And there's not a simple answer that can be given."

The next night Djokovic showed up late to the official party for the players. The Novak Cafe & Restaurant, a tony showplace for Family Sport's operations, across the Sava River in New Belgrade, threw open its doors and bar for dozens of models of the tall, short-skirted, high-heeled variety. This was John Isner's third time in town. "It's a pretty big party city," said the towering American. "And the girls are spectacular."

At first Djokovic hewed to the elite pro's playbook, retreating to a downstairs banquet room while the band boomed and everyone waited for something to happen. When he bounded up after an hour and grabbed the microphone, it figured that he'd say a few words and bolt. He had a match on Wednesday, after all. Instead, Djokovic launched into a supremely awful karaoke rendition of "Eye of the Tiger," his shout about *Risin' up to the challenge of our ri-val* sending an electric charge across the floor. Women danced, cheering men crowded toward their Nole, cameras flashed. The

song ended; Djokovic looked around. Isner had lost that afternoon. "This is for John Isner; it's his birthday today!" Djokovic
said. "It's a Serbian song: You won't understand the s—— we are
singing, but you will enjoy it."

After what turned out to be a soupy dirge, Djokovic insisted that
Isner join in singing the next song, a disco-polka in Serbian about
coital gymnastics. Thirty seconds in, the uncomprehending Isner
wandered off as Djokovic, joined by Davis Cup teammates Viktor
Troicki and Nenad Zimonjic, bellowed the refrain *"Ja volim taj sex!"*
("I love that sex!")

For those who like their athletes monkish, it was a disconcert-
ing sight. Djokovic had long been tennis's go-to guy on YouTube,
ripping off his shirt to sing "I Will Survive," mincing around to
imitate Maria Sharapova, mimicking the tics of Federer, Nadal,
and Andy Roddick with devastating accuracy. Fans and reporters
loved it, but the more stiff-necked of Djokovic's peers, such as Federer and Roddick, found it insulting. And for years this looseness
seemed of a piece with Djokovic's inability to break up the Rafa-
Fed duopoly. The two tennis gods radiated a sober intensity, and
despite Djokovic's occasional bite at big tournaments, he often
shrank when the time came to fully take them down. He lacked
gravitas. He seemed fated to go down as his generation's Marat
Safin, the prodigious Russian talent whose fearsome backhand was
undermined by a highly distractable mind.

But this year Djokovic has given every sign of being a changed
man. "He's crushing us," Mardy Fish said in April. Djokovic's serve
is one of the tour's best, and he's winning a ridiculous 43 percent of his return games; through Sunday he had lost just eight
sets since last November. He has summarily dismissed Federer the
last three times they've met, including a straight-sets slap in the
Australian Open semis. His four straight wins over Nadal, all in
tournament finals, are even more telling. Just when the Spaniard,
coming off a historic run in 2010, was expected to consolidate his
place at number one, Djokovic dealt him the kind of psyche-rat-
tling losses that Federer rarely could inflict. In the final at Madrid
on May 8, Djokovic beat Nadal for the first time on clay—hand-
ily—snapping his 37-match winning streak on the surface. "[My]
number-one ranking is not in danger—it's finished," Nadal said
after the match. "Let's not lie to ourselves."

In truth, Nadal will be number one when the French Open begins on Sunday, but few argued his concession. When Djokovic beat Nadal yet again in straight sets on Sunday in Rome, Rafa's status as the favorite in Paris began deflating—fast. The prospect of Nole tying Guillermo Vilas's all-time winning streak of 46 with a triumph in the Roland Garros final no longer seems unthinkable.

The first inkling that Djokovic had tunneled into Nadal's head came on April 3, when he beat the Spaniard in an extraordinary three-set final in Miami. That Djokovic should take Nadal on a hard court was scarcely a shock. But that the player Federer once called "a joke when it comes to injuries"—the player who once quit a Wimbledon semi against Nadal because of various ailments—had ground down the most relentless fighter in tennis left their peers slack-jawed.

"That was a game-changer for the locker room," says U.S. Davis Cup captain Jim Courier. "After the match Nadal went into a big cramp from dehydration and fatigue—and Djokovic didn't. That's remarkable. For someone to out-tough Rafa? I'd never seen that."

Djokovic hadn't either, and, yes, he takes massive pride in being the first. But he insists that none of his recent progress—the winning streak, his heightened fitness—is a matter of suddenly having become serious. At the party in Belgrade, as a video of Djokovic decked out as Ironman played on multiple screens, he mangled "Summer of '69"—"Nothing can last forever . . . forever: NO!"—and a man garbed as Superman swept in to dance and sing.

No other tournament is as tiring for Djokovic, but, he would say a few days later, "I look at it from the bright side: I want this to succeed. I want to help out, do my best to promote the tournament, to be with my family. As much energy as it takes, it takes. I love being around people who care about me, and I care about them. This is the purpose of living: being happy, being peaceful. Tennis is my life, obviously; I need to focus, I need to win. But it's not the only thing. I'm not going to play forever."

Midnight loomed. No one cared. Djokovic's Davis Cup cohorts have long been awed by what teammate Janko Tipsarevic calls "the switch," Djokovic's ability to transition overnight from lighthearted to hyperfocused. And even on off days, no other player monitors his diet and alcohol intake more strictly than the six-foot-two, 176-pound Djokovic, Tipsarevic says. His fixation on becoming number one has been legendary in Serbia for 15 years now.

Still, that was hard to picture, what with Djokovic howling "Livin' la Vida Loca" across the room. An old family friend, Zoran Krstic, insisted, "Yes, tonight he is like this, but tomorrow?" Krstic held out his hand level, added, "He will . . ." and slashed the air twice, like a sword hacking through anyone in the way.

After two days they'd had enough of the basement: too dank, too crowded with strangers and gypsies. The Djokovics had gone down there from the first-floor apartment of Novak's grandfather because, for most people in Belgrade in March 1999, news reports and frantic phone calls about NATO jets heading their way evoked hellish visions of World War II: Dresden, London, whole cities leveled and smoking. When the sirens began, all the adults in the apartment building in the hill neighborhood of Banjica fell into a panic: Where to go, where to take the kids? Will we be safe? Will we die?

The bombs kept falling—rattling windows, punctuating conversations with ominous echoes. But people adapt. Soon all the Djokovics and their friends decided to stay home, huddling fatalistically in the Djokovic apartment. "After one week we were doing [our] normal jobs, thinking, 'If it comes, it comes,'" says Goran Djokovic, Novak's uncle and the director of the Serbia Open. "And the family, we start again to play tennis."

Novak turned 12 that May. His parents, Srdjan and Dijana, had both been competitive skiers in the Yugoslav sports system, athletes who could just as easily pound a soccer ball or volleyball with power and grace, and they wanted their oldest son to follow their path on the slopes. What could be more natural? They lived most of the year in the mountain town of Kaoponik, where they ran the Red Bull pizza restaurant, and knew nothing about tennis. But at six, Nole had been entranced by the sight of Pete Sampras winning Wimbledon, and when a famous Belgrade-based youth coach, Jelena Gencic, began a summer camp on the new courts across the street from his mountain home, he insisted on attending.

Dijana helped pack his bag—towel, water bottle, cap, extra racket, and shirt—and Gencic, who had coached Monica Seles and Goran Ivanisevic as kids, still hasn't gotten over how carefully, how much like an adult, Novak unpacked it all. Soon, back in Belgrade, Gencic was feeding him balls, reading him poetry, telling his parents how special he was. "My second mother," Djokovic says. "The base of everything I have on the tennis court, and a lot of things off it, is from her. She took care of my life in general: what I was doing in school, what I was having to eat and drink. We were listening to classical music together. She wanted to teach me how I should behave on and off the court, how professional I should be."

Yet at seven it was he who insisted on a change that serves him still. Though determined to hit a one-handed backhand like Sampras, Djokovic found he was too weak to handle higher balls with it, so he began hitting with two hands. Such are the tweaks that determine tennis history. For along with his Gumby-like elasticity, it's Djokovic's alchemical backhand, the kind that transmutes the most defensive shots into hard, dipping winners, that helped him solve Nadal the way Federer never could. Djokovic has now beaten Nadal in seven of their last nine meetings, feasting on the same high, topspin-laced crosscourt forehands from Rafa that shred the Swiss maestro's one-hander.

Seven, too, was Novak's age when Gencic first put him on national TV. A child host asked the prodigy if his tennis was work or play. "Tennis is my job," Nole said. "My goal in tennis is to become number one."

Asked when he has time to indulge in normal childhood games, he answered, "I play at night."

By the mid-'90s Serbia had been shattered by the breakup of Yugoslavia and by a series of savage wars that left its populace economically isolated, socially shunned, and desperate for stability. Nole's goal to win Wimbledon "gave our family something we had to fight for," Dijana says. "It was a very bad time because our country was in a bad situation, so we were trying to do everything for our son."

For four years Gencic refined Nole's skills, but much of his drive came from his dad. Srdjan, with no tennis knowledge, became certain that his son would be number one someday—"believed Novak was an unbelievable player even when he was not unbelievable," says Niki Pilic, the Croatian former pro who is now a coach—and he told everyone who would (or wouldn't) listen. Critics put off by the sight of Srdjan and Dijana in matching T-shirts emblazoned with their son's face at the 2010 U.S. Open wouldn't be shocked to hear that nothing, not losing streaks, adolescence, or injuries, could shake Srdjan's faith. At each level he would look around at the opposition and tell Novak, "You're better than all of them."

At the Partizan Tennis Club, the most storied in Belgrade and the Serbian base for Tipsarevic and former world number-one Ana Ivanovic, Srdjan insisted on paying for the best coaches. Money was tight, and the Djokovic family, including Novak's younger brothers, Marko and Djordje, "were suffering," Goran Djokovic says, "because Novak had to have the top food, the top equipment, the priority of the priorities."

After the first week of NATO bombing the whole family began venturing out with Novak to practice, sometimes at Partizan, sometimes at courts near recent bombing targets, which, they reasoned, might not be bombed again soon. Five hundred combat missions were flown into Serbian territory each day, but the Djokovics put their heads down and kept hitting. "There was no way we are sitting at home and crying," Dijana says. "So we are on the tennis court from 10 in the morning to 6:00, 7:00, 8:00 P.M. Also our two other kids are practicing during the bombing. You are practicing and listening to sirens, but it was the only way. We were trying to find some way to get out."

On June 10, 1999, when the suspension of bombing finally was announced, Novak and his brothers spilled onto the terrace, hopping and hollering, "We are safe now! We are safe!"

Six months later Gencic asked Pilic, Ivanisevic's mentor, to consider Novak for his tennis academy in Munich. Pilic dismissed the idea at first; 12½ seemed too young for his grueling regimen. But Novak, accompanied by Goran, took his first plane ride to audition for Pilic, and the 1973 French Open finalist gave in. The boy arrived in midwinter with little cash; Pilic's wife dubbed him Jacket, because he didn't have one. Goran stayed five days. When he left Nole cried.

The stakes were high. Novak developed quickly, but the Djokovic restaurant depended on seasonal business—sometimes good, sometimes not. The academy cost more than $3,000 a month, and even when Pilic threw in a discount, the travel costs there and to tournaments near and far squeezed Srdjan. "He borrowed the money with high interest, from the loan shark, 10, 15 percent a month," Goran says. "Who knows how much? I don't want to count it."

No wonder Novak seemed like the oldest soul at the academy. One afternoon, 20 minutes before he was due to hit with Pilic, Novak passed Pilic's lunch table en route to warming up. Told that it seemed too early, Novak said, "I'm not going to waste my career." Pilic was stunned. "He was 13½!" the coach says. Serbs point to the bombing as the crucible of Djokovic's competitiveness, but he also had no choice. The family had put all its chips on him.

A year later Djokovic had just finished a grueling training regimen in the Austrian Alps, and all the players were readying for a party. He buttonholed his then-manager, Dirk Hordorff, and said, "If I go out tonight, would it be good for my tennis?"

"Just go," Hordorff said. "You worked hard, drink a glass of wine. . . ." Djokovic cut him off.

"I didn't ask you, 'Would this be good for me?' he said. "I asked, 'Would this be good for my tennis?'"

Novak became the top U-14, then the top U-16 player in Europe. He wasn't surprised. "Always he was very confident, and he was very sure that he was going to be on top," says Ernests Gulbis, the Latvian now ranked number 63 in the world, who met Djokovic at the Pilic Academy. "Nothing arrogant, but with all his thinking, all his work, he was really professional already at a young age. Me, at 16? I was a joke. I didn't take care about practice at all. And he was doing everything."

The family kept trolling for investors. No one bit. As a junior Novak won the third Futures (third tier) tournament he entered, then the second Challengers (second tier). But the Serbian Tennis Federation had no funds to give him. "Nobody cared," Goran says. "Srdjan is going around, trying to convince people, please invest. Like you are selling fruit or dairy: here's an investment for you. It was a very tough time." Junior tournaments came and went without Nole. There was no money for travel.

Early in 2006, the year after Djokovic had become the youngest man in the ATP's top 100, Srdjan was so disheartened that he had Dijana talk to England's deep-pocketed Lawn Tennis Association about the possibility of 18-year-old Novak and his brothers switching nationalities to play for England. (Marko, then 14, and Djordje, 10, were well-regarded prospects in Serbia.) "The decision in the end was mine," says Novak. "I never wanted to change countries; it's something that is part of me. We are all really proud of where we come from. And though we've been through tough times, it makes us stronger."

A month later everything changed. In Paris, Djokovic met the respected, serene Slovakian coach Marian Vajda, consulted with him informally, and reached his first Grand Slam quarterfinal at Roland Garros. That netted him $149,590. With Vajda as his full-time coach, Djokovic went on to win his first ATP titles—and a total of $104,000—in Amersfoort, the Netherlands, and Metz, France. He ended the year ranked number 16. Srdjan exhaled. He even tried congratulating his son for cracking the top 20, but Novak stopped him. "When I'm number one," he said, "then you can congratulate me."

Nobody in Belgrade likes to talk about how close Serbia came to losing a national treasure. In December, Djokovic led the country to its first Davis Cup win; he brought Serbian musicians into the locker room in Melbourne to celebrate his second Australian Open title in February; he hustled into a T-shirt stamped with the Serbian flag for the trophy ceremony after beating Nadal in Madrid.

There were plenty of less graffittied, less rubble-strewn cities Djokovic could have chosen for his tournament and tennis academy three years ago. Belgrade was his only choice. Such pride is a far cry from the attitude of the last great Serbian-born player, Seles, a native of Novi Sad who tiptoed around her heritage as if it were a box of nitroglycerin and finally took the step Djokovic couldn't. Seles changed her citizenship, becoming an American in 1994.

"Novak Djokovic," said Vladimir Petrovic, Serbia's ambassador to the United States, "is the single biggest positive PR this country's ever had. He's a positive face of the new democratic Serbia."

By Friday at the Serbia Open his voice had gone raspy and his eyes were rimmed with pink. Still, Djokovic kept rolling. His lingering cold was the one sign that Belgrade was taking its toll, but his wins in spite of it—not a set dropped—showed just how settled he is now.

A year ago Djokovic was a mess. An ill-conceived decision to hire coach Todd Martin to beef up his serving and volleying back-fired; Vajda eased into a part-time role, Martin and Djokovic didn't jell, and the result on court was the most disoriented number-two player you'll ever see. "The guy couldn't buy a second serve," Courier says. "He looked like he was throwing a javelin."

By April, Martin was gone and the new serve junked, but the damage lingered: a quarterfinal exit in Paris, a disastrous straight-sets loss to Tomas Berdych in the Wimbledon semis. But Vajda was back full-time, and in July, just as Djokovic began grooving his old service motion, he met the man who today may mean more to him than any other: a holistic nutritionist named Igor Cetojevic.

Throughout his career Djokovic had been plagued by respiratory problems and niggling injuries. "Bird flu, anthrax, SARS . . . common cough and cold," Roddick said mockingly at the 2008 U.S. Open. "He's either quick to call the trainer or he's the most courageous guy of all time." But Djokovic had long tried to find a solution, even to the point of doing breathing exercises with a Belgrade opera singer. Cetojevic, who says he studied traditional Chinese medicine at a college in Belgrade and earned a degree from the Indian Institute of Magnetotherapy in New Delhi, streamlined Djokovic's diet and cut out gluten altogether. Djokovic, child of a pizza parlor, shed a few pounds yet felt stronger.

"The whole allergy thing was coming from gluten," he says. "I didn't know. We grew up on gluten—bread, pasta—and I was consuming it in big, big amounts. I guess I'm very sensitive."

Cetojevic, who is also a member of the Serbia Messengers motorcycle club, is a fixture at Djokovic's matches, yelling huzzahs from the players' box, though he has little idea of what he's watching. "He doesn't even know the tennis terms: he calls a match a *game*," Djokovic says. "He's a very funny guy. He brought this positive energy to the team and a fresh voice."

With his entourage now solid, his body reset, and his nerve tempered by the fires of the Davis Cup, Djokovic's confidence soared. It sounds simple, a matter of just getting all the elements lined up, but few players figure out how to get the balance just right. That harmony includes his girlfriend of five years, Jelena Ristic. "Everything came into the right place," he says. "My mind-set is different now; I have a different approach to my life, to my profession. I'm more stable emotionally. I feel much tougher mentally: that's the learning and experience you get playing at the highest level. Physically, I've always tried to stay fit, I've been very dedicated—and that's what's paying off right now."

Still, it must be jarring to come back to the city of your youth, a place where you were once an unknown, and see your face plastered on billboards, your name on sugar packets and key chains. There's your brother wearing a T-shirt with your face on his chest. There's a life-sized faux terra-cotta statue of you. There's nearly every male in town sporting your peltlike hairstyle, like a scene out of a film called *Being Nole Djokovic*. "The restaurant is called Novak, the café is called Novak—even the water is called Novak," said an attendant on the tournament grounds. She laughed. "I'm the only thing here that is not called Novak."

It's a fight for him to remain normal in Belgrade, and Djokovic kept trying to connect with those who knew him before he became a national symbol. He called a boyhood pal he hadn't seen in four years, urging him to please come by. He took the most delight—"Time for revenge!"—in thrashing the Slovenian player Blaz Kavcic in the quarterfinals because Kavcic had beaten him at 14. The past, even the most distant, matters to him more than ever now. Without it, Djokovic would be adrift.

Srdjan and his family were born in Kosovo. Logic suggests that Serbia today wouldn't feel much connection to the region, if only because a mere 7 percent of Kosovo's population is Serbian. But Kosovo is where Serbian culture and the Serbian Orthodox religion began; it's central to the Serbian identity. Violence against the remaining Serbs and damage done to their churches by Kosovar Albanians—not to mention the U.S.-led recognition of an independent Kosovo by 75 nations—have, in the last few years, only inflamed Serbia's feeling of aggrieved impotence.

Djokovic has become even more involved in the issue since his famous 2008 speech. He has visited Kosovo repeatedly, dedicated victories to the Serbs there, and, in March, donated $100,000 to support its historic monasteries. For that, on Thursday, he received the Serbian Orthodox Church's highest honor, the Order of Saint Sava. "The most important award I'll ever get," he says.

"Imagine a part of the U.S.A., from which the U.S.A. started —where is the cradle of your history? This is Kosovo for Serbia," Djokovic says. "There are some stronger powers we can't fight. But the most important thing for me is that I know where I'm from, I know what's going on in that part of Serbia where my family's from. We are very righteous people. We want truth to come out.

That's why we're hurt. I'm being careful because it's very sensitive. But I have no reason to pretend. I know who I am."

Early Saturday evening Djokovic walked through the front door of the Partizan Tennis Club in Old Belgrade. The place was all but empty, drowsy with weekend indolence; a few elderly men laced up their shoes for doubles. Perfect: all week Djokovic had been seeking one chance to look back quietly, to center himself before the summer that seems certain to define his career. It had been seven years since he'd been there.

"This is the club that I grew up in, the club where I learned my first tennis footsteps," he said. His voice echoed in the narrow hallway as he rushed past the old stringing room, the faded team photos, toward the cramped locker room. At first he spoke easily of the titles the teams had won, about the other pros whose posters, like his, were now fading in the sun. But by the time Djokovic emerged from the club, something had changed.

He hadn't realized that every court, with its red clay freshly dragged and all but glowing, would unleash a new memory: that bee sting on his heel, the win over his archrival, Troicki, the wrenching decision to go to Munich. There was the spot where his dad would sit watching, the net where Gencic stood smiling, the hard courts from which, in 1999, he and everyone else watched the bombers streak the sky. "We weren't scared anymore," he said. "Everybody wanted to play." One minute he was giggling, the next he'd go silent and his eyes would begin to pool.

"You can't imagine," he said. "I have spent my good and my bad times in this club. I watched planes go over our heads, I celebrated my birthdays here, I cried, I laughed, I had the joy, I had sorrow—all the things you can experience as a human, I had here. Coming back, it's just overwhelming. It's too good to be true."

The next day Djokovic swatted aside López in the Serbia Open final for his 27th straight win of the year. Early in the second set, chasing down a deep, wide forehand, he slid into a full split that became a face-plant, his right wrist hammering the clay—the kind of crash that would give anyone pause. But Djokovic rose, won the next point, broke López, and took control of the match. The moment showed just how tough he has become.

Yet that was just tennis, a world Djokovic has handled with ease time and again this spring. The trip to Partizan, though, touched him in a way that no opponent has lately: suddenly, by his side was the old stringer whom he'd always begged for favors, his face lined and paler now; here came the club president, a man Djokovic once feared, hair gone whiter; here now his long-ago best friend, joking, "So, what have you been up to lately?"

A TV crew arrived, and Djokovic went to greet a 14-year-old boy whose only dream was to meet him. Djokovic hugged him, said that he understood how it felt to be young and struggling; the boy's mother stared, tears rolling down to her mouth. Her reaction seemed overwrought, until you remembered what Vlade Divac, the head of Serbia's Olympic Committee and a former NBA great, said on the first day of the tournament: "For years, especially the last 15 when there were wars, civil wars, people looked at us as bad guys. It was hard to raise kids to be proud Serbs. But Novak is giving the Serbian people that feeling now: to be proud."

Ten minutes later it happened again. Djokovic walked into the club café, and there she was, the same waitress who kept him in line when he was a boy, served him cake. Djokovic had forgotten about her, but now it all came rushing back; he moaned, his voice cracking, before pulling her close. "Just to hug you," he said. "You are still here!"

When Djokovic finally let her go, she was crying, and it became clear that the ambassador was wrong. Djokovic's isn't the face of Serbia now. Hers is: weathered, weary, and tearstained, yes, but when confronted with what their Nole has become, unveiling a tight but unmistakable smile.

JERÉ LONGMAN

Boy Genius

FROM THE NEW YORK TIMES

Brilliant!
   Magic!
      Aaaaaaaagh!
         Absolute genius again
From Messi!
   They tried
To kick him
They tried
   To plow him into the ground
   And what do you do then?
You try to put
         Fire out
   With gasoline!
Don't look for him
   In the X's and O's
   He doesn't live there.
   He doesn't live in
         The tactical world
Or the technical world
         He lives in the
Magnetic spectrum
               Of genuis
You could corral him with
   A dozen alligators
   And still he'd weave
   His way out.

BARCELONA, SPAIN — Given a rare night on the Barcelona
bench last Sunday, Lionel Messi yanked on the seat in front of

him, hunched his shoulders over the chair back, and kicked it with his cleats. He seemed not so much the world's best soccer player as a restless kid in a movie theater.

He is 23, with a grown-up's income reported to exceed $43 million this year. Yet Messi still has a boy's floppy bangs, a boy's slight build, and a boy's nickname, the Flea. Even the ball stays on his feet like a shy child clinging to his father's legs.

It is a boy's fearlessness, enthusiasm, calm, and humility, too, that help explain why Messi is already considered one of the greatest ever to play the world's game. In the space of 18 tense days from April to early May, Barcelona played four Clásicos against its archrival, Real Madrid. The Madrid strategy was to strangle beauty out of the matches, to use nasty muscle against Messi, to shoulder him down or shiver him with a forearm or take his legs in scything tackles. Once, he was sent rolling as if he had caught fire.

Messi made small appeals for fairness with his eyes and hands, but he remained unflappable and without complaint. He did not yell at the referee or clamp a threatening hand around an opponent's neck or fake a foul and dive to the ground. He remained apart from ugly words and scuffles and expulsions that marred the matches. Instead, he trumped cynicism with genius.

With a boy's ardor, Messi put Barcelona in the final of the Champions League in Europe—the world's most prestigious club tournament—to be played against Manchester United on Saturday at Wembley Stadium in London. He delivered both goals in Barcelona's 2–0 victory in the first leg of the semifinal round against Real Madrid. This gave Messi a startling 52 goals in his first 50 matches of a season in which he also leads the Spanish league in assists. The first goal was merely outstanding in its timing and clever anticipation. The second was a masterpiece of acceleration, power, balance, agility, vision, and darting virtuosity.

"I think this genius is impossible to describe," Pep Guardiola, Barcelona's manager, said. "That's why he is a genius. He has instinct. He loves to live with pressure. He is one of the best ever created."

That defining Champions League semifinal match was played April 27 at Estadio Santiago Bernabéu in Madrid. Nine months earlier, stars from Barcelona and Real Madrid joined to give Spain its first World Cup title. Together, they lifted the winner's trophy in South Africa. But now they played for club, not country. Temporary brotherhood fissured. Blood rivalry resumed. Madrid, the capital, was once the base of Franco's dictatorship and is now the seat of Spain's constitutional monarchy; Barcelona sits in the heart of the autonomous Catalan region, with its own language and cultural (and soccer) identity.

An Argentine, Messi was not born into these tensions. He came to Barcelona at 13, when the club agreed to pick up the costs of treatment for a growth-hormone deficiency. As the story goes, his contract was written on a napkin. At the time, he was about four feet seven inches. He now stands five-foot-seven. If his lack of size made him shy and self-conscious as a boy, his low center of gravity made him spectacularly elusive as a soccer player.

"We thought he was mute," said Gerard Piqué, the lanky Barcelona center back who played with Messi in the club's youth academy. "He was in the dressing room, on the bench, just sitting. He said nothing to us for the first month. We traveled to Switzerland to play a tournament, and he started to talk and have fun. We thought it was another person. He was really good, but he was really small and thin. His legs were like fingers. One coach said, 'Don't try to tackle him strong, because maybe you will break him.' And we said, 'Okay, but don't worry because we cannot catch him.'"

A decade later, Messi proved even more artful and cagey in the Champions League semifinals after the April match remained scoreless into the 76th minute. As Madrid sat and waited, Barcelona dominated possession with its elegant, patient attack, probing for an away goal that would serve as a tiebreaker if needed in the home-and-home series. It was a format meant to encourage aggressiveness in visiting teams and to discourage them from turtling into a defensive shell.

An opening came soon enough. Madrid was vulnerable. In the 61st minute, it had been reduced to 10 men after Pepe, a defender, was red-carded for a cleats-up challenge on Barcelona's right back, Dani Alves. Pushing into midfield, Pepe had been Madrid's most effective marker of Messi in two earlier matches during the month, one a tie in a Spanish league game, the other a Real Madrid victory for the Spanish Cup (which was unceremoniously dropped under the team bus during the celebration). But this match was more important, a chance to play for the championship of Europe. Pepe's eviction was a harsh blow that changed everything.

Madrid's impulsive manager, José Mourinho, was soon banished too. He clapped his hands mockingly at the referee's notice of Pepe's eviction and at what he considered Alves's theatrically pained reaction to a nonexistent foul.

In 2005, while managing Chelsea in the English Premier League, a suspended Mourinho reportedly evaded a prohibition on contact with his players by rolling into the dressing room while hiding inside a laundry basket. Now, against Barcelona, he was reduced to a child's classroom subterfuge of passing furtive notes to his assistant from the stands.

With 14 minutes remaining and the score still 0–0, Messi took what seemed an innocuous pass nearly 40 yards from the goal. It came from Xavi, Barcelona's brilliant playmaker, whose oiled pompadour and wide eyes evoke a young Jackie Gleason, though Gleason's comedy could be manic, even volcanic, while Xavi's art is restrained and surgical.

Messi stabbed forward with the ball, and Madrid midfielder Xabi Alonso tried to make a sliding tackle. Messi wobbled but shrugged off Alonso, keeping his feet. Still, he was not free. Madrid's defense engulfed him like white blood cells trying to fight off infection. His shot ricocheted off a clot of defenders at the top of the penalty area, but Messi remained alert and flicked the rebound back to Xavi.

It was no surprise that Messi connected so assuredly with Xavi. The three players who drive Barcelona's attack—Messi, Xavi, and the industrious midfielder Andrés Iniesta—all graduated from the club's youth academy. They are different ages, but they have been in one another's company for a decade.

The heart of Barcelona's defense, Piqué and Carles Puyol, also developed at the academy, which is symbolized by an 18th-century stone farmhouse, known as La Masia, that was remade into a dormitory just outside Camp Nou, Barcelona's stadium. The generic term for the academy is La Cantera. The quarry. It has become the world's model for mining young talent.

Messi grew homesick when he arrived with his father from Argentina, club officials said. He missed his mother and sometimes cried himself asleep. Quickly enough, though, he immersed himself in the Barcelona style, which demands flair and creativity, not mere utility. He played the keep-away game called El Rondo, in which one player stands inside a circle trying to steal passes made in tight spaces. He mastered the system known as tiki-taka, built around short, rhythmic passes and movement described by Iniesta as "receive, pass, offer," triangular exchanges that form a spellbinding geometry.

As Barcelona dispatched Arsenal in the 2010 Champions League quarterfinals, Gunners wing Theo Walcott marveled, "It was like someone was holding a PlayStation controller and moving the figures around."

In the first leg of this year's semifinals, Real Madrid must have felt the same wonder and helplessness, especially down a man. Barcelona completed an astonishing 713 of 788 passes in the match. Xavi alone was 107 for 112. In the 76th minute, upon taking Messi's short pass, Xavi turned his back to the goal and wheeled away from three defenders. Astutely, he played the ball on the right wing to the substitute Ibrahim Afellay. Messi took a few casual strides at the top of the penalty area, but this was a poacher's deceptive saunter.

Alonso put a forearm in Messi's chest for resistance, then backpedaled and turned his head to find the ball. Twelve yards from the goal, Alonso stopped, shuttling Messi off to the final line of Madrid's defense. Space opened in the briefest moment of hesitancy and indecision. That was all Messi needed.

"I knew Afellay would wait until the last second to cross the ball, so I kept running," he said.

He broke for the near goalpost, sprinting past defender Sergio Ramos, a boy's sprint, his short legs churning, his hands high and frantic. The cross from Afellay curled in low and precise. Before Iker Casillas, Madrid's goalkeeper, could react, Messi ran onto the ball and jumped and clipped it between Casillas's legs. Barcelona had a vital away goal. Messi jumped into his teammates' arms and pumped his fists. He raised the Barcelona crest on his jersey and pounded his chest.

"No one plays with as much joy as Messi does," Eduardo Galeano, the celebrated Uruguayan novelist and author of *Soccer in Sun and Shadow*, said in an e-mail. "He plays like a child enjoying the pasture, playing for the pleasure of playing, not the duty of winning."

He plays like a child, and, away from the game, he still possesses a child's reserve. Messi is seldom forthcoming. He even appeared distant last Sunday as Barcelona celebrated its latest Spanish league title with a belated festivity at Camp Nou. As confetti rained and his teammates danced and clapped and waved and threw peppers into the stands as a sign of strength, Messi mostly walked alone, his hands shoved into the pockets of his warm-up suit.

"Lio only wants to play," said Thierry Henry, a French star and a former teammate of Messi's at Barcelona who now plays for the Red Bulls of Major League Soccer.

On occasion, Messi does break his reticence. On Thursday, he said he played with the same eagerness that he did in Argentina when he improvised soccer balls from stones and women's tights and cans of cola. "I have fun like a child in the street," he said. "When the day comes when I'm not enjoying it, I will leave football."

Still, he is most often silent, leaving others to provide the soundtrack of his career. Watchers of the bilingual soccer channel GolTV are treated weekly to the cockeyed enthusiasm of the British commentator Ray Hudson. A blog, Hudsonia, was inspired by his ability to "coin phrases that defy both logic and belief" and by his unending quest to "invent a new language in English."

In Hudson's words, Messi has "chameleon eyes" and is as "slippery as an eel covered in Vaseline" and plays with the predatory appetite of a "zombie hunter looking for a Twinkie." Somehow, out of incomprehension comes clarity. Even poetry.

Robert Lalasz, the editor of the website Must Read Soccer, has assembled Hudson's verbal improvisations into verse, the way others previously did for the Yankees broadcaster Phil Rizzuto. One of the poems, "He Doesn't Live There," opened this article.

Here is another:

> "NEITHER WITH NET NOR TRIDENT"
> *The genius, the genius of*
> *Football*
> *In our modern-day life*
> *Utterly*
> *Unpredictable*
> *He doesn't know*
> *What he's going to do*
> *So how the hell*

> *Do the defenders*
> *You cannot contain him*
> *With a net*
> *Or a trident*
> *He's got pace*
> *He's got power*
> *He's got vision*
> *Technique!*
> *And he's got*
> *Finishing power*
> *His cup*
> *Runneth over . . .*
> *Magnificent Messi*
> *Wild man*
> *He doth bestride the Earth*
> *Like a Colossus*

A second goal by Messi followed in the 87th minute, this one with a slalom skier's pivoting and carving and shoulders squared to the fall line. The play began innocently enough, with a bland pass rolled out of the center circle from midfielder Sergio Busquets to Messi. Four Madrid midfielders and four defenders spread across the field ahead of Casillas in goal, an apparently safe but illusory deterrent.

What happened next is why players from the Costa Rican national team had lined up a month earlier for Messi's autograph in an exhibition against Argentina, reduced to mere fans.

Tall and lean, Busquets jogged languidly from the circle into the space between Madrid's central midfield and defense. Messi's return pass was sharp and direct. Busquets received the ball, pivoted, and tapped it lightly. What seemed unthreatening a few seconds earlier now became a menacing give-and-go.

"I saw some options," Messi said. "I always try to create danger."

During the careers of the greats to whom Messi is most often compared—Pelé of Brazil and Diego Maradona, a fellow Argentine—the pace of the game was slower, with more space to operate and more chance for flamboyant playfulness in the flowing dribbles known as gambeta.

Today, soccer increasingly relies on size and muscle and speed. The best players must be able to operate in claustrophobic spaces. That is the mesmerizing skill of Messi, slithering through these airless openings in top gear, changing direction, providing as well as scoring, his left foot tapping the ball on each stride with blurred and evasive touches. At such moments, the ball becomes an extension of his foot.

"You think of Gretzky playing hockey," said Bob Bradley, the coach of the U.S. national team, who sat in the stadium in Madrid, watching the play unfold. "It sticks with you. Everybody who watches Messi knows he is pushing the highest level of the sport ever."

Earlier in his career, Messi preferred to slash inside from the right wing, taking the ball on his dominant left foot. Now he is considered a center forward in Barcelona's 4-3-3 formation, but the position as he plays it is sometimes described as a "ghost center forward" or a "false number 9," a reference to the traditional jersey number worn by a striker. Instead, Messi wears number 10, the classic playmaker's number. He is free to drift and roam and handle the ball, to combine with Xavi and Iniesta, to seek out openings that he can exploit with his passing or his dribbling, with his chameleon eyes.

This puts enormous stress on central defenders. Do they stay put? Do they go with Messi and leave yawning holes on the back line? On this day, with Madrid short a man, every decision was precarious.

"Alarm bells didn't go off fast enough," Bradley said. "Everybody took for granted that they could get there."

Messi took the ball from Busquets about 45 yards from the goal. Four Madrid players surrounded Messi, but he deftly escaped. First, midfielder Lass Diarra was screened by Busquets. He caught up to Messi's right shoulder and reached for the ball, but Messi sensed Diarra's presence and touched it left. To keep from fouling, Diarra retreated with a dainty hop. Alonso quit after a few strides, also hopping in surrender.

Messi gathered speed and intent. Sergio Ramos charged at him, but Messi shielded the ball with the inside of his left foot, pushing it safely to the right. Taking the ball from him had become a blundering game, reaching for a dollar bill attached to a string.

"With someone like that, you want to move them one way, make them predictable, so if they do have a bad touch, you can win the ball," said Landon Donovan, the American star who has twice played against Messi and Argentina's national team. "The problem is, the ball is attached to him. Every stride, he's touching the ball. It's almost like a magnet is pulling it back in. You're waiting for the ball to get away, but it doesn't. If you foul him, his balance is so good, he keeps going. And he keeps going at speed, so you can't catch him. Sometimes, you run at him like, 'I've got him now,' and he'll make a onetime pass. You turn around and the ball comes back, and then he runs by you. There's a constant mind game that he's good at."

Raul Albiol now had his chance in the Madrid defense, but he is six-foot-two with a high center of gravity. He backpedaled and crouched, but his balance was all wrong and Messi was coming too fast. Futilely, Albiol thrust out a leg. Messi blew past and Albiol spun around and bent over, all his weight on his right leg. For a moment he seemed to be playing the wrong sport, appearing less a soccer player than a man who had just hurled a javelin.

With another touch, Messi pushed the ball five yards ahead into a vacant spot and sprinted into the penalty area. Marcelo, a defender, desperately rushed from behind, but a foul would have given Messi a penalty kick, so Marcelo pulled back, hands thrown up and knees bent as if parachuting from a plane.

Messi touched the ball with the outside of his left foot, once, twice, and Ramos made one last hustling charge, but he was too late. Sliding to the turf, Messi cuffed the ball with the inside of his right foot. A final drip of the honey, as Hudson sometimes says in his excitable commentary.

The ball seemed to roll under Ramos's foot, or between his legs. Beaten again, Ramos became tangled with Messi and tumbled in exasperation. Casillas moved to his left in goal, but the shot went to his right, squirting inside the far post. Real Madrid was all but finished in the Champions League. Casillas went to the ground on his backside and rose with his gloved hands upturned in a way that signaled disbelief and anger and resignation. And maybe awe.

On television and radio, Spanish-language broadcasters began their prolonged, ecstatic screams, "Gooooooooooooool!" extending the sound for an entire breath, but this was more than a goal, it was a supergoal, and so the shrieks became "Gooooooooooooooolazo!" as Messi again jumped into his teammates' arms.

"It was all instinct," Messi said. "Only when I watched it later on television did I know what happened."

"VINTAGE MESSI"
How many angels
Can dance on the head of a pin?
How magnificent
Is Messi?
There is no answer
It's like counting the bubbles
In a bottle of Champagne

With that goal, the question came again. Was Messi the best player ever? The novelist Eduardo Sacheri watched from Buenos Aires and knew that in Argentina, the answer was no. He wrote often about soccer because it reflected the joy and pain of daily life. He loved Messi. He took up for him when his own 14-year-old son, Francisco, asked, "Why is Messi never as good for Argentina as he is for Barcelona?"

But the fact remained: Messi had never won a World Cup, as Maradona had in 1986. And although Messi was influential at the 2010 World Cup, he did not score as Argentina exited meekly to Germany in the quarterfinals.

"Until Messi wins a World Cup, he doesn't stand a chance of being compared to Maradona," Sacheri said.

He still has plenty of time. Messi turns 24 next month. But his relationship with Argentina is complicated. He left when he was a teenager. For many, he is a remote figure.

"Maradona was born in the slums; he has had a chaotic life, anarchic," Sacheri said. "Failure and success, shadowy and brilliant. Those are things Argentines can relate to and empathize with. If Messi wins a World Cup, he will be an idol. But it might be more difficult for him to have a passionate relationship with the public."

The debate will never end. That is the beauty of soccer. It demands argument, abhors understatement. Goals are too few and too precious for restrained scrutiny. Entire nations swell and deflate at the sight of ball going into a net. But the next World Cup is not for three years. What to do until then?

"With Lio, the best thing is not to talk about him," Henry, his former teammate, said. "It is to watch him."

"COVERED WITH EYES"
What he is
He's like something
Out of Greek mythology, man
Little short-legged bull
Lionel Messi
Covered with eyes!

BEN MCGRATH

Queen of the D-League

FROM THE NEW YORKER

"IT's NOT EASY looking good these days," Nancy Lieberman remarked, her hair in curlers, as she eyed herself in the mirror of a Dallas hair salon. Once known as Lady Magic, for her skills on the basketball court, Lieberman is now 52, and comfortably beyond the tomboy phase that, back home in Queens, used to drive her mother to despair. While growing up, Lieberman idolized the Knicks stars Clyde Frazier and Willis Reed, and Muhammad Ali, whom she now considers a friend. (She calls him Muhammad.) She played tackle football with the neighborhood toughs, using a souvenir New York Jets lampshade for a helmet. She saved her paper-route money to buy a pair of Chuck Taylors, in defiance of the salesman, who told her, "It's not a shoe for girls." These days, she explained, "I tell people, 'Don't let my stilettos fool you. I still want to win.'"

Lieberman is the head coach of a minor league basketball team called the Texas Legends, an affiliate of the Dallas Mavericks in the NBA's Development League, or D-League, as it is more often known, which typically plays to crowds of a few thousand in cities like Sioux Falls, South Dakota, and Erie, Pennsylvania. Her charges are men, and as one of them, the captain, Antonio Daniels, told me recently, when they go out they inevitably get asked, "Oh, your coach is a girl? What's that like?" He paused a moment and shrugged. "What's it like? Same thing as if a guy was a coach, you know what I mean? Except you just don't undress in the locker room at the same time. And she's big on love, and she's big on hugs, and all that kind of stuff."

Chris Finch, the coach of the rival Rio Grande Valley Vipers, said, "I tell my players that I love their effort, but I wouldn't say that I love them."

"We're different," Lieberman acknowledged.

Lieberman was the first woman to play men's professional basketball. In 1986, she made $10,000 as a backup point guard with the Springfield Fame, of the United States Basketball League, which played its games in the late spring, after the conclusion of the NCAA season and before the start of the NBA summer leagues. She is not quite the first woman to be coaching men. In 2004, a 22-year-old Vanderbilt graduate with no prior coaching experience, Ashley McElhiney, was put in charge of the Nashville Rhythm, an expansion team in the American Basketball Association, which is a kind of poor man's D-League. (The team folded a year later.) But Lieberman is the first crossover coach with plausible aspirations to being taken seriously at the highest level. After she was offered the position, in late 2009, she went on a year-long listening tour, seeking advice from veteran NBA coaches and other wise men. "I was like, 'Holy cow, what the hell are you all talking about?'" she recalled. Lieberman had coached for a few years in the WNBA, in the late '90s, and then spent much of the intervening decade as an ESPN analyst, a job that consisted of explaining the game to a general audience. But in the pep talks with these would-be mentors she found the jargon impenetrable. It was as though the NBA spoke its own language. "They're talking 'two-nine,' 'cleanse,' 'shake,' 'ice it,' 'blue-blitz it,'" she said. "I knew I had to win that battle, so I had to educate myself on talking the talk."

She also had to find a way to connect with young, mostly African American men. "I tell these guys we have more in common than you think," she said. "Young black men don't want to be profiled, and old white women don't want to be profiled."

Lieberman is five feet ten and broad in the shoulders, but she retains a girlish face in spite of the corporate look—slacks, pumps—that she favors on game nights. At the salon, which she has been visiting with some regularity for the past ten years, she was wearing a sequinned sweatsuit and sneakers; she had come straight from practice. Her hairdresser, Sherry Gilderoy, stood beside her. The curlers wrapping Lieberman's red hair added two or three inches to her height. "Sherry owns me from the neck up,"

Lieberman said. Gilderoy apprenticed under José Eber, "the Michael Jordan of hairstylists," as Lieberman put it.

An hour passed before the curlers could come off and the blow-drying and spraying could begin. Lieberman started to fidget. "A little pain, a little beauty," another stylist drawled. "That's what my grandma says."

"So we lose opening night to RGV," Lieberman finally said, recounting the start of her debut season, last fall, against Coach Finch's Vipers, an affiliate of the Houston Rockets. "We go to Idaho, and we have two road games, and I'm thinking, I don't want to come back oh-and-three, because that's going to put a lot of questions on me and them. 'Does she know what she's doing?' Our first game at Idaho, we're down seven with about three minutes to go. You could just see this look of concern on Antonio's face. So I call him over—they're shooting a foul shot. I go, 'Antonio, come here.' 'Yes, coach?' He doesn't know how I work. It's our second game together. I say, 'Antonio, look, this is serious. Do you like my hair?'"

Lieberman likes to say that she has a Rolodex as long as the North Dallas Tollway. Every morning, she sends out a text message to a distribution list of friends and sports world dignitaries, from the Yankees manager, Joe Girardi, to the Mavericks coach, Rick Carlisle. "In reading the lives of great people," a recent one read, "I found that the first victory they ever won was over themselves." Most mornings, she gets a similar message in return from the former football and baseball player Deion Sanders: "The key ingredient 2a successful relationship isn't money, looks, or love. It's TRUST. 2be trusted is a greater compliment than anything." Before a recent game, she told me that she'd spent the afternoon seeking advice from Kevin Costner about a movie idea involving her life story. "Kind of like *The Blind Side,*" she said. "About overcoming all these challenges." Lieberman saw herself not as the Sandra Bullock character—a wealthy Southern woman who adopts and mentors a poor black teen—but as something closer to Michael Oher, the adoptee, who is now a 300-pound offensive lineman in the NFL.

Jerry Lieberman, Nancy's father, was a contractor, and he built the family home, on Bayswater Avenue, in Far Rockaway, as well as a house nearby for his parents; the two properties shared a large backyard that the local kids called Miniature Yankee Stadium. He moved out when Nancy was eight, and his absence—the loss of a male role model—usually marks the starting point in the capsule biography that she has honed in the retelling. There were unpaid electric bills. "We were one grandparent away from food stamps," she says. Her older brother, Cliff, was studious and not particularly interested in sports. (He later became a dentist.) Nancy, meanwhile, was a "hellion," as she puts it, and spent little time at home. She discovered basketball at PS 104, a couple of blocks away, and she and her friends played late into the evenings; when it got dark, they relied on the sound of bouncing rubber and called it "radar ball."

As a teenager, Lieberman began riding the A and the E trains after school to Harlem—at first, to play for a girls' team called the New York Chuckles, and then to compete against the boys who assembled for pickup games at Rucker Park, a proving ground for greats like Kareem Abdul-Jabbar, Dr. J., and Tiny Archibald. She wore extra layers of sweaters and stuffed T-shirts in the shoulders of her jacket to make herself look bigger and tougher. She was often the only white girl getting off at 155th Street. Fortunately, playground rules usually dictated that teams were frequently chosen through foul-shooting competitions, where she faced less of a physical disadvantage. "I get asked, you know, 'Tell me the horror stories,'" she says. "I don't have any, 'cause the guys were so good to me." Her first nickname, on account of her hair and her feisty temperament, was Fire.

In 1976, when she was 18, Lieberman became the youngest basketball player ever to win an Olympic medal. (The United States got the silver; the Soviet Union took the gold.) At Old Dominion University, in Virginia, she acquired more nicknames (SuperJew, Lieb the Heeb), and was also a three-time All-American and two-time national champion. After graduation, she moved to Texas to play for the Dallas Diamonds, of the fledgling Women's Professional Basketball League, a short-lived precursor to the WNBA. Next came the USBL, the men's league, where she struggled to keep up, averaging about two points a game during her season with Springfield before being traded to the Long Island Knights. With some initial reluctance, she accepted an invitation to join the Harlem Globetrotters' tour in the fall of 1987, playing for those perennial losers the Washington Generals and suppressing the constant urge to abandon the script and steal the ball during the famous three-man weave. "The guys on the Trotters were getting pretty old by that point," she says. "I think we had more talent on the Generals."

Lieberman's impatience with gender barriers extended into her personal life. In the early 1980s, she was romantically involved with Martina Navratilova, whom she worked for as a fitness coach. "We talked about the pro sport teams in Dallas, the playoffs, what so-and-so does on third-down-and-four when he calls an audible," Lieberman wrote, in her 1991 autobiography, *Lady Magic*. "I had never had that kind of conversation with another female before." In the late '80s, she married and had a son with her Washington Generals teammate Tim Cline. (They have since divorced.)

By the time the WNBA was established, in 1997, Lieberman was 39 and long since retired from playing anything other than pickup games at the gym in Dallas with guys like the former Slam Dunk Contest winner Spud Webb, now the Texas Legends' president of basketball operations, and the Utah Jazz star Karl Malone. Never one to pass up the chance for a reachable milestone, she signed a one-year contract with the Phoenix Mercury and became the oldest female professional, filling in off the bench.

The milestones are not insignificant, and may owe something to the grandiosity of Lieberman's choice of role models. "Rosa Parks—it took guts for her to say, 'I'm going to sit there,'" she told me. "It took guts, you know, for Martin Luther King Jr. to say, 'This is what I'm going to do.'" She added, "When I was up at the White House with President Obama, last May, he just looked at me and he goes, 'Change is hard.' I'm like, Don't you know, President, dude, don't you know."

Shortly after moving to Dallas, Lieberman paid a voice coach $2,000 to help her lose the Queens accent. "I yoused tuh tawk like dis," she told me. "You know, Whatchou lookin' at? Now I'm sophisticated and refined." She still drives like a New Yorker, however, and on the way home from the hair salon she maneuvered her Bentley in and out of traffic, shifting lanes and tailgating and generally ignoring the automated warnings her radar detector was issuing about red-light cameras ahead. Her cell phone rang, and she answered, using an earpiece. It was her first boyfriend, Tommy Conrad, a former Old Dominion point guard who is now a scout for the Orlando Magic. "Are you looking for a scorer, a defender—who you looking for?" Lieberman asked, and then began talking up a couple of her Legends players, Antonio Daniels and Justin Dentmon, as well as "a kid who's really good, down at Austin, with the Toros, Squeaky Johnson. Anybody named Squeaky, you got to wonder. But I like his game."

Jameer Nelson, the Magic's starting point guard, had apparently hurt his knee, and the team was looking to sign a replacement player—a "Band-Aid," as Lieberman put it—to help it through the playoff stretch. "I get these calls from time to time," she said, after the call ended. "I could tell them, 'I don't really have anybody on my roster.' Like, we're *done* if we lose Antonio or Justin." The Legends were in the middle of a playoff race of their own, a half-game out of the eighth and final spot, with three games to go in the regular season. "We need them," she went on. "But it wouldn't be fair, because I'm supposed to be their greatest promoter."

Therein lay the dilemma and the challenge of coaching in the D-League, where the ultimate goal is not winning per se but managing expectations and helping people move on to better things. The Legends' roster was a mixture of near-misses, dreamers, hangers-on, and guys who are "just thrilled to death that they're not playing in a rec league," as Lieberman said. It included the only Taiwanese-born player ever to be drafted by an NBA team (a power forward named Joe Alexander), the oldest man ever to play in the D-League (Antonio Daniels, who is 36), an NBA washout and former boyfriend of Khloé Kardashian (Rashad McCants), and an ex–high school standout from the Dallas area (Booker Woodfox) who worked last summer at Lieberman's basketball camp. Perhaps 20 percent of the players in the D-League can expect to see their names on the back of an NBA jersey at some point. The other 80 percent, Lieberman said, "we're coaching for life."

Daniels was an unusual case. He spent 12 years in the NBA, and won a championship with the San Antonio Spurs in 1999. He had reached that career stage where an athlete's sense of how much he has left to offer and the market's opinion are not aligned. "It's very humbling," he told me. "But I wouldn't trade this experience for anything. I feel like I'm back in college, to a certain degree. You know, the traveling, the hotels you stay in. When you have 12 years of the Four Seasons, and then you go to the Holiday Inn, it's a big difference. Having to take a commercial plane at five o'clock in the morning, as opposed to being able to fly out on a private plane out of your own hangar—it's a big difference. But to see some of these guys, and how hungry they are to get there . . . I believe in paying it forward."

At least they get to fly. "Back in the day, in the '80s, it was really buses and off-the-side-of-the-road hotels," Lieberman told me, recalling her own playing experience, and deeming her guys fortunate by comparison. "The D-League, we're at casinos!" The Legends took buses only for games in Austin and Tulsa, and Lieberman often found herself negotiating with airline ticket agents for special favors. "Oh, my gosh, you have never seen these guys cramped up like on some of these commuter flights," she said. "I'm like, 'Please, can you help my guys? I've got six-ten, six-eight, seven-four. I need exit rows. I need aisles. I need whatever you can get.'" One Delta employee was so accommodating that Lieberman gave her free tickets to a game.

Another time, at a morning coaches' meeting, I watched Lieberman phone in a sandwich order for an upcoming bus trip. "I like that I'm part coach, part mom," she said. "No job is too small. If our guys are sick, I'll go get 'em some soup and bring it to them."

Justin Dentmon wasn't sick, but Lieberman had promised to cook him crab cakes, and so, on a scheduled day off last month, Dentmon arrived at her house, in an unfinished luxury subdivision that backs up to the water tower in Plano, to call in the favor. "I bet Phil Jackson doesn't do this for Kobe," Lieberman said. Dentmon was accompanied by Jackie Fisher, the team's trainer—"and shrink and valet and masseuse and laundress," according to Lieberman. It was March Madness time, and Lieberman suggested that they try to find some games on TV while she attended to the stove. "Ain't no games today," Dentmon replied. "Just women's games."

"Did you say 'just'?" she asked. "Did you use the word 'just' women's games?" "Yeah, just women's games," he said, cracking a smile.

Dentmon, who is from Illinois, was a four-year starter at the University of Washington, as a guard, but went undrafted and played last season in Israel, for a club named Hapoel in the small northern city of Afula, near the West Bank. He led the Israeli league in scoring, and was impressed by the level of fan interest ("It was always packed"), but he characterized the overall experience as mixed. "What did my people do to you?" Lieberman teased. (She and her mother will be visiting Israel next month.)

"They didn't pay me on time," he said.

Lieberman's son, T.J., who is 16 and already six feet six, returned home from playing pickup basketball with some friends, and joined Dentmon and Fisher in expressing disappointment that there were tomatoes in the salad. Lieberman said grace, and T.J. began bombarding Dentmon with questions about playing in college and overseas versus in the D-League.

"So why'd you come here?" T.J. asked.

"Wanted to see if I could go to the NBA," Dentmon said. "You ain't never heard of me before I got here."

"Who can jump the highest on the team?"

Dentmon, who is six feet, suggested that he could. T.J. was skeptical. "All you need to do is YouTube me," Dentmon said.

After dinner, Lieberman grabbed a scrap of paper and began diagramming a new play that she'd seen while watching a Mavericks game the night before. "I would like to run this with you and Booker," she told Dentmon. "It's a great play, because they're going to be expecting that we're going to run the stagger, and that's going to be a great little counter."

"You're right," Dentmon said. "Quick hitter."

At one point, T.J. remarked, "Can you believe Antoine Walker is playing in the D-League?" Walker, a three-time All-Star with the Boston Celtics, had filed for bankruptcy after retiring and then contemplated resuming his career in Europe before signing with the Idaho Stampede, last December.

"How do you go through a hundred million?" Lieberman asked. "And he's only 34."

"Probably 'cause he thought the money would keep coming, so he was like, 'I'm going to spend, spend, 'cause I know it's going to be there,'" Dentmon said.

"Justin, you should do that," T.J. said.

"Justin will be putting his money away," Lieberman said, to which Dentmon assented.

First, of course, Dentmon has to make some money. D-League salaries range from $15,000 to $25,000 a season. Then, there was the matter of the looming NBA lockout, and what effect, if any, it might have on the pipeline. "I heard from some other coaches that they could increase the salary in the D-League to try to keep guys from going overseas," Lieberman said.

Dentmon shook his head, and said, "It's crazy that you've got to go overseas to get more money than in your own country." Before leaving, he turned to T.J. and reminded him to check out some YouTube highlights. "You'll see me dunk on six-eight, six-nine guys," he said.

Three years ago, Lieberman came out of retirement again and played nine minutes for the WNBA's Detroit Shock in a late-season game against the Houston Comets. She was 50 at the time, breaking by more than a decade her own record as the league's oldest player. ("I wanted T.J. to see what his mommy did," she told me.) She turned the ball over twice and registered two assists. Her knees no longer permit the kind of aggressive running and jumping that competitive sports require, but she hasn't lost her shooting touch. Before a recent practice, Lieberman was challenged by the Legends center Matthew Rogers to a game of H-O-R-S-E. Within a couple of minutes, she was ahead by two letters. Rogers, who is nearly seven feet tall, resorted to feats of acrobatics and strength, at one point hurling the ball against the gymnasium wall, jumping, catching the ricochet in midair, and dunking, as though in an alley-oop. Lieberman's throw didn't have enough force, and bounced once before she could retrieve it and convert a layup. "See, I can't do trick shots with her, 'cause she never does 'em right," Rogers complained, to no one in particular. Within the constraints of the possible, Lieberman was more consistent, however. "I'll keep winning as long as they keep playing me," she boasted, after finishing him off.

Lieberman ran a relatively subdued practice, without the punitive conditioning drills or the temper tantrums that you might associate with, say, Bobby Knight—another pal in the Rolodex. ("We're trying not to F-bomb our players and raise our voices," she'd warned me, of her style.) She introduced the new play that she'd diagrammed for Dentmon the day before, and oversaw a series of drills and controlled scrimmages that were aimed at improving defensive coverage. She occasionally interrupted the drills to demonstrate. After 47 games, and 22 wins, the Legends were the league's third-highest-scoring team but were also tied for the most points allowed. Earlier in the week, Lieberman had cold-called Tom Thibodeau, the head coach of the Chicago Bulls, and asked for help with her defense. He FedExed her a portion of the Bulls' playbook. "It's a fraternity, and I'm just glad the guys have allowed me to be in the fraternity," she said. "I bet you it's been 90 to 10, men to women, calling to congratulate me. 'What do you need? How can we help you?' Because women, we still have a little bit of, I think, that jealousy, or the pie's been so small in the past that we're petty in some cases."

Spud Webb, who appears no longer to be in dunking shape, looked on from the sideline and recalled a conversation he'd had back in 2009 with Donnie Nelson, the general manager of the Mavericks and the Legends' owner, about the vacant coaching position. "You know me, I'm a former player," Webb said. "I'm like, 'I got this guy, this guy, this guy.' He goes, 'Whatchou think about Nancy?'" Webb feigned an expression of surprise. "I been knowing Nancy for 27 years. Donnie's like, 'I think she'd be great for us. She's the whole works—personality, everything.'" Webb and Lieberman went out to a restaurant soon afterward to discuss the idea. "You really want to coach men?" he said. "You want to leave your job at ESPN to do this?"

Watching the practice, Webb marveled at how much attitudes had changed since his own playing days, when, he said, he and his teammates could never have imagined a female boss. "You see how organized she is," he said. "I mean, she's respected. You'll see a guy disagree here and there, and she'll tell him, 'This is my philosophy. This is the way we want to do it.' And that's what a coach should do."

Before sending the guys off to the showers, Lieberman reminded them that the team bus would be leaving immediately after the next night's game, for a three-day road trip to Austin. "Okay, look, so I'm pretty hard-line on this," she said. "Don't show up at the arena telling me you don't have your socks, or your jock, or your headphones, or your—"

"We don't wear jocks," one player interrupted.

"She thinks we wear jocks," another snickered.

When she was in her late twenties, Lieberman starred in a rarely seen movie, *Perfect Profile*. Its premise was that a computer whiz had taken over the Dallas Mavericks and come up with a formula for scouting the ideal basketball player, whose name turns out to be Terry Williams. The owner dispatches his aides to sign this Williams character to a multimillion-dollar contract, only to discover that the presumed "he" is in fact a "she," played by Lieberman. Despite strong resistance from the team's traditionalist coach, Williams is given a uniform, and helps the Mavericks defeat the Lakers in the championship.

Unlike the Mavericks, the Legends play their home games at the Dr Pepper Arena, a 4,500-seat venue in the town of Frisco, one of those North Dallas suburbs which have mushroomed in the past generation. They share the building with a Junior-A hockey team, the Texas Tornado, and the Dallas Stars, of the NHL, who use it as a practice facility. Standing at courtside during warm-ups before the Legends' final home game of the season, Lieberman mentioned that she'd just got a call from an ESPN reporter who wondered, in effect, whether *Perfect Profile* could ever come true—whether, five or ten years down the line, we might see a woman playing in the NBA.

"Heck no!" she said, and brought up the University of Connecticut senior Maya Moore, a three-time Wade Trophy winner as the NCAA Player of the Year. "Maya Moore's amazing, but she couldn't play in *this* league. The guys are too big and too fast and too strong." She also mentioned that she'd just got her nails done.

A high school band was practicing "Louie, Louie." A couple of players on the opposing team, the Springfield Armor, trotted by to say hello. Justin Dentmon looked over and gestured to the side of his head, causing Lieberman to fix her hair.

The Legends got off to a fast start, and weren't turning the ball over as much as they had been earlier in the season. ("We were like 501[c][3]s," Lieberman joked to me once. "We were very philanthropic.") D-League games are typically high-scoring affairs—the Legends, for instance, scored 68 points in the first half—but that, evidently, is not enough to hold fans' interest. The top 40 soundtrack seldom let up, even during play. A giant rock-climbing wall behind one of the baskets attracted restless spectators. During a stoppage in the third quarter, the owner, Donnie Nelson, got up and joined a color guard in a dance to "Whoomp! (There It Is)," waving a Mavericks sweatshirt around above his head. "You won't see that in the NBA," one of the team's radio announcers remarked, off air. At the conclusion of the game (Legends 132,

Armor 112), the public-address announcer invited everyone down onto the court to participate in an enormous team-and-community photo op.

A few nights later, in Austin, the Legends qualified for the playoffs with a thrilling double-overtime comeback win. Then, the following morning, they learned that the Philadelphia 76ers, having lost one of their guards to a hamstring injury, were interested in signing Antonio Daniels to a ten-day contract. Lieberman tweeted, "No greater feeling in the D-League than to have that conversation with ur guy and tell him he has gone to the show!" Without Daniels to run the point, however, the Legends sputtered in the opening round, against Tulsa. They were done. Lieberman's contract is up for renewal, but, with another milestone behind her, she hasn't disclosed whether she plans to return or what her next career move might be. By last week, she had settled naturally into the off-season jock routine of hitting the links and working on her short game.

WELLS TOWER

Welcome to the Far Eastern Conference

FROM GQ

ON HIS FIRST MORNING in China, former NBA point guard Stephon Marbury went to the lobby of his hotel to attend what his translator had described as a "banquet" thrown by the management of the Shanxi Brave Dragons, who'd brought in the player for a second consecutive season in the hopes of shedding their reputation as one of the worst outfits in China's not very distinguished league. Enticing Marbury, the biggest celebrity ever to play in the Chinese Basketball Association, should have been cause for jubilation. Yet it was hard to detect much joy at the "banquet," which was taking place in a room the size of a parking space off the hotel's dining hall. The guest list consisted of two grimly perspiring middle-rung executives and a translator. No food was served, just tea.

One got the sense that the finer points of graceful living didn't count much in the Brave Dragons' hometown of Taiyuan, an industrial city variously described in the online travel literature as "gritty," "smoggy," and "a fucking shithole." Outside, in the late autumn chill, the coal plants were going full tilt. Even with the windows closed, the air smelled like an emergency and had a salty chemical flavor you could taste with your eyes.

Still, Marbury seemed not to mind. "You get used to it," he told me before the meeting. "Really, it's not too bad, except this—" He gestured out the window at the unhandsome landscape of grease-blackened garages and industrial warehouses engulfed in the brown gloom. "And this—" He pointed at his mouth, indicating his distaste for the local cuisine. "When I first came here, for the first two weeks, I wanted to kill myself. But now I don't think about it."

Unlikely as it may sound to hear a multimillionaire athlete so emphatically resigned to a place like Taiyuan, it's worth recalling that by early 2010, when Marbury first cast his lot with the Dragons, he had reached a place in life where options did not abound. After leaving the NBA at age 32, the two-time All-Star's career had been defined not by his triumphs on the court but by what happened off it—a catalog of errors that included public spats with coaches, romancing a Knicks intern in his truck, and a series of candid Webcasts in which he wept, burst into song, ate Vaseline, and generally volunteered grist for broad speculation that he had gone out of his mind.

But then, when things looked dire indeed, associates put Marbury in touch with Chinese steel magnate Wang Xingjiang, who owned the Shanxi Brave Dragons. Until last year, Chinese law limited teams from paying their American players more than $60,000 per month (a sum Marbury characterized to me as "a little change"). As further enticement, Wang promised to crack China's growing market of 300 million basketball fans for Marbury's Starbury brand of low-cost apparel and shoes, a business that had been on ice since 2008. Promising an initial investment of $2.2 million, Wang and his associates would facilitate the selection of factories, coordinate construction of a nationwide franchise, and assist with the beleaguered point guard's rebirth in the fastest-growing economy in the world.

So Marbury left behind his family in genteel Purchase, New York, tried it out for a season, and found, to his great relief, a population of adoring fans willing to overlook his past. He drew record crowds to Brave Dragons games. At signings in Taiyuan within a month of his arrival, he moved 1,000 pairs of Starbury shoes in a few hours. He'd recently discussed with Shanxi a three-year contract and had not ruled out the possibility of retiring here.

"It's been unbelievable," he told me. "The fans there, they showed me so much love. They gave me a second chance." Here, Marbury raised his sleeve to show me where he'd had the characters of his Chinese name—Ma Bu Li—and a heart beside the word *China* tattooed on his arm. "Two years ago, no one would get near me," he continued. "Now I got [a major American bank] wanting to invest $50 million in my company. Man, China has changed everything for me. *Everything.*"

With the season opener 15 days away, Dragons management was eager to check in on the condition—physical and otherwise—of the team's six-foot-two point guard. But Marbury had more immediate concerns. The previous season, he'd stayed at the five-star World Trade Hotel, which sits on the toniest strip Taiyuan has to offer, convenient to Rolex and Burberry shops, with a half-dozen restaurants and a spa on the premises. This year, to his displeasure, he'd been stabled instead at the Grand Metropark Wanshi Hotel, whose sumptuousness was a notch or two below what you'd expect at the Omaha airport Sleep Inn.

Upon arriving, he'd complained to his handlers, to no avail. Marbury did not fancy the idea of spending four months in this hotel, whose rooms were carpeted in cigarette-pocked low-nap the color of earwax and whose mattresses would have registered respectably on the Mohs scale of mineral hardness. Nor did he want to stomach four months of meals at the Wanshi's restaurant, an undersea-themed eatery whose evening buffet included such dishes as Grab Stick, Intestine Duck, Best Thick Seam, Ear Rabbit, Black Fungus, Meat, and Duck Bloody Piece.

In the tiny meeting room, Marbury was ushered to his seat by the Brave Dragons deputy Mr. Song, an unsmiling man with close-mown hair gelled into tidy gleaming barbs. Through the interpreter, a nervous twentysomething who gave her name as Cindy, Mr. Song explained that he was in the process of finding a good factory to start minting Starbury shoes, but that many factories had powered down for the winter and production would likely have to wait until spring. "For now," he said, "we want to concentrate on basketball."

"The business stuff will work itself out," Marbury said serenely. "I'm not worried about any of that. Right now I want to talk about my living conditions. I don't want to be in this hotel. I want to be in the World Trade."

This set off a long, hushed caucus among the Chinese parties. At last Cindy very antsily explained that due to a legal dispute between the team's owner and the World Trade, the hotel issue was a matter of some delicacy.

Marbury offered another proposal: perhaps the team could

arrange long-term quarters. "A three-bedroom apartment," said Marbury. "With TVs and a chef, and a maid to come every day. I could do that as well. I'm gonna be here for three years. It'd probably be cheaper to rent a place anyway."

But Mr. Song pursed his mouth and nodded sourly, giving the impression that he was not in the habit of indulging fussy requests from players. Marbury's Chinese teammates, by way of comparison, didn't get to stay in a hotel at all. They lived by the team's rusting gym on the outskirts of town, in a dormitory of pink concrete with a big pile of coal in the yard.

Mr. Song agreed to take up the hotel upgrade—a $14-a-night proposition—with his boss, then he turned the conversation to basketball. The Brave Dragons, he said, were promising this year, having recently acquired a second American player, Jamal Sampson, late of the Denver Nuggets. The most important thing, Mr. Song said through Cindy, was that the 14th-ranked team finish in the top eight.

Marbury gave him a straight look and held up his index finger. "Number one," he said.

And Cindy went, "Yeeeeeeeeahh," part weird cheer, part dubious meow. "So you will, you will lead our team to the top eight? You promise that?"

"Don't worry," Marbury said.

"Okay! We believe you! Ha! Ha!" said Cindy, in a tone of forced enthusiasm. "So, ah, now Mr. Song want to know, before you come to China, you maintain the trainings?"

She cast a nervous eye over Marbury's middle, which was a tad softer and rounder than it had looked beneath the lights at Madison Square Garden. Marbury nodded.

"Every day?"

"Listen," said Marbury. "All you need to know: when December 10 comes, when they throw the basketball up, I'll be ready."

"Auch!" said Mr. Song, though whether he meant, *"Auch—what a relief"* or *"Auch—this person is completely full of baloney"* was not immediately clear.

"We believe in you!" cried Cindy.

"No problem," said Marbury. "All love."

Waking up in Taiyuan, a city of 3.5 million located 250 miles southwest of Beijing, was breathtaking in the literal sense. The city lay under an ochre fog of startling opacity. Even behind the fixed panes of my hotel windows, the air had a dizzying reek you could faithfully reproduce by sealing your head in a sack of Match Light charcoal. A walk around the neighborhood turned up symptoms of an industrial economy in transition: lots of people driving Mercedeses and Lexuses, yet still more people carrying multiple offspring and lumber on mopeds that seemed to be made mostly of tape. Sephora stores and Cadillac dealerships verged on aged tracts of cratelike concrete buildings Pompeian with particulate grime. Not a single window you couldn't have graffitied with a fingertip.

Inspecting the local firmament, I could see no birds in flight. "If you see one, let me know," said Marbury when I told him this. In fact, during my week in Taiyuan, I would not see a bird, or a rat, or an ant, or a cockroach, or any living creatures at all, except for human beings and a substantial population of upsettingly adorable and horny stray lapdogs.

Still, in the city's defense, "shithole," with its connotations of biotic robustness, was an unfair epithet. It was more like an engine, which was how Marbury regarded his adoptive home. Riding through Taiyuan, he pointed out the gleaming condominium towers going up along the custard-colored Fen River, and the storefronts where he imagined Starbury outlets opening their doors a few months from now. "This is one of the richest cities in China, and I'm here to be a part of it," he told me several times. The Starbury Corporation's future projects here might range from skyscraper construction to lumber and cotton, to "anything that's got anything to do with something being made." Even in the coal soot itself, Marbury saw future riches. "You just gave me an idea," he replied when I marveled at Taiyuan's grime. "Mobile car washes. Give these people a taste for being clean. I'm gonna get the schematics on that *immediately*."

Improbable as Marbury's schemes of merchandising/real estate/mobile car wash/import-export magnatehood might sound, it's worth considering that (a) Marbury is arguably the biggest star in the CBA, and (b) in China's increasingly basketball-obsessed but notoriously stingy consumer population, it's hard to imagine a product better poised for success than a celebrity-endorsed sneaker that sells for 15 bucks. It is also important to note that behind Marbury's lofty visions are three Starbury corporate offices (North Carolina, New York, Los Angeles) and a staff of 18—two attorneys, two MBAs, accountants, a designer, etc.—working full-time to make the dream real.

When I paid a visit to Starbury's operations center in Morris-ville, North Carolina, a village of office parks near Raleigh, I did, admittedly, half expect to walk into an empty room with maybe a big TV and a couple of guys playing Nerf hoops on the clock. In-stead I found a 10-room suite full of business-clad people hard at work. One woman was busy designing a line of Starbury camisoles. The in-house attorney was straightening out some particulars of Chinese copyright law. The rest of the staff was dealing with the financial intricacies of Marbury's real estate holdings, a $75 mil-lion portfolio leased to such disparate and unlikely tenants as a U.S. attorney, the Department of Homeland Security, the National Archives and Records Administration, and the Social Security Ad-ministration.

Starbury CFO Gustavus Bass told me that Marbury had so far sunk $10 million of his own pocket cash into Starbury Corpora-tion. Once production started in China, he said, the business was forecast to return profits within a year. Bass, a former Wachovia corporate banker, led me down a hall, past a boardroom with a table the size of a duckpin bowling lane, into Starbury's opera-tions center. He showed me whirring servers, flat files full of blue-prints and architectural designs for the Chinese retail stores, and a 25-station call center ready to be staffed. "We've been in the planning stages for a very long time," Bass said. "We're positioned to go."

In China, Marbury's famously erratic personality, too, seemed newly conditioned for popular consumption. Despite his renown as an arrogant megalomaniac outstanding in a field of arrogant megalomaniacs, in person he came across as a warm, even earnest man guilelessly fond of almost everyone around him. "I love the Chinese people" was his reflexive response to complaints about flying sputum on the streets or the sharp elbows of the sidewalk throngs. One night at dinner, he summoned the chef from the kitchen to embrace him. More than once Marbury would tell me, with a nearly uncomfortable directness of emotion, how glad he was that I'd come to China with him and that he'd miss me when I left. Nothing in his manner smacked of PR gamesmanship. Rather, he gave the impression of someone desperate to forget all the haters back home and see only a world full of new friends.

And in Taiyuan, his friends were legion. At one point, I remarked that it must get irritating not to be able to take two steps without some stranger panting on his neck. "Nah," said Marbury. "You never know when the day's gonna come when people stop wanting your autograph."

With no professional obligations pending this week, other than to ease himself through jet lag, Marbury designed his days around two fixed points: meals at American fast-food establishments and spa treatments across town at the World Trade Hotel. To my mixed relief, the massages were the opposite of the sort I'd been warned might be pressed upon me in China. For two hours, small, strong women tenderized our limbs and thoraxes, delivering a program of sensations that would have perfectly conveyed to a blind, deaf person the experience of being yelled at. Now and then the masseuses paused their assaults to take photographs of the point guard. My own attendant seemed put out that she'd gotten stuck working my unremarkable anatomy instead of Marbury's famous frame. She repeatedly expressed her frustration by pulling my hair and jamming her fingers into my ears.

Somehow the thrashings seemed to put Marbury in a reflective mood. So while the ladies assailed him, we talked about his early life in Brooklyn.

Marbury grew up in a housing project in Coney Island, in a four-bedroom apartment his parents shared with their seven children. His mother worked in a day care center. His father made his living "doing whatever he could to get money—construction, gambling, hustling." Marbury's three older brothers were all gifted basketball players who narrowly missed NBA careers. Shortly after Stephon's birth, the elder Marbury brothers set about molding him into a pro athlete. "I was like a lab rat. I was a science project," he said. "They put a ball in the crib with me. They said, 'Okay, we're gonna breed a point guard with Stephon, and we're gonna kick the door down with him.'"

The hazards of life in Coney Island made the project an urgent one. Marbury recalled more than once hitting the deck during games when shots rang out. Three cousins died in gunfights over the years; another served time for killing a man. "We all knew me getting to the NBA was my family's way out," he said.

Doubts about Marbury's future faded early. By the time he was six, he could shoot and dribble with both hands, and when he was 12, *The Hoop Scoop* magazine listed him as the top sixth-grader in the nation. College recruiters were scouting him at age 14.

After his freshman year at Georgia Tech, Marbury joined the Minnesota Timberwolves and began living out a career narrative the Greek tragedians would have liked. *Marbury Agonistes:* the story of a young and brilliant basketball player remembered for his bedeviling public contests with one after another of the deadly sins. First came the Parable of Envy of Kevin Garnett, in which Marbury, stricken, allegedly, by jealousy of his close friend's $126 million contract, forced a trade from the Timberwolves, breaking apart one of the most thrilling on-court partnerships in the NBA. Marbury then wandered to unsuccessful seasons with the New Jersey Nets, the Phoenix Suns, and his hometown Knicks. "He only played street ball growing up," says Tom Gugliotta, who teamed up with Marbury in both Minnesota and Phoenix. "In Minnesota, he struggled to find a balance between being aggressive and including the other guys. And in Phoenix, ironically, he had learned what he could and couldn't do, but they asked him to be the guy he always wanted to be, and that's a scorer."

The Knicks years, as his detractors see them, paid him the wages of Anger and Pride, plus the better part of $100 million for five losing seasons. His quarrels with coach Larry Brown vexed the fans and the tabloid press, who called him "the most reviled athlete in New York." In 2008, new Knicks coach Mike D'Antoni sidelined Marbury in the season opener against Miami, which caused him to weep in secret on the bench. The exile, apparently, was permanent, and the blow to his dignity was so grave that when D'Antoni surprised Marbury by offering to play him later in the season, the point guard declined and was punished with a $400,000 fine.

Let's pass over, shall we, the Lust Parable about the intern and the strip joint and the sports utility vehicle? The *New York Post* has already chronicled those details under the cover story headline "Knicks Intern: My Sex in a Truck." That was in the autumn of 2007, when he was entering a period of unpleasantnesses of nearbathetic excess. The Knicks tied a record for season losses that year, and in December, his father suffered chest pains while watching a game at Madison Square Garden. Marbury didn't find out until after the game that his father had died. "It still upsets me that I didn't get to see him," he said. "And it was hard on my family—bringing my wife to his funeral when there's reporters everywhere and the whole world knows I just fucked another woman. There's nothing harder than that."

The lone bright spot for Marbury was the Starbury brand, which in 16 months on the market sold more than 10 million shirts, shorts, and $15 sneakers. The sports media briefly relented their hostilities to acknowledge Marbury's decency in selling sufficiently inexpensive footwear that inner-city youths wouldn't need to kill or rob anyone in order to own. And then, in 2008, Steve & Barry's, Starbury's retailer, went bankrupt. Not long after, the Knicks released Marbury, and he was banished from the Garden. "People were saying, 'The brand is over,'" said Marbury. "'His basketball career is over. He's done.'"

Marbury is so persistently haunted by the public version of his poetic decline that it isn't necessary to ask him about it. Talk to him for more than five minutes and he'll compulsively revisit the story's details, like someone who can't stop picking at a sore.

On Kevin Garnett: "They said I was jealous because he made $126 million, but the league changed the ceiling [of a max contract to $71 million, the price of Marbury's extension]. How could I be jealous of that?"

On refusing to play: "I refused to play? After y'all said to the whole world y'all not playing me and embarrass me on opening night? Have me sitting there in front of my hometown? They exiled *me!*"

On YouTube-inspired reports of his insanity: "I was just having a good time, playing, yelling, screaming, enjoying myself, and people took from that, 'Marbury's crazy. He's losing his mind.'"

On the Vaseline-eating thing, specifically: "I had a sore throat. My friend's grandmother said to take Vaseline. I did, and it went away."

Crucified is the word Marbury uses to describe his treatment. And you have to wonder how you could possibly resist developing a Christ complex if you were born to a family who had, for decades, been waiting in faith for a magical child to come along and work miracles from way outside the three-point line, to make more money than God, and to shepherd his loved ones out of Coney Island and into comfortable homes in the suburbs.

Marbury, a recently born-again Christian, saw his resurrection as imminent in China, from which his name and brand would spread across the globe, to India, then through unspecified African nations, then possibly, back to the United States. When I asked him what anyone would do with so much money, he described a corporate vision inspired by the Rapture, not the Robb Report.

"I want to build my own city," he said. The settlement, he explained, would be built on a 4,000-acre cotton farm in South Carolina he had his eye on. The citizens would be "all my family members. They gonna have their own businesses, companies that will feed off of my company. I want to build my own Walmart-style store. I want to build my own hospital and school system. I'll take all the people where I'm from in Coney Island and tell them to leave everything they got inside their homes and move into our new homes. We'll have all the people sign up to be Starbury employees before they move. This is my vision of what I want to do if this thing really pops off the way I think it will if we continue to stay on the path."

And yet, so far, Marbury's days in Taiyuan seemed curiously devoid of the meetings and factory tours you might expect of someone building a billion-dollar empire. Save a single one-on-one workout and a few treadmill sessions, Marbury didn't seem all that concerned with getting in shape. So while the Chinese members of the Brave Dragons were off playing exhibition matches and training twice a day, the preseason stretch in Marbury's entourage was a purgatorial study in petit-opulent torpor: usually emerging from quarters near the two o'clock hour for a meal at McDonald's, Pizza Hut, Subway, or Kentucky Fried Chicken; then to the World Trade Hotel for another bruising massage; then dinner at said American franchises.

The only break in the monotony came one evening when the American members of the Brave Dragons coaching staff mounted a plan to go out on the town. In the lobby, I waited for the others with a young guy named Wes, a former player for Oregon State, who was picking up a few bucks as a freelance assistant coach of the Brave Dragons junior squad.

I asked him how the team was looking. "They got this one kid who's *good*," he said. "You don't understand. They keep these motherfuckers in a dorm and make them lift weights three, four hours a day."

If the Chinese were such rigorous cultivators of talent, I asked him, why had China produced only one international basketball star, the pituitary marvel Yao Ming?

"This next generation, they'll probably have a few more. You don't know. They're probably breeding the motherfuckers from petri dishes."

We were soon joined by Patrick Sellers, a former UConn coach who'd come to Taiyuan after being implicated in a recruiting scandal. "I got thrown under the bus, and here I am. It's weird here and everything, but man, I think it's a gold mine."

At last Marbury came down, and—by coincidence—we ran into one of the Brave Dragons' chief sponsors, "Brother Wong," an elfin man in Gucci loafers. Brother Wong, who had supposedly amassed a fortune as a builder of local roads, was very pleased to see Marbury. He kept laying hands on Marbury's arms and shoulders and seemed to want very badly to climb into the point guard's lap. He insisted we go immediately to his favorite karaoke bar.

Marbury and I caught a lift in Brother Wong's chauffeur-driven Audi SUV. "You starting to see the Starbury movement," Marbury said. "Brother Wong's like Mark Cuban without being the owner. He wants to buy the team." Wong, said Marbury, was well connected with China's Communist Party, pointing out large yellow O's in the corners of the Audi's windshield, evidently emblems of officialdom. Then, at Marbury's prompting, Brother Wong hit a switch on the Audi's dashboard and a siren on the roof blared and wailed. "Police! Police!" cried Brother Wong, laughing madly. Traffic scurried from our path, and the Audi made for the karaoke bar at a desperate speed.

No one sang at the karaoke bar, a place the term *bar* is inadequate to describe. It was a fantastic labyrinth of mirrored hallways, astrobe with neon accents and red and blue LEDs, generally creating the effect of inhabiting a giant article of robot lingerie. In a room twice the size of my New York apartment, a rotund older woman dressed in a plaid field-hockey skirt led in a cadre of young women and briskly directed them, singly and in pairs, to sit beside us on the couch. The girls wore an unhookerly mufti of jeans or miniskirts or T-shirts or Annie Hall–style sweaters and, as far as I could tell, were not quite prostitutes but merely young women who drew a paycheck to ply lonely men with beer and grapes, and pinch them on the knee. The only hitch in the distribution came when the field-hockey lady ushered in a girl resembling an Asian Julia Child whose eyes happened to be crossed. There was no immediate clamor for her company. She stood before the room for a painful length of time. Finally, Marbury, who'd been obliviously drinking Sprite and BlackBerrying through the whole escort disbursement procedure, looked up and invited the big girl to his area of the sectional, a quiet act of valor that put the rest of us to shame.

I was partnered with a girl in an ivory body sock who knew enough English to claim her name was Apple. Further attempts at conversation foundered. Apple, who seemed to have mistaken me for a basketball pro from the American mean streets, periodically flashed what looked like gang signs at me and put her mouth to my ear to murmur, "I love basketball." At one point, Brother Wong grew concerned that things between Apple and me were not progressing at a proper clip. He crossed the room and reached out, as though for a handshake. Then he pulled the old grade school stunt of clapping my palm to the girl's breast and shrieking with laughter.

Mercifully we departed, honor intact, well before dawn. I, for one, was glad to escape, though Wes had sipped a few beyond his limit and was bereft to be going home empty-handed. "Can't we get some bitches?" he kept saying. "Can't we? Can't we?"

The hired friends also seemed glum to see the last of us, or of Marbury anyway. A few of them gathered by the exit. "Ma Bu Li, Ma Bu Li," they were moaning as we made our way into the benzene-scented night.

In the days after our night on the town, something odd happened: Marbury more or less dropped out of sight. He hardly stirred from his quarters. He canceled appointments or simply did not show up in the lobby at the times we'd planned to meet. I got the clear sense he was avoiding me.

Then, after two days of near-invisibility, he e-mailed me, asking me to come to his room. When I entered, he was on the phone with a travel agent, booking a hotel room in Beijing for the following night. "Yeah, sure, the Marriott. I'm just looking for the cheapest thing," he said.

He hung up and gave me an unhappy look. "I'm leaving Taiyuan," he said. "I been compromised." Management, he told me, had informed him that his services as a player were no longer required for the regular season. "If they make the playoffs, then they'll use me, is what they said. Otherwise, they want me to help coach."

He was, in other words, being asked to recapitulate his humiliating final season riding the bench for the Knicks. It was hard to understand this "offer" as anything but a ploy to force Marbury to quit the Dragons, which, he told me, was what he had done.

The source of the trouble, said Marbury, was that the team had recently hired a new general manager named Zhang Aijun, who was cleaning shop. "He didn't like me from the beginning," Marbury said. He gazed out the window. A tatter of Hefty bag danced on the wind. "The Knicks tried to hold me hostage," he said, apropos of nothing. "They fined me 400 grand and said that I refused to play! Refused to play? D'Antoni said I wasn't playing! He said that to the world! What I refuse to do is compromise. I understand what's right and what's wrong."

The old outrage wore on for a time and then exhausted itself. Marbury leaned back in his chair.

"It's bullshit," he said. "But you know, the good thing about this situation, at least I know it wasn't anything I did. You know what I've learned in my trials and my errors in the last three years? You can't let anguish derail you. People are gonna say, 'Oh, Stephon went to China. He messed up, and look what happened.' But I know the truth. This is a time of growth right here. This will work out for the best. I'm just gonna go to Beijing and find another team."

But this seemed an impossible ambition. The season started in less than two weeks, and presumably all the contracts for foreign players had been settled months ago. Marbury's position was, I felt, sad. Surprisingly so. Or, rather, it was really surprising to find oneself suddenly sickened with sympathy for an international sports celebrity with more money to his name than many American small towns.

Then again, it's never pleasant to see anyone's dream collapse, and Marbury's dream of China was about the vastest, most ornately bespired cathedral of ambition I'd ever met anyone trying to build. It contained, so far, $10 million of his own personal cash, one year of his life, the adoration of some number of thousands of Chinese people, putative fame and wealth in India and unspecified countries throughout Africa, his own personal city in South Carolina, skyscrapers, and Marbury's left arm, indelibly inscribed I ❤ *China*.

When such an extraordinary volume of wishes comes abruptly to earth, you can't help but feel the ground quiver the tiniest little bit.

There was little left to say. We sat awhile in silence. Then Marbury said he had to call his wife, Tasha. He hadn't yet given her the news, and he wasn't going to now. Their six-year-old son was sick with impetigo. Tasha was exhausted, and he didn't want to add to her burdens right now. He dialed. Through the receiver, I could hear the fatigue and anxiety in Tasha's voice. "I know it's hard, Boo. I know you're challenged, but it's gonna be all right, I promise," said Marbury, sounding oddly calm and assured for someone whose ultimate hope to redeem himself in the eyes of the world had almost certainly fallen apart.

The following day, a platoon of solemn well-wishers gathered at the Taiyuan airport to say good-bye. Marbury posed for a few last photos. He told his fans how sorry he was to leave Shanxi but said little else. In the meantime, the Brave Dragons' GM, Zhang Aijun, was handling the breakup with considerably less aplomb. Since the rupture had become final, Zhang made a spirited public effort to saddle Marbury with blame for the split. What helped poison the contract, Zhang said, was Marbury's insistence on a $30,000 health insurance policy for himself and his family and, *and,* his request for a $14 upgrade to the World Trade Hotel.

Before Marbury's plane had touched down in Beijing, ecstasies of Schadenfreude at his failed Chinese experiment broke out on American sports sites: "Stephon Marbury: Wearing Out His Welcome in Yet Another Continent," one headline ran. "Hide yo Vaseline, hide yo webcams," a blogger warned. "Marbury is on his way back to the United States of America."

But as it happened, reports of Stephon Marbury's professional collapse were premature. Within days of his departure from Shanxi, he secured a spot with a fledgling team in Foshan, on China's southern coast. While not a stellar club, Foshan wasn't much worse than the Brave Dragons. With Marbury, who in March made headlines scoring 55 points in a single game, Foshan took down Shanxi in both their matchups, helping to scuttle Shanxi's hopes of a top-eight season finish.

Nor did the split with Shanxi deal a mortal blow to Starbury. To cover the $2.2 million promised by the owner of the Brave Dragons, Starbury Corporation briskly liquidated Marbury's $75 million real estate business. They recently engaged Apple's marketing firm to handle the build-out of their shops and, according to Bass, have already started churning out a Chinese line of shoes at a cautious volume of 5,000 pairs per month.

In Marbury's opinion, the shake-up in Taiyuan could not have worked out better. Shortly after I'd returned from my trip, he called from Foshan. His enthusiasm was so forceful, I had to turn down the volume on my phone. "Man, you wouldn't believe it!" he said. "It's like Florida here! Grass! Sun! Blue sky. Did you see what they said about me? How I got exiled out of China? How I lost a second home? Man, they were just *waiting* for it. But it shall be well. I'm here, and I'm happy. I've landed. Both feet."

JON MOOALLEM

The History (and Mystery) of the High Five

FROM ESPN: THE MAGAZINE

Part One: Invisible Marks the Court

WHEN I FIRST PHONED Lamont Sleets this spring, I knew only the following: he is a middle-aged man living in the small town of Eminence, Kentucky; he played college basketball for Murray State University between 1979 and 1984; and he reportedly created one of the most contagious, transcendently ecstatic gestures in sports — and maybe, for that matter, American life.

I was calling Sleets because I wanted to talk to the man who invented the high five. I'd first read about him in 2007 in a press release from National High Five Day, a group that was trying to establish a holiday for convivial palm-slapping on the third Thursday in April. Apparently, Sleets had been reluctantly put in touch with the holiday's founders, and he explained that his father, Lamont Sleets Sr., served in Vietnam in the First Battalion, Fifth Infantry — a unit nicknamed "The Five." The men of The Five often gathered at the Sleets home when Lamont Jr. was a toddler. They'd blow through the front door doing their signature greeting: arm straight up, five fingers spread, grunting "Five." Lamont Jr. loved to jump up and slap his tiny palms against their larger ones. "Hi, Five!" he'd yell, unable to keep all their names straight. Years later, Sleets started high-fiving his Murray State teammates, and when the Racers played away games, other teams followed. In short, Lamont Sleets was both the inventor of the high five and its Johnny Appleseed.

The low five had been a fixture of African American culture since at least World War II. It might seem impossible to pinpoint when the low five ratcheted itself upright and evolved into the high five, but there are countless creation myths in circulation. Magic Johnson once suggested that he invented the high five at Michigan State. Others trace it to the women's volleyball circuit in the 1960s. But the Sleets story quickly shot around the Internet and into local newspapers, displacing, or at least undermining, all other claims. Sleets was budging his way atop the high-five hierarchy.

When he answered my phone call, Sleets sounded tired. He was on his way to work, he said, and told me to try back at 4:30 that afternoon. So I did. But he never picked up my call again. In the following weeks, I dialed him more than a dozen times. I pleaded in voice mails and texts. I combed local newspaper archives and funeral notices, looking in vain for someone who knew him. Gradually, the man attained an elusive, gurulike aura in my mind.

"He was kind of a private person" was all his Murray State coach, Ron Greene, could tell me. (Greene said his memory is so fuzzy that he "couldn't confirm or deny" the high-five story.) Old-timers in Eminence, I was told, still point to invisible marks on the high school basketball court from where Sleets routinely sank jumpers—spots well beyond where the three-point line has since been painted. Steve Frommeyer, Eminence High's principal, said everyone asked about the high five when the school inducted the guard into its hall of fame four years ago, but Sleets didn't show up for the ceremony. Years ago, Frommeyer added, the school retired Sleets's jersey, but it was mysteriously stolen off the gymnasium wall shortly thereafter.

In search of a definitive lead, I reached out to the founders of National High Five Day: Conor Lastowka, a comedy writer, and Greg Harrell-Edge, who was once named "Laziest Person in America" in a nationwide search by *Jimmy Kimmel Live!* Talking to them, I suddenly had the good sense to ask whether the Sleets story was even true.

"You know," Harrell-Edge said, "you are actually the first person to ask us that."

It was all a hoax, a publicity stunt. They'd concocted the whole story, then scoured college basketball rosters to plug in a name. "We just found the guy and made up a story about his dad,"

Lastowka said. He seemed amused that I'd gotten the actual Lamont Sleets on the phone, if only briefly.

Part Two: The High Five of Life

If this prank has a victim, it's Glenn Burke, a young outfielder for the Los Angeles Dodgers in the late 1970s whose astonishing physique and 17-inch biceps earned him the nickname "King Kong." For at least a generation before the Sleets story surfaced, the conventional wisdom had been that Burke invented the high five on October 2, 1977, in front of 46,000 screaming fans at Dodger Stadium.

It was the last day of the regular season, and Dodgers left fielder Dusty Baker had just gone deep off the Astros' J. R. Richard. It was Baker's 30th home run, making the Dodgers the first team in history to have four sluggers—Baker, Ron Cey, Steve Garvey, and Reggie Smith—with at least 30 homers each. It was a wild, triumphant moment and a good omen as the Dodgers headed to the playoffs. Burke, waiting on deck, thrust his hand enthusiastically over his head to greet his friend at the plate. Baker, not knowing what to do, smacked it. "His hand was up in the air, and he was arching way back," says Baker, now 62 and managing the Reds. "So I reached up and hit his hand. It seemed like the thing to do."

Burke then stepped up and launched his first major league home run. And as he returned to the dugout, Baker high-fived him. From there, the story goes, the high five went ricocheting around the world. (According to Dodgers team historian Mark Langill, the game was not televised, and no footage survives.)

The high five was a natural outgrowth of Burke's personality. The Oakland native was an irrepressibly charismatic man who, even as a 24-year-old rookie that season, had become the soul of the Dodgers' clubhouse. He did Richard Pryor stand-up from memory and would stuff towels under his shirt and waddle bow-legged around the dugout, imitating Dodgers manager Tommy Lasorda. "He was a joyous, gregarious person," sports agent Abdul-Jalil al-Hakim says of Burke, a friend since childhood. "He could high-five you without necessarily going through the motion with his hand."

What most people didn't know was that Burke was gay. Following his retirement in 1980, he became the first major leaguer to come out. Even though he tried to keep his sexuality a secret during his playing days, there had been rumors in the clubhouse. And as the 2010 television documentary *Out: The Glenn Burke Story* revealed, Dodgers executives scrambled to squash those rumors at all costs: in the off-season of 1977, team VP Al Campanis offered Burke $75,000 to get married. (The Dodgers executive later explained the offer not as a bribe but as a "helpful gesture" to pay for Burke's honeymoon.) According to a friend, Burke rejected the marriage deal with a mix of wit and rebelliousness. He told Campanis, "I guess you mean to a woman."

It was around that time that Burke struck up a relationship with Spunky Lasorda, aka Tommy Lasorda Jr. Spunky was a lithe young socialite who frequented West Hollywood's gay scene, smoking cigarettes from a long holder. A 1992 *GQ* profile of Spunky portrays his homosexuality as an open secret. But his father was in staunch denial and remained so even after Spunky's death in 1991 from pneumonia. *GQ* reported that the death certificate said his illness was likely AIDS-related. "My son wasn't gay. No way," Lasorda Sr. told the magazine.

Burke and Spunky's relationship didn't become public until years later and remains ambiguous. Burke's sister, Lutha Davis, insists the two men were just close friends. In his 1995 memoir *Out at Home*, coauthored with Erik Sherman, Burke went out of his way to leave the true nature of their relationship unclear. "That's my business," he wrote. He also explained that Lasorda Sr.'s homophobia was something he and Spunky commiserated about. Burke described them turning up together at Lasorda's house one night, done up in pigtails and drag, hoping to stage a kind of gay *Guess Who's Coming to Dinner.* They chickened out before knocking on the door.

Whatever the case, Burke's association with Spunky marks the point at which his big league career took an irrevocable left turn. Lasorda stopped being amused by the player's dugout antics and, according to Burke, once turned on him and chewed him out. "Glenn had such an abundance of respect and love for Tommy Lasorda," says Burke's sister. "When things went bad at the end, it was almost like a father turning his back on his son." Early in the 1978 season, the Dodgers abruptly dealt Burke to the Oakland A's, among the most lackluster teams in baseball, for Billy North, an outfielder past his prime. LA sportswriters described the trade as sucking the life out of the Dodgers' clubhouse. A couple of players were seen crying at their lockers.

To be fair, North was a proven player, whereas Burke wasn't yet delivering on his potential. And that's how Campanis explained the deal at the time. But for Burke, and several teammates, the trade had everything to do with his sexuality—though the out-fielder sounded off to the press about it in only the most cryptic terms. "I never got a chance here," he said. "I felt I was supposed to kiss ass and I didn't. As far as getting along with Lasorda, that didn't work out too well."

After unproductive years in 1978 and '79, Burke hoped for a fresh start in 1980 under new A's manager Billy Martin. But the gay rumors followed him to Oakland. Martin threw the word "fag-got" around the clubhouse and didn't play Burke. Some team-mates even avoided showering with him. Burke, accustomed to be-ing the heart of the clubhouse, felt crippled by the discomfort he was causing. His unhappiness was compounded by a knee injury and a demotion to Triple A. After playing just 25 games in the mi-nors in 1980, he abruptly retired, feeling it was his only option. He was 27 years old. "It's the first thing in my life I ever backed down from," he later said.

Burke started hanging around San Francisco's Castro District. He became a star shortstop in a local gay softball league and domi-nated in the Gay Softball World Series. "I was making money play-ing ball and not having any fun," he said of his time in the majors. "Now I'm not making money, but I'm having fun." Jack McGowan, a friend in the Castro who has since passed away, once said of Burke: "He was a hero to us. He was athletic, clean cut, masculine. He was everything that we wanted to prove to the world that we could be."

In the Castro, Burke's creation of the high five was part of this Herculean mystique. He would regularly sit on the hood of a car—whichever one happened to be parked in front of a gay bar called the Pendulum Club—flash his magnetic smile, and high-five everyone who walked by. In 1982, Burke came out publicly in an *Inside Sports* magazine profile called "The Double Life of a Gay Dodger." The writer, a gay activist named Michael J. Smith, appropriated the high five as a defiant symbol of gay pride. Rising from the wreckage of Burke's aborted baseball career, Smith wrote, was "a legacy of two men's hands touching, high above their heads."

By that time, however, Burke was struggling with a drug habit. It escalated in 1987, when a car plowed into him as he was crossing a street, breaking his right leg in four places and stealing his athleticism. He couldn't hold a job. He went broke. He did some time at San Quentin for grand theft. Then in 1993, he tested positive for HIV. He passed away on May 30, 1995, after a sharp and grisly decline. One obituary noted that, at the end, the man who invented the high five "could barely lift his arm."

As Burke's life sputtered downward, the high five madly ascended. Even by 1980, the Dodgers were selling "High Five" T-shirts with a trademarked logo of two upraised hands connecting. A promotional poster explained: "The 'High Five' salute has become the Dodgers' standard salute during the 1980 season. It is given customarily following a home run, good defensive play or Dodger victory."

It wasn't just L.A. The high five was being celebrated as a welcome injection of style throughout sports. In 1981, the Canadian magazine *Maclean's* noted that, thankfully, "when a black guy has hit a home run," the players scoring ahead of him don't just stand around anymore and "shake his hand like a bunch of Rotarians at lunch on a Tuesday."

Burke's friend Abdul-Jalil al-Hakim argues: "The high five liberated everybody. It gave you permission to enjoy your high points." And not just in sports but at your kid's spelling bee or your office after a killer PowerPoint presentation. In this interpretation, Burke didn't just add a bit of flair to baseball—he uncorked a repressed longing for personal expression and connection in all of American society.

Burke's sister, Lutha Davis, says Burke himself was pleased to see the high five spilling out of sports to punctuate smaller, everyday joys. "Now when something great happens in life, people do the high five," she says. "I call it 'the high five of life.'"

Years after her brother died, Davis was watching *Jeopardy!* when a question about the inventor of the high five popped up. People who knew Glenn have always known "the truth," she told me, but it was gratifying to watch some anonymous, Midwestern-looking contestant buzz in right away and say, with unflappable certainty, "Who is Glenn Burke?"

Part Three: The Four-Fingered Man

Burke died believing the high five was his legacy, and the more I learned about him, the more tragic the Sleets hoax seemed. It's nice to believe that something as magnificent as the high five could be invented only once, in a romantic, unforgettable flash. The truth is, such things are invented many times, by many people—there are multiple mythologies rewritten over time. I've come to realize this because I happened upon a third, entirely credible story of the high five. It goes like this:

At a University of Louisville basketball practice during the 1978–79 season, forward Wiley Brown went to give a plain old low five to his teammate Derek Smith. Out of nowhere, Smith looked Brown in the eye and said, "No. Up high."

The Cardinals were known as "the Doctors of Dunk." They played above the rim. So when Smith raised his hand, it clicked for Brown: he understood how the low five went against the essential, vertical character of their team. "I thought, yeah, why are we staying down low? We jump so high," says Brown, now head coach at Indiana University Southeast. Brown insists it's Smith who invented the high five and Smith who spread it around the country.

In fact, high fives turn up in highlight reels of the 1978–79 Louisville team. Occasionally, they're jerky, thrusting fives—more like spears thrown perpendicularly at the other guy's torso—but they're clearly among the first high fives ever broadcast into American living rooms. Midway through the second half of the 1980 NCAA Final against UCLA, Brown posted up against Kiki Vandeweghe and overpowered him, banking in a shot and drawing the foul. In footage of the game, Brown immediately rams his left arm up to slap Smith five. (Brown always made a point of high-fiving with his left hand because as a kid he had his right thumb amputated and it somehow didn't feel right to high-five with four fingers.) The announcer, Al McGuire, shouts: "Mr. Brown came to play! And they're giving him the high-five handshake. High five!"

Both Derek Smith and Wiley Brown grew up in small, poor towns in southern Georgia. Smith is said to have arrived on the

Louisville campus as a shy stutterer with all of his possessions in one bag. According to Brown, Smith was always blown away that someone with an undistinguished background like his could make an indelible impact on the entire world. "He'd talk about the high five constantly," Brown says. "It was one of those things he was most proud of, right up there with getting his degree, having his kids, and marrying his beautiful wife."

I couldn't ask Derek Smith about his invention of the high five. After a respectable NBA career, he died suddenly in 1996 from an undiagnosed heart condition. (His son, Nolan Smith, was drafted out of Duke by the Trail Blazers in June.) But Brown told me about one particular day at Louisville, after Smith got a call about the high five from a big-city newspaper. "Derek was talking about how this was going to go down in history," Brown says. "It would be something we could tell our kids and grandkids about. I've got a smile on my face now just talking about it."

I think I found the newspaper story: a tiny item in the *New York Times* on September 1, 1980, about a burgeoning fad called the high five and the man who apparently invented it, Derek Smith. There's no mention of Glenn Burke, even though he also apparently invented the high five three years earlier. In fact, aside from Smith and his teammates, there's only one other person mentioned in the story. The piece begins: "Manager Tom Lasorda of the Los Angeles Dodgers has joined the growing list of 'high-fivers.' . . . But the veteran of 35 years in baseball admits he does not know where it all began." It's just one of those things, Lasorda told the paper. "Who knows?"

So here's the question: Did Lasorda purposefully not mention Glenn Burke? Or did Lasorda just forget? I don't know what to believe. (Through an assistant, Lasorda reiterated that he doesn't know who invented the high five but didn't respond to requests for an interview.) Ultimately, the story of the high five is a ghost story, about how we remember and how badly we want to be remembered.

Glenn Burke walked away from baseball after four seasons with a career .237 batting average. But as he told a newspaper reporter years later: "You think about the feeling you get when you give someone the high five. I had that feeling before everybody else."

Contributors' Notes

ALEX BELTH has written about sports and culture at his New York City lifestyle site Bronx Banter (www.bronxbanterblog.com) since 2002. He is a contributor to *Sports Illustrated* and the author of *Stepping Up,* a biography of Curt Flood as well as the editor of *The Best Sports Writing of Pat Jordan* and *Lasting Yankee Stadium Memories.*

JOHN BRANCH was a reporter for the *Colorado Springs Gazette* and a sports columnist at the *Fresno Bee* before joining the *New York Times*. A native of Redondo Beach, California, he earned both a bachelor of science degree in business and a master of arts degree in journalism from the University of Colorado at Boulder.

TAYLOR BRANCH is the author of, among other works, *America in the King Years,* a three-volume history of the civil rights movement, for which he won the Pulitzer Prize and the National Book Critics Circle Award.

A longtime writer-at-large for *Runner's World* and contributor to many national publications, JOHN BRANT is the author of *Duel in the Sun: Alberto Salazar, Dick Beardsley, and America's Greatest Marathon* and coauthor of *14 Minutes: A Running Legend's Life and Death and Life.* This is his fifth appearance in *The Best American Sports Writing.* His story in this edition was made possible by the extraordinary courage and grace of Frank Shorter and his sisters.

BILL DONAHUE has been working as a journalist since 1987 and his work has appeared in many publications, including *The Atlantic, The New Yorker, Wired, Runner's World,* and the *Washington Post Magazine.* A two-time nominee for the National Magazine Award, his work has also been reprinted in

The Best American Sports Writing, The Best American Travel Writing, and many
other anthologies.

ROBERT HUBER is features editor for *Philadelphia* magazine. His work
has also appeared in *Esquire, GQ,* the *New York Times Magazine,* and many
other publications. This is his third appearance in *The Best American Sports
Writing.* Currently at work on a novel about difficult moral choices engen-
dered by the dying arena of print media, Huber lives with his wife and two
sons in Philadelphia.

THOMAS LAKE is an Atlanta-based senior writer for *Sports Illustrated* and
cofounder of the Auburn Chautauqua, an annual writers' conference in
Ludowici, Georgia. In 2011 he gave a speech at Gordon College on the
story of his life. It can easily be found on YouTube. He can also be e-mailed
at thomasglake@netscape.net.

JEANNE MARIE LASKAS is the author of six books, including her newest work of narrative nonfiction, *Hidden America,* the award-winning tril-
ogy of memoirs, *Growing Girls, The Exact Same Moon,* and *Fifty Acres and a
Poodle,* and her collection *The Balloon Lady and Other People I Know.* Most
of her long-form journalism appears in *GQ,* where she is a correspondent. Formerly a contributing editor at *Esquire* and a weekly columnist
at the *Washington Post Magazine,* her stories have appeared in numerous anthologies, including *The Best American Magazine Writing* and *The
Best American Sports Writing.* Laskas is the director of the writing program at the University of Pittsburgh, where she is an associate professor.
She lives in Scenery Hill, Pennsylvania, with her husband and two daughters.

Sports Illustrated senior writer TIM LAYDEN joined the magazine in 1994.
He previously worked at *Newsday,* the *Albany Times-Union,* and the *Sche-
nectady Gazette.* During his three decades in journalism, Layden has won
multiple sports writing awards, including an Eclipse Award for coverage of thoroughbred horse racing. A native of Whitehall, New York,
Layden graduated in 1978 from Williams College, where he was an
English major and a member of the basketball team. He lives in Connecticut.

JERÉ LONGMAN is a sports reporter for the *New York Times* whose books
include the national best-seller *Among the Heroes: United Flight 93 and the
Passengers and Crew Who Fought Back* and *The Hurricanes: One High School
Team's Homecoming After Katrina,* chosen by *Slate* magazine as one of the
best books of 2008.

BEN MCGRATH has been a staff writer at *The New Yorker* since 2003. He lives in Brooklyn with his wife.

JON MOOALLEM is a contributing writer to the *New York Times Magazine,* and his work has appeared in many publications as well as in *The Best American Science and Nature Writing 2011.* He lives in San Francisco.

MICHAEL J. MOONEY is a staff writer at *D Magazine* and also writes for *GQ, Outside,* and *Grantland.* His story about poker appeared in the 2009 edition of *The Best American Sports Writing,* and his story about a surgeon who operated on both John F. Kennedy and Lee Harvey Oswald was selected for the penultimate edition of *The Best American Crime Reporting.* He lives in Dallas with his fiancée and their retired racing greyhound.

S. L. PRICE has been a senior writer at *Sports Illustrated* since 1994. This is his sixth appearance in *The Best American Sports Writing.*

DAVE SHEININ is a sports and features writer for the *Washington Post,* where he has worked since 1999. A graduate of Vanderbilt University with a degree in English and music, he lives in Maryland with his wife and two daughters.

PAUL SOLOTAROFF lives in New York and is the author of *The Body Shop, Group,* and *House of Purple Hearts.* A contributing editor at *Men's Journal* and *Rolling Stone,* he has written features for *Vanity Fair, GQ, Vogue,* and the *New York Times Magazine.* This is his seventh appearance in *The Best American Sports Writing.*

RICK TELANDER is a sports columnist for the *Chicago Sun-Times* and the "Basketball Evangelist" for *SLAM* magazine. He is the author of nine books, including *Heaven Is a Playground,* which has been in print for 36 years. This is his seventh appearance in *The Best American Sports Writing.*

WRIGHT THOMPSON is a senior writer for ESPN.com and *ESPN: The Magazine.* He lives with his wife, Sonia, in Oxford, Mississippi. This is his seventh appearance in *The Best American Sports Writing.*

From 1997 to 2012, TOMMY TOMLINSON wrote a local column for the *Charlotte Observer* before joining a new joint venture between the USA Today Sports Media Group and Major League Baseball Advanced Media. He studied journalism at the University of Georgia, was a finalist for the Pulitzer Prize in commentary in 2005, and was named best local columnist in America by *The Week* magazine in 2004.

WELLS TOWER is the author of the short story collection *Everything Ravaged, Everything Burned*. His short stories and journalism have appeared in *The New Yorker, Harper's, McSweeney's,* the *Paris Review, The Anchor Book of New American Short Stories,* the *Washington Post Magazine,* and elsewhere. He has received two Pushcart Prizes and the Plimpton Prize from the *Paris Review*. He divides his time between Chapel Hill, North Carolina, and Brooklyn, New York.

Notable Sports Writing of 2011

Selected by Glenn Stout